Japan Works

JOHN PRICE

Japan Works

POWER AND PARADOX

IN POSTWAR INDUSTRIAL RELATIONS

ILR Press AN IMPRINT OF

Cornell University Press

ITHACA AND LONDON

The publisher gratefully acknowledges a grant from the Japan Foundation
that aided in bringing this book to publication.

First published 1997 by Cornell University Press.

Number 30 in the Cornell International Industrial and Labor Relations
Report series.

Library of Congress Cataloging-in-Publication Data

Price, John, 1950–
    Japan Works : power and paradox in postwar industrial relations /
John Price.
        p.   cm. — (Cornell international industrial and labor
relations reports ; no. 30)
    Includes bibliographical references and index.
    ISBN 0–8014–3285–5 (alk. paper). — ISBN 0–8014–8360–3 (pbk: alk.
paper)
    1. Industrial relations—Japan.   2. Industrial management—Japan.
3. Employee empowerment—Japan.   4. Quality control—Japan.
5. Automobile industry and trade—Japan.   6. Japan.—Foreign economic
relations—United States.   7. United States—Foreign economic
relations—Japan.   I. Title.   II. Series.
HD8726.5.P75   1996
331'.0952—dc20   96–8953

Printed in the United States of America

This book is printed on Lyons Falls Turin Book, a paper that is
totally chlorine-free and acid-free.

In memory of
Agnes C. Jones
poet and grandmother

CONTENTS

TABLES

FIGURES

ACKNOWLEDGMENTS

Many people have contributed to this book and I sincerely appreciate the help, kindness, and advice offered by so many on both sides of the Pacific. This work would not have been possible without extensive cooperation from many people in Japan. I would like to offer special thanks to Harada Yōzō, Iribe Shōji, Kamehara Yoshiaki, Katō Toshio, Kōno Kazuo, Kubota Takeshi, Kurumi Yoshiaki, Matsui Susumu, Matsuo Kamachi, Michiyama Fusahito, Nishimura Yasunori, Ogawa Keizō, Sanada Noriaki, Sugita Tomoji, Uchiyama Tashirō, Watanabe Akinori, Yamada Shin, and Yamamoto Kikue, all of whom helped me gain a basic understanding of work and workers in Japan.

For their advice and kindness while I was in Japan, I thank Yamamoto Kiyoshi, Totsuka Hideo, Hyōdō Tsutomu, Hirai Yōichi, Matsuzaki Tadashi, Kamii Yoshihiko, Kumazawa Makoto, Hirota Osamu, Watanabe Ben, and Kenmochi Kazumi. Without their support this work would not have reached fruition. My gratitude also goes to the Wada family, Nina Raj, the Naniwa family, and Neil and Ayako Burton, who provided sustenance and encouragement while I was in Japan.

On this side of the Pacific, my appreciation to Colin Gordon and David Edgington for their close reading of the manuscript. Thanks also to T. G. McGee, Joe Moore, E. Patricia Tsurumi, and Donald Burton for their support and inspiration. A deep bow to Professor William D. Wray, whose patience, attention to detail, and knowledge of Japan's economic history kept me on track. And particular thanks to Steve Babson and Andrew Gordon, whose criticisms were both constructive and motivating. My thanks to Dick Woodworth and Jean Valino, who through example both taught and inspired me, and to Sid Shniad, whose company on the racquetball courts over these many years was as helpful as his enthusiasm for the manuscript.

My appreciation to Fran Benson, Elizabeth Holmes, and Barbara Salazar of Cornell University Press, who, during a challenging period of amalgamating the ILR and Cornell University presses, skillfully shepherded this book to completion. John LeRoy's meticulous editing of the manuscript was concise and creative— thank you. I am also indebted to Gillian Boyd, who helped reproduce the book's figures. My thanks to *Fortune* magazine for permission to reproduce in Table 1 its assessment of the lean-mass production distinctions, and to St. Martin's Press and Routledge for permission to reproduce in Figures 5 and 6 comparative levels of bargaining from Ron Bean's *Comparative Industrial Relations*.

Fellowship support from the University of British Columbia and the Social Sciences and Humanities Research Council of Canada was instrumental in allowing me to pursue the research that formed the basis for this book.

Finally, I thank my family—my parents, Gwen and Bernie Price, my partner, Margaret McGregor, my children, Tom and Mae, and Maurice McGregor and Margot Becklake for their support throughout this endeavor.

J. P.

Abbreviations

AFL	American Federation of Labor (U.S.)
AJPMUF	All-Japan Prefectural and Municipal Union Federation (Zen Nihon Jichi Dantai Rōdō Kumiai or Jichirō)
CIO	Congress of Industrial Organizations (U.S.)
CLRB	Central Labor Relations Board (Chuō Rōdō Iinkai or Churōi)
ICFTU	International Confederation of Free Trade Unions
ILO	International Labour Organization
JCL	Japan Confederation of Labor (Dōmei Kaigi and then Dōmei after 1964)
JCP	Japan Communist Party (Nihon Kyōsan Tō)
JCU	Japan Coalminers' Union (Nihon Tankō Rōdō Kumiai Rengō-kai or Tanrō)
JFL	Japan Federation of Labor (Dai Nihon Rōdō Sōdōmei or Sōdōmei);
JPC	Japan Productivity Center (Nihon Seisan Sei Honbu)
JSP	Japan Socialist Party (Nihon Shakai Tō)
JTUC	Japan Trade Union Congress (Zen Nihon Rōdō Kumiai Kaigi or Zenrō)
Keidanren	Federation of Economic Organizations (Nihon Keizai Dantai Renmei)

Keizai Doyūkai Commitee for Economic Development

LRB   Labor Relations Board (Rōdō Iinkai)

MITI   Ministry of International Trade and Industry (Tsūshō Sangyō Shō)

MMF   Mitsui Miners' Federation (Mitsui Tankō Rōdō Kumiai Rengōkai or Sankōren)

MSF   Mitsui Staff Federation (Mitsui Tankō Shain Kumiai)

NCIU   National Congress of Industrial Unions (Zen Nihon Sangyō Betsu Rōdō Kumiai Kaigi or Sanbetsu)

Nikkeiren   Japan Federation of Employer Organizations (Nihon Keieisha Dantai Renmei)

NPA   National Personnel Authority (Jinji In)

NRWU   National Railway Workers Union (Kokutetsu Rōdō Kumiai or Kokurō)

OECD   Organization for Economic Cooperation and Development

SCAP   Supreme Commander of the Allied Powers

SCUF   Satellite City Union Federation (Eisei Tōshi Shokuin Rōdō Kumiai Rengōkai, or Eitōren)

Sōhyō   General Council of Trade Unions of Japan (Nihon Rōdō Kumiai Sōhyōgi Kai)

TUC   Trade Union Congress (Britain)

TUL   Trade Union Law (Nihon Rōdō Kumiai Hō)

UAW   United Auto Workers (U.S.)

WFMCU   Western Federation of Mitsui Coalmine Unions (Nishi Nihon Mitsui Tankō Rōdō Kumiai Rengōkai)

WFTU   World Federation of Trade Unions

Japan Works

1   Introduction

In an episode of *The Simpsons*, that dastardly American animated cartoon, Bart's bumbling dad, Homer, is promoted from a lowly technician to top management. Obliged to deliver a lecture on administration, Homer begins his presentation by writing *jiko kanri* in large letters on the blackboard. This Japanese term meant "self-management," explained Homer, and it represented the new direction for American business. That a consultant helped Homer prepare his lecture does not detract from the message; in fact it nicely captures not only the message but the human dynamic as well—Japanese management techniques have become so widespread as ideals or fads in North America that they have penetrated popular culture.

Since popularity has been building for two decades, Homer's reference to *jiko kanri* comes as no surprise. From a historical perspective, however, the popularization of Japanese management within the citadel of international capitalism indicates that the postwar world has indeed come to an end. That world took shape after World War II, when the United States transformed its military might into economic leadership and came to epitomize the power of mass production and the appeal of mass consumption. Today, however, the United States no longer monopolizes that role. Germany and Japan, two of the nations defeated in World War II, have risen from the ashes to challenge the United States economically in significant respects. Japan, in particular, has broken the U.S. grip on economic leadership. Japan's automobile industry, which by the 1980s accounted for nearly 30 percent of total world production, has played a significant role in a global game of musical chairs, to the point that it has inspired a worldwide review of production management.

Two decades ago, automobile producers in North America introduced quality circles into the workplace as a means to improve their quality and productivity, which had fallen behind that of Japanese producers. By the early 1980s, it had become clear that quality circles alone were not enough.

The year 1985 was a watershed in the worldwide ascent of Japanese production management. The first Japanese-directed assembly facility in North America, New United Motor Manufacturing Incorporated (NUMMI), a General Motors–Toyota joint venture, began its first full year of operation in Fremont, California. And the Massachusetts Institute of Technology began a $5 million, five-year study on the future of the automobile, the International Motor Vehicle Program (IMVP).

By 1990 the results were in. Using an American work force, NUMMI was producing vehicles at quality and efficiency levels similar to those in Japan, proving once and for all that Toyota production methods were not contingent on cultural traits found uniquely among Japanese workers. The IMVP study team published their findings in a best-selling book, *The Machine That Changed the World.*[1] The Japanese, declared the researchers, had developed a new form of production management they dubbed "lean production," which, they asserted, would supersede the old way of producing automobiles. According to the authors of the IMVP report, "Lean production (a term coined by the IMVP researcher John Krafcik) is 'lean' because it uses less of everything compared with mass production—half the human effort in the factory, half the manufacturing space, half the investment tools, half the engineering hours to develop a new product in half the time. Also, it requires keeping far less than half the inventory on site, results in many fewer defects, and produces a greater and ever growing variety of products."[2] *Fortune* magazine summarized its perception of the advantages to be gained from the "lean/flexible" system (see Table 1).[3] As the table indicates, managers in North America envisaged a new production model based on Japan's production methods. The trend that had begun as an effort to mimic quality circles had mushroomed into a full-scale movement to promote Japanese production systems.

This movement has spread far beyond manufacturing. Lean production has inspired a resurgent quality movement in North America that has spread from the factory to the warehouse and even into health care and educational facilities. Often appearing under the labels Total Quality Management (TQM) or Continuous Quality Improvement (CQI), the quality movement is based largely on the model of lean production. It has been inspired by gurus such as Edward Deming and J. M. Juran, both of whom made their reputations as quality experts in Japan in the 1950s but who remained largely peripheral in North America until the 1980s.

1. James P. Womack, Daniel T. Jones, and Daniel Roos, *The Machine That Changed the World* (New York: Macmillan, 1990).

2. Ibid., p. 13.

3. Many names have been assigned to the model: lean production, innovation-mediated production, management-by-stress, post-Fordism, and flexible production are among the best known.

Table 1. *Fortune* summary of production systems: Two ways of making things

The lean/flexible system (new Japanese style)	The buffered/rigid system (traditional American style)
Can be profitable making small batches of products.	Profitable only when making large batches.
The product and process for making it are designed concurrently.	The process is designed after the product has been designed.
The lean inventory turns over fast.	The fat inventory turns over slowly.
Suppliers are helped, informed and kept close.	Suppliers are kept at arm's length.
Engineers search widely for ideas and technology.	Engineers are insular, don't welcome outside ideas.
Employees learn several skills, work well in teams.	Employees are compartmentalized.
The company stresses continuous small improvements.	The company looks for the big breakthroughs.
The customers' orders pull the products through the factory.	The system pushes products through to the customers.

Source: Fortune, "Manufacturing the Right Way," May 21, 1990, p. 60. © Time Inc. All rights reserved.

The quality movement catapulted them and the quality message—customer service, *kaizen* (constant improvement), waste elimination, and teams—into the lexicon of North American workplaces whether staffed by steelworkers or nurses. And if one traces the roots of the most recent management trends, be they re-engineering or agile manufacturing, one eventually comes back to lean production.

Despite its apparent success, lean production has had its critics. As early as 1985, scholars in Germany criticized the emerging management theories that attributed Japan's success in automobile production to alternative forms of industrial organization including worker participation in quality circles.[4] In 1988, the Canadian Autoworkers Union adopted a policy statement criticizing Japanese management methods.[5] That same year Mike Parker and Jane Slaughter published *Choosing Sides: Unions and the Team Concept,* a biting critique of lean production.[6] Victor Reuther, one of the founders and former leaders of the United Autoworkers Union (UAW) along with his brother Walter Reuther, condemned the new

4. Knuth Dohse, Ulrich Jurgens, and Thomas Malsch, "From 'Fordism' to 'Toyotaism'? The Social Organization of the Labor Process in the Japanese Automobile Industry," *Politics and Society* 14, no. 2 (1985): 115–146.

5. Canadian Autoworkers Union (CAW), "Statement on the Organization of Work" (Willowdale, Ont.: CAW, 1989).

6. Mike Parker and Jane Slaughter, *Choosing Sides: Unions and the Team Concept* (Boston: South End Press, 1988).

systems: "Where the team concept was born and has become dominant, in Japan, workers no longer turn to the union for help." And from Sweden, Christian Berggren contested the humanist claims of lean production by showing how Volvo's Udevalla plant had actually abolished the assembly line and humanized work to a degree unknown in Japanese assembly plants.[7]

These critics might have been dismissed, particularly after Volvo closed its Udevalla and Kalmar plants in 1993, had it not been for two other salient facts: workers in some of the North American plants where lean production had been introduced displayed persistent, and at times rancorous, dissatisfaction with significant aspects of the new systems.[8] Also important, however, was the fact that lean production has come under fire from within. In Japan itself, automobile makers and unions increasingly questioned these same production methods and objectives. In a startling 1992 statement, the Japan Automobile Workers Union (JAW) conceded: "The automobile industry for example, is bogged down of triple sufferings: the employees are exhausted; the companies make only little profit; and the automobile industry is always bashed from abroad."[9] The union's advisor and noted scholar, Shimada Haruo, echoed this refrain: "Workers have lost out due to long working hours, which are unimaginable for workers in advanced countries." Shimada also recognized that Japan's auto unions had somewhere gone amiss: "Trade unions cooperated in this desperate competition for a share. Working hard, they lost their vision about for whom and what growth should be achieved."[10] These statements are an indication of the serious reflection taking place in Japan about production issues. New works by Japanese scholars such as Totsuka Hideo, Kamii Yoshihiko, and Nomura Masami also exposed a side of Japanese management that the IMVP task force either failed to detect or ignored.[11]

7. Christian Berggren, *Alternatives to Lean Production: Work Organization in the Swedish Auto Industry* (Ithaca: ILR Press, 1992).

8. For recent critical insights into the effects of lean production see Steve Babson, ed., *Lean Work: Empowerment and Exploitation in the Global Auto Industry* (Detroit: Wayne State University Press, 1995), and Mike Parker and Jane Slaughter, *Working Smart* (Detroit: Labor Notes, 1994).

9. Confederation of Japan Automobile Workers' Unions (JAW), "Japanese Automobile Industry in the Future" (Tokyo: JAW, 1992), p. 1.

10. Ibid., pp. 31–35. Shimada today is less inclined to see enterprise unions in a positive light. He still tends to see the issues from an organizational perspective (Japan's enterprise unions are unique) but he has at least recognized that they have problems that go beyond organizational issues. He postulates that they have become captive to an "industrial culture": "And, second, they are mentally restricted by the narrow scope of enterprise-level labor-management relations." See Shimada Haruo, "Japan's Industrial Culture and Labor-Management Relations," in K. Kumon and H. Rosovsky, eds., *The Political Economy of Japan*, vol. 3, *Cultural and Social Dynamics* (Stanford: Stanford University Press, 1992), pp. 267–291.

11. See Totsuka Hideo and Hyōdō Tsutomu, *Rōshi kankei no tenkan to sentaku* [Transition and choice in industrial relations] (Tokyo: Nihon Hyōron Sha, 1991); Totsuka Hideo and Tokunaga Shigeyoshi, *Gendai Nihon no rōdō mondai* [Labor issues in contemporary Japan] (Tokyo: Mineruba

This book attempts to contribute to the debate about lean production by documenting the conditions within Japan that gave rise to the new production systems. More generally, this book is a historical study about postwar Japan. It attempts to integrate four spheres: labor history, industrial relations, production management, and economic history. Its main focus is not lean production per se, although that is also directly examined, but rather the postwar industrial relations system that has played a key role in its genesis. To document this, and at the same time provide a theoretical and comparative framework, I have adopted an interdisciplinary approach that I hope is comprehensive enough to satisfy the specialist, yet broad enough to appeal also to the general reader.

Lean Production: The Issues

It would be one thing if the advocates of lean production argued simply that the new production process is more efficient than traditional assembly plants and left it at that. But they go much further, arguing that lean production is not only more efficient but more humane for employees. Lean production, they argue, represents a new, progressive phase of capitalism in which workers are finally empowered to use their brains as well as their brawn.

Two of the most eloquent advocates of this thesis are Martin Kenney and Richard Florida. In 1988, these two argued that Japan's production regime "replaces the task fragmentation, functional specialization, mechanization, and assembly-line principles of Fordism with a social organization of production based on work teams, job rotation, learning by doing, flexible production, and integrated production complexes."[12] Kenney and Florida's later work *Beyond Mass Production* represents the most thorough and sophisticated articulation of the post-Fordist thesis. They have now dubbed the new production paradigm "innovation-mediated production" and declare that it will define "the future of the advanced capitalist world."[13]

I share Kenney and Florida's assessment of Japan's importance. In attempting to present a cohesive portrait of the origins of the system, they have provided a thoughtful and reasoned interpretation. The interpretation, however, is flawed.

Shobō, 1993); Nomura Masami, *Toyoteizumu* [Toyotism] (Tokyo: Mineruba Shobō, 1993); Kamii Yoshihiko, *Rōdō kumiai no shokuba kisei* [The influence of the enterprise union on the shopfloor level] (Tokyo: Tokyo Daigaku Shuppan Kai, 1994).

12. Martin Kenney and Richard Florida, "Beyond Mass Production: Production and the Labor Process in Japan," *Politics and Society* 16, no. 1 (March 1988): 122.

13. Martin Kenney and Richard Florida, *Beyond Mass Production: The Japanese System and Its Transfer to the U.S.* (New York: Oxford University Press, 1993), p. 316.

The flaw becomes evident in the way the authors downplay evidence that contradicts their thesis, even when the evidence comes from their own research or from other advocates for lean production. The IMVP study, for example, admits that the work pace is harder in lean production plants such as Toyota's Takaoka plant than at GM's Framingham plant.[14] Kenney and Florida make similar admissions: "Life on the Japanese assembly line is stressful, difficult, and at times even unhealthy."[15] Why, one might ask, should workers have to work harder if the system is more efficient? Yet instead of explaining this contradiction, the authors wish it away by portraying the new production paradigm as the result of a voluntary accommodation between labor and management. Workers don't mind working harder because they have input into production, or so the argument goes.

To prove their point, however, Kenney and Florida are obliged to construct a historical schema explaining the origins of this grand labor-management compromise. In the process, they distort the dynamics of postwar class relations in Japan and end up relying on a caricature of the industrial relations system—the alleged three pillars of permanent employment, seniority-based wages, and enterprise unions—to justify their views.

Kenney and Florida quite rightly point out, however, that critical studies can easily fall into the trap of portraying Japan's development as a return to the despotism of coercive capitalism, or of dwelling on the theme of superexploitation. The extreme polarization in the debate represents a general difficulty in coming to terms with the paradox of Japan's production politics: On one level, workers get involved in production, work in teams, and rotate jobs; yet on another level the system maintains a strong bias toward mass production and exploitation.

This book acknowledges that both aspects developed integrally; it attempts to explore the paradox, not dismiss it. I examine postwar labor-management relations based on three case studies, one in the public sector and two in industry—coal and automobiles. The research results reveal that a major feature of the industrial relations system in postwar Japan was the extensive control employers enjoyed over work and workers. This control has never gone unchallenged. Some unions succeeded in modifying the system, but they were a minority. In general, the postwar compromise ended up a lopsided affair with employers exercising powers that both differed from and exceeded those of employers in North America. This control did not, however, lead to anything resembling the despotic regimes of early capitalism, despite such a tendency during the 1950s. Instead, the regime evolved into a variant of a Fordist system, similar in its high productivity–high wage formula to Fordist regimes in other countries but with some distinctive attributes, notably, worker participation in quality circles.

---

14. Womack, Jones, and Roos, *Machine That Changed the World*, p. 80.
15. Kenney and Florida, *Beyond Mass Production*, p. 10.

Japan's production system retained the stamp of extensive employer control, however, and the regime that developed was unique in that it allowed for employee involvement without altering the norms of the Fordist labor process. Instead, the regime shaped the input that workers had in production matters, and it undermined workers' ability to articulate their own independent agenda for the workplace. This, in the end, diminished labor's capacity to extract the benefits one might have expected from such an efficient system. Thus Japan's contemporary factory regime could not break with Fordism. The assembly line, repetitive and routine jobs, and standardization remained at the heart of the production process in the automobile industry. But it was a dynamic system, one that continually renewed itself in response to competitive pressures. In referring to this dynamic system I have adopted the term "lean production" although other terms, including "management by stress," are just as appropriate. I also accept that lean production represented a higher stage in the evolution of capitalist productivity, one that must be studied and learned from. To do so, however, requires that we return to its origins and that we come to terms with the paradox of Japan's production politics by reexamining the historical relationship between industrial relations and production norms as they evolved in postwar Japan.

Lean Production and Industrial Relations

This book is essentially an attempt to explain why worker participation in Japan could occur without transforming the system into a worker-friendly environment. It is fundamentally about control in the workplace and how employers in Japan came to exercise control in ways that differed from those that became institutionalized in the United States or Canada. In a broad sense, it is a historical account of the emergence of the postwar industrial relations system (or "employment system" as some would term it). Understanding the nature of Japanese industrial relations is essential to understanding lean production. The advocates of lean production understood the importance of this linkage and provided their own interpretation.

The IMVP team, for example, contend that at Toyota, a strike in 1946 gave workers lifetime employment and seniority-based wages. These rights supposedly made Toyota workers full members of the enterprise and "went far beyond what most unions had been able to negotiate for mass-production employees in the West."[16] This account conveys the perspective that the new deal gave workers considerable power in the workplace and in exchange workers saw fit to contribute their brains as well as their brawn in production. As we shall see, this account may

16. Womack, Jones, and Roos, *Machine That Changed the World*, p. 54.

fit the image the authors were trying to create, but it has little to do with the reality of industrial relations as they evolved at Toyota or in other automobile plants.

A similar but more sophisticated perspective is provided by Kenney and Florida. They provide some depth to their analysis and devote a whole chapter ("Beyond Fordism") to their views on the historical relationship between Japanese industrial relations and lean production:

> The basic contours of the argument are as follows. The rise of innovation-mediated production in Japan was tied in large measure to the specific constellation of political and economic forces acting on Japan in the immediate postwar years. During this crucial period, intense industrial unrest at the point of production, popular struggle, and class conflict unleashed a set of forces that altered the balance of class power or "class accord," produced a distinct pattern of capital-labor accommodation, and resulted in a dramatic restructuring of work and production organization.[17]

Key in this early period (1946–47) were the struggles for production control which, according to Kenney and Florida, "essentially, established the roots of the Japanese system of team-based work organization." The authors recognize that the early "laborist" period was superseded by a managerial offensive in 1949, but they contend that "many of the characteristics now interpreted as indicating capital's control of labor were initially labor demands. Like the postwar accords of the United States and Western European countries, only later were these demands integrated into the logic of capitalist accumulation." This postwar accommodation was reflected in the new system of industrial relations that "revolved around guaranteed long-term employment, a seniority-based wage system, and enterprise unionism for the core of the labor force."[18]

It is no coincidence that the MIT researchers and Kenney and Florida come to similar conclusions. Their research on lean production in Japan was based mainly on secondary sources, and although their work reflects a new appreciation of Japan's economic strength, their perceptions of the reasons for that strength remain based on old interpretations. The conventional "three pillars" interpretation of Japan's labor-management relations, adopted in a modified form by advocates of lean production, has tended to perpetuate a stereotype of workers in Japan as loyal employees bound to the company through paternalistic employment practices of cradle-to-grave employment, wages that increase with seniority, and unions that are focused on the enterprise. Although not entirely lacking in substance, this portrait of industrial relations in Japan is more caricature than reality. Furthermore, as a generalization it leaves little room for digression. The three pillars typology, in the end, prevents us from exploring the intricate web of Japan's

17. Kenney and Florida, *Beyond Mass Production*, pp. 23–24.
18. Ibid., pp. 28–29.

work life and, when integrated as part of the new production model, promotes a vision for workers that, from a comparative perspective, cannot be justified.

It is understandable that policy analysts and overseas commentators, when looking to understand the new factory order, would quickly refer to the three pillars theory of Japan's industrial relations. That the system is supposedly structured around the three institutions of lifetime employment, seniority-based wages, and enterprise unionism has become conventional wisdom. For the past thirty years, it has been offered up as standard fare with few exceptions. And, as we shall see, even recent historiography has been unable to break with this stereotype.

James Abeggelen was among the first of many scholars and industrial relations specialists to elaborate the three pillars interpretation of Japan's industrial relations. In his 1958 classic, *The Japanese Factory*, he postulated that jobs were permanent and that wages were based on seniority.[19] Japanese employers themselves began to promote a similar interpretation to Abegglen. In 1963, Sakurada Takeshi, representing Nikkeiren (Federation of Employer Organizations), used the Japanese term "three golden treasures" to describe the main features of the labor relations system. Since the 1960s, citing the three pillars has become *de rigueur* for any account of labor relations. Astonishingly, adherence to these features transcends phases of interpretations, academic fields, and even the political spectrum. Whether in OECD reports or in leftish journals in the United States, the three pillars apparently provides support for every interpretive bent.[20]

Of all the works in English based on the three pillars interpretation none has been more influential than that of Ronald Dore, the eminent British sociologist. In his classic work, *British Factory–Japanese Factory*, Dore offered the most sophisticated schema of the three pillars theory as well as a treatise on Japan's labor relations history. According to Dore, employers were convinced of the necessity of working with unions from 1922 on, and they were able to shape union-management relations before unions became too strong. Thus Japan was able to avoid the fate of Britain, where the early and drawn-out process led to acute class conflicts and "the antique inflexibility of her trade union institutions."[21]

Immediately after the war, according to Dore, Japan underwent a social-democratic revolution and employers unquestioningly accepted unions and abol-

19. James Abegglen, *The Japanese Factory: Aspects of Its Social Organization* (Glencoe, Ill.: Free Press, 1958).

20. In his literature survey Shimada posits that the three pillars terminology is derived from the Japanese term "three golden treasures." Three treasures (jewels, a mirror, and a sword) were bestowed upon the gods Izanami and Izanagi according to folk legend. Sakurada Takeshi uses the same terms in reference to lifetime employment, seniority-based wages, and enterprise unionism. For a leftist view, see David Levine's article "Japan's Other Export," *Dollars and Sense* (September 1990), pp. 17–24.

21. Ronald Dore, *British Factory–Japanese Factory* (Berkeley: University of California Press, 1974), p. 420.

ished the status differences between staff and manual workers. This gave rise to the postwar "enterprise-as-community" pattern of industrial relations based on the three pillars of lifetime employment, seniority wages, and enterprise union- ism. As a consequence of this "late development" syndrome, industrial relations in Japan have leapfrogged ahead of Britain on the road to "democratic corporatism."

If anything, Dore's recent publications reinforce his initial contentions and constitute aggressive advocacy of the Japanese model.[22] According to Dore, the "firm-as-community" has been influenced by Japan's Confucian roots. It has given employees an equal if not superior footing with managers and shareholders, en- terprise proceeds are fairly divided, and decision making is from the bottom up. In comparative terms, Dore associates his "firm-as-community" model with Swedish social-democratic institutions and sees in it the future direction of inter- national work life.[23] Although Dore's view is not couched in the same terms as Kenney and Florida's, he in fact projects a post-Fordist vision of Japan similar to the one they espouse.

Dore's works are important, and I and many others have learned from them. But this does not mean that we should necessarily accept their interpretive bent. Dore may be correct that Confucian values emphasize community, but there is also a strong case to be made that Confucian values emphasize hierarchy and pa- triarchy. This book will not explore the ideological dimension so much as the functional, and on that level, as we shall see, the analogy Dore makes between Japan's workplaces and those in Sweden, for example, is difficult to accept.

To be fair, in the past decade a number of other scholars have taken issue with the three pillars paradigm or at least cautioned us about its limits. Mary Brinton does this in *Women and the Economic Miracle*.[24] So do other comparative scholars such as Koike Kazuo, for example, who directly criticizes the concept of perma- nent employment.[25] And in an extensive survey of English-language literature on Japan's industrial relations, Shimada Haruo warns that the three pillars stereotype "tends to overshadow facts that do not conform with it and to discourage alterna- tive interpretations."[26] Yet Shimada himself seemed to forget his own admonitions

22. One of Dore's more recent works is *Taking Japan Seriously: A Confucian Perspective on Leading Economic Issues* (Stanford: Stanford University Press, 1987). Note Dore's use of the term "Confucian." Dore explicitly reaffirms his adherence to the three pillars paradigm on p. 9. Another relevant study is Dore's *Flexible Rigidities* (London: Athlone Press, 1986).

23. Dore's works represent only the sophisticated cutting edge to what has become a deluge of ma- terials that advocate Japanese-style institutions in production systems, education, and labor relations.

24. Mary Brinton, *Women and the Economic Miracle: Gender and Work in Postwar Japan* (Berkeley: University of California Press, 1993).

25. Koike Kazuo, *Understanding Industrial Relations in Modern Japan* (London: Macmillan, 1988).

26. Shimada Haruo, "Japanese Industrial Relations—A New General Model?", in Shirai and Shi- mada, eds., *Contemporary Industrial Relations in Japan* (Madison: University of Wisconsin Press, 1983), p. 10.

when it comes to dealing with one of the pillars, the so-called enterprise unions. "For Japanese workers the enterprise union was the only, and most *natural*, form of organization because their basic common interest as industrial workers had been formulated within an individual enterprise."[27] Not only did Shimada continue to uphold the validity of the enterprise union model, until recently he assailed any critique of enterprise unions:

> An interesting example is Galenson (1976). He analyzed the operation of the Japanese labour market and industrial relations system and concluded in effect, that Japanese unions have not generated the strength necessary to represent workers' demands properly or to protect their interests, and that they have failed to secure the workers' due share of the gains from economic growth. A view of this kind apparently assumes that American or Anglo-Saxon trade unionism is almost the sole ideal type and dismisses some differing but important attributes that make Japanese-type unions effective.[28]

This vicious cycle of pointing out limits only to reinforce them illustrates the underlying persistence of the three pillars typology, not to mention the nationalist pitfalls of comparing and evaluating different labor relations institutions.

Even Andrew Gordon, despite the insights in his book *The Evolution of Labor Relations in Japan*, accepted the three pillars framework. Nevertheless, Gordon's study constituted a benchmark in English-language scholarship on Japan's labor history and deserves further comment, especially since Kenney and Florida rely on it for much of their analysis of Japan's industrial relations.[29]

Gordon's study attempted to discover the nature and origins of industrial relations patterns in Japan through case studies of several firms in heavy industry. Its tremendous strength derives from the way it traces patterns of industrial relations at these firms over the course of a century, from its emphasis on the role of workers' struggles in shaping the labor-management relationship, and from its refusal to be bound by convergence theories. Gordon concluded that there were many aspects of continuity in industrial relations institutions (the bonus system, for example) from the prewar to the postwar period. He also posited that for men in large enterprises, "the postwar settlement emerges as a far-reaching transformation of the labor relationship."[30] Male workers in large enterprises were finally given

27. Shimada Haruo and Shirai Taishiro, "Japan," in Dunlop and Galenson, eds., *Labor in the Twentieth Century* (New York: Academic Press, 1978), p. 258 (emphasis added).

28. Shimada, "Japanese Industrial Relations," p. 8.

29. Andrew Gordon, *The Evolution of Labor Relations in Japan: Heavy Industry, 1853–1955* (Cambridge: Harvard University Press, 1985). Kenney and Florida base their interpretation of postwar labor relations in Japan on Gordon, although it is not clear if Gordon agrees with the particular spin they have given his study. See their acknowledgment in *Beyond Mass Production*, p. 27.

30. Andrew Gordon, *The Evolution of Labor Relations in Japan*, p. 411.

"membership" in the enterprise community and given the benefits of the three pillars. Gordon cautions against attributing too much importance to culture or pitting conflict against culture, however. Both workers and managers manipulated culture to promote their own interests.

Gordon's study had its own specific framework and its limitations. For example, his conclusion that the postwar settlement represented a significant transformation of labor relations was specifically *relative* to the prewar and wartime regimes. He also concluded that

> workers did become part of the organization to a far greater extent than before or during World War II. Although managers rejected their program of control, participation, contractually secure jobs, and explicit livelihood wages, they conceded the status of 'employee,' the respect and security of a monthly wage, and the right to use all facilities to an expanding pool of workers. And they worked out an implicit system of job security and livelihood wages acceptable to most employees. From the perspective of the late twentieth century, this may look like a cheap set of concessions, largely symbolic, often imposed from above, and actually in management interest. But remember how different the situation had been in the 1930s and during the war.[31]

In other words, Gordon's conclusions were strictly in relationship to Japan's domestic evolution. Today, when Japan's industrial relations and production processes are being cast as a potential model for other countries, such conclusions must be reassessed from a comparative perspective. As we shall see, such a perspective exposes the analytical weakness of the three pillars theory.

Although he adopted the three pillars analogy, Gordon was aware of the potential risks associated with invoking this typology. Regarding jobs, for example, Gordon concluded that the terms "permanent employment" and "lifetime job" were misleading.[32] He also acknowledged that wages were contingent on much more than seniority. Yet despite these qualifications he continued to accept the designation of the wage system as seniority based. Furthermore, Gordon never seriously explored the enterprise union pillar, and by equating enterprise unions with company unions he perpetuated confusion.[33] The greatest limitation of his work, however, is that he examines postwar developments only in a single chapter, and his exclusive emphasis on heavy industry narrows the scope of his postwar investigation. The idea that Japan's industrial relations system consolidated between "the late 1940s and the mid-1950s . . . to endure relatively unchanged for at least three decades" obliges Gordon to omit such institutions as annual bargaining from his narrative and undermines the construction of an appropriate periodiza-

31. Ibid.
32. Ibid., p. 2.
33. Ibid., p. 3.

tion for the postwar era. Nevertheless, Gordon's study will remain a classic in delineating the origins of the employment system in Japan.

This book is not about the origins of the employment system. It is an attempt to clarify the nature of the postwar industrial relations system as it functionally evolved and to demonstrate its role in the genesis of lean production. In taking a comparative approach, it challenges the three pillars interpretation of Japan's industrial relations as well as Kenney and Florida's general post-Fordist thesis. Where they stress continuity between the early labor triumphs and the post-1949 period, I find discontinuity and qualitative changes, particularly in the nature of the wage system, union orientation, and union input on job levels. In fact, in defining the contours of postwar industrial relations, this study fundamentally challenges the conventional wisdom about Japan's industrial relations. It argues not only that the three pillars interpretation has limited scope (most commentators now acknowledge that employees enjoying permanent employment status represent less than 30 percent of the work force) but that even within the limited confines of large enterprises it provides an inaccurate and inadequate description of employer-employee relations.

In reexploring the history of postwar labor relations, it became clear that the dominant pattern of industrial relations in Japan reflected greater employer domination and, consequently, greater market influence over workplace values than in other industrialized countries. This was the result of labor's defeat in an intense class struggle in the early postwar period, a defeat that led not to an accommodation of labor's demands but in fact to their reversal and to a long-term weakening of labor's ability to shape the Fordist compromise of the 1950s and 1960s. Although labor did regroup in the 1950s and played a role in instituting annual bargaining, for example, its relative weakness meant that outcomes for workers in the miracle economy were relatively small, particularly from a comparative perspective. This helps explain why, after leading the world in productivity growth in the 1970s and 1980s, Japan's workers were putting in longer hours than employees in any other industrialized country.

To be sure, some of the features of the postwar accommodation, such as joint consultation committees, harked back to the management councils of 1946 to 1948, in which labor had representative equity and exercised a right to veto layoffs. But joint consultation committees were a pale imitation of the former management councils and, given the overall relation of forces between labor and management, did not resemble, for example, the forms of codetermination that emerged in continental Europe in the postwar period.

Instead, the system of industrial relations that emerged reflected the impact of this strong employer influence and undermined workers' capacity to remove their employment conditions from the competitive market and employer control. Taking one specific area as an example, wage determination in Japan's workplaces be-

came subject to employer control through an extensive system of regular personnel evaluations. In other words, instead of wages being calculated on the basis of
strict objective criteria (age or accumulated service or jobs) they became the subject of unilateral management evaluation of a worker's worth. Other researchers,
including Gordon and Dore, have noted this point, but few have stressed how
widespread this procedure had become, and even fewer have understood or analyzed its fundamental implications. Instead we have been indulged with the constant refrain of the "seniority-based" character of Japan's wage system.

The ability of employers to manipulate the industrial relations environment
gave them some important advantages in maximizing capital accumulation. I argue that Japan's Fordism, although allowing for higher wages, achieved its rapid
development partially through a greater degree of labor exploitation than in other
industrialized countries. This is most easily perceived through the position of
women within the work force, as Brinton and others have pointed out. But even
within the large, male-dominated workplaces, employers were able to use labor
more flexibly than in automobile plants in North America. This led to certain
economic efficiencies, but it also exacted a harsh toll from the labor force.

Furthermore, because the industrial relations environment differed from that
of the United States or Canada, for example, the organizational innovations that
occurred in the automobile industry displayed important variations from Fordist
norms in the United States. These variations did not provoke a break with fundamental Fordist standards of work organization. Instead, what evolved in the automobile industry at least was a leaner, more intense version of Fordism. That the
system was more efficient is recognized. That some of the changes were positive
and have opened up room for progressive reform is also within the realm of discussion. What is questioned, however, is the proposition that the new production
model, whether we dub it "lean," "innovation-mediated," or "post-Fordist," represented a qualitative step forward for labor.

This book dwells on Japan's postwar labor history and its impact on industrial
relations, production management, and economic history—issues that can be
complex. Because this is an interdisciplinary study and since many readers may
have limited knowledge of Japan, the next part of this introduction spells out the
theoretical and comparative framework used in analyzing the issues.

History: Critical and Comparative Approaches

To move beyond the three pillars stereotype and to provide some depth to
our understanding of work in Japan, we need to develop a more comprehensive
understanding of the postwar history of labor-management relations. It will be
helpful to take advantage of recent theoretical insights into labor and industrial

relations under capitalism. It is also necessary to ground the discussion with an explicit, comparative reference point in order to avoid inappropriate assumptions. This approach differs from the cultural orientation that has often dominated Japanese studies recently. The intent in taking a comparative, structuralist approach, however, is not to deny the extremely valuable and important role of the study of indigenous culture and ideology. Indeed, many questions that arise from this study can be answered only through further research on cultural issues. But given the confusion about the nature and function of industrial relations in postwar Japan, I try to clarify some of the issues from a comparative perspective.

Although the contemporary debate about lean production shapes the issues addressed in this book, this is first and foremost a historical study of labor relations as they evolved at the point of production. My earlier research into the coal industry in Japan acquainted me with the Miike coalminers in Kyushu and their momentous fight for survival, which galvanized the whole country in 1960. The relative absence of strike activity in the post-1960 era, it seemed, was a new development. I became convinced that no account of contemporary labor-management relations was worth its salt if it could not document and analyze the role workers and unions played in the postwar period and if it could not explain the tremendous labor-management conflicts that marked the years from 1945 to 1960.

This, then, is a study of labor history, of industrial relations and of production management mainly in the 1945–73 period. This particular period was chosen because, despite important continuities between the prewar and postwar periods, defeat in World War II and the American occupation marked the beginning of a new era for Japan in economic, social, and political terms. The cutoff is about 1975. By this time, Japan had put its own stamp on its development, and many of the contemporary features of industrial relations and production management were installed. The 1973–74 oil crisis marked an important socioeconomic watershed, which has been given some attention, but the period deserves much more exhaustive study than was possible in this work. Finally, twenty years provides the distance necessary to obtain some historical purchase on the often slippery slopes of socioeconomic analysis.

A Crisis of Theory

It is one thing to use history to challenge current assumptions and quite another to overcome them. I suspect that one of the reasons the three pillars typology persists, despite numerous recent qualifications and challenges, is because there has not been an adequate theoretical framework to construct an alternative, coherent analysis. And so we in the English-speaking world have, for the most part, been left to debate Japan's institutions from the outmoded or limited perspectives of convergence theories, late development, or strategic choice, among others.[34] That a radical framework of analysis has been, until recently, next to nonexistent in the English literature on Japan is hardly surprising. And even where it has developed, the radical perspective has not been without its problems.

Braverman did resuscitate an interest in a radical analysis of the labor process. His work has achieved classic status and inspired sustained research in this specific area.[35] Unfortunately the same cannot be said for the arena of industrial relations. The Marxist tradition has until recently failed to articulate a cohesive theory that speaks directly to this issue. In some cases it has gone to the point of even questioning the plausibility of industrial relations as a specific field.[36] This narrow Marxist approach has perpetuated a dichotomy between theories of the labor process and of industrial relations. Marxists study the labor process or political economy, academics study industrial relations. Fortunately, the abyss is beginning to disappear as capital globalization stimulates international and comparative studies. These in turn are forcing Marxism into the twentieth century. This study suggests that one part of that transition requires continually specifying what we mean by the labor process. It may mean simply the study of the division of labor, that is, how work is organized (a micro approach), or it may invoke a macro approach to socioeconomic analysis.

In the latter, the French school of regulation theory and Burawoy's theory of production regimes are two key elements that have helped to resuscitate a constructive Marxist critique of capitalist development. Both help us comprehend the macrodynamics of the labor process.[37] Together, they constitute the theoretical heart of this thesis. The former has provided a Marxist economic analysis that challenges traditional Keynesian economic theory and permits a deeper understanding of Fordism, that is, the regimes of advanced capitalism (intensive capital accumulation) and the mechanisms that govern them. Burawoy, on the

34. For an overview of these perspectives see Chapter 1 of Greg Bamber and Russell Lansbury, eds., *International and Comparative Industrial Relations* (London: Allen & Unwin, 1987), pp. 3–29.

35. Harry Braverman, *Labor and Monopoly Capital* (New York: Monthly Review Press, 1974).

36. See R. Hyman, "Theory in Industrial Relations: Towards a Materialist Analysis," in P. Boreham and G. Dow, eds., *Work and Inequality*, vol. 2, *Ideology and Control in the Labour Process* (Melbourne: Macmillan, 1980), p. 55.

37. For a review of regulation theory see Michel Aglietta, *A Theory of Capitalist Regulation* (London: Verso, 1987); Alain Lipietz, *The Enchanted World: Inflation, Credit and the World Crisis* (London: Verso, 1985), and *Towards a New Economic Order: Postfordism, Ecology and Democracy* (Cambridge: Polity Press, 1992), and "Towards Global Fordism?" *New Left Review*, no. 132, (March-April 1982); Robert Boyer, *The Regulation School* (New York: Columbia University Press, 1990), and Robert Boyer, ed., *The Search for Labour Market Flexibility* (Oxford: Clarendon Press, 1988). For Canadian pespectives see Rianne Mahon, "Post-Fordism: Some Issues for Labour," in D. Drache and M. Gertler, eds., *The New Era of Global Competition* (Montreal: McGill-Queens University Press, 1991), pp. 316–332; Martha MacDonald, "Post-Fordism and the Flexibility Debate," *Studies in Political Economy* 36 (autumn 1991): 177–201. On production politics see Michael Burawoy, *The Politics of Production* (London: Verso, 1985).

other hand, posits a theory of "relations in production." These relations arise not only from the nature of work organization but also from the class conflicts and compromises that shape specific production regimes on a sectoral and national scale.

The combination of these two strains in recent Marxist theory permits, indeed demands, a perspective that embraces both convergence and divergence in understanding capitalist development on an international scale. They will help us understand how industrial relations in postwar Japan facilitated innovation in production process yet did so without empowering Japan's workers. To fully understand Japan's system, however, we must first backtrack and explore what is meant by "Fordism."

Fordism as Work Organization

This book and other works that attempt to analyze the production or labor process often introduce the term "Fordism." This term has different meanings depending on the context and on the writer. In this section I summarize the uses of the term, particularly as it is employed in this book.

The crux of the issue is the production system that Henry Ford introduced into his operations with the Model T between 1908 and 1913. These changes culminated in the introduction of the chassis assembly line production at Ford's Highland Park plant in 1914.[38] Most commentators today agree that the Ford system was, in its embryonic form, the prototype of modern mass production. It was based upon "deskilling, but also product standardization, the use of interchangeable parts, mechanization, a moving assembly line, and high wages."[39] This quote represents what we might call the popular, macro definition of Fordism. It captures not only how work is organized but the necessity of investment and the possibility of relatively high wages.

What had happened in the automobile industry, in fact, was a revolution in the organization of work based on the capitalist imperative of an ever increasing efficiency and on a technical revolution in steel manufacturing. The development of high-grade steel and Ford's insistence on using standard gauges created the possibility for the standardization and interchangeability of parts. Ford's managers used these developments to push the division of labor. According to Ford, time study of the work process revealed, for example, that assembly of pistons and rods for engines with one worker doing the whole process required nine hours, of which

38. The most detailed study of this process is Stephen Meyer III, *The Five Dollar Day: Labor Management and Social Control in the Ford Motor Company, 1908–1921* (Albany: State University of New York Press, 1981).

39. Ruth Milkman, "Labor and Management in Uncertain Times," in A. Wolfe, ed., *America at Century's End* (Berkeley: University of California Press, 1991), p. 134. This citation contains what I term the functional description of the generic Fordist regime.

fours hours were consumed in walking to fetch or move parts. The work was re-organized so that "instead of one man performing the whole operation, one man then performed only one-third of the operation—he performed only as much as he could do without shifting his feet."[40] In 1908, just prior to the introduction of the Model T, the average fitter's cycle time—the time between repetition of the same operation—was 514 minutes.[41] Ford reorganized the production process so that workers narrowed their job into short, repetitive operations. By August 1913, just prior to the introduction of the assembly line, the cycle time had been re-duced to 2.3 minutes.[42]

These nominal productivity increases were impressive, and the new division of labor required Ford to hire thousands of new workers. But realizing the potential productivity gains was not so easy. Coordinating production to capture the economies of scale was difficult at best. Furthermore, the intense pace and rou-tinization of work created new bottlenecks, and automobile workers demonstrated their resistance with their feet. Absenteeism and turnover at Ford reached astro-nomic levels. To address this issue, the automaker introduced in 1914 the five-dol-lar day, a profit sharing/bonus scheme that effectively doubled wages for semiskilled workers. The only hitch was that Ford workers had to agree to submit to an investigation by Ford's "sociological" department. This group conducted home visits to ascertain the moral character of employees. This paternalistic regime lasted only until 1920, at which time the sociological department was dissolved. Ford instead combined the carrot—a year-end bonus system based on skill and length of service—with the proverbial stick—a network of spies to report on slack-ers and union organizers.[43] A point seldom emphasized, however, is that Ford's wage system had for the most part abolished any form of individual or collective production bonus or incentive payment that was tied to overall output. Instead wages were paid on a straight time basis; adjustment for skill was incorporated into the wage scale through a classification system tied to specific jobs.[44]

With Ford's production system as a prototype, short cycle times, repetitive job routines, and detailed operations charts became legion in the U.S. automobile in-dustry. Little has changed since. Meyer, for example, documented the changes in the Fordist regime within the U.S. auto industry after 1920.[45] The two major changes he points to were the introduction of flexible specialization allowing for

40. As cited in Meyer, *Five Dollar Day*, p. 21.
41. Womack, Jones, and Roos, *Machine That Changed the World*, p. 28.
42. Ibid.
43. Meyer, *Five Dollar Day*, p. 197.
44. For details of the new job hierarchy see ibid., pp. 101–104.
45. Stephen Meyer, "The Persistence of Fordism: Workers and Technology in the American Auto-mobile Industry, 1900–1960," in Nelson Lichtenstein and Stephen Meyer, eds., *On the Line: Essays in the History of Auto Work* (Urbana: University of Illinois Press, 1989), pp. 73–99.

annual model changes under GM's president, Alfred Sloan, as early as the 1920s, and the advent of extensive automation in the postwar period prompted by union institutionalization of high wages and influence over job assignments. Despite these innovations, Meyers concluded that "Fordism remained a managerial strategy for the control of workers and the reduction of labor costs." For workers, the strategy "diluted skills, intensified work, and eliminated possible jobs."[46]

The Fordist norm for work organization, the type of repetitive and routinized work that developed in the automobile industry, was a classic example of what became known as "Taylorism." At the same time that Ford was introducing his new form of work organization at Highland Park, others were conducting time and motion studies of the work process in sectors outside the automobile industry. The most famous of these consultants was Frederick Taylor.[47]

Frederick Taylor and his associates Henry Gantt, Carl Barth, and Horace Hathaway were active in the American Society of Mechanical Engineers at the turn of the century. They began to do contract work for employers, scrutinizing the work process of both craft workers and laborers and submitting them to rigorous standards of efficiency.[48] The movement grew in scope, and in 1911 Taylor and his many associates founded the Society to Promote the Science of Management (renamed the Taylor Society in 1915 upon Taylor's death). The growth of Taylorism and "scientific management" signified the elevation of the study of the labor process to a separate discipline in order for employers to gain complete control over how work was organized and to maximize efficiency through exact instruction of detail work.

To be sure, as Braverman observes in his seminal study of the labor process, the long-term impact was to reduce the control and power of the craft worker. The continuous re-division of labor in the early twentieth century had tremendous repercussions on the composition of work skills. Non-craft workers began to predominate in assembly operations and, as David Montgomery points out, "skilled workers in large enterprises did not disappear, but most of them ceased to be production workers. Their tasks became ancillary—setup, troubleshooting, toolmaking, model making—while the actual production was increasingly carried out by specialized operatives."[49] Clearly, Taylorism and scientific movement had a pro-

---

46. Ibid., p. 94.

47. Taylor himself acknowledged that Ford independently developed repetitive and restricted work procedures when he congratulated six hundred Detroit automobile industry managers for being the "first to install the principles of scientific management without the aid of experts." Meyer, *Five Dollar Day*, p. 20.

48. For a mainstream account of Taylor's experiments see Daniel Nelson, *Frederick W. Taylor and the Rise of Scientific Management* (Madison: University of Wisconsin Press, 1980).

49. David Montgomery, *The Fall of the House of Labour* (Cambridge: Cambridge University Press, 1987), p. 215.

found impact on the organization of work, particularly in mass production industries. But for a number of reasons its influence remained partial.

For one thing, Taylorism provoked organized resistance from many union
workers. Molders at the Watertown Arsenals walked out in protest against Taylor's
experiments and prompted a congressional investigation of Taylorism. Congress
in fact prohibited time studies in government arsenals and navy yards in 1915.[50]
Since the scale and nature of the production process varied according to the product and the size of mill, this left some room for the skilled worker and restricted
the ability of managers to exert control through work organization. Productivity
growth brought forth huge increases in the number of workers in certain crafts.
Furthermore, the redivision of labor also created new forms of crafts and skills
over which management had only partial control.[51] And as movements, Taylorism
and scientific management themselves went through important transformations,
particularly after Taylor's death.[52] Despite these limits, many aspects of scientific
management persisted, mainly in the modern guise of industrial engineering. Its
symbols were, and continue to be, the stopwatch, time-and-motion studies, and
the detailed operations chart, which remained prevalent especially in the automobile industry.

The relevance of this discussion to the work at hand is twofold. First, the noted
Japanese industrial engineer Ishikawa Kaoru, among others, contends that Japanese employers did not adopt Taylorist work methods. As well, a number of Western scholars, such as Kenney and Florida, assert that the Toyota production system
(lean production) has broken with the Fordist labor process and reached a new
level of post-Fordist development. The findings of this book contradict such
views. The evidence from a historical review of labor process in Japan's automobile industry (summarized in Chapter 6) indicates that, up to 1975 at least, Taylorist forms of work organization were alive and well, as was assembly-line
production. Although we discovered significant differences between the Fordist
forms of work organization as they evolved in Japan and in the United States, we
have found none that lead us to qualify the Toyota system as post-Fordist, however. The variations, including flexible production and extensive employee involvement through quality circles, were significant and can be attributed to a

50. Ibid., p. 221.

51. In *Labor and Monopoly Capital*, Braverman posits that these trends "simply mask the secular
trend toward the incessant lowering of the working class as a whole below its previous conditions of
skill and labor" (pp. 129–130). This seems to overstate the case and ignores the dynamics of capitalist
productivity. It also sets linear standards of skill (handicraft equals best, operative equals worst) which
can easily be interpreted to mean that the goal of even modern labor is craft production methods.

52. For details see chapter 10 in David Noble, *America by Design* (Oxford: Oxford University Press,
1979), and Steve Fraser, "The Labor Question," in S. Fraser and G. Gerstle, eds., *The Rise and Fall of
the New Deal Order, 1930–1980* (Princeton: Princeton University Press, 1989), pp. 55–84.

number of factors. Early postwar circumstances in Japan did not allow for the direct application of mass production techniques as they were being used in U.S. automobile plants, for example. Small batches had to be integrated into a continuous flow process. Furthermore, although employers were enamored with the mass production system and Taylorism, they did not necessarily embrace the industrial relations practices (the wage system, job descriptions, and so forth) that had evolved under the influence of the U.S. union movement. They were therefore able to use labor more flexibly. As these examples illustrate, understanding the distinction between work organization and industrial relations and, at the same time, their interrelationship is crucial for understanding the convergence and diversity within Fordism as it evolved in Japan and other parts of the world.

Fordism and Regulation Theory: A Macro Approach

French Marxists Michel Aglietta and Alain Lipietz go beyond a functional description of Fordism to articulate a general theory of capitalist regulation based on a historical assessment of the U.S. experience. They make the following points:

1. Fordism embraced and went beyond Taylorism through the use of the semi-automatic assembly line, which became a core component of the new labor process. Ford's assembly line created a new benchmark for continuous flow operations, requiring a standardized, repetitive cycle of movements over which labor had almost no control.

2. The resulting productivity increases articulated a new relationship between the process of production and mode of consumption. In other words, Fordism both created and demanded the development of mass consumption, but the employers' short-term perspective (and anti-labor bias) prevented the establishment of the mass consumption norm until after the Depression.

3. The articulation of an independent labor agenda through unions and political parties demanded a new form of relationship between capital and labor. This new relationship was hegemonic, that is, based on the consent of labor to the continuing existence of the regime in return for an independent voice at the workplace.

4. The necessity of mass consumption and stable labor-capitalist relations gave rise to the Fordist state that, to one degree or another, regulated industrial development, socialized a part of the expense of reproducing labor power (through social insurance, schooling, health care, and so forth), and created a framework for hegemonic labor-capital relations.

5. In economic terms, mass consumption created a balance between the producer goods and consumer goods sections of the economy (heavy and light industry) and facilitated the passage of capitalist accumulation from an extensive phase (extended working hours) to an intensive one (accelerated work dependent on an ever increasing investment in fixed assets).

6. Problems in the labor process remained, including balancing the assembly line (standardizing each work routine to a specified period), the negative effects of routinized work and speed-ups on workers, and the potential dangers of creating a workforce with a shared experience.

Regulation theory offers significant insights as a labor-based, inclusive, and comprehensive framework for understanding capitalist development. It affords the wage relationship between labor and capital a centrality that conventional social science denies and that some state-oriented Marxists at times ignore. By describing it as inclusive, I mean it acknowledges that labor, employers, and the state were all key players in elaborating the specific regulatory mechanisms necessary for capital accumulation. For example, it correctly identifies the historical role of labor's struggle for a shorter workweek as a key determinant in pushing employers to find alternative means of accumulation through extension of the division of labour and mechanization.

Regulation theory also illuminates the complex nature of capital accumulation. The locus of regulation can be found not only in the labor process or in the state but also in the modalities that link production and consumption and in the interactions between labor and capital at various stages of the valorization of capital. In other words, it allows for the integration of politics and economics at every level.

Regulation theory also accommodates the Gramscian notion of hegemony, which holds that capitalist control cannot, in the long term, be exercised by authoritarian means alone and that some sort of deal must be worked out between labor and capital. This requires that employers relinquish some degree of power over the workplace. On the other hand, wage workers, through their union or shop representatives, must accept many facets of an oppressive industrial order in return for some say over the terms of employment and working conditions. Labor's concessions and influence are often contained in work rules or collective agreements. Thus, while struggling against exploitation, labor also consents to it, but this consent is extracted by a coercive economic system based on private ownership of the means of production. As we shall see, Japan did develop a hegemonic regime, and it also passed into the Fordist phase of capital accumulation; but this system did not crystallize until the 1960s.

Although not always conducted under the rubric of regulation theory, the study of national variations in Fordist regulatory mechanisms has become the focus of an increasing number of studies. Charlotte Yates and Nelson Lichtenstein have helped establish one important point of demarcation in Fordist regimes in their studies of labor in Canada and the United States.[53] Their work illuminates

53. Charlotte Yates, *From Plant to Politics: The Autoworkers Union in Postwar Canada* (Philadelphia: Temple University Press, 1993); Nelson Lichtenstein, "From Corporatism to Collective Bargaining," in Fraser and Gerstle, *The Rise and Fall of the New Deal.*

INTRODUCTION

how Canada and the United States were unable to pursue the social-democratic route that culminated in the corporatist mediation (labor/business/state) that became the hallmark of Fordism in Sweden, for example. Yates terms this noncorporatist model a "liberal-pluralist" form of regulation in which the regulatory mechanisms are integrated into and diluted by the private market and not universalized by public control through the state. Such insights are suggestive and can help to explain Japan's particular form of Fordism. They are related to the attempts by Michael Burawoy to develop a theory of production regimes.

Burawoy and the Politics of Production

Regulation theory has directed our attention to the universal aspects of Fordism as an intensive regime of accumulation that demands the creation of the regulatory state. Burawoy, on the other hand, directs us to examine the variations in the nature of production regimes as they are reproduced at the workplace.

Burawoy begins his thesis by refuting Braverman's proposal that the fundamental aspect of capitalism is its control of the labor process through the division of labor and the concomitant division of conception from execution. While upholding the classic status of Braverman's work as critique, he contends that it cannot stand as a framework for analysis. Braverman misses the essence of capitalist control because his framework remains within capitalism: "Braverman takes his standpoint from within capitalism, alongside the craft worker—the embodiment of the unity of conception and execution."[54] Braverman also fails to capture a relative notion of capitalist control because he does not articulate a potential alternative model of worker control. Socialism "is deduced for Braverman by inverting a picture of capitalism taken from within."[55] In contrast to Braverman, Burawoy contends:

Capitalism can and did survive under conditions of the unification of conception and execution. Their separation is not at the core of the capitalist labour process per se but is something that emerges and disappears in an uneven fashion as capitalism develops. The craft worker was, and indeed in some places still is, a part of capitalism. Thus, to identify the reunification of conception and execution with socialism is to confuse job control with workers control, relations in production with relations of production. It risks not going far enough and, in the process, mistaking a nostalgia for the past for a nostalgia for the future.[56]

Burawoy demands that we go beyond Braverman and broaden our understanding of labor. First we must stop reducing the labor process to the division of labor and

54. Burawoy, *Politics of Production*, p. 23.
55. Ibid., p. 24.
56. Ibid., p. 54.

work organization.[57] The labor process encompasses both the organization of work and what Burawoy terms the "relations in production," that is, the apparatus of production which regulates labor-management relations at the point of production. Thus any examination of the labour process must entail not only how work is organized but the entire scope of employment relations including wage and job determination, hours of work, dispute resolution, and so forth.[58]

Another critical factor is correctly discerning the relationship between labor and the specific factors that might condition it. For example, the labor process can be affected by the nature of specific industries, interfirm competition, technological developments, labor market conditions, gender and race issues, and ideology, not to mention the degree and nature of state intervention.

Taking a broader approach and allowing for a multifactor analysis of variables allow us to examine how capitalist development varies in time and space. Burawoy does this for both old capitalism—the regimes of the early industrial period—and for advanced capitalism, the hegemonic regimes. In his analysis of the former, Burawoy concludes that Marx was incorrect when he implied that capitalism could give rise to only one type of regime, market despotism. Many types of production regimes existed even in the early period of capitalism including the "company state" (early throstle mills in England), paternalism (Lowell Mills in 1830–60), patriarchy (mule spinning in England), and market despotism (New England mills after 1860).[59] More relevant to the discussion at hand is Burawoy's characterization of advanced capitalist regimes.

Burawoy places considerable emphasis on the role of the state in shaping the regimes of production in advanced capitalist countries. Using the development of state welfarism (support for reproduction of labor power, that is, maintenance support allowing workers to subsist without employment) and the degree of direct state regulation in production as variables, he develops a distinctive analytical approach. Buraway's comparative framework is based exclusively on the degree of state intervention and is not, therefore, a comparison of regimes per se (such a comparison would have to take into account other factors). Nevertheless, Burawoy's schematization is interesting in that he poses Japan and Sweden as two opposite poles in relation to state intervention in the labor process. The findings from my own study confirm Burawoy's perspective and refute Dore's association of Japan with Sweden. In trumpeting the benevolence of Japan's employers and the progressive aspects of Confucianism, Dore attempted to create a resonance be-

---

57. Burawoy is at times confusing on this issue, sometimes equating work organization and the labor process. See *The Politics of Production* at p. 8 and the definition on p. 31.

58. Burawoy understood this through his comparison of work at Allied and Jay's. Even though the work process, that is, what people did in the machine shops, was organized in a similar manner, the relations in production were quite different.

59. Burawoy, *Politics of Production*, p. 91.

tween East and West. This is a laudable objective, but it should be based on an actual harmony achieved, not an imagined one.

The last points concerning the theory of variable production regimes are related to concepts of the state and notions of employer control. The general thrust of Burawoy's analysis is to combat what he considers to be the underpoliticization of production and the overpoliticization of the state—the latter are theories that stress the state's "autonomy, dislocating it from its economic foundations."[60] Burawoy sees an organic link between production apparatuses and the state and goes so far as to suggest that, from a historical perspective at least, these apparatuses determine the shape and role of the state. My own study confirms this theory and goes a little further. Japan's politics of production definitely shaped the Fordist regime of the 1960s. The key question from labor's perspective, however, was (and is) to what degree was it the production regime or the state that allowed the separation of the reproduction of labor power from the market and employer control?[61] In simpler terms, to what degree can labor de-commodify itself within the confines of a commodity-based capitalist system? This, I contend, is one index against which we can assess the role of the state and also the particular nature of any given production regime. In Japan, as we shall see, the divisions in the labor movement and the ascent of enterprise unionism weakened labor's ability to de-commodify itself, both at the level of the state and the workplace.

Notions of capitalist control can neither be reduced to a single dimension nor understood statically. Capitalism can only survive so long as capital is capable of extracting surplus value. For this it needs labor. But because labor resists exploitation, capital would prefer to rid itself of it or control it absolutely, both of which are impossible. As a result we have the ultimate in codependent relationships. There are thus both economic and political aspects to the labor process, and the essence of capitalist control is, as Burawoy puts it, to secure surplus value and at the same time keep it hidden. This is an important formulation because it captures both the economic and political moment of capitalist relations. Employers must secure the maximum surplus value possible but at the same time not overly exacerbate the exploitative relationship inherent to the enterprise.

This tension was indeed at the heart of production politics in Japan. Using these theoretical insights, this study traces the evolution of the relations in production (industrial relations) in Japan and examines the impact of the dominant pattern on the organization of work, particularly in the automobile industry. It also attempts to reconstruct Japan's economic history in a manner that includes workers and labor organizations.

---

60. Ibid., p. 122.
61. Gosta Esping-Andersen designates this separation as the de-commodification of labor. See his work *The Three Worlds of Welfare Capitalism* (Princeton: Princeton University Press, 1990).

A Specific Comparative Framework

Before proceeding to the body of research, I propose to offer a specific comparative reference. This is necessary for two reasons. First, Fordist theory has been related mainly to the issue of work organization or to a general theory about capital accumulation. Second, the impact of specific forms of industrial relations can be fully understood only when they are evaluated from a specific comparative perspective. We need, therefore, a reference point in industrial relations. Indeed, understanding different regimes often requires overcoming not a single stereotype but a pair, the thesis and antithesis often associated with different countries. Take unions, for example. To many, the Japanese trade union is an "enterprise union," and its counterpart is the "industrial union" epitomized by a national union like the United Auto Workers (UAW). The juxtapositioning of the two creates a dynamic, an attempt to define one or the other as superior. But how quickly we can slide into assumption! By counterposing the terms "enterprise union" and "industrial union," presto! we have supposedly defined them both. This is an a priori deduction at best, and the problem is amplified when we juxtapose two entities and associate them with two different countries. The reality is always much more complex. Both enterprise and industrial unions come in a variety of configurations that defy simplistic comparisons. Thus even before we delve into the history of Japan's production regimes it is essential to provide some details about our comparative frame of reference.

Given the limitations of this work, I have chosen Canada and the United States as the specific points of reference. The reasons for this are fairly obvious and have, I should state, nothing to do with convergence theories. Neither the United States nor Canada is the gold standard. But they will serve as a reference point for a number of reasons. First, it was in these two countries that Fordism first matured. Second, they are the regimes that I know well, and we can avoid conflicting assumptions if I state my own perceptions about these regimes. Finally, the choice of the United States seems appropriate given the extraordinary influence Americans have exerted on Japan beginning in the Occupation period and continuing with the development of close economic ties thereafter. In discussing these two regimes, however, I shall provide some other international comparisons as well.

Historical Background

Kim Moody has argued that the major features of labor-capital relations in the United States since World War II have been "national pattern bargaining, grievances procedures designed to remove conflict from the shop floor, and bureaucratic unionism."[62] As a historical polemic, Moody's arguments are powerful and extremely useful in explaining some of the weaknesses that have dogged the U.S. labor movement in the last 20 years. As a comparative frame of reference, however, Moody's analysis requires modification.[63] For the purposes of this study, I contend that the primary features of the industrial relations system in the United States and, to a large extent, in Canada include

- the partial triumph of industrial as opposed to craft unions, which allowed for the organization of all workers on the basis of "one shop, one union";
- a regime of compulsory union recognition in exchange for a bureaucratic-legalistic method of dispute resolution;
- institutionalized collective bargaining on wages and working conditions every one to five years in which single-enterprise bargaining is the norm but centralized bargaining in the form of pattern or joint-bargaining also occurs;
- extensive and legalistic collective agreements based on a system of industrial jurisprudence in which residual managerial rights predominate (i.e., management controls anything not spelled out in the collective agreement);
- an occupation- and classification-based wage system founded on the principles of "equal pay for equal work" and comparability, under which incentive systems play a secondary role;
- union job controls ("restrictive work practices") including extensive seniority rights, detailed occupational classifications, job descriptions, bumping rights, and so forth, enforceable by shop stewards but subject to bureaucratic grievance procedures in cases of dispute.
- the feminization of the labor force and labor movement, particularly within Canada, which has signficantly affected equity issues on many levels.

---

62. Kim Moody, *An Injury to All: The Decline of American Unionism* (London: Verso, 1988), p. 20.

63. The following account of labor relations is based on the following works. For the *United States:* David Brody, *Workers in Industrial America* (New York, Oxford University Books, 1993); C. Gersuny and G. Kaufman, "Seniority and the Moral Economy of U.S. Automobile Workers, 1934–1946," *Journal of Social History,* Spring 1985, pp. 463–475; Harry C. Katz, *Shifting Gears* (Cambridge: MIT Press, 1987); Edward Levinson, *Labor on the March* (New York: University Books, 1956); Fraser and Gerstle, *Rise and Fall of the New Deal;* Nelson Lichtenstein and Stephen Meyer, eds., *On the Line: Essays in the History of Auto Work* (Urbana: University of Illinois Press, 1989); Leon Litwack, *The American Labor Movement* (New York: Simon & Schuster, 1962); Montgomery, *Fall of the House of Labor;* Moody, *An Injury to All.* For *Canada:* John C. Anderson et al., *Union-Management Relations in Canada* (Don Mills, Ont: Addison-Wesley, 1989); Craig Heron, *The Canadian Labour Movement: A Short History* (Toronto: James Lorimer, 1989); L. S. MacDowell and I. Radforth, *Canadian Working Class History: Selected Readings* (Toronto: Canadian Scholars Press, 1992); Desmond Morton, *Working People* (Toronto: Summerhill, 1990 edition); Bryan D. Palmer, *Working-Class Experience* (Toronto: Butterworth, 1983); Gerald E. Phillips, *Labour Relations and the Collective Bargaining Cycle* (Toronto: Butterworth, 1981); James Rinehart, *The Tyranny of Work* (Toronto: Harcourt Brace Jovanovich, 1987); Julie White, *Sisters and Solidarity: Women and Unions in Canada,* (Toronto: Thompson, 1993); Yates, *From Plant to Politics.*

This system of contemporary industrial relations in Canada and the United States matured in the 1935–50 period, although there were important supplementary developments in the 1960s particularly in feminization. On the whole, the Fordist mechanisms of workplace regulation that developed in the two countries were similar with some notable exceptions. Here are some key points for comparative purposes.

Industrial Relations: United States and Canada

Henry Ford revolutionized the labor process with the changes brought about by the re-division of labor and the introduction of the assembly line. This restricted the development of craft skills and obliterated individual control over work. At the same time the new form of work organization substantially increased productivity and created the conditions necessary for the incorporation of millions of workers into production. These changes initially occurred in the 1908–20 period, yet Fordism did not mature at this time. On the whole, employers, including Ford himself, remained dedicated to the open shop and maintained a fundamentally antagonistic attitude toward collective bargaining.[64] High wages never became institutionalized, and this, among other factors, precipitated the economic crisis that began with the crash of 1929.

The Depression brought forth the Roosevelt administration, which passed the National Recovery Act in 1932 and the Wagner Act in 1935. The reforms represented by these two acts constituted a watershed in U.S. regulation of labor. They marked the triumph of a new vision of industrial relations which, although hardly supported by a majority of employers, became the standard for decades to come. This new standard provided for compulsory employer recognition of independent unions on the condition that they fulfilled certification requirements.

Historical circumstance played an important role in establishing the new regime. Mass production industries had created a new type of working class, which traditional craft unionism, as typified by the American Federation of Labor, was unwilling to embrace. The economic backdrop to this legislation was of course the Depression and the subsequent political perception that capitalism, left unregulated, was unable to sustain itself. This put employers on the defensive and created the momentum for the election of Roosevelt. But the labor relations component of the New Deal had been forming even prior to Roosevelt's election. As Steve Fraser has shown, even in the 1920s a small minority of employers and consultants (many of them in the Taylor society!) had begun to articulate a new mode of regulation that accorded independent representation for workers through

64. See Montgomery, *Fall of the House of Labor*, pp. 269–275.

unions and collective bargaining.[65] These people worked with union leaders such as Sidney Hillman of the mens clothing union in elaborating a new labor-management deal. The essence of that deal was an acceptance of scientific management and employer rights, tempered by a bureaucratic form of regulation encompassed by a collective agreement.

Capitalism's first failure, the Great Depression, precipitated the meteoric rise of regulationists within Roosevelt's New Deal administration. But as historians such as Lichtenstein and Brody have documented, the labor movement faced tough going even after passage of the Wagner Act in 1935 and the establishment of the Congress of Industrial Organizations in 1936–37. Only U.S. entry in World War II created the exceptional conditions that allowed the state to actively promote the consolidation of unions and regulate wages and prices. The war represented the peak of collectivist influence within the liberal U.S. state.

The 1946 defeat of the bid of Walter Reuther and his autoworkers for a wage increase without an increase in the price of cars, along with the enactment of the regressive Taft-Hartley Act in 1947, marked the end of the wartime regime and the resurgence of conservative business in the postwar era. The failure of the CIO to break with the Democratic Party in 1947–48 marked the incorporation of progressive unionism into a postwar order based on "alignment with the government in the battalions of the new cold war and exclusion of the Communists from the political arena."[66]

In Canada's case, legislation similar to the Wagner Act was introduced only in 1944. Mackenzie King, leader of the Liberal government, had been long associated with the company union movement and was adamantly opposed to compulsory recognition of unions. It took the Wagner Act in the United States, a 1943 strike movement that surpassed all previous levels of strike activity, and the rise of the social-democratic Co-operative Commonwealth Federation (CCF) to convince King that it was time to embrace the politics of the New Deal, including union recognition. Privy Council order 1003 (PC 1003), which more or less embodied the Wagner Act, was enacted in April 1944.

The essence of both pieces of legislation was that employers were, theoretically at least, obliged to recognize and bargain with unions that had obtained certification as worker representatives. In return, unions were obliged to agree to dispute-resolution mechanisms that would prevent job action during the life of the collective agreement.[67] Prior to this, unions existed in a state of limbo. Although

65. Steve Fraser, "The 'Labor Question'," in Fraser and Gerstle, *Rise and Fall of the New Deal*, pp. 55–84.

66. Nelson Lichtenstein, "The Eclipse of Social Democracy," in Fraser and Gerstle, *Rise and Fall of the New Deal*, p. 141.

67. Two important points of divergence between the U.S. and Canadian examples must be noted. First, in the Canadian instance, provinces exercised almost exclusive jurisdiction over labor relations

many of the master-servant or conspiracy laws that had bedeviled unions in the nineteenth century had been struck down, employers were not obliged to recognize or bargain with unions. The Wagner Act and PC 1003 changed the political climate, but the labor movements in both Canada and the United States had to wage relentless struggles to make use of the new legislation.

Mass production, the Depression, new labor legislation, and war converged to create the context for the partial triumph of industrial unionism that took place in the 1937–50 period. The first upsurge in the organization of the mass production industries began in the 1935–37 period in both the United States and Canada. This early spurt was more dramatic in the United States but was not sustained in either country. World War II was a crucial period for union expansion in the United States and to a somewhat lesser degree in Canada. It was only in the early postwar period (1945–48) that Canadian union densities reached the 30 percent plus figures that had already been achieved in the United States. Union densities reached their peak levels (34–35 percent) around 1955 and then declined over the next decade in both countries. In 1965, union densities in Canada began to recover and have hovered close to the 40 percent level since 1978, whereas in the United States union densities continued to fall.[68]

The rise of industrial unionism was predicated on a significant shift in union philosophy. Prior to 1935, the predominant form of union had been the craft type, that is, organizations of workers with a defined trade. The shift to organize the non-craft workers in the mass production industries required a new organization, the Congress of Industrial Organizations, because of the hidebound haughtiness of the craft unions (organized in the American Federation of Labor) towards non-craft workers. Industrial unionism rose in opposition to craft unionism. It is quite true that many of the unions, including the autoworkers, steelworkers, rub-

---

after 1925. PC 1003 applied to most private sector workers only because the federal government had appropriated much provincial power through federal wartime controls. Most provincial governments in Canada passed legislation similar to the Wagner Act after 1948, however. They did not necessarily emulate the Taft-Hartley amendments, which weakened many of the provisions of the Wagner Act. This has resulted in a second divergence in the labor-management environment in Canada, namely somewhat easier certification procedures in some Canadian provinces, extensive use of conciliation/mediation prior to strike action, stricter controls on grievance procedures, and relatively stronger union security regulations. For details see Donald Carter, "Collective Bargaining Legislation in Canada," in Anderson et al., *Union Management Relations in Canada,* pp. 34–35.

68. As mentioned above, part of the reason for Canadian union vigor can be attributed to a relatively favorable legal context. This appears to have had some bearing on the rise of unionism in the public sector in Canada, which most studies point to as one of the most significant divergences from the United States and the reason for sustained union power in the post-1965 period. A second notable feature of the Canadian situation has been the gradual Canadianization of unions in Canada. Most unions in Canada were so-called "international" unions, that is, U.S. unions with Canadian locals. The reign of "international unions" in Canada lasted until 1977, by which time the majority of union members belonged to Canadian unions.

berworkers, and so forth, were national in scope, but then too so were many of the craft unions. The essential difference between craft and industrial unionism was the idea that all workers, regardless of craft, should be organized in one union, whether it be by industry, enterprise, or plant.[69] This dynamic is crucial to any understanding of industrial unions in North America and, as we shall see, begins to undercut the organizational dichotomy between industrial and enterprise unions that is so commonly assumed by adherents to the three pillars interpretation of Japan's industrial relations. This dichotomy is further challenged if we move to the level of collective bargaining.

The unit of bargaining certification issued by labor relations boards in Canada or the United States was usually not a whole industry but rather the plant or enterprise (single company with multiple plants). Nor should industrial unionism be equated with industry-wide bargaining because, with very few exceptions, seldom did industry-wide bargaining ever exist. As a matter of fact, in a Canadian study of bargaining structures in units of five hundred employees or more, less than 20 percent of the cases (40 percent of workers) involved multiemployer bargaining in 1965.[70] If units of less than five hundred employees were included, the ratio of multiemployer bargaining dropped even further. In other words, for better or worse, the plant or enterprise remained the center of industrial relations in Canada and the United States in the postwar period.

Recognizing the centrality of the plant or enterprise in Canadian and U.S. industrial relations should not blind us, however, to the fact that other forms of bargaining did develop, and although they did not become the standard, they were important. Except for the construction industry, there was almost no legal provision for certification of industry-wide bargaining units for either employers or employees in Canada. In one of the most centralized bargaining units, the coastal lumber mills of British Columbia, employers formed a voluntary bargaining council which signed a master agreement with the corresponding union bargaining agents. Even this agreement was supplemented by locally negotiated agreements on plant-level issues. In Canada and the United States, a well-known form of horizontal bargaining was the "pattern bargaining" that evolved in the automobile industry. This practice consisted of choosing one enterprise—Ford, General Motors, or Chysler—as the bargaining target and subsequently pursuing collective bargaining with the target enterprise, up to and including strike action, until a settlement was reached. Similar settlements would then be demanded of the other two major automakers. Pattern

69. To understand the organizational principle behind the ascent of industrial unionism, see "Minority Report of the Resolutions Committee on Organization Policies: A.F. of L. Convention" (1935), in Litwack, *American Labor Movement*, pp. 49–51.

70. John C. Anderson, "The Structure of Collective Bargaining," in Anderson et al., *Union Management Relations in Canada*, p. 218. By 1982, the level of centralization had dropped further below 1965 levels.

bargaining in this case was a form of multi-plant, enterprise-level bargaining. Even under pattern bargaining, the agreements struck on the enterprise level (master agreements concerning wages, pensions, and so forth) were supplemented by local agreements regarding working conditions negotiated at the plant level.

A third type of bargaining structure involved coordinated bargaining. This type of bargaining did not culminate in a master agreement. Instead the agreements reached were incorporated in local agreements. It should be stressed, however, that these trends toward centralized bargaining never became the standard, and the plant and enterprise remained the organizational center of collective bargaining and industrial relations.

The outcome of collective bargaining in Canada and the United States was a detailed collective agreement, which could run into hundreds of pages. This type of collective agreement only developed with the rise of industrial unionism under the legalistic Wagner-type industrial relations system. Many of the early craft contracts were only a few pages long. The detailed collective agreement arose first as a response to residual rights theory, that is, the theory that what was not in the contract remained the prerogative of management, and second, in response to the legalistic arbitration process for resolving grievances arising from differing interpretations of the collective agreement.

The detailed collective agreement contains stipulations regarding hundreds of items. Two of specific importance for our purposes are the detailed wage schedules and job control rules. While many variations emerged according to industry and union, on the whole wages were pegged to occupations or job classifications.[71] Incremental steps or a wage ladder often existed, but on the whole unions demanded equal pay for equal work and an end to favoritism in wages. The role of performance evaluations declined, seldom having a major impact on wage determination. Furthermore, in automobile plants, for example, the wage gap between a production worker and a trades person narrowed, with the hourly rate only about 20 percent higher for the latter.

Job control rules refer to the web of contract clauses that determine the specific tasks and rights of every employee. Job descriptions determined the content of work, and because different jobs had different pay rates, job switching was frowned upon. Seniority became a major factor in determining the outcome of bidding on jobs; no longer did supervisors determine who would be posted where. Nor could they arbitrarily decide which employees to lay off.[72] As we shall

71. The job-based wage system, which subsequently gave rise to the often complex classification codes, dates back at least to Ford's 1914 labor relations reform. It probably was institutionalized by the tripartite U.S. wartime regime.

72. In the 1937 GM-UAW agreement, clauses related to seniority constituted 35 percent of the contract, followed by grievance procedures at 30 percent. All that time the contract was still relatively short: 186 lines of typescript. For further details see Gersuny and Kaufman, "Seniority and Moral Economy."

discuss later, this notion of seniority, as a means of restricting employer discretion by limiting choice to measurable determinants such as length of service, is crucial in understanding why the term "seniority-based wages" is so inappropriate from a comparative perspective in describing Japan's wage system. While managers in the United States and Canada controlled the labor process in theory, in practice the collective agreement regulated the regime, and workers were able to put an indelible if incomplete mark on the organization and regulation of work.

Finally, the feminist contribution to our understanding of industrial relations must be recognized.[73] Many of the attributes of postwar industrial relations, including seniority, embodied the discriminatory norms of a patriarchal society. Women under this system were often hired last and fired first. Wages, although nominally equal, remained vastly inferior for job classifications in which women predominated. The feminization of the labor force and the labor movement, which accelerated in the 1970s when issues such as pay equity and affirmative action began to take hold, has had a profound impact on industrial relations.

Many of the points made above are generalizations and as such are subject to wide variations depending on the industry, region, and workplace. But on the whole they represent, in my opinion, a valid summary and an explicit starting point for comparing the practice of industrial relations and production management in Japan with that in the United States and Canada. In particular, the decentralized form of industrial unions, the basically egalitarian wage system, notions of seniority, and feminization are fundamental to any serious comparative discussion. I will refer to them frequently as we proceed through the material.

Case Studies

Many scholars would agree that Fordism, as defined by regulation theory, is a universal trend among industrialized countries (a form of convergence) although its realization differs according to the country and the particular stage of economic development. In the case of Japan, the social and economic dimensions of the Fordist paradigm were adopted only after a period of extensive accumulation in the 1950s. The nature of Japan's hegemonic regime can be understood only by tracing its origins back to the politics of production at the workplace.

Three sites form the core of the primary research conducted for this study: the Miike coal mines (part of the Mitsui Mining group) in Kyushu, Suzuki Motors in Hamamatsu, and Moriguchi City Hall, just outside Osaka. These case studies

73. Recent works that have had an important influence on my thinking include White, *Sisters and Solidarity*; Linda Briskin and Patricia McDermott, *Women Challenging Unions: Feminism, Democracy, and Militancy* (Toronto: University of Toronto Press, 1993); Judy Fudge and Patricia McDermott, *Just Wages: A Feminist Assessment of Pay Equity* (Toronto: University of Toronto Press, 1991).

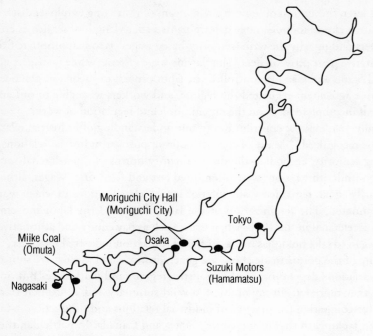

Figure 1.   Location of case studies

were chosen partly through design and partly through good fortune. Miike was chosen specifically because I had earlier studied the bitter, year-long dispute that occurred there in 1960 and that became a landmark in Japan's labor history. It seemed that any solid interpretation of the postwar period had to capture and explain the nationwide conflict centered at Miike—a conflict so broad in scope, so intense, and so divergent from the image of labor-capital harmony—which is the image usually offered to the Western labor relations specialist—that it cannot be dismissed simply as an exception that proves the rule. Suzuki Motors and Moriguchi City Hall became case studies more through fortuitous circumstances than by design. I had, for other reasons, made contact with these two enterprises, and thus they offered themselves as potential victims of scrutiny. It should be said, however, that together they conformed to an explicit standard of my research: these two enterprises were characterized by diversity in the production process. Too often labor relations models have been based exclusively on case studies in a single economic sector, thus depriving our construct of the insights from other angles. Moriguchi provided a window into the public sector workplace in Japan. Suzuki Motors offered the added attraction of being part of Japan's automobile industry, the sector that spawned much of the lean production paradigm being emulated today. The diversity of labor relations in these three sectors—resource, manufacturing, and service—affords a greater appreciation of the variation in industrial relations that developed and continues to evolve in Japan today.

My research at these sites, which focused mainly on workers and their unions, is intended as a contribution to a growing body of scholarship that examines history "from the bottom up," as Harvey Kaye puts it.[74] This tradition has long been upheld in Japan by scholars such as Yamamoto Kiyoshi, Totsuka Hideo, Hyōdō Tsutomu, Hirai Yōichi, Matsuzaki Tadashi, and Kawanishi Hirosuke, who in their voluminous works have stressed the history of workers' struggles in Japan. It is only in the past decade, however, that works in English by such scholars as Andrew Gordon, Joe Moore, E. Patricia Tsurumi, and Norma Chalmers have revived this more balanced view of labor history and labor-management relations in Japan.[75] They have, in their particular ways, "brought workers back in," as Gordon puts it.

The case studies mentioned above form the research base, but the book ranges through a series of people, institutions, and struggles that I considered important to an understanding of postwar labor-management relations, and hence to a new conceptualization of contemporary lean production systems. Apart from the three detailed case studies, I also discuss events of wider importance that occurred in the specific periods under discussion. In particular, I have tried to integrate the role of peak managerial organizations such as Nikkeiren and labor organizations such as Sōhyō (General Council of Trade Unions of Japan). Given the significance of the automobile industry, an effort was also made to compare Suzuki with Toyota Motors in order to provide a broader perspective on the origins of lean production. These excursions have posed certain difficulties in the flow and structure of the narrative, but I believe the results make them worthwhile.

Having said this, however, the reader should be cautioned. This study remains a partial reconstruction of the postwar period and has its limitations. It remains centered on large, unionized enterprises, which employ less than 20 percent of paid workers in Japan. Obviously I feel the study of this stratum is important, particularly because it forms the basis for hegemony within society at large. However, it can easily distort our image of work in Japan by ignoring the majority of work-

74. Harvey J. Kaye, *The British Marxist Historians* (Cambridge: Polity Press, 1984).

75. See Joe Moore, *Japanese Workers and the Struggle for Power, 1945–1947* (Madison: University of Wisconsin, 1983); Gordon, *Evolution of Labour Relations;* E. Patricia Tsurumi, *Factory Girls: Women in the Thread Mills of Meiji Japan* (Princeton: Princeton University Press, 1990); Norma J. Chalmers, *Industrial Relations in Japan: The Peripheral Workforce* (London: Routledge, 1989). Moore documents a period when workers and unions were setting the agenda in production politics in Japan. Tsurumi gives us a valuable cultural-feminist portrait of Meiji textile workers. Gordon shows the workers' role in the evolution of labor-management relations. Chalmers provides an important contribution with her analysis of the peripheral workforce in postwar Japan.

ers, (80 percent or more) who are employed in small and medium businesses. Recently, other scholars have given this sector some attention, but, given its magnitude, it remains woefully underrepresented in our understanding of production relations in Japan.[76] The same can be said for the issue of gender. While I have attempted to integrate gender issues as they arose in the course of research, the treatment is far from systematic.

The methodology is basic. I have relied extensively on primary institutional histories by both management and labor for the case studies. This was supplemented by fieldwork carried out at each site during a number of visits to Japan from 1985 through 1995, including visits to the workplaces where possible and numerous interviews with rank-and-file workers, union officials, and management representatives (see the Bibliography for details). These visits also provided me with supplementary, firsthand accounts of important events. Discussions with scholars of Japan's labor history have provided me with additional scope and comparative reference points that helped me find my bearings in this complex field.

76. See Chalmers, *Industrial Relations in Japan.*

2 Testing the Limits: Workers' Challenge (1945–1948)

Revolution from the Top

When Canadian diplomat Herbert Norman and U.S. foreign service officer John Emmerson headed for a prison on the outskirts of Tokyo in mid-October 1945, they carried with them authorization for the release of political prisoners held by the Japanese government: two communists jailed for almost twenty years, two Korean independence leaders, anti-Fascist intellectuals, and religious leaders. Effecting their release was, reported Norman, "the most exciting experience of my life."[1] This release, authorized by General Douglas MacArthur, Supreme Commander of the Allied Powers (SCAP), symbolized the onset of political revolution in Japan, a revolution whose liberal-democratic outcome was predetermined because of the American Occupation, but whose dynamics were shaped by the fierce class conflict that raged in Japan between 1945 and 1950.[2] The outcome of this conflict left an indelible imprint on Japan's workplace regimes as they evolved after the war. This chapter examines the rise of production regimes that were shaped mainly by an insurgent labor movement in 1946–1947.

The political revolution launched by SCAP in the fall of 1945 created propitious conditions for the revival of the labor movement. In a detailed study of American Occupation policymaking, Michael Schaller concluded that "during the initial reformist stage of the Occupation, lasting through early 1947, Washington encouraged SCAP

---

1. As recounted in Roger Bowen, *Innocence Is Not Enough: The Life and Death of Herbert Norman* (Vancouver: Douglas and McIntyre, 1986), pp. 118–119.

2. In theory SCAP derived its authority from the Far Eastern Commission, which had eleven members states including the Soviet Union. However, the postwar division of the world, worked out among the Allies, allowed the United States, through SCAP, to dictate policy.

to pursue a program that reflected the most progressive tendencies of the New Deal. Even as American domestic and foreign policy lurched to the Right, MacArthur and his aides remained committed to a reform agenda abhorrent to most of the general's conservative constituency in the United States."[3] To be sure, the reform agenda had already been diluted by the American government's decision to retain the monarchy (the emperor) and to work through the established Japanese government. Nevertheless, SCAP sponsored political and economic structural changes that reverberated throughout society.[4] On the political level the changes included the proclamation of basic rights in October 1945, which released over three thousand political prisoners; the passage of the Trade Union Law in December of the same year; the drafting and passage of a new constitution in November 1946, which invested sovereignty in the people, embraced a no-war clause, extended the franchise to women, and articulated a Fordist social charter that guaranteed state assistance in welfare as well as the right to an education, labor rights, and gender equality.

SCAP also pursued a punitive course by arresting and trying suspected war criminals (both military and civilian) and by "purging" from public office over 200,000 people who allegedly helped direct Japan's militarization. On the economic level, the Occupation began to dismantle industry as a reparation payment in kind to Asian countries victimized by Japan. It implemented a trust-busting policy including obligatory stock sales to the public, antimonopoly laws, and an initial attempt to break up large companies. Land reform allowed tenants to purchase their properties and ended absentee landlordism.

The purpose of citing these reforms is neither to tout nor to justify them but rather to sketch the early Occupation landscape. The fact is, the early antimilitarist and democratic tone of the Occupation put the prewar and wartime Japanese elite on the defensive, if not in jail, and left them chafing at the bit of reform. Labor, on the other hand, was liberated—free to organize and to play an independent role within the emerging liberal-democratic structures of the day. The state, under the control of the United States, had set new ground rules for society and for politics. In the first three years of the Occupation there were three governments: the nonelected Shidehara cabinet (October 1945–May 1946); the first Yoshida Liberal cabinet (May 1946–May 1947); and the Katayama coalition cabinet (May 1947–March 1948).

The early postwar situation was further complicated, however, by economic dislocation. The political structures may have conformed to an advanced capitalist country, but economically Japan was in turmoil. Although Allied bombing had destroyed only 30 percent of Japan's industrial capacity, actual production for 1946 was

3. Michael Schaller, *The American Occupation of Japan: The Origins of the Cold War in Asia* (New York: Oxford University Press, 1985), p. 25.
4. This overview on Occupation reforms is based on Schaller, *American Occupation of Japan;* John Dower, *Empire and Aftermath* (Cambridge: Harvard University Press, 1979); Howard B. Schonberger, *Aftermath of War* (Kent: Kent State University Press, 1989).

down 70 percent from 1934–36 levels. Tokyo and Osaka were bombed out, with nearly 60 percent of all buildings destroyed. Air attacks had decimated shipping capacity. Rice production was seriously deteriorating. For city dwellers starvation was not only possible but imminent. Food shortages, a black market, and excessive currency provoked a serious bout of inflation, with prices doubling between October 1945 and October 1946. The dislocation was further complicated by what may be termed a capital strike, when major business leaders turned their backs on production efforts. Why invest or produce when one might be jailed, purged, or otherwise compromised? Economic chaos, political freedom, and a defensive capitalist class conspired to radicalize a working class that was in constant flux.

Labor Law

Democratic reforms were imminent in the fall of 1945. In October the Shidehara cabinet authorized the formation of a tripartite commission to draft a trade union law. The labor representatives on this commission's core working group included Matsuoka Komakichi and Nishio Suehiro of the prewar JFL (Japan Federation of Labor, Nihon Rōdō Sōdōmei), Mizutani Chōzaburō of the JSP (Japan Socialist Party, Nihon Shakai Tō), Koizumi Hidekichi of the Japan Seamen's Union (JSU, Kaiin Kumiai). Other members included Mitsui Mining Company director Fukagawa Masao and University of Tokyo legal expert Suehiro Izutarō.[5]

The committee quickly drafted labor legislation, and on December 22, 1945, the Diet passed the first Trade Union Law in Japan's history. It contained five sections and one addendum.[6] Section I (Overview) declared that the purpose of the law was to stabilize the economy by elevating the status of workers and guaranteeing their rights to unionize and bargain collectively. Article 2 under this same section defined employees and excluded from union membership employers and their representatives, organizations whose administrative expenses were provided by employees, mutual aid societies, charitable groups, and groups whose main purposes were political or social.

Section II (Unions) provided details of accreditation; union bylaws had to be submitted to the appropriate administrative agency (gyōsei kanchō). Any disputes about union certification would be settled by the administrative agency based on a recommendation by the Labor Relations Board. Unions were not liable for damages arising from reasonable actions during disputes. Unions were not accorded exclusive bargaining agent status, so the door was open to multiple certifications at a single workplace.

5. Rōdō Shō hen, *Shiryō rōdō undō shi, 1945–1946* [Materials from the history of the labor movement] (Tokyo, 1947), p. 689. This yearly series is hereafter abbreviated as *SRUS*.

6. This analysis is based on the full text of the law as reprinted in Rōdō Shō, *SRUS 1945–1946*, pp. 771–774.

Section III dealt with collective agreements. These were to have a three year limit (Article 20); were to be based on a spirit of improving efficiency and maintaining industrial peace (Article 21); were to be applied to all employees in cases where more than three-quarters were under a collective agreement (Article 23); could be applied, at the discretion of the Labor Relations Board, to all workers in a given industry of a specific region if a majority were already unionized (Article 24). The parties could not resort to job action until after any mediation or arbitration procedures inscribed in the collective agreement had been exhausted (Article 25). Section IV outlined the provisions for Labor Relations Boards, which were to be tripartite (employer, union and public representatives on the board) and established at both the central and regional levels (Article 26).

The passage of the Trade Union Law was followed by passage of the Labor Relations Adjustment Law in September 1946 and the enactment of the Labor Standards Law in April 1947. The former outlined regulations for the conduct of the central and regional Labor Relations Boards and the latter outlined minimal labor standards. These three laws affected labor relations both directly and indirectly. On the one hand, they made unions legitimate both legally and socially. Furthermore, the creation of the Labor Relations Boards as the administrative agency for the law would itself create specific dynamics for the labor movement. This will become evident when we examine the unionization process as it evolved at Miike, Suzuki, and Moriguchi.

A Reconstituted Working Class

When the employees of Suzuki Looms, a textile manufacturer that converted to arms production during the war, gathered at the Hamamatsu headquarters on the last day of August 1945, there was little rejoicing. Suzuki Michio, the founder and president of the enterprise, announced they would all be permanently laid off and thanked them for their years of service. Suzuki's main facility and headquarters in Hamamatsu, Shizuoka prefecture, had been 95 percent destroyed by American bombing. The glitter of gold was markedly absent from this final handshake for the nearly 2900 regular employees of whom nearly 1300 were women. As for the 800 conscripted workers and 110 Korean prisoners of war that Suzuki had also employed during the war, there is no record.[7] Yet within a few days of laying off all its employees, Suzuki rehired a select few, restarted operations at its Takatsuka facility, which had remained unscathed, and in the last half of the financial year (October 1945–March 1946) had sales of over ¥5.7 million.[8]

7. Suzuki also employed over one hundred Korean prisoners of war, but nothing has been recorded about their fate. See Suzuki Jidōsha Kōgyō, *40 nen shi* [Forty years in the making] (Hamamatsu, 1960), p. 86.

8. Ibid., p. 88.

As at Suzuki, there was a shakeout of the work force at the Miike mines in Kyushu. Miike was the largest coal mine in Japan and had been owned and operated by Mitsui Mining as part of the Mitsui conglomerate since 1888. Over 24,000 miners were working Miike's shafts at war's end. But conditions at Miike were so bad that the miners abandoned the coal seams en masse. By November 1945, 13,000 miners had abandoned the pits, including 6,000 Chinese, Korean, and Caucasian prisoners of war.[9] For these miners, defeat for Japan supposedly implied liberty, but while Caucasian prisoners of war were quickly repatriated, Chinese and Korean miners at Miike had to riot before they were able to leave the mines.[10] In many cases, the Occupation policy was to force non-Caucasians to dig coal immediately after the war.[11]

Coal production had been targeted as a priority industry early in the Occupation, and as massive numbers of wartime workers abandoned the mines, the coal operators were hard pressed to stabilize the labor force. Over 12,000 new miners were hired in 1946, but of that number nearly 8,000 quit or were discharged within the year.[12] By December 1948, the workforce multiplied to reach its postwar peak of 28,960. Of this total, however, only 1,000 had worked at Miike prior to 1932.

Moriguchi employees did not experience such a severe shakeout in employment. Still not incorporated as a city, the few dozen employees in Moriguchi district remained at their post.

Revolution in Labor Relations

The Trade Union Law came into effect on March 31, 1946, by which time the labour movement was already galvanized for action. The pace of organization was frantic, and by 1948 over six million workers were in unions. To be sure, some unions were little more than paper organizations, but just as certainly there were many unions that were dynamic and member driven. As the labor movement confronted employers, it displayed a heterogenous mix of political proclivities, demands, and tactics, many of which failed to correspond to the norms that the Trade Union Law had hoped to establish. Further confounding the situation was the resistance to unionization displayed by employers. In some cases, workers and unions moved to take control of the workplace as it became increasingly evident that some employers were finding it difficult to break with their past paternalism

9. Mitsui Kōzan Kabushiki Kaisha, *Shiryō: Miike sōgi* [Documents: The Miike dispute] (Tokyo: Nihon Keieisha Dantai Renmei, 1963), p. 16.

10. Ibid., p. 16.

11. See Moore, *Japanese Workers*, pp. 33–35.

12. Mitsui, *Shiryō: Miike sōgi*, pp. 16–18.

and were proving resistant to democratizing the workplace. In this confused and complex clash of interests, workers began to create new forms of regulation.

Miike

At Miike, management attempted to preempt the formation of an independent union by creating a company union. Shortly after war's end, Mitsui ordered new elections for Sanpō committeemen at each mine site, who then elected delegates to a union preparatory committee for each site.[13] This process was well under way when miners at the Mikawa shaft (one of three main shafts at Miike, see Figure 2) rudely disrupted the process by demanding an immediate 30 percent wage increase, a minimum wage, and an eight-hour day.[14] As confrontation brewed, worker representatives undertook to form a single union for Miike miners.

On February 3, 1946, approximately 10,000 miners congregated in an Ōmuta park to found the Miike union. Also attending the gathering were city notables, management representatives, and delegations from other unions. The union announced its main demands: immediate participation in management, abolition of taxes on salaries, large increases in severance pay, adequate money and materials to live on, the dismissal of foremen who stymied the workers' will to produce, an end to discrimination between staff and miners, severance pay for workers who quit, and an end to the black market.[15] The company gave each participant ten yen for pocket money to show its good will toward the union. At this point the staff (*shokuin*) were not included in the union.

Mitsui's reply to the union demands was piecemeal; it proposed the formation of a labor-management council in response to the union's demand for participation in management, but on monetary issues it equivocated. This led to a strike beginning on March 9 (the miners at Mikawa struck on March 7). This action against Mitsui invited labor solidarity, and unions at Tagawa and Yamano joined the Miike union in a joint council (Sanzan Kyōgikai) on March 4. The miners at these two Mitsui mines partially joined in the strike action. On the other hand, the Miike union decided against occupying the mine and taking over production themselves (*seisan kanri* or production control) and condemned the Japan Communist Party (JCP) members who appeared at the Mikawa shafts advocating such a takeover for their "inflammatory attitude."[16] The strike ended on March 13 with the company making some lim-

13. Sanpō was the government-initiated and -controlled Patriotic Labor Front, which was modeled after the German wartime regime. It had committees in every workplace.
14. See Mitsui, *Shiryō: Miike sōgi*, pp. 28–29, for details of management's early attempts to control the union. According to Mitsui's account, prewar JFL organizers working at Mikawa precipitated the early demands and union formation.
15. Ibid., p. 29.
16. Miike Tankō Rōdō Kumiai Jū Nen Shi Hensan Iinkai, *Miike jū nen* [Miike's ten years] (Ōmuta: Miike Tankō Rōdō Kumiai, 1956), p. 66.

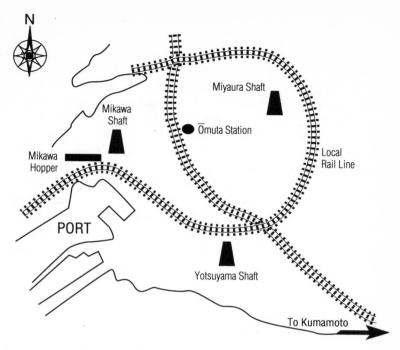

N

Miyaura Shaft

Mikawa
Shaft

Ōmuta Station

Mikawa
Hopper

Local
Rail Line

PORT

Yotsuyama Shaft

To Kumamoto

Figure 2. Mitsui's Miike facilities (Ōmuta, Kyushu)

ited concessions. The coordination among the unions at the three Mitsui mines during the March strike led to the creation on May 19 of the Western Federation of Mitsui Coal Unions (WFMCU Nishi Nihon Mitsui Tankō Rōdō Kumiai Rengōkai), a regional federation of coalminers working at Mitsui's three Kyushu mines.

The following month, the Miike local signed its first collective agreement with Mitsui. The contract was modeled after Section III (Collective Agreements) of the Trade Union Law but in addition gave the union important powers. The union won formal recognition, a closed shop, a clause giving it a virtual veto over layoffs (Article 3), the right to equal participation in a management council, and automatic renewal of the collective agreement.[17]

By this time, however, workers in Japan were facing severe poverty and food shortages and the new collective agreement provided little in wage increases. At Miike, miners were going into the mines without having eaten a meal, and the regional miners federation, the WFMCU, called for an immediate wage hike. Mitsui gave a one-time bonus that averaged ¥250 per employee.[18]

17. The entire contract has only eight clauses and was less than one page in length. It is reprinted in its entirety in Miike Kumiai, *Miike jū nen*, p. 58, appendix.
18. Ibid., p. 73.

The regional links developing among Mitsui mineworkers in Kyushu did not stop at the company gates. Although Tagawa and Yamano miners had left a regional federation that had included coalminers from other companies to take up affiliation with Miike, this was not because of some predisposition towards "enterprise union-ism" but rather because of political differences with that regional federation and because of the proximity with other Mitsui miners working in Kyushu.[19] In fact, the Mitsui miners in Kyushu became active in helping found a "neutralist" federation of Kyushu coalminers with workers drawn from a number of regional employers.

The impulse for regional and industrial affiliations came from diverse sources. For example, on August 12 the acting director of the Central Labor Relations Board met with leaders of unions in the Ōmuta region and encouraged them to form industry-wide affiliations.[20] The WFMCU took the lead in establishing the Kyushu Federation of Neutral Coalminers' Unions (Kyūshū Tankō Rōdō Kumiai Chūritsu Renmei) on October 4. As evident in the name, this federation attempted to avoid political affiliation with either the communist or social-democratic trends in the union movement.[21]

Parallel to this political polarization, an attempt was made to overcome the resultant schisms through the formation of an umbrella group that would mount a united front against the employers. On the regional level this manifested itself in the formation of the Fukuoka Prefectural Council of Coalminers' Unions (Fukuoka-Ken Tankō Rōdō Kumiai Kyōgikai) on October 21 (see Figure 3). On the national level, a similar umbrella group loosely affiliating the three trends (neutral, social-democratic, and communist) was established on January 25, 1947. This was the Japan Coalminers' Council (Tankō Rōdō Kumiai Zenkoku Kyōgikai or Tankyō). This federation, representing 340,000 miners or 83.4 percent of the coal labor force, began negotiating with the national coal employers group immediately. At this time, the union advanced a proposal for a social wage; it demanded a sliding wage that would allow the miners to purchase a daily quota of 2,400 calories. The interim agreement signed on March 7 went only halfway to meet the demand, and all hell broke loose as the left-leaning unions wildcatted in protest. This led to the demise of the regional and national umbrella federations. The right and center federations consequently consolidated and united to form the Japan Coalminers' Union (JCU, Nihon Tankō Rōdō Kumiai Dōmei or Tanrō) in October 1947, and the left-leaning unions organized the All-Japan Coal Federation (Zen Nihon Sekitan Sangyō Rōdō Kumiai, or Zen Sekitan).[22]

19. Mitsui, *Shiryō: Miike sogi*, p. 31.

20. Miike Kumiai, *Miike jū nen*, p. 74.

21. This organization later changed the "Neutral" component of its name to "Democratic" after being criticized for attempting to stake out a middle ground between employers and employees. See ibid., pp. 74–75.

22. Nihon Tankō Rōdō Kumiai Dōmei, *Tanrō ju nen shi* [Ten years of the JCU] (Tokyo: Rōdō Junpō Sha, 1961), p. 162.

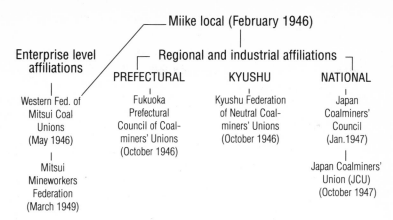

Figure 3.   Miike union's affiliations

A number of significant points emerge from this brief sketch of union organization and conflict in the coal mines. Miners at Miike evidently wanted an organization that was independent of company control; politics played an important role in the alignment, disintegration and realignment of union federations; and regardless of political stripe, miners wanted affiliations with other miners across the enterprise, both regionally and nationally. This natural inclination to develop horizontal linkages with other miners was given further impetus by the call from the Labor Relations Board encouraging the formation of cross-union linkages. The coal unions also took up the demand for a social wage. In a sense this was hardly surprising. For workers in Japan to accept that wages should be pegged to an almost nonfunctioning market would have meant starvation in the immediate postwar period. Politics and economics converged, propelling many unions to conceive of workers' interests independent from the state of the market.

Suzuki

The tendency towards independent unionism was as spontaneous as it was organized. Suzuki workers also formed a union in early 1946. After having dismissed all its employees at war's end, the company proceeded to hire back 350 workers. On January 18, these employees turned around and formed the Suzuki Loom Workers Union. Documentation regarding the original union is scanty, but according to one source the inspiration behind the union came from supervisors.[23] This notwithstanding, horizontal affiliations began immediately as the

23. This information comes from Sugiura Kiyoshi, one of the founding members of the union, cited in Suzuki Jidōsha Kōgyō Rōdō Kumiai Shi Henshū Iinkai, *Nijū go-nen shi* [Twenty-five years] (Hamana-Gun: Suzuki Jidōsha Kōgyō Rōdō Kumiai, 1976), p. 225.

union was one of the founding affiliates of a regional federation (Eishū Regional Labour Federation, Eishū Chihō Rōdō Kumiai Kaigi, founded on February 25) which undertook to coordinate union activities for May Day and to deal with the sharpening food crisis that had begun to grip the country. The president of the Suzuki union, Kawai Kasaku, became a leader of the regional federation.[24]

As in the coalminers' case, the impetus for horizontal links among metalworkers was the Trade Union Law. Promulgated on March 1, 1946, the new law called for the creation of regional labor boards composed of representatives of employers, labor, and the public. The Shizuoka Labor Office (Shizuoka Ken Rōseika) subsequently pushed for unions to join together to choose prefectural representatives.[25] Thus, on February 6, union representatives from across the prefecture, including Suzuki's Kawai, gathered at the first meeting of the Preparatory Committee of the Shizuoka Labour Federation (Shizuoka Ken Rōdō Kumiai Rengōkai Junbi Kai). The meeting not only designated labor representatives to the labor board but also began deliberations for a permanent labor federation that would coordinate activities for both industrial and regional unions. On March 2, 1946, the Shizuoka Labor Council was founded with Kawai elected as vice-president. The Suzuki union thus developed strong regional links early in 1946. Industry-based affiliations also began in this period. In Shizuoka, unions from the metal industries began meeting in May 1946, and in October the Japan Machine Tools Union–Shizuoka District was founded with the Suzuki-Style Loom Union affiliated as one local.[26]

Management at Suzuki was adamantly opposed to the union's affiliation to the left-leaning Machine Tool Union and this led to the first postwar confrontation at the plant. In November 1947, the union local demanded that Suzuki conclude a new collective agreement and recognize the new union. Suzuki declined but did begin to "consult" (*kyōgi suru*) on the issues of wages and year-end bonuses. Internal conciliation efforts failed and on January 8, 1948, the union struck for twenty-four hours. On the same day local union members crashed a meeting between union representatives and Suzuki Michio. Barring all exits, the militant unionists forced Suzuki to bargain from 4 P.M. on the 8th until 3:30 the next morning, when a tentative agreement was reached. This agreement fell through prior to the official signing on the afternoon of the 9th, and the union immediately occupied the plant and entered into production control (*seisan kanri*), a dispute tactic widely used in 1946–47 in which workers continued production without management. Suzuki finally concluded a new wage agreement on Janu-

24. Shizuoka Ken Rōdō Undō Shi Hensan Iinkai, *Shizuoka ken rōdō undō shi* [A history of the labor movement in Shizuoka prefecture] (Shizuoka: Shizuoka Ken Rōdō Kumiai Hyōgikai, 1984), pp. 292–295.
25. Ibid., p. 277.
26. Ibid., pp. 296–298.

ary 15, raising the base wage to ¥3,800 per month with an average ¥2,000 year-end bonus.

In August 1948, Suzuki agreed to sign a new collective agreement that included provisions for a union shop (Article 4), a union veto over hiring and firing (Article 5), and changes in compensation and personnel (Article 15) as well as the right to automatic renewal of the collective agreement should a new agreement not be concluded prior to the expiration of the existing agreement (Article 22) and equal participation in a managerial council (*keiei kyōgikai*).[27]

The nature and achievements of the Suzuki union, with its growing regional and industrial affiliations, its gains in employment security, and its strong say at the workplace were strikingly similar to those of the Miike miners. These similarities cannot be attributed to a common leadership, since the two unions were affiliated with different labor federations both regionally and industrially. Union politics also differed, with the Miike union taking a distinctly neutralist tone while the Suzuki union was moving into the left camp.

In both cases, the unions took on a distinctively independent flavor and developed affiliations with workers on both a regional and industrial basis. There was no stopping at the company gates. Early achievements seemed to reflect a spontaneous drive for secure, independent organizations to represent them in dealings with management for secure jobs and for a say at the workplace. In other words, unions reflected workers' dissatisfactions and their unwillingness to let employers sort them out. The Trade Union Law and its administrative organs acted as both a guide and a catalyst, channeling the spontaneous movement into distinct directions.

The Moriguchi City Union

Moriguchi was incorporated as a city in November 1946 through the amalgamation of two local districts. According to the city workers' union history, the union's beginnings can be traced to a dispute related to wage discrimination between employees of the two districts.[28] Kiyomizu Yasuji, director of the economics department, led a group of twenty disenchanted employees to confront city officials over the discrimination in pay. Subsequently Kiyomizu and others met in a local school to found a union to represent all city hall employees (including supervisors and foremen). Little has been recorded about the union's activities in this

27. The entire collective agreement is reproduced in Shizuoka Ken Rōdō Undō Shi Hensan Iinkai, *Shizuoka ken rōdō undō shi, shiryō (Ka)* [Documents, vol. 1, History of the Shizuoka labor movement] (Shizuoka: Shizuoka Ken Rōdō Kumiai Hyōgikai, 1981), pp. 399–402.

28. Morigichi-Shi Shokuin Rōdō Kumiai, *Moriguchi-shi shokurō sanjū go nen shi* [Thirty-five years of the Moriguchi Employees Union] (Moriguchi: Moriguchi Kumiai, 1981), pp. 82–83.

early period except that the Moriguchi union did develop horizontal affiliations with other public sector unions in the Osaka region, probably in 1948.[29]

National Labor Federations and the Winter of Discontent

The issue of class became clearly defined in this early postwar period. Workers in these three case studies formed unions precisely because they were free to do so and because they felt some form of collective power was necessary to counterbalance the power of their employers. In the case of Mitsui, the employer displayed a paternalistic response by offering employees beer money to celebrate the founding of the union. But this paternalism quickly evaporated as the parties got down to brass tacks in bargaining.

The propensity to form horizontal linkages, characteristic of unions at all three work sites was a distinctive feature of most unions at this time. One reason for this was a spontaneous desire for relations with other unions. Regional and industrial affiliations were given further impetus by the Trade Union Law. Politics also played a role as union activists of various political persuasions attempted to organize on a national scale in an effort to effect change at levels beyond the enterprise.

In this early period, the Miike, Moriguchi, and Suzuki local unions had both regional and industrial affiliations, while the Suzuki union was also affiliated with a national labor federation. Through its affiliation with the national Machine Tool Union, it became part of the National Congress of Industrial Unions (NCIU, Zen Nihon Sangyō Betsu Rōdō Kumiai Kaigi, or Sanbetsu). The impulse for this labor federation came from the newspaper unions and the Kant labor committee. On February 20, 1946, these groups helped found the Preparatory Committee for a National Congress of Industrial Unions. The heterogeneous but left-leaning NCIU was formally established in the summer of 1946 and the Machine Tool Union affiliated soon after. The more conservative labor center, the Japan Federation of Labor (Nihon Rōdō Kumiai Sōdōmei, or Sōdōmei) was also founded that summer. Although the two federations reflected prewar divisions between left and right, both centers were politically diverse. An intense economic crisis accompanied by raging inflation sharpened class distinctions and drew unions together, creating favorable conditions for united labor action.

In the fall of 1946, private sector unions mounted a series of wage struggles to counter the effects of inflation. This coordinated wage offensive was inspired by the formation that summer of the two major union centers. Encouraged by victories in the rail and shipping industries earlier in the year, the NCIU called

---

29. The union's history cites confusing data on this issue but according to the Satellite City Federation, Moriguchi City Hall employees affiliated with it in May 1948.

for a coordinated wage offensive to begin in October 1946. Workers at Tōshiba led the charge, followed by unions in the communications, electricity, printing, power, and a host of other industries.[30] The fall offensive saw a number of unions gaining substantial wage increases, but of these struggles the most important was that in the power industry. For the first time, the union in the electrical power industry (Zen Nihon Denki Sangyō Rōdō Kumiai Kyōgikai, or Densan) called not only for a wage increase but for a fundamental change in the wage structure. After a series of job actions, including one that led to a five-minute power outage, the workers won what became know as the Densan wage structure, a ¥500 minimum monthly wage, an industry-wide collective agreement, a seven-hour day, time off for union activities, and controls over hiring and firing.[31]

The achievements of the October offensive gave the NCIU an edge over the JFL as the leading labor center in the country. These private sector gains amplified, however, the degree to which workers in the public sector had fallen behind in the fight against inflation. Government workers' wages remained at about only 60 percent of the private sector level.[32] But the conservative Yoshida cabinet refused to discuss any wage increases until it completed an investigation into public sector salaries. Thus out of the October offensive grew a winter catch-up drive by public sector workers.

Playing a leading role were employees in the education field, mainly teachers. At a special conference on October 18 they demanded a minimum monthly wage of ¥600 and an end to wage discrimination according to region or gender. Communication workers also demanded a minimum monthly wage but upped the ante to ¥800 per month. Finally, the rail workers, meeting in convention in November, also demanded a base salary scale beginning at ¥650 per month and called for a general strike as a last resort to back up their demands. These three unions joined with the civil service employees' unions to form a joint struggle committee in late November. By January 1947 this committee represented 2.6 million workers in thirteen unions.

The deepening crisis opened an opportunity to bridge the gap between the labor centers, the NCIU and the JFL. While the initiative for the general strike was clearly came from NCIU affiliates, the trade union committee of the Japan Socialist Party, which supported the JFL, also initiated the formation of a coalition to back the strike movement and joined with the unions in a massive antigovern-

---

30. On the October offensive see Kawanishi Hirosuke, *Kigyō betsu kumiai no riron* [A theory of enterprise unionism] (Tokyo: Nihon Hyōron Sha, 1989), pp. 170–172, and Shiota Shobei et al., eds., *Sengo rōdō kumiai undō no rekishi* [History of the Postwar Labor movement] (Tokyo: Shin Nihon Shuppan Sha, 1970), pp. 47–51.

31. Shiota, *Sengō rōdō kumiai undō no rekishi*, p. 50.

32. Miriam Farley, *Aspects of Japan's Labor Problems* (New York: John Day, 1950), p. 137.

ment demonstration on December 17. In Tokyo alone 500,000 demonstrated, while inside the Diet the JSP introduced a motion of nonconfidence in the government. This motion was defeated, but the unity in action of the pro-labor forces illustrated the relatively high degree of solidarity around both the demands for wage increases and for the resignation of the Yoshida government. This cohesion was further enhanced with the creation of a broad-based coalition of private sector unions and community groups to support the strike movement. Finally, on January 18, the public sector unions announced their intention to begin an unlimited general strike on February 1.

The burgeoning extra-parliamentary movement threw a scare into Yoshida and SCAP. Yoshida attempted to seduce conservative social-democrats into joining him in a coalition cabinet early in the New Year, but these attempts failed. In the meantime, SCAP, through its Labor Division, began to intervene to derail the general strike movement. MacArthur met personally with General Marquat, head of Economic and Scientific Section and the direct supervisor of the Labor Division, and instructed him to meet the union leaders and convince them to call off the strike.

On January 22, Marquat summoned leaders of the unions involved in the general strike plan and ordered them, verbally, to call off the strike. At this point the JFL leaders succumbed, and a few days later informed Marquat that they would abide by the strike prohibition and, significantly, would also work to stop other unions from striking. The majority of the strike preparatory committee, however, refused to go along. On the 30th, Marquat once again summoned strike leaders to his office and ordered them to call off the strike and report to him the following day to explain the concrete measures they had taken to stop it. Marquat refused to issue a written order banning the action, however, and the strike leaders again balked on calling off the strike. On January 31, MacArthur issued a written order banning the strike. Strike leaders were summarily brought to the Labor Division and ordered to broadcast an order to union members. After being escorted by military guard to commercial radio stations, they issued statements recognizing MacArthur's order. Only then were they released from what was effectively military custody. While scattered walkouts still occurred, the general strike was effectively crushed.

The abortive general strike came to symbolize labor's high tide mark—a line strewn, however, with the debris of recrimination and reprisal. But it would take some time before the union tide would recede. As at Suzuki, some sectors of the union movement continued to wage successful local or sectoral struggles into 1948. But on the whole the labor movement had reached its zenith, and within eighteen months employers, backed by SCAP, would launch a counteroffensive to push the unions back. In the meantime, however, unions at the local, regional, and national levels had made some impressive gains.

Labor's Achievements

Despite the setback of February 1, the labor movement's accomplishments in 1945–47 were substantial and of a magnitude similar to those of the Congress of Industrial Organizations (CIO) in 1935–38 in the United States. The dramatic spread of unionization, the organization of national union centers, and the challenge to management rights all testify to the strength of organized labor. Indeed, the unionization and contract struggles at Miike, Suzuki, and Moriguchi were a microcosm of the greater movement. The richness and diversity of these struggles reflected the vigorous, heterogeneous workers' movement of the period. Some of the particular features of this period which merit special attention are union organization, union rights, and the Densan wage formula.

Union Organization

Unionization during 1945–47, as Table 2 indicates, soared in an unparalleled fashion. The 6.5 million union members represented over 50 percent of the labor force. Of course, as our case studies reveal, not all unions were of the same type. The Moriguchi union was relatively inactive, the Miike union was active but independent of both the NCIU and the JFL, and the Suzuki union was active and affiliated with the metalworkers federation, which was in turn affiliated with the NCIU. Nevertheless, the scale and speed of this organization of the working class in Japan certainly compares with that of workers in the United States and Canada a decade earlier. Numerous parallels in conjuncture which no doubt contributed to the rise of unionism in all three countries, economic dislocation and a favorable political situation being among the more important.[33]

Of particular interest, however, is the organizational basis of the union movement, given the contention of Shimada and others that Japanese are by nature predisposed to enterprise unions as opposed to "industrial" unionism. As we have already established by looking at the United States, the key aspect to industrial unions was that they were organized according to industry as opposed to craft or trade, whether it be at the enterprise, regional, or national level. In Japan, to the extent the issue came up, all groups regardless of affiliation agreed that craft unions were not viable in Japan.[34] But from this point, workers and management parted ways.

33. If one looks at unionization rates in the three countries, the most notable feature is that unionization in Canada was delayed by several years. This delay may be attributable to the fact that the legal framework recognizing union rights (an integral part of the Fordist paradigm) was not established until 1944 with the passage of PC 1003.

34. Sakurada Takeshi states that he and Matsuoka Komakichi of the JFL had early on agreed that craft unions were out as a basis for union organization. See Ōtani Ken, *Sakurada Takeshi no hito to tetsugaku* [Sakurada Takeshi: His person and philosophy] (Tokyo: Nihon Keieisha Dantai Renmei Kōhō

Table 2.   Union formation, 1945–1948

Date	Unions	Union members
August 1945	0	0
December 1945	707	378,481
June 1946	11,579	3,748,952
December 1946	17,265	4,849,319
June 1947	23,323	5,594,699
December 1947	28,013	6,268,432
June 1948	33,900	6,533,954

Source: Ōhara Shakai Mondai Kenkyū Jō (hereafter Ōhara Shaken), *Nihon rōdō nenkan, 1951 nenban* [Japan labor yearbook, 1951 edition] (Tokyo: Jiji Tsūshin Sha, 1951), p. 55.

The heart of the debate about union organization centers on enterprise versus industrial unions and whether or not Japanese workers were predisposed to vertical relations (with their employer) or horizontal relations (other workers). For this period under study at least, the answer apparently lies with the latter. No matter how one shapes the dynamics, the fact that workers organized at all amounted to an implicit critique of employers. Furthermore, in each of our case studies unions did not limit themselves to a single enterprise but actively searched for affiliations with other workers. The solidarity developed within enterprises and spread within the region, often by industry. To the extent that any debate on the issue of organization did take place, it was between the NCIU and JFL.

The NCIU emphasized from its inception the idea that unions should be organized by industrial grouping, whereas the JFL stressed regional federations across industrial lines. The relative success of the NCIU would seem to indicate that the majority of organized workers agreed with the stress on industrial lines of organization or at least did not object to it. Furthermore, when one looks at the bargaining structure for this period, one sees that by the spring of 1947 it was moving away from the enterprise and becoming increasingly centralized. In the first quarter of 1947, for example, 64 contracts covering 1.9 million workers were negotiated in some form of centralized bargaining, compared to 881 contracts covering 244,000 workers conducted on an enterprise basis.[35]

During this period, as exceptional as it might seem, workers and unions were clearly predisposed to working class solidarity that transcended the enterprise. If this was so, as I think it was, the contention that workers in postwar Japan were

Bu, 1987), p. 148. Furthermore, the 1945 Trade Union Law was clearly biased against craft unionism.
   35. Statistics from Rōdō Shō, *SRUS 1945–46*, p. 650.

"naturally" predisposed to enterprise unions and spurned industrial or regional affiliations becomes untenable.

Labor Rights

Workers' rights were legally enshrined in the immediate postwar period, not as a direct result of workers' struggles but rather as a part of the democratization process.[36] As mentioned earlier, the government passed the Trade Union Law in December 1945. In September 1946, the government enacted the Labor Relations Adjustment Law regulating the operations of the labor relations boards and also announcing potential restrictions on strike actions in essential services. On November 3 of the same year, the Diet adopted a new constitution for Japan. Articles 25, 27, and 28 specified the people's rights to a minimum livelihood, the right and obligation to work, and the rights to organize, bargain, and act collectively. Finally, in April 1947, the government enacted the Labor Standards Law, which prohibited discrimination, proclaimed gender equality, and detailed minimal standards for hours of work, health and safety, and so forth.[37] The constitution and these three basic labor laws established the original legal framework for industrial relations in postwar Japan. Although they are therefore significant, they did not necessarily reflect the dynamics of conflict and compromise in the workplace at the time.

The fruits of unionization and collective bargaining at the workplace in this period were summarized at the time by the Ohara Institute's *Japan Labor Annual Review*, which underscored the following features as being specific to early collective agreements. *(a)* clauses defining working conditions were abstract—wage agreements simply stated that the company guaranteed a "living wage" and specifics were left to later bargaining; *(b)* personnel matters (hiring and firing) and major managerial decisions required the union's agreement; *(c)* unions obtained a closed shop or union shop clause; *(d)* union activities were sanctioned during working hours; *(e)* collective agreements often did not contain a "no strike" clause; *(f)* workers gained the right to participate in management through management councils; *(g)* contracts were automatically and indefinitely extended at expiration unless replaced with a newly negotiated agreement.[38]

These features indicate the extent to which union rights expanded in this period, often at the expense of managerial rights. While workers in both Japan and the United States organized unions as a means of improving their situation, the

36. This brief summary of legal changes is based on Sugeno Kazuo, *Japanese Labor Law* (Seattle: University of Washington Press, 1992).

37. The law prohibited night work and underground mining for women, as well as other measures that might be considered paternalistic today.

38. Ōhara Shakai Mondai Kenkyū Jō, *Nihon rōdō nenkan, 1951 nenban* [Japan labor yearbook, 1951 edition] (Tokyo: Jiji Tsūshin Sha, 1953), p. 346.

goals and methods often differed. Two distinct features of the unions' achievements in this period were the extensive incursion by workers into what had traditionally been considered exclusive managerial rights and the nonlegalist tone of collective agreements. Specifically, the veto over hiring and firing and equal participation in managerial councils (which potentially could make decisions on investment, technology, and so forth) were unprecedented achievements for Japanese labor and find no parallel in the labor history of the United States or Canada.

The collective agreements that emerged resembled what in today's industrial relations parlance are know as "framework agreements," that is, outlines for conducting labor-management relations that were subject to elaboration through letters of understanding on specific issues. Evidence of this is the absence of no-strike clauses during the life of the collective agreement and the fact detailed wage settlements were also left to negotiation outside the contract. What factors gave rise to these particular features of collective agreements?

Factors including discredited management, a fractured economy, and a growing democratization created fertile conditions for the rise of radicalism and the movement for independent unionism. But chance also played a role. For example, the U.S./Canadian model of two- or three-year collective agreements including wage increases clearly could not have coped with the ravages of inflation occurring at this time. Wage agreements were constantly under review and revision, and unions were also using the bonus system, historically reserved mainly for management, as a wedge for further wage increases. Thus collective agreements and wage agreements in many cases ended up being negotiated separately.

Production Control and Management Councils

In 1946, workers at Miike had rejected the idea of production control, that is, occupying and running the workplace, while workers at Suzuki indulged in it as late as 1948. But it was in the period between December 1945 and June 1946 that production control became most prominent. The first worker takeover occurred at the Yomiuri newspaper in the fall of 1945.[39] The Yomiuri occupation culminated in an arbitrated settlement that forced the owner to resign his position and sell a majority interest to disparate shareholders. More important, employees were accorded almost equal partnership in managing the firm through the establishment of management councils in which both sides had equal rights. Ironically, as radical as this compromise might appear in comparative terms, in fact it represented a necessary hedge against the specter of

39. See Moore, *Japanese Workers.*

outright appropriation, which was looming in the spring of 1946, as production control tactics proliferated.

It was precisely this specter that motivated the conservative Shidehara government to condemn production control in the so-called four ministry declaration of February 1946. This declaration failed to win enthusiastic SCAP support, however, and the government attempted appeasement by promoting managerial councils as an alternative to production control. Managerial councils, which were seen as a means of overcoming production control and stopping managerial "sabotage" (by withholding capital), were officially sanctioned in October 1945 and given substance by the Central Labor Relations Board (CLRB) in its July 17th memorandum calling for managerial councils.[40]

In its November 1946 guidelines for union contracts the NCIU agreed to the formation of managerial councils as a means of democratizing the workplace. It cautioned its affiliates, however, that such councils could easily become the site of labor-management collusion, and it emphasized the importance of collective bargaining and the collective agreements as the chief means of guaranteeing union rights. Most parties backed managerial councils, but for radically different reasons. For the government, managerial councils would forestall revolution; for the JFL, they were a means of institutionalizing labor-management cooperation; and for the NCIU they would democratize the workplace. It was no wonder then that such councils proliferated, as Table 3 indicates.

At both Miike and Suzuki, managerial councils were established in what became a national trend. Eighty percent of the 2,692 collective agreements signed in the first half of 1948 contained provisions for such a committee.[41] The committees met on average less than once a month, however, and how effective they were in ensuring labor rights is questionable. The right to veto in hiring and firing contained in collective agreements was probably much more important.

The Wage Structure

Unionization also had an impact on wage structure in 1945–48 in Japan, but it did not follow the U.S. pattern. As discussed in the introduction, the wage or compensation system that evolved in Canada and the United States had a number of peculiar features. The most important transition, which occurred in the 1930–45 period, was from a management-controlled piecework or job-rated system to a job-rated, straight-time system. In manufacturing in particular, there was a difference between production workers, who were paid an hourly rate, and front office or staff who were on a weekly or monthly salary. Among production workers, the most im-

---

40. Rōdō Shō, *SRUS 1945–1946*, p. 804.
41. Ōhara Shakai Mondai Kenkyū Jō, *Nihon rodo nenkan, 1951 nenban*, p. 396.

Table 3.   Managerial councils in 1948

Industry	Unions (all)	Unions with management councils	Percent
Primary	814	170	20.9
Mining	1,376	980	71.2
Construction	1,854	465	25.1
Manufacturing	13,190	6,912	52.4
Utilities	747	432	57.8
Commerce	1,293	522	40.4
Finance	779	411	52.8
Transportation and communication	4,312	2,285	52.9
Service	358	111	31.0
Education	2,882	924	32.1
Public service	5,928	1,704	28.7
Other industries	367	93	25.3
Total	33,900	15,005	44.3

Source: Ōhara Shaken, *Nihon rōdō nenkan, 1951 nenban* (Tokyo: Jiji Tsū-shin Sha, 1951), p. 395.

portant distinction was between trade and production or line workers, the former holding specific "tickets" or accreditation and receiving higher wages. But for all production workers, the most important feature of the wage system was that it was based on specific job descriptions within which there evolved steps or grades determined by seniority and ability. In general the impact of unionization was to "narrow wage differentials that reflect such factors as skill, education and experience."[42]

In Japan, on the contrary, the wage system was almost unilaterally controlled by management during eighty years of capitalist development.[43] Management attempted to divide and rule by ranking employees according to social status, qualifications, occupation, education, gender, and so forth. They also attempted to break labor solidarity by inculcating workers with the idea that what was good for the company was good for workers. Employees thus competed with workers at other companies and relied on management for their livelihood.

The wage agreement won by the electrical utility workers' union, Densan, in the fall of 1946 changed this pattern and set a precedent for workers in postwar Japan. Until then, unions had concentrated on winning a minimum base rate and

42. Morley Gunderson, "Union Impact on Compensation, Productivity, and Management of the Organization," in Anderson, *Union-Management Relations in Canada*, p. 360.
43. Kawanishi, *Kigyō betsu kumiai no riron*, p. 177.

cost-of-living increases to combat inflation, but management control over the system remained intact from the prewar period. In the Densan union, a wage committee devised a new wage system that did away with much managerial discretion in the wage system. As outlined in Figure 4, the only element of the Densan wage system over which management exercised some control was the merit or ability-based pay (*nōryoku kyū*), and this was not to exceed 20 percent of the total pay package.[44] Furthermore, the union wage committee would have some say in the evaluation of ability. Unions usually looked at the cost of living, caloric intake, housing, and so forth to determine the minimum wage, which was then divided according to the categories. Few unions were able to achieve the full Densan system but the general outlines of the future wage system date from this model.

The Densan wage system makes an interesting comparison with the job-attached comparative worth system that evolved in the United States or Canada. The Densan formula was certainly egalitarian in outlook, trying to wrest control of the system from subjective employer discretion by establishing a livelihood component based on age and family size. But this form of family wage was mainly intended for regular (male) employees and may have invited institutionalized discrimination against women. Although unions in Canada had called for a family wage to justify their demands for higher wages (and in Canada, at least, had at times opposed family allowances provided by the state because it undercut their demand for wages high enough to provide for a family), in Japan the concept of a family wage influenced the structure of the wage system. Furthermore, the elements in the wage categories (age, family size, and so forth) could be determined without reference to workers in other industries doing similar work. Perhaps in this indirect sense, the Densan wage formula may have been less effective in developing horizontal linkages between workers than the comparable system in the United States or Canada, although this is speculation. If, as Kim Moody concluded, the comparative worth factor reduced the wage gap between workers in large and small plants in the United States, then the whole issue of comparative wage determination should be considered an important area for further investigation in international industrial relations.[45]

Other forms of compensation dramatically different from the Densan wage structure were also under consideration in this early period. In November 1947, the Central Labor Relations Board established a special commission to reform the wage structure for government employees. Its recommendations, examined in detail in the next chapter, included the establishment of an occupation-based, incremental wage scale that closely resembled the compensation system for government workers in the United States. The wage system would be contested by

44. Ibid., p. 178.
45. Moody, *An Injury to All*, p. 25.

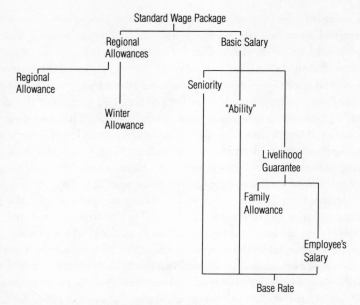

Figure 4. The Densan wage formula. From Kawanishi Hirosuke, *Kigyō bestsu kumiai no riron* [A theory of enterprise unionism] (Tokyo: Nihon Hyōron Sha, 1989), p. 178.

both labor and management, and in the end neither the Densan nor the American system would endure.

Shift in Alignments

The abortive general strike of 1947 constituted a landmark in Japan's labor history. Why did MacArthur ban the strike? Why had he taken so long to issue a written order to that effect? One might justifiably assume that the conservative general would be antilabor, but this is an insufficient explanation. For these were exceptional times. This same antilabor general had also allowed unions substantial power and legal rights. He had even tolerated production control in a number of important cases. In the case of the general strike, however, MacArthur no longer had room to maneuver. For one thing, a general strike would have definitely left the impression, particularly internationally where the cold war was gaining steam, that MacArthur had lost control of the situation in Japan. With a delegation of U.S. newspeople visiting Tokyo in January, MacArthur would not tolerate the specter of a general strike. He was also under pressure from business and the Yoshida government to resolve the crisis. Adding their voices to the hysteria were the hawks in the army and in intelligence.

MacArthur saw the political demands of the strike movement as a communist conspiracy and an affront to the U.S. liberal democratic ideal where public policy and lawmaking were the exclusive reserve of representatives elected every few years. He hoped to resolve the crisis informally by having the Labor Division persuade the strike leaders to abandon the movement. After the Labor Division failed to deliver the goods, however, MacArthur was obliged to issue a formal prohibition order. In his order MacArthur implicitly outlined what would become the standard interpretation of labor disputes: "The persons involved in the threatened general strike are but a small minority of the Japanese people. Yet this minority might well plunge the great masses of the people into a disaster not unlike that produced in the immediate past by the minority which led Japan into the destruction of war."[46]

The Labor Division chief, Theodore Cohen, was more explicit in his correspondence at the time. Writing to Mark Starr, educational director of the International Ladies Garment Workers' Union, Cohen blasted the Japan Communist Party:

Since you left the Communists have gotten very active in the Japanese unions. They have organized in almost every large union a Youth Action Corps into which they have recruited ex-officers and right extremists. Their people are threatening the union leaders with physical violence in case they are not aggressive enough, are disrupting union meetings and are otherwise raising Hell. This is the crowd which is pretty directly run by Tokuda, Secretary General of the Communist Party, that is behind the general strike threat on 1 February.[47]

What bothered Cohen in particular was the extra-parliamentary nature of the movement. As he expressed it later: "With no one to govern except on the strike leaders' sufferance, revolutionary unionism would replace the ballot box and representative democracy. The Occupation's 'democratization express' was heading for derailment."[48] What particularly galled the liberals in the Labor Division was that they were unable to control the strike leaders. While JFL leaders had abandoned the strike movement under pressure from Labor Division, militant union leaders—some of whom were communists—refused to buckle until ordered to call off the strike by MacArthur himself. This undermined the Labor Division's stature within SCAP.

46. Labor Division, Economic and Scientific Section, "Reports Concerning Activities of the Labor Movement Culminating in the 1 February 1947 General Strike Threat in Japan," 1 April 1947, Valery Burati Papers, box 2, folder 2, p. 6, Archives of Labor and Urban Affairs, Walter P. Reuther Library, Wayne State University, Detroit (hereafter cited as Burati Papers).

47. Ted Cohen to Mark Starr, 7 February 1974, Mark and Helen N. Starr Collection, Archives of Labor and Urban Affairs, Walter P. Reuther Library, Wayne State University, Detroit. Cohen remained remarkably consistent in his views over the years and maintained the myth that the JCP alone had instigated the general strike, in his memoirs. Theodore Cohen, *Remaking Japan: The American Occupation as New Deal*, ed. Herbert Passim (New York: Free Press, 1987); see p. 278.

MacArthur's prohibition of the general strike caused much anger and confusion. How could the Occupation—midwife to the union movement's rebirth—now spurn its offspring? In less than two years the union movement had risen from the ashes of illegality under militarism, organized and innovated, and stood up—only to run smack into the limits of liberal democracy as defined and enforced by an autocratic SCAP. As one historian commented later, "no organization, not even the JCP, was able to utter any criticism of General MacArthur's prohibition of the general strike. The words were on the tip of the tongue but could go no further in the presence of the Occupation forces who had the authority of the Almighty."[49] In this difficult context, workers and union leaders had to choose: either the Occupation was antilabor or perhaps—as MacArthur and the Labor Division asserted—the strike leaders had taken things one step too far. MacArthur did not leave the choice to chance. Instead, SCAP embarked on a campaign to convince the public that the threat of a general strike was a result of a communist conspiracy.[50]

The general strike prohibition of January 31, 1947, marked a turning point in Occupation labour policy.[51] Prior to the general strike threat, Occupation policy had principally been to support unions as a legitimate force in society and to limit employers' ability to suppress them. After February 1, however, the principal pillar of labor policy shifted from liberalization to anticommunism. Significantly, militant unionism became identified as communist-inspired, and thus the thrust of Occupation labor policy was not only to hound communists but also to restrict militant unionism, communist or not. The change in labor policy, although nuanced at first, can be clearly documented.

First, MacArthur was obliged to shuffle personnel in the Labor Division. Its chief, Theodore Cohen, was removed while he was away in the United States. Cohen among others had been identified by conservative U.S. reporters in Japan as a New Dealer. In his memoirs, Cohen recounts how Roy Howard, head of United Press and the Scripps-Howard newspaper chain, denounced him along with his

48. Cohen, *Remaking Japan*, p. 278.
49. Shiota, *Sengo rōdō kumiai undō no rekishi*, pp. 60–61.
50. *Newsweek* faithfully reflected the new line. In its edition of February 10, 1947, it stated: "The general strike was primarily designed to undermine the conservative Yoshida Cabinet. Working with the Social Democrats and the small Japanese Communist party, labor leaders had hoped to install a pro-labor government although the conservative parties won the last elections." A week later the magazine had concluded: "Moderate leftists now recognized that the strike threat and the fiasco that followed were engineered largely by Communists" (*Newsweek*, 17 February 1947).
51. Historians have different views about the beginning of the change in Occupation labor policy. Some assert that the change in policy began in 1946; others see the general strike prohibition as the turning point, while a third school sees the 1948 ban on strikes in the public sector as the key event. For an analysis of these trends, see Yamamoto Kiyoshi, *Sengo kiki ni okeru rōdō undō* [The labor movement in the postwar crisis] (Tokyo: Ochanomizu Shōbō, 1978). For a more recent account in English see Endo Koshi, "Reflections on the Turnabout in Labor Relations Policy in Occupied Japan," *Annals of the Institute of Social Science* (Tokyo), no. 26 (1984), pp. 78–101.

division's labor policy in an interview with MacArthur during the general strike melee.[52] MacArthur subsequently replaced Cohen with James Killen, a U.S. labor official who had been scheduled to join the Labor Division as an advisor on the recommendation of the American Federation of Labor.[53]

Suddenly promoted to chief, Killen's first assignment was to make sure that anticommunism became the axis of Occupation labor policy, the second clear indication of policy change after the February general strike. With the help of Richard Deverall and Paul Stanchfield, Killen drafted a program titled "Counteracting Communist Activities in the Japanese Labor Movement" in May, 1947, which was adopted as general policy the following month.[54]

According to the new policy, "Communist influence is in many cases disproportionate to the numerical strength of Communists . . . and it is often exerted and maintained by undemocratic and undesirable means."[55] The problem existed at every level of union organization and communists had attempted to prevent a "peaceful settlement of the abortive general strike of 1 February 1947." There was a clear need to support and encourage noncommunist labor groups. Finally, the program asserted that communists were preventing peaceful settlement of labor disputes because they "insist on acceptance of *all* union demands and emphasize the use of strike tactics as a normal procedure rather than as a last resort." The program recommended restrictive changes in the Trade Union Law, use of Labour Relations Board mediation to resolve labor disputes, and a broad anticommunist education program to encourage unions to purge themselves of communist influence. Closer liaison between Labor Division staff and unions was authorized, despite admonitions that the anticommunist program had to be carried out by the unions themselves.

Although changes to the Trade Union Law would not come until 1949, other parts of the program were implemented immediately. Writing to AFL president William Green in November 1947, Labor Division staffer Richard Deverall could report: "I only recently returned from a trip through Northern Honshu and Hokkaido, during which trip we addressed some 20,000 local labor leaders in 18 major cities of Japan. . . . One of the key points on our speeches up in the North were outright attacks on the principles of Marx-Engels' Leninism, the conclusion

52. Cohen, *Remaking Japan*, pp. 117 and 299.

53. For a detailed account of Killen's background and his role within the Labor Division, see Howard Schonberger, *Aftermath of War*, Chapter 4.

54. The original document is Paul Stanchfield, "Comment and Recommendations for Counteracting Communist Activities in the Labor Movement," 25 May 1947, Economic and Scientific Section, Labor Division, box 8497, National Archives Depository, Suitland, Md. (hereafter cited as Labor Division Papers). The final version is W. F. Marquat to Chief of Staff, "Program for Counteracting Communist Activities in the Japanese Labour Movement," 27 June 1947, Labor Division Papers, box 8497.

55. Paul Stanchfield, "Comment and Recommendations," p. 2.

being that a good trade unionist could not possibly be a trade [*sic*]."⁵⁶ (He probably meant to write, "could not possibly be a red.") Deverall, a former unionist and avid anticommunist, confidently predicted the elimination of communist influence by the middle of 1948.

Democratization or Witch-hunt?

The Labor Division's plan to encourage anticommunist groups quickly bore fruit and consolidated into what became known as the "democratization movement" (Mindō Undō).⁵⁷ The movement actually began within the railway workers' union, where anticommunists led by Katō Etsuo established the Railway Workers' Anticommunist League (Kokutetsu Hankyō Renmei) in the fall of 1947. It only later renamed itself the Democratization League. This group, or at least sections of it, played an extremely negative role within the rail union when it accepted government layoffs in order to purge the union executive of leftist elements.

It is important to note, however, that a second major component of this movement emerged from within the left wing of the NCIU itself. Hosoya Matsuta, an NCIU official and member of the JCP, had led an internal critique of the national federation and the party. In essence, his critique accused the union of being strike-happy and the party of attempting to use the union as a transmission belt. When these criticisms were rebuffed, Hosoya created an NCIU Democratization League (Sanbetsu Minshūka Dōmei) in February 1948. The rail and NCIU groups were later joined by the JFL to form a national organization in the summer of 1948.

These developments prompted G-2 (Military Intelligence) to report to the Labor Division in March 1948 that "anti-communist organizations are springing up in some of the most strongly Communist-dominated of the Japanese labor unions. Though these organizations are as yet weak and lack coordination on a nation-wide basis, there is every indication that the anti-communist trend in labor unions may be expected to increase."⁵⁸ It should be noted that the movement at this time was not strong, had a heterogenous character, and was not directly controlled by the Labor Division.

56. Dick Deverall to William Green, 19 November 1947, AFL Manuscripts, Office of the President, Florence Thorne Papers, file C, convention file, box 6, State Historical Society of Wisconsin, Madison.

57. This account of the Mindō is based on Takano Minoru, *Nihon no rōdō undō* [Japan's labor movement] (Tokyo: Iwanami Shoten, 1958); *Zenro ju nen shi* [Ten years: The Japan Trade Union Congress] (Tokyo: Zenrō Kaigi, 1968); and Takemae Eiji, *Sengo Rōdō Kaikaku* [Postwar labor reform] (Tokyo: Tokyo Daigaku Shuppan Kai, 1982).

58. Military Intelligence Section, General Staff, "Communist Leadership of National Congress of Industrial Unions," 15 March 1948, Labor Division Papers, Record Group Number 331, box 8497.

Employers Come Up for Air

Even more indicative of the post–general strike change in labor policy was the Labor Division's assistance to employers. In late 1947, John Harold instructed Paul Jackson to "contact Kanto Employers, Chamber of Commerce and any other Employers Association—to assist or advise them in respect to *broad* problems of labour relations."[59] In early December 1947, Jackson forwarded a check sheet to Killen outlining his program of advice for employers. Titled "Advice to Employers on Fighting Typical Communist Tactics," Jackson suggested that Occupation staff advise employers to (1) refuse to negotiate if unionists packed the negotiating room; (2) go over the heads of the negotiating committee and contact workers directly (through mass meetings, personal interviews, letters, and newspaper ads) about recent contract negotiations; (3) refuse to negotiate if the union leaders refuse to modify their bargaining position; and (4) split the union from communist leadership.[60] Concretely, Jackson advised the following steps to accomplish the split:

> Where such leadership has brought about a strike, even though management has made the best possible offer under the circumstances and where such offer has not been submitted to the rank-and-file for vote thereon, management may be advised that it can open its plants to any of the workers who wish to return to work on the basis of the last offer made by management. Other workers may be recruited elsewhere, if obtainable. If there is a group within the union that desires to accept the offer of the company and the company ascertains that the group represents a majority, management may conclude a tentative agreement with such group.[61]

Prior to the prohibition of the general strike, labor policy had been supportive of union formation and informally proscribed formation of overtly antilabor employer groups. With the shift in policy however, employers found the space to regroup. As the official history of Nikkeiren (Federation of Employer Organizations) later put it, "What was decisive in changing the situation was MacArthur's statement banning the general strike."[62]

With the help of the Kanto Employers' Association, two employers' organizations specifically dealing with labor relations began operations in 1947, the Federation of Employers' Organizations (Keieisha Dantai Rengō-kai or Keiei Rengō) and the Coordinating Committee for Employers' Organizations (Keieisha Dantai Renraku Kaigi). Both organizations (formed in May and July 1947 respectively) brought employers together to discuss strategy, a process that culminated in the

59. Handwritten note from John to Paul, undated, Burati Papers, box 1, folder 6.

60. Jackson to Chief, ESS/LA, "Advice to Employers on Fighting Typical Communist Tactics," Burati Papers, box 1, file 6.

61. Ibid., p. 3.

62. Nikkeiren, *Nikkeiren Sanju Nen Shi* [Nikkeiren: thirty years] (Tokyo: Nikkeiren, 1981), p. 189.

formal founding of Nikkeiren (Nihon Keieisha Dantai Renmei) on April 12, 1948, under the motto, "Managers: Be Fair and Firm." It marked the triumph of conservative employers over liberals in labor relations and the beginning of a concerted class attempt to take away the gains labor had made in 1945–47.

Prior to the founding of Nikkeiren, a liberal employers' group, the Committee for Economic Development (Keizai Dōyūkai), had achieved some stature among younger executives who wanted to emulate the Fordist system of the United States or Europe. They gained a "radical" reputation early in the Occupation when they refused to forthrightly condemn production control. This has led some academics in North America to portray the liberal Keizai Dōyūkai as a symbol of a new employer approach to labor relations.[63] However, with the change in Occupation policy after the aborted February 1 general strike, conservative employers became more aggressive and began to challenge the liberal trend within their ranks.

The main issue in the liberal-conservative confrontation was managerial rights. As explained earlier, workers had gained a major role in running enterprises through the creation of management councils in which they had equal representation with managers. Through these councils workers could effectively exercise a veto over hiring and firing, investment plans, and other crucial facets of what had hitherto been considered managerial prerogatives. The liberal trend among businessman embraced this new situation by calling for a new deal between labor and management. Liberal executives such as Ōtsuka Banjō, a Kansai businessman and president of Yawata Steel Pipe, called for enterprise democratization, tripartite power sharing, and a strong separation of managerial and stockholder authority.[64] In July 1947, a special Keizai Dōyūkai committee headed by Ōtsuka published a research report titled "A Draft Proposal for Democratizing Enterprises—A Modified Capitalist View." This report was a watered down version of Ōtsuka's views, but conservative businessmen remained adamantly opposed even to this version of power-sharing. Indeed, one businessman concluded: "Ōtsuka's modified capitalism is nothing more than the shrieks of middle-class managers who have lost

---

63. North American academics often incorrectly point to the Keizai Dōyūkai as a symbol of enlightened management that came to govern the workplace after the war. As one labor lawyer described it, "Japanese management has never viewed its work force and union representatives with the same negative attitude. The famous 1947 Doy Kai Declaration set the tone of union-management relations when it recognized the essence of a Japanese enterprise to be a coalition of three equals—managers, workers and shareholders," Joseph M. Weiler, "The Japanese Labour Relations System, Lessons for Canada," in W. Craig Ridell, ed., *Labour-Management Co-operation in Canada* (Toronto: University of Toronto Press, 1986), p. 123.

64. Ōtsuka's original views are contained in the April 1947 issue of *Zaikai* [Business] under the title, "Economic democratization and ways to achieve it" [Keizai minshūka to sono gutaisaku]. It is reproduced in full in Hazama Hiroshi, ed., *Zaikaijin no rōdō kan* [Business views of labor] (Tokyo: Daiyamondo-Sha, 1970). Ōtsuka basically calls for the formation of works councils but avoids the issue of the union's role within them.

confidence in face of the intense labor offensive."[65] And the president of Keidanren (Federation of Economic Organizations), the main business lobby, concluded that Dōyūkai was a bastion of communism in this period.[66] Opposition was so great that even the Dōyūkai's executive board refused to endorse Ōtsuka's views. The committee report was eventually released as a draft committee proposal but quickly faded into oblivion. As the Keizai Dōyūkai official history admitted: "That this report should stir up controversy was natural. 'Modified Capitalism' became the symbol of the Doyūkai and there was a time when these views were regarded as partially heretical by one section of the *zaikai*."[67]

One person who epitomized the conservative business element that was so opposed to the Dōyūkai's liberalism in postwar Japan was Maeda Hajime. A personnel manager in a Mitsui-related coal mining firm from before the war, Maeda helped establish Nikkeiren and suggested the motto "Managers: Be fair and firm." In his memoirs, Maeda recalled how his prewar fascist associations inured him against the democratization process during the Occupation: "Being one of the founding members of the Kōkoku Dōshikai (a prewar, militaristic youth group), I often went on outings with student friends from this group during summer vacations. Since my student days, my views were predisposed in this direction, and so I always had difficulty adjusting to the democratic thought that was bestowed on us by the Occupation after we lost the war."[68]

Given the ostensible liberal-democratic slant of the Occupation, Maeda and other conservative businessmen could not easily revert to their prewar practice of simply having unions outlawed. They recognized they had little choice but to live with them. Where they did have a choice was in deciding what type of unions they would work with. Early Nikkeiren documents clearly reveal their concern for reestablishing managerial control within the factories.[69] While paying lip service to "mutual respect for managerial and worker rights," Nikkeiren demanded

---

65. Hazama, *Zaikai no rōdō kan*, p. 366.

66. See Solomon Levine, "Employers Associations in Japan," in J. Windmuller and A. Gladstone, eds., *Employers Associations and Industrial Relations* (Oxford: Clarendon Press, 1984), p. 326. Despite these admonitions, the liberal limits of the Dōyūkai were apparent as early as October 1946, when it denounced the National Congress of Industrial Unions in the following terms: "To use a general strike for political struggles is anti-democratic. Labor disputes and workers political activities should reflect this restriction." Keizai Dōyūkai, *Keizai Dōyūkai sanjū nen shi* [Keizai Dōyūkai: Thiry years] (Tokyo: Kaizai Dōyūkai, 1971), p. 31.

67. Keizai Dōyūkai, *Keizai Dōyūkai sanjū nen shi*, p. 37. This account is affirmed in the biography of Sakurada Takeshi published by the Public Relations department of Nikkeiren. See Ōtani Ken, *Sakurada Takeshi no jin to tetsugaku*, p. 128.

68. Maeda Hajime, "Tōshō Ichidai" (Ge), *Bessatsu chuō kōron, keiei mondai* 8, no 2 (Summer 1964): 305.

69. These documents include the Nikkeiren founding statement, "An Opinion on Securing Managerial Rights," and "A Fundamental Plan for Revising Labor Contracts." These documents were all elaborated in April–May 1948 and are summarized in Nikkeiren, *Nikkeiren sanjū nen shi*, pp. 200–208.

unions be responsible and allow responsible management in order to achieve industrial peace and improved productivity. The founding statement even contained elements of self-criticism: employers had not stood their ground in the postwar period, and this had invited the erosion of managerial rights. To redress the situation, Nikkeiren called for absolute managerial control over all personnel issues, accounting, administration, organization, systems, supervision, production methods, work rules, and even safety. They also called for labor-management councils to be downgraded to consultative bodies.

Nikkeiren was not just a think tank. A few nights after Nikkeiren was established, top managers gathered at Yawata Steel's Yoyogi villa to discuss with the directors of Tōhō Movies the possibility of making Tōhō a test case to reestablish managerial rights.[70] Tōhō had come to symbolize the ascent of workers' control. As Maeda explained it: "Take the example of the union in the Tōhō struggle— when the current vice-president, Mabuchi Norikazu, left the Labour Relations Board to become an executive with Tōhō, he couldn't believe the internal memoranda. If the union president's stamp was not in the appropriate column, nothing could be decided regarding personnel—hiring, firing, transfers—nothing. . . . Thus recovering managerial rights was the main preoccupation of managers."[71]

Soon after this clandestine meeting, Nikkeiren published its "Guaranteeing Managerial Rights—Our View," in which it committed the organization to support Tōhō managers in their fight for concessions from the union.[72] In August, the Tōhō battle came to a head when the company obtained a court injunction forbidding the occupation of the production studios by about one thousand workers and their supporters. Soon after, 1800 police supported by U.S. tanks and warplanes routed the workers. As Sakurada Takeshi's biographer later put it: "The special significance of Tōhō is that this was the first time the Occupation army had directly and publicly intervened where labor had gone too far, and this gave police the determination to exercise their authority in cases of inappropriate strikes or where managerial rights had been violated."[73] With the defeat of the Tōhō union, conservative employers had scored a significant victory—one that would pave the way for a major managerial offensive in 1949.

70. The meeting at the Yawata villa is described in two reliable sources: Ōtani Ken, *Sakurada Takeshi*, p. 132, and Nikkeiren, *Nikkeiren sanjū nen shi*, p. 721.

71. Maeda Hajime, "Nikkeiren ni Ikita Nijū nen," *Bessatsu chūō kōron, keiei mondai* 8, no. 3 (Fall 1969): 355.

72. Under the 1947 contract at Tōhō, workers recognized managers' ultimate responsibility over hiring and firing, but this was mitigated by clauses which required the company to obtain the union's consent for each case. For contract details as well as information on the *Tōhō* struggle see *Tōhō sōgi (1948) shiryō* (Tokyo: Tokyo Daigaku Shakai Kagaku Kenkyū Jō, 1986), and *Tōhō sōgi (1948) shiryo (sono ni)* (Tokyo: Tokyo Daigaku Shakai Kagaku Kenkyū Jō, 1989).

73. Ōtani Ken, *Sakurada Takeshi*, p. 133.

3 The Japan–U.S. Business Alliance: Capital Retaliates (1948–1951)

The period from February 1, 1947, to the summer of 1948 constituted a transition from labor's high tide to the onset of the ebb. After this period ended Japan's employers began an offensive which, over the next three years, pushed labor back and reestablished managerial prerogatives in the workplace. The Japanese government, under instructions from SCAP, wrenched collective bargaining and strike rights from most public sector employees in the summer of 1948. Capital in Japan then followed up with a coordinated and planned offensive against the labor movement, an offensive that was endorsed by big business in the United States and which SCAP also supported. This renewed U.S.-Japan business alliance had been forged the previous year after business circles in the United States became alarmed at the spectre of workers' power generated by the threatened February 1 general strike and the Occupation reforms.[1] And as the cold war heated up in 1949 only to break out in a hot war in Korea, this offensive culminated in a spasm of unmitigated repression.

This chapter documents the causes and scope of the antilabor offensive and, in the process, shows how labor's achievements in the earlier period were eliminated or transmuted into pale imitations of the past, which superficially resembled the early days of radical reform but in substance reflected the resurgence of managerial control. The managerial offensive of this period had a lasting impact on the framework for labor-management relations as it evolved in the 1950s and 1960s.

---

1. Howard Schonberger has meticulously documented the forging of this alliance in his book *Aftermath of War* (Kent: Kent State University Press, 1989).

Public Sector Attacked

Despite MacArthur's prohibition of the February general strike and the resurrection of managerial prerogatives through Nikkeiren, the workers' movement retained substantial vigor into 1948. Public sector unions in particular pressed demands for wage increases and civil service reform in late 1947 and early 1948. Their demands were a contributing factor in the March 1948 downfall of the JSP-led coalition government that had been in power since May 1947.[2]

SCAP at this time was taking a hard line against strikes. Disputes in coal, electricity, and communications had been halted by Occupation fiat in the spring. That May, the resurrected coalition cabinet, under the leadership of the Democratic Party's Ashida Hitoshi, was determined to bite the bullet and rein in labor.[3] Its conservative faction conspired with bureaucrats in SCAP's government section to have MacArthur issue an order directing the Ashida cabinet to rescind the public sector's right to bargain and strike.[4] On July 22, 1948, MacArthur did exactly that, creating an uproar within the labor movement. This was followed by Cabinet Order 201, which prohibited all public sector strike action and ordered an end to CLRB attempts to mediate in public sector disputes.[5] Specific laws were subsequently passed in December 1948 and in 1950 that formally deprived all public sector workers of the right to strike and prohibited most of them from bargaining collectively. Table 4 illustrates the impact of the 1948 measures and subsequent legislation on the legal framework for collective bargaining.

The restrictions on union rights in the public sector came about for two reasons: a convergence of opinion between Japanese officials in the Ashida government and SCAP officials in the Government Section and MacArthur's desire to send a strong message to labor that he would not brook work stoppages in the public realm. SCAP's Labor Division opposed the scope of the changes, but James Killen, the head of Labor Division, was overruled by MacArthur after a dramatic showdown on the issue in June 1948.[6] Killen subsequently resigned. An important

2. For an account of this period see Koyama Kōtake and Shimizu Shinzō, *Nihon shakai tō shi* [History of the Japan Socialist Party] (Kyoto: Hōka Shoten, 1965), pp. 58–60. In English, see Farley, *Japan's Labor Problems*, pp. 172–183.

3. In discussions with Under Secretary of the Army William Draper in March 1948, Ashida clearly indicated he wanted labor restrained through changes in the labor laws. See Schonberger, *Aftermath of War*, p. 186.

4. For details on the conspiracy, see Takemae Eiji, *Sengo rōdō kaikaku*, pp. 230–231.

5. The crackdown on the public sector and the overwhelming use of force during the Tōhō dispute in August would seem to make summer 1948 a decisive period, when what I call the period of realignment ends and the managerial offensive takes shape. However, the coalition government (especially with the left-leaning Katō Kanju as Labor Minister) was not the most effective vehicle for a concerted attack on labor. This problem was resolved in October.

6. For an inside account of the showdown see Cohen, *Remaking Japan*, pp. 390–392.

Table 4.   Union members by labor law jurisdiction

Total	Trade Union Law	Crown Corp. Labor Relations Law	National Civil Servants Law	Regional Civil Servants Law
5,686,774	3,815,144	463,795	511,031	896,804

Source: Ōhara Shaken, *Nihon rōdō nenkan, 1951 nenban* [Japan labor yearbook, 1951 edition] (Tokyo: Jiji Tsūshinha, 1951), p. 71.

Note: (1) These statistics are from 1950. Most of the union members covered by the TUL were in the private sector. Those under the CCLRL were mainly railway workers. (2) The TUL allowed the right to unionize, bargain, and strike. The CCLRL allowed the right to unionize and bargain. The National and Regional Civil Servants Laws allowed for unionization but denied the right to bargain for a collective agreement.

factor that is often overlooked in this matter is that the union rights accorded to public sector workers in Japan clearly exceeded those of their counterparts in the United States or Canada, for whom striking continued to be prohibited in the main. Thus, in MacArthur's eyes, his actions during the summer simply redressed what he saw as the excesses of the early postwar reforms. But for public sector employees, union rights hardly seemed an excess, and for years public sector unions unsuccessfully challenged these measures in court and filed complaints to the International Labour Organisation to little avail. The restriction on union rights shaped the production regimes in the public sector in ways not shared by the private sector.

Besides the prohibition of union rights another development was occurring within the public sector that would also have long-term implications for Fordism in Japan. The outline of a new wage and classification system, one dramatically different in structure from the Densan system, was being constructed in the civil service.

Through his work in the Occupation's Government Section, Blain Hoover, chairman of the Civil Service Assembly of the United States and Canada, played an instrumental role in reforming Japan's civil service. Not only was Hoover responsible for insisting that the Government Section repeal the right to strike for civil servants, he also advised that Japan adopt the American system of occupational classifications for civil servants.[7] This system, while reflecting inherent biases regarding gender and replete with bureaucratic pitfalls for labor, did reflect an attempt to implement the principle of equal pay for equal work by endeavoring to evaluate the actual work that employees performed. Thus as early as 1947, when the National Public Service Law was enacted by the JSP-led coalition government,

7. Based on information in Jinji In, *Jinji gyōsei nijū nen no ayumi* [Twenty years of personnel administration] (Tokyo: Ōkura Sho, 1968), pp. 70–73.

the legislation adopted the principle that jobs should be classified and weighed against each other through a standardized evaluation of job content (responsibility, duress, and so forth).[8] At the same time as the job classification scheme was being introduced, the government and the CLRB were attempting to initiate major changes in the wage structure for civil servants.

After the prohibition of the February general strike, the JSP-led Katayama cabinet came to power and referred demands for wage increases to CLRB mediation. Reporting back in November 1947, the CLRB recommended that government employees receive a special inflation bonus worth 2.8 months of salary and that a special commission be formed to reform the wage structure.[9] Of all the unions in the government sector, only the rail union (NRWU) accepted the CLRB recommendations, and it was the lone union to sit with the government and the CLRB on the special wage commission. The main points of the wage reform package, introduced in May 1948 and amended some months later, were (a) the abolition of the four employee levels (officials, employees, daily paid workers, and monthly paid workers) and establishment of two wage scales, one standard and one daily paid; (b) the establishment of the principle that employees would be paid on the basis of the quantity and quality of their work; (c) the adoption of a fifteen-tier classification scale with six to ten incremental steps in each; and (d) the creation of five such scales for particular government sectors (general, taxation, police, railways).[10] This compensation system was very close to the American model. A key feature was that employees had to go through an evaluation process in order to change classifications or to win promotions. The issue of how to measure performance was a point of major divergence between U.S. and Japanese officials.

In 1949, Andō Tamao began work for the Efficiency Bureau of the National Personnel Authority, which administered the new wage system for government workers. He recalled that U.S. Occupation officials stressed the difficulty of measuring performance objectively and that they insisted that employee evaluation be restricted to work performance. Andō could not accept the American position:

> For my part, well—as you can see how we translated "Jinji Kōsa Ka" as the Employee Evaluation Section, not the Service Rating Section, we stressed that it wasn't enough to base our evaluation simply on employee work performance and that if we didn't plan to also fairly measure such things as character, ability and aptitude the evaluations would be useless in deciding such things as assignments and transfers. I said the

8. Ibid., p. 71. The fact that the official number of job classifications peaked at 449 in January 1952—while Japan was still under occupation—and thereafter declined is an indication that job classifications were largely a result of U.S. influence. For statistics on the job classifications see ibid., pp. 86–87.

9. Ibid., p. 219.

10. Ibid., pp. 220–221.

purpose of the so-called personnel evaluations was about character and, compared to the U.S. performance evaluation which had a history of only 50 years, my country's [practice of] personnel evaluations actually date back over 1200 years ago to the idea of "evaluating" [kō] found in the regulations of the Taihō legal code.[11]

Whether one classifies Andō's musings as the expression of tradition or simple rationalization, the fact remains that there existed divergent views on the scope and appropriateness of evaluations. Americans officials had come to recognize the difficulty of evaluating performance. Managers such as Andō did not see any difficulties and went so far as to add character assessment to the work rating. Clearly, the idea of using personnel evaluations had struck a resonant chord among some Japanese officials. The idea of establishing a hierarchical wage and promotion ladder based on pseudo-scientific, bureaucratically controlled measurements took hold and expanded into the private sector during the next few years.

The Employer Offensive (1948–1950)

The appointment of Yoshida Shigeru to form a new cabinet in October 1948, after the Ashida coalition government fell due to scandal, signaled the onset of an employer offensive that significantly altered labor relations in Japan. If 1946–47 represented the high tide of union power, then 1948 marked a transition. The next two years, 1949 and 1950, can only be regarded as a coordinated employer/government offensive against labor. We will first examine the contents and effects of this managerial offensive through a case study at Suzuki. This is followed by a broader examination of the 1949–50 layoffs and strikes and by a discussion of the timing and nature of the 1949 reform of the Trade Union Law. The section concludes with a synopsis of the intent and basis of the managerial offensive.

The Suzuki Lockout

A surge in loom demand in 1948 sustained relatively tranquil labor relations at Suzuki after the turmoil early in the year. In the second half of 1949, however, sales began to drop dramatically. At the same time Suzuki came under intense pressure from its banks to retrench and regain managerial control in the workplace—control that had weakened by union gains.

On November 23, 1949, the company submitted what it considered a "reconstruction" proposal to the union. The proposals, although vague at first, included

11. Ando Tamao, "On Setting Up the Plan for a System of Performance Evaluation," in Jinji In, *Jinji gyōsei no nijū nen no ayumi*, pp. 313–314.

demands for major wage cuts and personnel reductions. The next day Suzuki officially demanded a 35 percent wage reduction. This marked the beginning of a dispute that would escalate into a major confrontation between Suzuki and its
employees. Suzuki explained its decision to embark on this collision course with
the union this way:

> The origins of our decision (reconstruction through personnel consolidation) can be
> traced to the fact that both domestic and overseas orders had dropped sharply, and
> profits stagnated leading to a surplus in personnel; but our banks forced our hand
> telling us: "you must deal with redundant personnel, eliminate radical elements from
> the union, reduce the scope of operations and restart your operations on a healthy ba-
> sis or we cannot lend you money." With this they also refused to discount our note.[12]

The instructions Suzuki had received from its bank were not simply a result of a
tight-money policy; they reflected an escalation in the attempt by the highest echelons of big business to purge the unions of an adversarial approach to labor relations.

At Suzuki, the union responded to the company's proposal with a counterplan
to deal with the ostensible economic aspects of the crisis. The union proposal contained major concessions including a proposal to reduce wages by 20 percent for
regular employees and 35 percent for managers. The company declined this offer
and instead began to solicit "volunteer retirees" (kibō taikshokusha). By December
15, fifty-four employees had decided to accept early retirement.

The company continued to press in the management council for further concessions from union representatives during January. It also informed the union
that if a new collective agreement was not in place by January 20, it would consider the existing collective agreement void (1949 amendments to the Trade Union
Law banned the perpetual duration clause for contracts). On January 26 the union
received company notification that the collective agreement had expired but remained optimistic that a new contract would be worked out. By February, however, the union began to loose confidence in a negotiated settlement and issued
an emergency notice to its members warning them of impending layoffs.

Discussions in the management council ended at this time and collective bargaining began. In one sense this was a formality, because the same people were still
meeting. Collective bargaining represented an escalation in the conflict, however,
because the contradictions were now public and an informal agreement to end the
dispute became impossible.

On March 10 the company unilaterally reduced the base wage rate from ¥9,000
to ¥7,000 per month and one week later announced it would layoff 282 employ-

---

12. Suzuki, *40 nen shi*, p. 100.

ees of its own choosing.[13] Severance pay was set at ¥30–40,000. The union responded with a twenty-four-hour strike on March 22. On April 11 Suzuki broke off collective bargaining and the next day it sent by registered mail layoff notices to the 282 employees. On the 17th, the union members occupied the plant and began production control. Katō Toshio, a veteran employee from this era, recalled the conflict: "The union decided that they would swallow the wage cut, but they insisted that somehow the layoff of 282 of their members must be rescinded . . . this was the origin of the confrontation. As it was however, the union was really strong, and even if layoff notices were given to individuals, they were all returned. They gathered up the notices and sent them back to the post office. Finally, the company publicly revealed the layoff notices and there was no turning back."[14] The layoff notices were returned to Suzuki on April 21 at which point the company applied for a temporary injunction banning the laid-off employees from entering the plant.

On May 15 the Japan Machine Tools Union declared a twenty-four-hour general strike to protest layoffs at Hitachi and Tōshiba as well as at Suzuki. The workers barged into the executive offices and tried to force Suzuki Michio and others to restart collective bargaining. During the confrontation, the workers attempted to hoist Suzuki's chair into the air, at which point a scuffle occurred. Suzuki fell and lay prostrate, but ten minutes later he got up and left without further hindrance from the union members. He reported to a local hospital where he was told he was not seriously injured.[15] Suzuki reported the incident to the police and on May 21 fourteen union activists including the local's executive were arrested.[16] The day after the arrests Suzuki locked out its employees. On June 8, the Shizuoka Regional Labour Relations Board offered to mediate the dispute and the two parties accepted this proposal.

As the confrontation escalated, dissension grew within the local and on June 8 and 9 union members opposed to the local's militant tactics met to form a breakaway union. On June 10 the second union was founded and quickly gained 132 adherents. According to the original union, the new union members visited each member's residence and said, "Even if you are not one of those laid off this time, if you stick with the Metalworkers the next time there are layoffs you'll definitely get

---

13. Suzuki Jidōsha Kōgyō Shashi Iinkai, ed., *50 nen shi* [Fifty years in the making] (Hamana-Gun: Suzuki, 1970), p. 30.

14. Katō Toshio, interview by author, 7 March 1990. Katō Toshio was a veteran of the 1950 strike who later became active in the Suzuki union. He was elected to the executive in 1955 and became president in 1960.

15. Moto Zen Kinzoku Rōsō Suzuki-Shiki Shokki Bukai, *Sōgi kiroku* [A record of the dispute] (Hamamatsu: Suzuki, 1951), as reproduced in Shizuoka-Ken Rōdō Kumiai Hyōgikai, *Shizuoka-ken rōdō undō shi shiryō (Ka)*, p. 353.

16. Shizuoka-Ken Rōdō Undō Shi Hensan Iinkai, *Shizuoka-ken rōdō undō shi*, p. 640.

the boot. If you join the second union now you'll be okay."[17] The breakaway union obtained an old building from the company to use as its headquarters, and an all-out war between the factions began. Katō Toshio, who later became active in the second union and went on to become president in 1960, recalled the dilemma that workers faced: "Those who weren't targeted for layoff, as you can imagine, they would gradually get weaker. That's how factions occurred and the union gradually split up. That's when the second union was formed. As long as things weren't resolved things got worse. Debts, the union was going into debt, and there was no place to turn. You were damned if you did and damned if you didn't."[18] On June 21, a U.S. military officer responsible for labor affairs in the Civil Affairs Section of the Kanto Division of the Occupation Forces visited the Suzuki factory, ordered all the workers to assemble in front of the factory gates, and proceeded to lecture them on the importance of maintaining production and keeping the peace. Inspired by the speech, some members of the breakaway union breached the picket lines and entered the factory.[19] Fearing further violence, mediators and prefectural officials pressured Suzuki to get the dissident workers to withdraw from the factory grounds, and Suzuki in the end complied with these requests.

The regional LRB stepped up its mediation efforts and on June 25 submitted its proposals to resolve the dispute. Among other things, the LRB recommended that the number of layoffs stand but that the company allow some leeway in who was to be laid off. That is, if certain volunteers stepped forward, then others who had been designated for layoff could remain. This compromise proposal was based on the union contention that the company was attempting to break the union and that it was guilty of an unfair labor practice because it had designated the majority of the union executive to be laid off.

The company responded to the effect that it would have the final say about who was to be laid off, thus rejecting any possibility that union leaders might retain their jobs. The union, for its part, demanded that all layoffs be carried out through attrition or voluntary early retirement. Mediation continued until July 5 and then broke off. Later the same day, Suzuki concluded an agreement with the breakaway union based on the mediation proposals but eliminating those clauses that allowed for the original union executive to possibly retain their jobs. With this memorandum of agreement in place, Suzuki decided to lift the lockout and thereby served notice that it was prepared to have its new union break the strike.[20]

The LRB mediators, fearing new clashes if the breakaway union members attempted to cross the picket lines, made one final effort at settlement. On the key

17. Moto Zen Kinzoku, *Sōgi kiroku*, p. 356.
18. Katō Toshio, interview.
19. Suzuki, *50 nen shi*, p. 31.
20. Ibid., p. 32.

issues of jobs, it proposed reducing the number of workers to be laid off by twenty. The company accepted this new proposal because it maintained control of who was to be laid off. The union was in a difficult position. Workers could sense the changing relation of forces through the intervention of the military, the police, and the company's support for the breakaway union, and an increasing number had shifted allegiance to the breakaway union. In a dramatic general meeting on July 8, over three hundred members of the original union met to vote on the mediator's proposal. The outcome: 212 in favor and 111 against.[21] Suzuki reopened its doors on July 10 and, with the full support of management, the breakaway union gradually gained exclusive jurisdiction at the plant. Needless to say, the new union had no affiliation with the Japan Machine Tool Union and from 1950 on followed a policy of cooperation with the company.

The 1950 strike at Suzuki, which has not been investigated by researchers in Japan, constitutes a microcosm of the changing relation of forces in labor-management relations from 1948 to 1950. To fully grasp its significance, one must situate it within the general experience of the period.

Layoffs: Scope and Motivations

Table 5 illustrates the scope of layoffs in the private sector that occurred in this period. Major corporations including Mitsui Mining, Tōshiba, Hitachi, Toyota, and Yamaha laid off thousands of their employees in 1949 and 1950. Nor were the layoffs restricted to the private sector.

In May 1949, the Yoshida government introduced a legislative package to reduce employment in the public sector. The package called for Japan National Railways (JNR) to dismiss about 90,000 workers and for reductions in the civil service at all levels. The layoffs in rail were massive and hotly contested by militant sections of the rail union. Unfortunately, the summer of 1949 is remembered not for the wanton dismissal of so many workers but for a series of violent events related to the dispute: the Shimoyama, Mitaka and Matsukawa incidents, which took the lives of ten people.[22]

Job cuts among employees in regional governments were not of the same scale because the prefectural and city authorities had already been reducing staff levels. In fact, many of the layoffs constituted paper savings, although the new standards

---

21. Ibid., p. 33.
22. The Shimoyama case refers to the death of the president of the JNR, Shimoyama Sadanori, whose mangled body was found on rail tracks in the Tokyo area on July 6, 1949. In the Mitaka incident a sabotaged electric train became a runaway and smashed into the Mitaka station, killing six people. In the Matsukawa case, a passenger train derailed, killing the three engineers in the steam-driven locomotive. The rail tracks had been deliberately sabotaged. For details in English, particularly on the latter incident, see Chalmers Johnson, *Conspiracy at Matsukawa* (Berkeley: University of California Press, 1972).

Table 5.   Private sector layoffs, 1949

Month	Enterprises	Layoffs
February	218	7,480
March	479	15,349
April	513	26,295
May	833	31,911
June	941	40,840
July	1,241	99,629
August	1,330	73,546
September	1,071	44,264
October	748	33,552
November	645	32,468
December	795	30,132
Total	8,814	435,466

Source: Rōdō Shō, *Shiryō rōdō undō shōwa 24 nen* (Tokyo: Rōdō Shō, 1951), p. 86.

Note: The statistics are for less than one year and are not complete.

did imply lower job levels in the long run. Table 6 shows the effects of layoffs in the civil service at the regional level. Moriguchi, one of our case studies, was not affected by the layoffs that occurred in this period.

Recognition of the relatively limited scope of the layoffs among regional government employees should not blind us to the pain suffered by the 20,000 who were given the sack. Nor should it lead us to underestimate the importance of analyzing the nature of these layoffs. Many scholars regard the layoffs in this period as simply an economic function of the Dodge line, a policy of fiscal retrenchment imposed by the United States on the Japanese government in 1949. However, the evidence from the Suzuki case study and related materials suggests that the layoffs that occurred in this period were more than simply a case of temporary dislocation due to government fiscal policy.

The directive that Suzuki received from its bank clearly indicated that one objective of the layoffs was to eliminate what it called radical elements from the union. Forty years after the dispute, Katō Toshio recalled how Suzuki went after the militants: "Two hundred eighty-two heads were to roll, but they began with the reds, so there was an element of an anticommunist purge."[23] In the Toshiba dispute this was clearly one of the objectives as well, as Occupation documents made clear and as Joe Moore confirmed in his study of that dispute.[24] In the pub-

23. Katō Toshio, interview.
24. Valery Burati, a former CIO staffer, joined the Labor Division in late 1948 and quickly became involved in the Toshiba dispute. In a report to his superiors he explained that the existing collective

Table 6. Employment adjustment standards for regional public sector

	Prefectural	Five metros	Cities	Town/ village	Total
Previous em- ployment standard	293,786	77,566	95,461	206,022	672,835
Reduction	52,881	11,635	9,546	10,301	84,363
New employ- ment standard	240,705	65,931	85,915	198,721	588,473
Actual layoffs	9,443	3,568	5,324	4,120	19,455

Source: Jichi Rōdō Undō Shi Henshū Iinkai, *Jichi rōdō undō shi* (Tokyo: Keisō Shobō 1974), p. 138.

lic sector, the layoffs explicitly targeted union activists and communists. According to one study of layoffs at sixty-nine prefectural, metropolitan, and city or town bargaining units, at fifty-four of the sites the layoffs included executive members of the union.[25] In light of these indications, one is hard pressed to avoid the conclusion that the 1949 layoffs had as a major objective the purge of militant unionists. When linked to other political events at this time, and put in the context of the realignment of U.S. and Japanese business interests, it becomes blindingly clear that the management offensive of 1949–50 was, in the main, a political act on the part of Japanese capital. It certainly had the blessing of U.S. business and SCAP, but Japan's employers needed little coaching on how to tame an unruly labor force; they had a half century of practice and their antilabor bias was as home-grown as miso soup. Further evidence for this perspective comes from the history of Nikkeiren policy proposals leading up to the 1949 assault on labor.

Trade Union Law (TUL) Reform

A key ingredient in Suzuki's successful attempt to restructure as well as break its militant union was its ability to lay off employees at its own discretion. The 1948 collective agreement (Section 2, Clause 5) explicitly prohibited layoffs unless

---

agreement gave the union "almost managerial authority." The Labor Division's plan was to have the Tōshiba management revoke the collective agreement and renegotiate a new agreement with a second union. See Val Burati to Chief, Labor Relations and Education Branch, "Strike in Tokyo Shibaura Electric Company," 15 March 1949, Economic and Scientific Section, Labor Division Papers, box 8477, pp. 1–2. Joe Moore has done a more thorough review of the Tōshiba dispute. See "The Tōshiba Dispute of 1949: The 'Rationalization' of Labour Relations," *Labour Capital and Society* 23, no. 1 (April 1990): 134–159. Moore emphasizes that Toshiba management was the principal actor in the offensive and not Occupation officials.

25. Jichi Rōdō Undō Shi Henshū Iinkai, *Jichi rōdō undō shi dai ikkan* [A history of the labor movement among local government workers] (Tokyo: Keisō Shobō, 1974), pp. 143–145.

agreed to by the union, however. In order to get around this major problem, Suzuki served notice that it was refusing to renew the collective agreement. This in itself was a violation of Section 5, Clauses 22–24, which provided for automatic renewal of the contract (perpetual duration) until a new collective agreement was in place. According to clause 24, the terms and conditions of the collective agreement would remain in place until such time as a new collective agreement was signed. In May 1949, however, the conservative Yoshida government had revised the Trade Union Law and prohibited perpetual duration clauses in collective agreements. Suzuki was thus able to take advantage of the new law, revoke the collective agreement, and thereby void the clauses that prohibited layoffs.

The correlation between the revisions to the TUL and Suzuki's revocation of the collective agreement six months later is far from coincidental. In fact, employers had begun to plan for changes in the TUL shortly after July 1948, when MacArthur authorized the government to attack public sector unions by lifting their right to collectively bargain and to strike. Nikkeiren, for example, had secretly formulated its demands for changes in the TUL prior to September 7, 1948, when they were formally adopted. Nikkeiren submitted its reform proposals for Labor Division scrutiny on October 27.[26]

In introducing its reform package Nikkeiren summarized its perspective on the labor-relations scene: "A few far-left elements, who have a political blueprint for Japan's labor movement but who have no democratic union consciousness or experience, have repeatedly taken control of the country, pushed the economy into chaos while ignoring the economic well-being of the people."[27] It recommended (1) banning strikes that endangered the economy including general strikes, political strikes, sympathy strikes, production control, etc., (2) widening exclusion provisions to prohibit managers and others (including even health and safety personnel) from union membership, (3) cessation of subsidy for union activities, (4) restriction of collective bargaining to economic issues and restricting the bargaining unit to enterprise units, (5) invalidating the closed or union shop, (6) reinforcing management's right to fire for cause, (7) clarifying unfair labor practices and making each party liable for these actions, (8) obliging unions to submit decisions regarding dispute actions, for example, to a secret ballot at general meetings, (9) inserting a peace clause (similar to a no-strike clause), collective bargaining procedures, and establishing a grievance committee within collective agreements, (10) dividing the Labor Relations Board function into two separate divisions, one for arbitration and one for mediation.[28]

    26. Takemae Eiji, Sengō rōdō kaikaku, pp. 279–280.
    27. Nikkeiren, "Rōdō kumiai hō kaisei ni tai suru ware no kenkai," as cited in Takemae Eiji, Sengō rōdō kaikaku, p. 408.
    28. Takemae Eiji, Sengō rōdō kaikaku, pp. 409–411.

The resurrection of a Yoshida-led government by SCAP in October 1948 was a direct signal of the imminent changes in Occupation policy, economic and otherwise. Nikkeiren moved quickly to take advantage of the situation by lobbying the new administration. In a memorandum submitted to major governmental departments on October 20, the employers' association called for wage stabilization, reinforcement of the workers' sense of duty by establishing a productivity-based wage system, measures to cope with the unemployment produced by rationalization programs in both the public sector (*gyōsei seiri*) and private sector (*kigyō seibi*), reform of labor laws to bring radical unions into line, educational measures to democratize unions and to promote managerial and technical skills, and creation of a social welfare system.[29] Clearly this plan for wage restrictions and layoffs (rationalization) predates the Dodge directive of December 1948.

Yoshida heeded Nikkeiren's call for government intervention and immediately began to exert pressure on militant unionism through administrative fiat. In October, for example, the Labor Ministry issued an internal memorandum stating that the banning of communists from unions or union positions was legal.[30] This was followed by other minor changes, and then on December 22 the ministry issued a major internal memorandum to prefectural authorities. Titled "Circular from the Deputy Minister for the Promotion of Democratic Unions and Democratic Labor Relations," the notice called for close supervision of individual unions by the civilian authorities in conjunction with the corresponding Military Civil Affairs officials in order to break militant unions.[31] Concretely, the circular outlined changes the government would require in union bylaws and collective agreements. The latter included the following provisions: (1) strengthening managerial rights, (2) restricting the scope of collective agreements, i.e. excluding all managers from its provisions, (3) halting union activities on company time and payment of union officers, (4) spelling out provisions of the collective agreement in detail, (5) establishing grievance committees, (6) inserting if possible no-strike clauses for the duration of the collective agreement or, minimally, inserting a clause to peacefully resolve disputes during the term of the agreement, (7) no payment of salaries during work stoppages, (8) an end to perpetual duration clauses.[32] It was this memorandum which authorized the dispatch of a U.S. offi-

---

29. Nikkeiren, "Rōdō seisaku ni kan suru Yoshida shin naikaku e no yōbō iken sho," reprinted in Ōhara Shakai Mondai Kenkyū Jō, *Nihon rodo nenkan, 1951 nenban*, p. 825.

30. Rōdō Shō, *SRUS 1949*, p. 921.

31. The entire document is reprinted in ibid., pp. 923–928, with the comment: "This measure played an extremely important role in the preparatory process of revising the Trade Union Law and the Labor Relations Adjustment Law."

32. Rōdō Jikan, "Minshū teki rōdō kumiai oyobi minshū teki rōdō kankei no jōchō ni kan suru jikan tsūchō," as cited in Rōdō Shō, *SRUS, 1949*, pp. 927–928.

cer from the Military Civil Affairs section in Shizuoka to intervene in the Suzuki dispute.[33]

The December 22 circular was an administrative precursor to the actual reform of the Trade Union Law, which took place six month later. The complex process leading to revision has been minutely examined by Takemae Eiji.[34] A series of initiatives to reform the Trade Union Law, each reflecting the nuances of the respective sources, had surfaced during the previous two years.

The first impulse for revision had come from reformers such as State Department staffer Phillip Sullivan, who as early as 1946 had called for revision of the Trade Union Law (TUL) because it allowed for too much government interference and gave management too much leeway to interfere in union affairs. This first call for revision was, in the main, a call for further democratization, albeit based on the American model of labor regulation. The second impulse for revision came in the anticommunist plans of the Labor Division of May–June 1947.[35] This plan called for amendments in the TUL to provide for stricter internal union functioning through revision of union constitutional and bylaw provisions because, according to the Labor Division's post–general strike analysis, communists were able to control the unions from the top using bureaucratic manipulation. As Takemae has demonstrated, however, any plans to amend the TUL were postponed under Killen's tenure as chief of the Labor Division.[36] But MacArthur's decision to restrict public sector employees' union rights in July 1948, Killen's subsequent resignation, and the resurrection of the Yoshida government led to a major review of the TUL within both SCAP and the Ministry of Labor.

A first draft of proposed amendments was circulated within the Labor Division on October 1, and on October 27 Nikkeiren submitted its own recommendations for revision.[37] At the end of 1948 the Labor Division instructed the Japanese government to set up a commission to oversee the revision process and on February 14 a draft bill was made public. Until this point, labor had no input whatsoever into the revision process. Public hearings into the revisions took place that spring, but despite protests by labor groups of all political hues the revisions to the TUL passed the Diet in May. The revisions resulted in the prohibition of all perpetual duration clauses, weakened the protection of unions under the civil

33. In examining Nikkeiren's recommendations and the Labor Ministry's circular it becomes clear that both agencies were influenced by the U.S. model. The call for grievance committees, for example, seems to be based on the U.S. model of regulating shop floor disputes, but there was no call for the strict grievance procedures that would have been necessary to make grievance committees work.

34. Takemae Eiji, *Sengō rōdō kaikaku*.

35. W. F. Marquat to Chief of Staff, "Program for Counteracting Communist Activities in the Japanese Labor Movement," 27 June 1947, Labor Division Papers, box 8497.

36. Takemae Eiji, *Sengō rōdō kaikaku*, p. 255.

37. Nikkeiren's recommendations for revising the TUL are reprinted in ibid., pp. 408–412. Interestingly, Nikkeiren makes no mention of this document in its own official history.

codes, and forced unions to abide by stringent rules of secrecy in strike votes and internal elections. By this time, however, the management offensive was already in full swing.

The Meeting of Japanese and American Business Minds

Given the series of events in this fateful period, it seems reasonable to conclude that the management offensive was planned and carried out in the main by a resurgent Japanese business elite in coordination with the government and the Occupation forces. Control in this offensive appeared to reside with the banking community and Nikkeiren. As the Suzuki example demonstrated, the banks controlled the levers of finance; but they could not accomplish their objectives without the support of the Japanese government and SCAP.

This was why the "reverse course" in Occupation policy was so significant. Howard Schonberger has meticulously documented the process that led to the change in Occupation policy.[38] While the Occupation had its own conservative ideologues, such as intelligence chief Charles Willoughby, on the whole their views did not predominate in Occupation policy. The initial period reflected the proposals of democratic reformers. By early 1947, however, conservative policymakers and businessmen such as *Newsweek*'s foreign affairs editor Harvey Kern and Wall Street lawyer James Lee Kauffman assailed Occupation policy for being prolabor and antibusiness. They successfully organized a Japan lobby whose opinions began to make inroads among U.S. government officials such as Under Secretary of the Army William Draper and Defense Secretary James Forrestal, both of whom came from the Wall Street law firm Dillon, Read and Company.

One of the key moments in this process was the March 1948 meetings between Draper and then Prime Minister Ashida Hitoshi. Ashida, while still in a coalition government with the Socialist Party, railed against workers and unions and asserted that industrial recovery in Japan depended on "better control over labor, revision of the Occupation's liberal labor laws," and appeals to "labor asking greater moderation in its demands."[39] Accompanying Draper on this visit was an economic mission of American businessmen led by Percy Johnston, chairman of the Chemical Bank and Trust Company of New York and a close friend of MacArthur's (he had handled the general's investments). While Draper met with Ashida, the businessmen met with Japanese business leaders, including the purged Asano Ryōgyō and Tōshiba president and Keidanren chairman, Ishikawa Ichirō, who impressed upon the U.S. tycoons the need for a change in Oc-

38. Chapters 5, 6, and 7 in Schonberger's *Aftermath of War* carefully document the roles of Harry Kern, William Draper, and Joseph Dodge in the change in Occupation policy.
39. As cited in ibid., p. 186.

cupation policy. The Johnston report of April 1948, calling for a curtailment of a program to deconcentrate the *zaibatsu* (conglomerates), signaled the new meeting of minds between the business elites of Japan and the United States. This collusion was engineered by Draper, who had told Ashida that balancing the government budget was the key to dealing with labor and inflation. Prior to returning to the United States, Draper informed MacArthur that he would recommend that Joseph Dodge, the Detroit banker who had devised Germany's currency stabilization program, be sent to Japan to assure that an austerity program was implemented. Draper faced numerous obstacles in getting U.S. government approval for the antilabor austerity program (it was finally obtained in December 1948 and Dodge subsequently arrived in February 1949); but businessmen in Japan and the Yoshida government were already beginning to implement the new agenda even prior to the December 1948 directive from Washington.

This pan-Pacific meeting of business minds allowed Nikkeiren to play a key role in policy formation after its founding in April 1948. As the business community's major lobby group on labor issues, it was able to bring the government and SCAP together for crucial aspects of the offensive, in particular the assault on collective bargaining. Nikkeiren itself summarized the events in this period in the following way:

> On December 23, 1948, the government, through the Ministry of Labor, clarified that it would promote democratic labor-management relations and nurture democratic unions through administrative means. On December 23, 1948, it published a memorandum, "Concerning the promotion of democratic trade unions and democratic labour relations." As part of "leadership methods" it takes up the issue of revising union bylaws and collective agreements, and regarding collective agreements it puts forward eight new measures. Many of these measures were similar to the new direction Nikkeiren was advocating. This broad current would be tied to the application of the revised Trade Union Law beginning on June 10, 1949.[40]

Of course, the business elite was searching for new forms of regulation and often turned to U.S. forms for inspiration, as in the case of its demand for grievance committees. But at its heart, the offensive was aimed first and foremost at regaining managerial control in the workplace, and thus unions that had challenged that control were the main target in the attack. And precisely because the new forms of labor control—including vetoes over hiring and firing, equal representation on management councils, perpetual duration clauses, and so forth—differed from the U.S. form of regulation, the assault on these forms was endorsed even by those La-

---

40. Nikkeiren, *Nikkeiren sanjū nen shi*, pp. 211–212.

bor Division types who were not completely committed to support of SCAP's antilabor policies.[41] The end result was that the form of regulation appeared to conform to U.S. norms, but in fact, as employers gained increasing control, the substance of labor relations was developing in ways that would weaken labor's ability to counter managerial power.

The Effects on the Labor Movement

In the United States the great unionization wave led by the CIO was able to finally consolidate itself only during World War II, after union leaders had proven themselves willing to work with capital in accomplishing the war objectives of the government. In Japan, the labor movement never had that luxury. After a scant two or three years of relatively favorable conditions, the union movement faced an assault on a scale unequaled in the United States or Canada. Ranged against the new Japanese unions were the forces not only of capital but of the state, the latter under the control of both the conservative Japanese government and a belligerent United States determined to stamp out any resistance to its plans to integrate Japan into its Asian empire as a beachhead against communism. The labor movement in Japan lost the great battle of 1949.

Contracts: Revision and Revocation

If the Tōshiba contract struggle that broke out in February 1949 marked an initial managerial sortie into contract revocation, the revision of the trade union law in June heralded a wholesale onslaught against those collective agreements that enshrined many of labor's gains of the immediate postwar period. In the June 2 edition of *Nikkeiren Times*, a column titled "Automatic renewal no longer recognized—stage set for revising contracts" sounded a clarion call for a general offensive against labor: "However, once the revised law regulations are at last promulgated, the power derived from the law will be used extensively. So whether one likes it or not, we should consider that the time has come for a decisive battle to revise collective agreements."[42] According to the article, the law reform would permit employers to expand the number of occupations that could be excluded from the union, weaken the closed shop or union shop system, restrict their financial contributions to unions, eliminate union activities during work hours, and

41. For an example of the complexities involved in understanding individual roles in this period, see John Price, "Valery Burati and the Formation of Sōhyō during the U.S. Occupation of Japan," *Pacific Affairs* 64, no. 2 (summer 1991): 208–225.

42. *Nikkeiren Taimusu*, 2 June 1949, cited in Rōdō Shō, *SRUS 1949*, p. 833.

stop automatic renewal of contracts.[43] Nikkeiren's focus on collective agreement revision reflected a legalistic approach that corresponded with the general labor orientation under the Occupation. But there were many variations, and in some cases employers simply got rid of unions and collective agreements altogether.

Under the guidance of the government and the Labor Division, major industrial federations including the Japan Federation of Iron and Steel Employers, the Communications Industry Employers, the Federation of Private Railway Employers, and the Association of Cotton Spinning Employers drafted model collective agreements between February and April, 1949, to be used by their constituent members.[44] These models followed the revised Tōshiba contract that this employer had succeeded in forcing on the union during the dispute in this period.

These proposed collective agreements were the legal edge of the employers' offensive and led, for the most part, to a vitiation of workers' hard-won rights. Employers used varied means to accomplish this. At Miike, for example, Mitsui served notice that it would not renew the contract set to expire on April 30, 1949, because the Mitsui miners were opposed to the company's proposal to lay off miners. The company used the "no contract period" to implement its rationalization program.[45] As with the Suzuki and Toshiba agreements, the Miike contract had contained a "no layoff without consent" clause as well as a perpetual duration clause. Local negotiations were held at Miike from April 13-19, at which time company negotiators revealed their demands. According to the union they included elimination of the word "democratic" from the phrase "the purpose of this agreement is to aid in the democratic development of the company" in the introduction to the union's contract, elimination of the union shop clauses, company control over eligibility for union membership, reduction of the management council to a consultative body, and introduction of a complicated grievance procedure.[46]

Negotiations were put on hold in May and June and then were further complicated by the All-Japan union's demand for joint bargaining for the Kyushu and Hokkaido districts. The company refused this proposal for enterprise-wide bargaining, and regional negotiations restarted in July, 1949, with Mitsui's three Kyushu mine managers negotiating with Western Federation leaders. Negotiations ended in a deadlock, however, and Mitsui miners remained without a formal contract until December 1951. In the interim, labor-management relations were resolved on the basis of a series of memorandums of agreement. The 1951 contract

43. Rōdō Shō, *SRUS 1949*, p. 833.
44. For further information on these model contracts, see Ōhara Shakai Mondai Kenkyū Jō, *Nihon rōdō nenkan, 1951 nenban*, pp. 366–367.
45. Miike Kumiai, *Miike jū nen*, p. 167.
46. Ibid., p. 179.

Table 7. Contract coverage, 1948-1950

Year	Unions with a contract	Total unions	%	Union members covered	Total union members	%
1948	12,484	33,900	37	3,152,806	6,533,954	48
1949	14,099	34,688	41	3,744,763	6,655,483	56
1950	7,655	29,144	26	1,831,335	5,773,908	32

Source: Ōhara Shaken, *Nihon rōdō nenkan, 1950–1952 nenban* (Tokyo: Jiji Tsūshin Sha, 1950-1951 editions).
Note: Statistics for 1948-49 are from June; for 1950, from May.

incorporated these memorandums in what the union officially considered not a bad collective agreement for the time.[47]

If the final contract at Mitsui was, in the union's opinion, not bad, such was not the case for the majority of contracts signed after June 1949. According to the Labor Ministry's account of that period, revised contracts were signed at twenty-six major companies after the revised Trade Union Law was put into effect in June 1949.[48] According to the same report these contracts were longer than earlier contracts, having over one hundred clauses, and represented a substantial victory for management in each case.

Even more significant than these contracts, however, were those that were not renewed at all. This was what had happened at Suzuki. As Table 7 indicates, in the one-year period between June 1949 and May 1950, the number of unions with collective agreements fell from 14,099 to 7,655, and the number of union members covered by collective agreements fell by over one-half (3.77 million to 1.83 million).[49] This gave rise to the "no contract era" from 1949 to 1951. By May of 1951, 2.2 million of 4.1 million total union members (54 percent) were still without collective agreements.[50] Indeed, the Suzuki workers who returned to work in July 1950 returned under a memorandum of agreement but without a formal contract. For them the "no contract era" lasted until 1967. Only then was Suzuki willing to formally institutionalize the labor-management relationship.

Unions: Decline and Divisions

Workers did not lay down and roll over in the face of the employers' onslaught. As evidenced by the Suzuki strike, workers resisted the layoffs and the attempt to

47. Ibid., p. 738.
48. Rōdō Shō, *SRUS 1950,* p. 836.
49. Ōhara Shakai Mondai Kenkyū Jō, *Nihon rōdō nenkan, 1951 nenban,* p. 370.
50. Ōhara Shakai Mondai Kenkyū Jō, *Nihon rōdō nenkan, 1952 nenban* (Tokyo: Jiji Tsūshin Sha, 1954), p. 494.

Table 8.   Decline in unions and union membership, 1949–1951

	Unions	Union members	Change in members
June 1949	34,688	6,655,483	-21,944
June 1950	29,144	5,773,908	-881,575
June 1951	27,644	5,686,774	-87,134

Source: Ōhara Shaken, *Nihon rōdō nenkan, 1951 nenban* (Tokyo: Jiji Tsūshin Sha, 1951), p. 65.

purge their unions. Employers, however, had a host of tactics by which they could regain control over production and, for that matter, the country. First, they used layoffs as a means to purge unions of advocates of adversarial unionism, communist-led or not; second, they used anticommunism to fire union militants; third, where workers resisted the layoffs or witch-hunts, management sponsored or supported breakaway unions; and finally, in many cases, employers simply got rid of unions altogether. Table 8 illustrates the drastic reduction in both the number of unions and union membership that occurred from 1949 to 1951 period. More significant for the future of labor-management relations, however, were the splits within unions, both local and national, that occurred in this period. As early as the fall of 1947, democratization cells had been formed in many unions. For most of 1948 they were unsuccessful in gaining much influence within national unions, but as the 1949 employers' offensive took its toll, the democratization movement came to the fore. Although certainly not a political monolith, the democratization movement was united on the basis of anticommunism, and as the employers' offensive developed, unions began to split into rightist and leftist factions or were taken over by anticommunists. Major unions federations began to disaffiliate from the NCIU, and this led to its rapid decline as Japan's national union center by 1950.

The Suzuki strike in 1950 was one example of how a dual union emerged on the local level. Its birth was a result of a coercive process. The union clearly had a large degree of support at the beginning of the dispute, that is, in the period from November 1949 to April 1950. The formation of the second union in May represented internal cleavages within the union, but the victory of the second union was mainly the result of coercion. The arrest of union leaders, the intervention by the U.S. Army, the lockout and resulting monetary hardship, the threats of job loss if workers stuck with the first union, not to mention the general anti-left social tenor of the Occupation—all contributed to the defeat of the original union.

The Suzuki experience was not uncommon in Japan in this period. Fujita Wakao, one of Japan's most noted labor scholars, conducted a survey of the formation of dual unions between 1946 and 1952, from which he concluded that dual unions resulted from cleavages within a segmented workforce but that the origin of the contradictions was the attempt by management to control the production process.[51] And recall Japan's labor law permitted multiple union certifications in a single workplace.

The 1949 managerial offensive precipitated many splits but the 1947 Mindō movement had already signaled the political cleavage that, in these new circumstances, resulted in the rupture of the working class movement. As explained earlier, the Moriguchi union was affiliated with a regional organization, the Federation of Satellite Cities, which regrouped city hall employees in the greater Osaka area, as well as with a national organization, the All-Japan Prefectural and Municipal Union Federation (Jichirō). Splits within the regional and national federations began in August 1948 after MacArthur banned strikes and collective bargaining for government and crown corporation employees. On August 18 eleven members of the national executive announced the formation of the Renovation Society (Sasshin Dōshikai) in Tokyo newspapers. Their statement explained: "Unions, without a doubt, should serve the interests of all affiliated union members and not serve a specific person or political party. Using the union as the milieu for implementing their own political beliefs, a small number of leaders have brought this union to the brink of disaster with their endless destructive agitation and senseless theorizing, which they have persisted with while disregarding the realities around them. Their crimes should be strictly examined and they should be censured in the spirit of an eye for an eye."[52]

This conservative faction gained substantial support but was unable to overturn the Left's influence. In October, an attempt to censure the leftist-dominated struggle committee was defeated in the executive by a vote of 71 to 55. The conservative faction eventually split, forming a rival federation (Jichi Rōkyō) on November 28, 1949. Of 230,000 union members in 1949, the rival federation garnered 150,000 by 1953, leaving the original union with 50,000 members. Another 30,000 members withdrew from the original union but did not join the rival federation. On the regional level, the Federation of Satellite City Employees also split along similar lines. The Moriguchi union affiliated with the conservative factions on both the regional and national levels.[53]

Splits or takeovers by conservative union leaders were commonplace in this period, but enterprise unionism did not gain complete control. In the coal mining industry, the left-leaning coal union dissolved to join with the heterogeneous JCU in March 1949.[54] This testified to the weakness of the left wing, but amalgamation at least afforded the possibility of future united action.

---

51. Fujita Wakao, *Dai ni kumiai* [Dual Unions] (Tokyo: Nihon Hyōron Shinsha, 1955), p. 148.
52. Jichi Rōsō, *Jichi rōdō undō shi*, p. 127.
53. Moriguchi Kumiai, *Moriguchi shi shoku rō sanjū go nen shi*, p. 105.
54. For a full account see Nihon Tanrō, *Tanrō jū nen shi*, pp. 230–234.

Perhaps the most important example of union splits was in the railway union. The conservative anticommunist caucus in the union took advantage of the layoff of 90,000 railway workers in July 1949 (part of the government's austerity program) to take over the union. Among those laid off were seventeen members of the Central Struggle Committee. Usurping the exclusive right of the struggle committee to call special executive meetings, the president of the union, Katō Etsuo, a conservative Mindō leader and favorite of the Labor Division, called a special meeting of the union executive that excluded those who had been fired. This led to the formation of a conservative railway union executive. Although the railway union did not actually split, the left wing was purged through government layoffs and with the collaboration of the Mindō leaders.[55] At last, Mindō leaders had attained a leading role within the trade union movement. But it was a dubious triumph: management's offensive had robbed the union movement of the fruits of earlier victories.

The Ironies of Anticommunism

Anticommunism played a significant role in the 1949 assault on labor and led to the demise of the NCIU, the largest labor federation in the early postwar period. It also created the basis for the creation of a new, national labor federation in 1950. But as the assault proceeded, new divisions occurred. Factions within the noncommunist left, that is, the union supporters of the Japan Socialist Party, engaged in an all-out battle to replace communist leadership within the labor movement. As communist influence waned, the antilabor agenda of employers and the Occupation became clearer. The outbreak of the Korean War in June 1950 and escalating repression further polarized the situation. The Japan Socialist Party lurched to the left and the labor movement followed. By 1951, hopes for a moderate, pro-American national labor federation dissolved as independent unionism emerged from the ashes of anticommunism.

From the NCIU to Sōhyō

Prior to leading the coup within the railway workers' union, Katō Etsuo had been nominated by the Labor Division to represent Japanese labor at the 32d General Assembly of the ILO (International Labour Organisation) in the summer of 1949. Using this ILO meeting as a forum, U.S. labor leaders were preparing the terrain for the formation of a new international trade union federation. A few months earlier, in January 1949, the American CIO (Congress of Industrial

---

55. This account of the struggle in the rail union is taken from Rōdō Shō, *SRUS 1949*, p. 383.

Table 9. National union affiliations, 1948–1951

	1948	1949	1950	1951
NCIU	1,228,151	1,020,190	290,087	46,708
JFL	873,470	913,827	835,115	313,448
Unaffiliated national unions	3,087,400	3,403,086	3,194,404	912,764
Other	1,488,406	1,318,380	1,461,265	1,675,257
Sōhyō	—	—	2,764,672	2,921,228

Source: Ōhara Shaken, Nihon rōdō nenkan, 1953 nenban (Tokyo: Jiji Tsūshin Sha, 1952), p. 73. Note: Sōhyō was formed in July 1950. Other 1950 figures were for June so there is some overlap in affiliation figures.

Organizations) and the British TUC (Trade Union Congress) broke from the existing international federation, the WFTU (World Federation of Trade Unions) over the Marshall plan.[56]

Sponsoring Katō to attend the 32d ILO convention was a brilliant move, killing two birds with one stone. Domestically, it lent conservative union forces tremendous legitimacy, and on the international level Katō gave backing to the proposal for a new, U.S.-sponsored, international labor federation. Katō attended the backroom meetings to prepare for the new federation as well as the regular ILO sessions.[57] Out of the backroom dealings came the call for a new, anticommunist international labor federation (later named the International Confederation of Free Trade Unions, or ICFTU) to be created at a founding session in London in late November 1949.

The politics involved in the founding of a new world labor federation became closely intertwined with Japan's domestic labor scene and the eventual formation of Sōhyō in 1950. Katō attempted to use his Occupation-sponsored role internationally to unite the noncommunist Japanese union movement around the issue of affiliation with the ICFTU.

Parallel or even prior to these developments on the international scene, employers and breakaway unions had done everything in their power to weaken the largest union federation in Japan, the NCIU. Table 9 traces the decline of the NCIU and the rise of Sōhyō in its place in 1950. As at Suzuki, the employers' offensive was a main factor in the decline of the NCIU. But another important player was the democratization or Mindō movement. In the summer of 1949 the

56. For details of the split within the WFTU and the formation of the ICFTU, see John P. Windmuller, American Labor and the International Labor Movement, 1940 to 1953 (Ithaca: Cornell University Press, 1954), and Ronald Radosh, American Labor and United States Foreign Policy (New York: Random House, 1969).
57. Katō wrote an account of the June meetings in Atarashii jiyū sekai rōren [The new world labor federation] (Tokyo: Kokutetsu Rōdō Kumiai Bunka Kyōiku Bu, 1949), p. 77–80.

Mindō movement was gaining strength at the expense of the JCP, but it was becoming increasingly divided. While some noncommunist union leftists had resisted the employers antilabor offensive, many others had refused to follow the JCP's political orientation and had ended up splitting with them. Uchiyama Tashirō, a communist at the time who went on to become a Sōhyō official, recalled the debate that continues to this day about Mindō:

> Regardless of whether Ōta Kaoru [a former Sōhyō leader] now says that because the Mindō movement had an anti-communist component and so was off track, I think that there were two aspects to this. The Communist Party says that the Mindō movement was based on the Occupation's power, or used the power of employers, and thus was an anticommunist, antiunion formation, but I don't think this was always the case. Of course there was that aspect; the Occupation helped the Mindō movement, or helped the creation of Sōhyō. And employers thought it was good, and didn't obstruct it or gave it help. So there was that aspect. But if you look at it from the overall history of the labor movement, it shouldn't be completely condemned. It taught us that the union movement should not be controlled by a party and there were positive aspects to it.[58]

Perhaps the most important problem with a blanket condemnation of Mindō was that it masks the important cleavages among the noncommunist unionists. These divisions were most clearly articulated by factional lines within the JSP. A series of events—the involvement of Nishio Suehiro, a conservative JSP Diet member, in the Shōwa Denkō scandal in late 1948, the secession of one section of the JSP's left wing to form the Labor-Farmer Party in December, and the abysmal JSP election performance in January 1949—converged to galvanize the left wing of the party. At the JSP convention in April, left social-democrats made substantial policy and leadership gains. Although these divisions were partly based on personal power politics, substantive policy issues were also at stake, issues that would split the JSP completely in 1951.

The growing division within the JSP led to serious breaches within the noncommunist labor movement. For example, conservative union leaders such as Matsuoka Komakichi (JFL) and leaders of the railway Mindō group helped sponsor the creation of the Independent Youth League (Dokuritsu Seinen Dōmei) within the JSP in July 1949. Under the leadership of ex-communist Nabeyama Sadachika, this group hoped to counter the growing strength of left unionists such as Takano, Hosoya, and others.

In the wake of these divisions, it was perhaps not surprising, that the initiative for a new labor federation to replace the NCIU came from unions less involved in the factional infighting. Unity proposals first surfaced among the leaders of several nonaffiliated unions—among them the JCU (Tanrō), the Japan Seamen's Union

58. Uchiyama Tashirō, interview by author, 10 October 1988.

(Kaiin), and the private railways union (Shitetsu)—that had formed a discussion group, the Rōdō Kumiai Kenkyū Kai (Rōken), in July 1949.[59]

The Labor Division was also directly involved in the emerging plans for a new national union federation. The chief liaison officer between SCAP and the trade unions was Valery Burati, a former CIO official who began work with the Labor Division in late 1948. Burati was informed and supportive of emerging plans for a new, national labor federation that would include what he termed "progressive" elements in the JFL. In a report prepared for the Labor Relations Branch in August 1949, Burati alerted the Labor Division:

> The most significant development, however, is still in the formative stage. Under the leadership of Mutō, those progressive, anti-Communist elements represented in Sanbetsu, Sōdōmei and the large independent group of unions are now in the process of organizing a committee which will guide the formation of a new federation of industrial organizations. Only unions which are committed to democratic principles and which declare themselves specifically in opposition to the World Federation of Trade Unions will be admitted.[60]

Through SCAP efforts, this trend towards noncommunist unity first coalesced around affiliation to the ICFTU. On September 2, the U.S. Army and the State and Labor Departments wired SCAP to recommend that a Japanese delegation be allowed to attend the founding convention in London. This prompted a review of SCAP policy, since overseas labor delegations had been forbidden, although they could send labor representatives as observers to ILO meetings. Burati made the initial policy review, noting the emerging trend towards an anticommunist union federation within Japan: "This new federation, if present plans are successful, will be established by January 1950 and will include the great bulk of the Japanese labor movement independent of both the extreme left and extreme right. Unions and their leaders will be judged by their declared alliance with either the new Free World Trade Union Organization or the old World Federation of Trade Unions."[61] Burati recommended that SCAP permit a Japanese delegation to attend the London conference in order to further align Japanese labor with the international anticommunist program.

While the review proceeded, Katō Etsuo helped establish the Committee to Promote Affiliation with the ICFTU in early September. After SCAP gave the go-

59. Zenrō, *Zenrō jū nen shi*, p. 43.

60. Valery Burati, "Report of Burati for Voorhees Meeting," 19 August 1949, Labor Division Papers, box 8481, p. 1.

61. C. W. Hepler (drafted by Burati), memo for record, "Attendance of Japanese Delegation at London Conference to Organize New Free World Trade Union Organization," 6 September 1949, Labor Division Papers, box 8477, p. 2.

ahead to send a delegation (funded by SCAP and escorted by Robert Amis, the new chief of the Labor Divison), unions in the committee nominated five delegates to go to London. Matsuoka Komakichi, the conservative leader of the JFL was among the five nominated, but Burati, acting through the Labor Division, vetoed his nomination because he considered Matsuoka too pro-company. Matsuoka wrote to AFL president William Green prior to the London Conference to complain about Burati and Amis's action.[62] A JFL delegation visited Burati on December 2 to inquire why the Labor Division had scuttled Matsuoka's participation in the Japanese contingent to go to London. According to the transcript of this meeting, Burati tried to play down the affair, but when pushed he cited Matsuoka's backing of the Independent Youth League at the JFL'S convention as evidence that Matsuoka represented the old guard. "However, I must say as I remember, the convention, to use one example, opposed the Youth League and as I remember it, Mr. Matsuoka was in favor of the Youth league. Therefore, it would seem there is some difference between the new policy and the old and that Mr. Matsuoka is not representative of the new policy."[63] In fact, Burati had received numerous reports about the activities of the Independent Youth League and its association with rabid anticommunist figures such as former communist leader Nabeyama Sadachika. According to Labor Division advisor Hara Meijirō,

> With regards the character of the Independent Youth League, repeated appraisals have been made in our past reports that clarified personality and political motives of the league leader Nabeyama as well as the league's rightist political design. Ex-communist Nabeyama is a close associate of Nishio and Matsuoka, the noted old-timers and political bosses within the Socialist right-wingers. He develops a most positive attack on the Communists, and is in close relationship to Nikkeiren (Japan Operators Association).[64]

Thus even SCAP attempts to bring anticommunist unions together through affiliation with the ICFTU were subject to factionalism. Although the movement for affiliation with the ICFTU and the drive for a new national federation moved along parallel tracks, they remained distinct because of domestic factional struggles. Thus the formal proposal to begin a new federation was first tabled in October within Rōken, the nonaffiliated unions' discussion group.[65] It was decided then that the new federation could not limit itself only to unions that had affiliated to

62. Matsuoka Komakichi to William Green, personal letter dated 23 November 1949, AFL Office of the President, Green Manuscripts, convention file, box 14.

63. "Report of Conference with JFL Delegation in Mr. Burati's Office," 2 December 1949, Labor Division Papers, box 8478, p. 3.

64. Meijiro Hara to chief, Labor Division, "Anti-Dokusei Stand by New CIU within General Council," 27 February 1950, Labor Division Papers, box 8481.

65. Zenrō, Zenrō jū nen shi, pp. 48–49.

the ICFTU.[66] The private railways union (Shitetsu) would be the sponsoring organization. Private sector affiliates held formal discussions on November 1 and a broad unity conference was slated for November 14. The JFL held its fourth annual convention in early November, at which time it decided to join in the unity conference.

Thirty representatives from nineteen unions (including the JFL and the New CIU) met on November 14, and preparations for the new federation were officially launched. On November 21 the group was officially designated the Preparatory Committee for Unity of Japan Trade Unions (Zenkoku Rōdō Kumiai Tōitsu Junbikai), and subcommittees were established to prepare a constitution, bylaws, a budget, and an action plan. At this point, however, differences cropped up. For example, affiliation with the ICFTU was not made compulsory in the constitution or bylaws as had been intended.[67] Instead, promotion of the international body was relegated to a part of the action plan. As well, changes were made to the draft constitution which, according to some later critics of Sōhyō, left it open to class struggle politics.[68] Delegates to the preparatory conference to found Sōhyō held on March 11, 1950, debated the basic plan, constitution, and action agenda for the new organization. Since these documents already embraced important compromises and were only drafts to be adopted at the founding convention set for July, however, major conflicts were avoided—with one exception: the New CIU group (led by Hosoya) announced that it would not participate in Sōhyō because it was SCAP-controlled. The New CIU group later reversed this view and participated in the founding meetings only to withdraw later.

Thus after a year of factional infighting, Sōhyō finally came into being. Although it had been originally cast as a conservative, anticommunist labor federation, the reemergence of center-left forces (neither communist nor conservative but aligned with the left wing of the JSP) made Sōhyō a volatile force. As events unfolded, it would become a thorn in the side of the United States.

Anticommunism and the Korean War

The last two years of the Occupation witnessed a virulent spasm of anticommunist witchhunts as well as Japan's integration into the U.S. Pacific sphere of influence, a fate sealed with the outbreak of the Korean War in June 1950. Continued coercion, however, only exacerbated tensions within the noncommunist labor movement.

66. In the Sōhyō account of its own formation, at the Nov. 1 meeting called to discuss the Rōken proposal it was specifically stated that a new federation could not limit itself to unions affiliated to the ICFTU. See Sōhyō, Sōhyō jū nen shi [Sōhyō: Ten Years] (Tokyo: Rōdō Junpō Sha, 1963), pp. 167–173.

67. Zenrō, Zenrō jū nen shi, pp. 48–49.

68. Ibid., p. 49.

U.S.-Soviet tensions escalated dramatically in late 1949 and early 1950. On January 6, the Cominform issued a critique of the JCP for pursuing a strategy of peaceful revolution. This was accepted and the party prepared for further confrontation with the Occupation. It was not long in coming. During the spring of 1950, SCAP and the Japanese government increased their surveillance and scrutiny of the JCP. On May 3, MacArthur publicly postulated that the Party might lose its constitutional rights. Using a scuffle between demonstrators and GIs on May 30 as a pretext, SCAP invoked powers originally intended to be used against war criminals and initiated a purge of the JCP central committee and the *Red Flag* editorial board on June 6 and 7 respectively. The outbreak of the Korean war on June 25 led to an escalation of repression. On July 24, SCAP ordered the firing of suspected communists in the media followed by a general purge of suspected communists in important industries on August 10. On August 30, SCAP ordered the dissolution of the All-Japan Federation of Workers (Zenrōren), a loosely organized national labor coalition that included leftist and rightist factions of the labor movement. The escalating repression was too much for Valery Burati, who commented, "I think that the Generals acted under the impulse of their anti-labor bias. They want to smack labor every chance they get."[69]

Nikkeiren went quickly to work to take advantage of the situation. On October 2 it published a "Guide for Expelling the Red Elements," in which it gave detailed instruction on how to carry out a purge. Maeda Hajime recalled, "At work at Nikkeiren, every day was a busy one because of the red purge."[70] Documents from SCAP files indicate that G-2, SCAP's intelligence unit, was feeding employers information on who precisely was to be fired. Corporations filed standard reports with SCAP on how the witchhunt was being carried out at their respective work sites. Nikkeiren acted as a clearing house for information and advised employers how best to implement the firings.

Mitsui, for its part, tabled detailed criteria for its witch-hunt to the Mitsui Miners' Federation on October 12. The union opposed Mitsui's proposals because the criteria were too broad and open to abuse. After three days of negotiations, however, the union agreed to the layoff of "communists who obstruct the normal operations of the plant, or others who do the same."[71] As a result 197 miners were fired and 8 took early retirement. In the private sector as a whole, 10,972 workers in 537 companies were fixed, and in the public sector 1,777 workers in 14 ministries or corporations.[72] These statistics do not include a major purge of the pub-

---

69. Burati letter to Philip Sullivan, 6 September 1950, Burati Papers, box 1, folder 12, p. 6.
70. Maeda Hajime, "Tōshō ichidai," p. 358.
71. Mike Kumiai, *Miike jū nen*, p. 209.
72. Rōdō Shō, *SRUS 1950*, p. 1078.

lic sector that took place in 1949, and the private sector statistics understate the extent of the firings since they reflect only official reports.

In hindsight, the Miike union recognized problems in its position. Its official history shows how the company used the witch-hunt to rid itself of militant workers. The situation at the time was complex, however. As early as July 1950, Mitsui had indicated that it intended to rationalize its operations through major layoffs. Many workers no doubt hoped that the layoff of suspected communists would forestall their own walk out the door. As well, union leaders were not unhappy to see the end of activists critical of their stewardship. But another factor must be understood if one wants to avoid rationalizations and facile condemnations: the culture of the period. Japan was in a de facto state of war with North Korea, the conservative elite was consolidating its control under the protection of the Occupation, and communists became convenient scapegoats.

Layoffs hit Miike the following month in the form of "voluntary retirement." But it was hardly voluntary, and those that the company wanted out were soon made aware they would be retired. Between September and December, 4,612 workers were laid off, many of whom were workers with disabilities.[73]

Suzuki management did not participate in the fall witch-hunt because the defeat of the Suzuki union in the 1950 strike and the subsequent firing of over two hundred employees had eliminated the union activists and communists. The witch-hunt hit the public sector in November; over 1,100 employees at prefectural and national offices were fired under section 78 of the public service law. There were fewer firings at the local level and existing documentation indicates that Moriguchi and other cities escaped this particular phase of the purge.[74]

After helping to implement the anticommunist witch-hunt in the fall of 1950, Nikkeiren attempted to sustain its coercive strategy through its Workshop Defence Movement. Ostensibly to counteract communist reinfiltration into factories, the movement was mainly used for anticommunist indoctrination and for strengthening the right-wing trend within the union movements.[75] Nikkeiren directly employed Mitamura Shirō and other former communists in this movement and published their views regularly in the *Nikkeiren Taimusu*, the organization's weekly paper.

---

73. Miike Kumiai, *Miike jū nen*, p. 217.

74. According to Jichirō, *Jichi rōdō undō shi*, the 1949 layoffs eliminated many left-wingers on the local level. See pp. 148–149.

75. For details of this movement see Rōdō Shō, *SRUS, 1951*, pp. 716–724. If anything this account underestimates the importance of the movement. In its own history of the 1960 Miike strike, Mitsui Mining Company points out that the Labor Ministry's history (cited above) erred when it stated the workshop defense movement came to an end in April 1951; the movement continued at Mitsui until late 1952 at least. See Mitsui, *Shiryō: Miike sōgi*, p. 113.

Independent Labor

The Korean war and the related antilabor repression exacerbated tensions among the noncommunist factions of the labor movement. Disputes escalated both within the JSP and the newly founded labor federation, Sōhyō.

The JSP had elaborated its international relations platform as early as December 1949, when it called for a comprehensive peace treaty (including China and the Soviet Union) and neutrality for Japan. Serious debate on international issues climaxed at the party's January 1951 congress after the outbreak of the Korean War, however. Delegates handed a resounding blow to the right wing when they defeated, by a vote of 342 to 81, a motion proposing a partial peace treaty (excluding China and the Soviet Union) and integration into the Western camp.[76] The defeated motion had been introduced by Nishio Suehiro, one of the leaders of the right wing of the JSP. Convention delegates then proceeded to adopt the left wing's four peace principles: adoption of an overall peace treaty, neutrality, opposition to foreign bases, and no rearmament.

The left-right split over international relations precipitated an end to noncommunist unity over a host of other issues. At Sōhyō's March 1951 convention, delegates adopted the left's four peace principles and defeated a resolution to affiliate en bloc to the ICFTU. Takano Minoru, a part of the left faction within the JFL, was elected general secretary. Shortly thereafter the JFL, in which Takano had played a leading role, voted to dissolve and join Sōhyō.

The establishment of Sōhyō as the national labor federation, its adoption of an independent foreign policy, and the election of Takano all heralded the reemergence of an independent labor movement. The politics of anticommunism had, ironically, allowed the center-left forces within the labor movement to take the initiative. The costs, however, were high.

Although an independent movement did emerge, labor had suffered a tremendous setback. Not only did tens of thousands of union activists lose their jobs, many local unions were split and new enterprise unions were established. Contracts were revised or done away with, the labor code was gutted, and the major national union federation, the NCIU, was obliterated in the process. The scale of the setback should not be underestimated. What would industrial relations in the United States look like today if, for example, major sections of the Wagner Act had not been upheld by the Supreme Court, if there had been no collaborative labor-management effort in World War II, and if big business had attacked the new industrial unions and succeeded in destroying the CIO?

---

76. This account of the JSP debate on peace is based on Koyama and Shimizu, *Nihon shakai tō shi*. For an English-language account see J. A. A. Stockwin, *The Japanese Socialist Party and Neutralism* (London: Melbourne University Press, 1968).

Given the scale of the assault in Japan, it seems ironic that American scholars such as Kenney and Florida would conclude that "the undermining of the radical forces made it easier to integrate many worker gains into the evolving framework of capitalist accumulation."[77] The evidence from this study does not support such a contention. To a large extent, the gains of the earlier period were extinguished or seriously jeopardized. Big business in Japan, by reestablishing an alliance with a U.S. business community irked by the scope of Occupation reform, had managed to escape from under the cloud of war responsibility. The alliance pursued its own antilabor agenda, and the Occupation's "reverse course" and the Dodge line represented the culmination of interaction between the Japanese and U.S. business elites. The fact was, big business in both Japan and the United States quickly put World War II behind them in order to deal with labor on both sides of the Pacific.

77. Kenney and Florida, *Beyond Mass Production*, p. 30.

4 Forms and Substance of Labor-Management Relations (1951–1955)

Through the antilabor offensive of 1949–50 many employers regained substantial control within the workplace. Many militant unions were broken, communist and noncommunist activists were fired, collective agreements were revoked or revised to assure managerial authority, and the changes in the public service and trade union laws regulating collective bargaining were dramatically amended in favor of management.

Paradoxically, though, the employers' offensive and Japan's imminent independence obliged the labor movement to reassess the divided profile it had assumed during the management offensive. On both the national and local levels, several important unions overcame their divisions, began to reassert their independence, and challenged employers' agendas for labor-management relations.

A defined system of labor-management relations did not exist as yet. Workers and managers alike inherited a hodgepodge of institutions that had evolved under the Occupation but now bore the scars of the managerial offensive. Much of the dynamic of this period revolves around the attempt to redefine these institutions, with labor and management jockeying to gain maximum advantage. Where management had the upper hand, specific institutions such as the compensation system developed in a certain direction. Where independent unionism gained a strong base, institutions took on a different flavor.

It was not only the relation of forces that determined the outcome, however. Labour-management relations reflected different patterns of production according to the type of product, the nature of the work, and the legacy of cultural institutions including paternalism, patriarchy, and so forth. Coal mining differed from automobile production, textiles differed from the public sector. Specific production regimes added their own dynamics to the conflict over evolving institutions.

For different reasons we find that neither Nikkeiren, for example, nor Sōhyō were able to shape the workplace regime exactly as they hoped. Instead what emerged was a diverse set of labor relations within which some common features began to appear. But even then, one had to be careful in making assumptions about apparent similarities. For example, at both Miike and Suzuki, labor-management councils became institutional features, but the actual role of the councils differed because of the different strengths and orientation of the unions.

Employers, for their part, did not pursue a central plan. Initially, Nikkeiren advocated largely American-style labor relations institutions, including formal grievance mechanisms and a wage structure based on job classifications. It gradually relented when it realized that labor relations institutions forged at the point of production were equally workable.

One constant, however, was the employers' unending devotion to managerial control within the workplace. As in the Occupation period, Nikkeiren persisted in its efforts to break any union that posed a threat to managerial prerogatives on the shop floor. The bitter confrontation at Nissan in 1953 and the 1954 Muroran dispute in the steel industry were important instances of Nikkeiren machinations on this level. On the other hand, the challenge posed by women strikers in the Ōmi textile dispute led some Nikkeiren leaders to realize that the overtly antidemocratic, paternalistic regime that had dominated in the textile industry was no longer viable. These leaders put pressure on textile employers to give in to the strikers at Ōmi.

Independent unionism bounced back at the national level with Sōhyō's turn to the left in 1951–52. On the local level, some unions continued to defend the gains of the workers' control period (1946–1947) while others attempted to carve out some space within the emerging regime. In both cases, these unions accepted an adversarial perspective of labor relations and promoted militancy on both economic and political issues. There were also important divisions within the various groups that supported independent unionism, however, and this diversity was reflected in Sōhyō's change of leadership in 1954–55. These factors also weighed heavily in the history of labor-management relations.

The independent orientation adopted by some unions in the early 1950s had a direct impact on labor relations, particularly the forms of wage bargaining that consolidated in the last part of the decade. The new forms of horizontal bargaining that emerged did not, however, challenge managerial rights in the workplace, as had the adversarial trend in the immediate postwar period. Independent unionism continued to erode as enterprise unionism gained strength, often through the establishment of breakaway unions such as at the Nissan plant in 1953. The resurrection of adversarial unionism in the 1950s provoked a conservative backlash within the national labor movement. Differences in attitudes towards wages, strikes, and political action culminated in an organizational schism in 1954 that persisted, albeit in altered forms, until 1989 when Sōhyō itself finally dissolved. The conservative union federation that emerged from the 1954 schism—the Japan Trade Union Congress (Zenrō Kaigi)—constantly undermined the independent union trend, which won it the grudging approval of even Nikkeiren.

Nikkeiren and the Managerial Arena

The 1949–50 employers' offensive had allowed managers in many large corporations to regain control over production and reestablish the primacy of managerial rights. This altered temper of the times was acknowledged in 1950 by Yamamoto Asamichi, a Mitsui Mining director and head of Nikkeiren's Labor Management Committee:

> The fact that management of labor in our enterprises has experienced a long period of confusion over the past three or four years was to some extent unavoidable. The origins of this confusion was the social and economic instability immediately after war's end, the sudden rise of the labor movement, and the successive passage of a series of labor laws. These circumstances have gradually evolved towards normalization and stabilization in the last year, however, through the policies of financial and economic disinflation, rectification of the far left trend in the unions, and revision of the trade union laws. At the same time we have clarified the issue of managerial rights, which at the level of the enterprise had been relinquished in the storm of confusion stirred up by the labor movement.[1]

In the early 1950s, conservatives within Nikkeiren continued to advance the theory of exclusive managerial rights and to intervene aggressively in labor-management relations to enforce this premise.[2] While upholding managerial prerogatives, however, some managers like Yamamoto attempted to find an appropriate institutional formula that would permit the evolution of a stable union-management relationship.

These two trends were not fundamentally contradictory but reflected subtle differences in approach. Conservative managers and organizations such as Nikkeiren were mainly concerned with purging the unions of adversarial elements (initially identified mainly as communists) and establishing firm managerial

---

1. Yamamoto Asamichi, "Shin rōmu kanri ni kan suru kenkai," in Nikkeiren Sōritsu Jū Shū Nen Kinen Jigyō Iinkai, *Jū nen no ayumi* [Ten years: Nikkeiren] (1950; Tokyo: Nihon Keieisha Dantai Renmei, 1958), p. 145. First published by Nikkeiren on 9 May 1950.

2. This evaluation of Nikkeiren's role is confirmed by other scholars. See Ōtake Hideo, "The Zaikai under the Occupation," in R. Ward and Y. Sakamoto, eds., *Democratizing Japan: The Allied Occupation* (Honolulu: University of Hawaii Press, 1987).

authority within the workplace. Others, such as Yamamoto and members of the Keizai Dōyūkai, on the other hand, directed their energies towards institutionalizing a collaborative labor-management relationship with those unions that accepted the narrow role assigned them by management, that is, as a consultative mechanism.

The difference in approach may well have reflected that contradictory essence of capitalism—the need to at once secure and obscure the appropriation of surplus value. Roughly speaking, the authoritarian trend represented the "secure" side, which in the concrete, historical, national circumstances of postwar Japan was interpreted as meaning the exercise of nearly absolute managerial control over the shop floor. Forms of job control, which grew in the United States under totally different circumstances, were not to be tolerated. Coercion was this trend's forte. The downside was that the heavy hand tended to expose and sharpen class differences and in the long term could undermine employers' control.

Modern managers such as Yamamoto represented the complementary yet contradictory component, the obscurity within the equation. Although they accepted and indeed actively supported the coercive managerial response to the workers' challenge to management rights, they saw this as a short-term expedient. They concerned themselves more with the long term and searched for structural means to develop a collaborative relationship with unions, but—this was important—they accepted the conservative premise that adversarial unionism on the shop floor was beyond the pale.

Employers Debate Labor Relations Institutions

As part of the 1949 managerial offensive, Nikkeiren had advocated the abolition of managerial councils (*keiei kyōgikai*) because, in its opinion, they had been part and parcel of the erosion of managerial rights that had occurred in 1946–47. The chair of Nikkeiren's Subcommittee on Institutions for Regulating Labor-Management Relations, Yamamoto Asamichi, explained Nikkeiren's rationale at the time: "The management councils strayed from their original purposes and became a place where [labor] meddled and unduly interfered with managerial rights."[3] The councils had also become the site for negotiations and grievance resolution and had generally created confusion, said Yamamoto; they therefore had to reevaluated. In the meantime, Nikkeiren recommended the establishment of three institutions—collective bargaining, grievance resolution through a grievance committee, and a production committee to deal with production issues—as a

3. Yamamoto Asamichi, "Rōdō kankei chōsei ni kan suru shishin," in Nikkeiren, *Jū nen no ayumi*, p. 125. First published by Nikkeiren on 9 June 1949.

three-track institutional formula for conducting labor relations.[4] This position was also advocated by the Labor Ministry in a directive issued on July 6, 1949.[5]

By the following year, however, Nikkeiren had reevaluated its position regarding the management councils. In its May 1950 statement, "An opinion regarding the new labor management," Nikkeiren advocated the inclusion of an institutional form of cooperation within collective agreements. It was to be neither a forum for collective bargaining nor a grievance committee but an organ that would permit "a mutual exchange of ideas and proposals" with a view to "creating a peaceful and co-operative workplace".[6] Nikkeiren cautioned that such an institution must not be allowed to disturb discipline on the shop floor and that its decisions had to be implemented through normal supervisory structures. Nikkeiren thus envisaged transforming the postwar management committees, through which labor during its ascendancy had achieved an equal voice with management over traditional managerial rights, into consultative organs with no power or authority.

A second element in Nikkeiren's perspective on institutional reform was its proposal for wage determination. This issue surfaced repeatedly in management and governmental literature during the early 1950s as employers and officials attempted to counter labor's claim for a social wage, that is, a wage that reflected the right to a decent livelihood. The most important employer initiative regarding the wage system was the proposal for a classification system advocated by Yamamoto in 1950.[7] According to this proposal, modern labor management could no longer be based simply on past practice and tradition; mass production demanded new scientifically determined standards. The most important of these was the introduction of a classification system whereby standards for personnel would be inserted into the work content. By classifying the jobs performed by individuals, employers could achieve high efficiency and, theoretically at least, pay higher wages.[8] This was classic Fordist theory combined with the American system of industrial relations.

The Labor Ministry took up the substance of Yamamoto's proposals and conducted an educational campaign about a scientific wage system in 1952. A 1953 Nikkeiren report complained bitterly, however, that unions and many companies were ignoring the new proposals, that large companies were agreeing to excessive wage increases, and that a wage gap was emerging between workers in small and medium-size industries.[9] Furthermore, moaned the employers' association, wages

4. Yamamoto Asamichi, "Rōdō kankei," pp. 126–127.

5. Rōdō Shō, SRUS 1949, p. 892.

6. Yamamoto Asamichi, "Shin rōmu," p. 148.

7. Ibid., p. 149.

8. Ibid.

9. Nikkeiren, "Kihon teki rōdō taisaku ni kan suru iken," in Nikkeiren, Jū nen no ayumi, pp. 199–207. First published on 4 June 1953.

were not being inscribed as part of collective agreements and instead negotiations were constantly taking place over wages, summer bonuses, winter bonuses, and special allowances, and this was causing an increase in disputes. Some unions, stated the report, had even gone so far as to recommend that wages not be included as part of the collective agreements so that unions could renegotiate wages as often as necessary!

Clearly, Nikkeiren had only a limited amount of control over the process, and labor-management institutions evolved mainly from the workplace. Two distinct features that emerged in this period were labor-management councils and the classification system of wage determination. The former would prove to be an enduring institution, while the latter would not.

Labor-Management Councils (Rōshi Kyōgikai)

The trend toward the institutionalization of labor-management councils, as opposed to grievance or production committees as originally advocated by Nikkeiren, can be documented both statistically and through our case studies. Grievance committees were established, but they often remained essentially paper institutions with little function. Although more than half of a representative sample of contracts reported the existence of grievance committees (569 out of 1026), of these nearly 75 percent had never met! (Another 20 percent met fewer than ten times.)[10] The reason for this is, in one sense, obvious: What gave life to such committees in the United States or Canada was the formal grievance procedure, often prescribed by law, which required stages of labor-management discussions up to binding arbitration to resolve such disputes. This mechanism had never been inscribed within the regulatory system in Japan.

Management councils dated from the workers' control period, during which labor had equal representation with management. At that time management councils, theoretically at least, could deal with anything and everything including investment decisions and grievances. But with the exception of the production control movement, unions had seldom developed the potential of these councils. The power unions brought to the councils in this early period rested mainly in the support they had among workers and the collective agreement clauses that gave them a veto over hiring and firing.

In one sense, then, the downgrading of the management councils simply reflected the new relation of forces. In other words, because employers insisted on their unilateral right to run the enterprise, the potential for labor-management councils to become a serious exercise in co-determination was lost. It was precisely

---

10. Rōdō Dijin Kanbō Rōdō Tōkei Chōsa Bu, *Rōdō kumiai kihon chōsa hōkoku sho (1953)* [Report of the basic survey of labor unions, 1953] (Tokyo: Rōdō Daijin Kanbō, 1954), p. 35.

because of this that employers subsequently embraced the councils as a consultative forum and they became widespread. According to a 1953 Labor Ministry survey of 1026 collective agreements, 835 contained clauses calling for a labor-management council and of these 655 met regularly.[11] Depending on the union-management relationship, there was some variation in the character of the consultative forums.

A labor-management council operated at Suzuki in the early 1950s despite the fact there was no formal collective agreement in place. For the most part it operated as a mechanism in which management transmitted its positions to the union on wages and other issues. At Miike, a labor-management council was inscribed as part of the collective agreement, but it was not a transmission belt for management. Instead it became the meeting ground for negotiations over anything and everything. The distinction between the two modes of operation indicates that these councils took on the characteristics that the parties imparted to them.

From a comparative perspective it is significant that neither labor nor management rushed to adopt the two-track system of grievance resolution (based on a collective agreement) and intermittent collective bargaining for a detailed collective agreement that had become the norm in Canada and the United States. Different patterns of labor relations arose. In many instances collective bargaining (usually translated as *dantai kōshō*, although this term literally translates as group bargaining) began to take on two quite distinct meanings. In one, a single collective bargaining session was formally convoked to sign an agreement as the concluding step after a process of consultation; in the other, collective bargaining was invoked because the process of consultation had broken down and serious confrontation seemed inevitable. In either case collective bargaining took on an air of formality, even though the actual circumstances in discussions were dramatically different. Consultations, on the other hand, were construed as belonging to the informal phase of discussion, so these often took place in the labor-management committee. It is only when inserted within the framework of a general collaborative labor-management system that these committees took on a specific dynamic.

Wage Fixing, Classifications, and Seniority

The ban on government workers' strikes and collective bargaining made the public sector an arena where the government largely controlled the wage-determining mechanism. Base wages were fixed by government decree and released in an annual report by the National Personnel Authority (Jinji In). Table 10 shows the results of this process from 1948 to 1955. From 1946 to 1948 govern-

11. Ibid., p. 36.

Table 10. National Personnel Authority reports and government implementation, 1948–1955

Year	NPA		Government	
	Wage recommendation	Bonus recommendation	Wage decree (¥)	Bonus decree
1948	6,307	—	6,307	—
1949	7,877	—	6,307	—
1950	8,058	—	7,981	—
1951	11,263	1 month's pay	10,062	0.8 month's pay
1952	13,515	1 month's pay plus diligence allowance of 0.5 month's pay	12,820	As proposed
1953	15,480	Increase bonus by 0.5 month's pay	15,483	Bonus and diligence allowance both up by 0.25 month's pay
1954	No recommendations		No changes	
1955	—	0.25 month's increase in bonus and diligence allowances	—	Bonus up by 0.25 month's pay

Source: Moriguchi Kumiai, *Moriguchi shi shoku rō sanjū go nen shi* (Moriguchi: Moriguchi Kumiai, 1981), p. 138.

ment workers had attempted to win cost-of-living bonuses, another source of the contemporary bonus system, but this was discontinued between 1948 and 1950.

As mentioned above, Nikkeiren promoted a wage system based on job classifications in the early 1950s. At Miike and Suzuki job classifications did exist to some degree and had some bearing on wage rates. But it was in the public sector that job classifications became the main factor in wage determination, if only for a short period. As described in Chapter 3, a classification-based wage system was introduced for government employees in May 1948. It was this system that some Nikkeiren leaders first envisaged as the basis for the future wage system in Japan.

For a short period, it appeared that this might indeed be the case, particularly in the public sector. In November 1950 there were 151 job classifications for government workers. By January 1952 this number had increased to 449.[12] At this time, however, the National Personnel Authority began to move away from job classification as a basis for wage determination and introduced regular performance evaluations (*kimmu hyōtei*) which in 1953 became integrated with promotion up the incremental wage scale.[13] Performance evaluation, based on

12. Jinji In, *Jinji gyōsei nijū nen no ayumi*, pp. 86–87.
13. Details on performance evaluations used for national government employees are contained in ibid., pp. 292–302. The relationship of performance evaluations to the wage system is described in some detail on p. 228. In 1953, the performance evaluations were first used as a means of winning accelerated promotion up the wage scale. Their role is explained in the next chapter.

American models, had begun as early as 1948 within the national civil service and became institutionalized in 1950 and 1951 as part of the classification system but they only came to play a key role in the wage system in the 1953–58 period. Japan's historians of the civil service describe the performance evaluation developed in the early 1950s as "the motive force behind the promotion of performance evaluations for private enterprises and for regional public enterprises."[14] In this, Japan's employers seem to agree. Here is how Nikkeiren summed up the wage-determining mechanism in this period:

> Japanese-style, *nenkō* labor control, based on the two pillars of lifetime employment and *nenkō* wages (if one adds enterprise unions it includes three elements), was reestablished during the 1949–54 period, after coming out of the chaotic immediate postwar period. Accompanying the influx of American methods of business administration, the classification system was promoted for personnel in 1949–50. The use of the classification-based wage system began in the public sector and existed even in the private, but it did not necessarily take root. In the early 1950s a general compensation package (a base wage salary) came to predominate. At the same time, moreover, job performance evaluations were introduced for national civil servants in 1952, and in the private sector a system of personnel evaluations [*jinji kōka*] began. By mid-decade, a system of regular incremental increases based on assessments was added, creating the framework of yearly personnel administration. This system of annual personnel administration consolidated in the 1955–59 period with progress in the reinvestigation of personnel evaluations.[15]

The importance of these descriptions cannot be overemphasized. Here we have employers describing, more or less accurately in my opinion, an evolving wage mechanism in which yearly assessments of personnel begin to play a substantial role in wage increases. This was in dramatic contrast to the unionized sector in the United States or Canada, where industrial unions in particular had successfully reduced management discretion in assigning wage increases and made even incremental increases contingent on length of service or seniority. In other words, where an incremental wage grid existed in Canada or the United States, an employee usually moved up automatically after a fixed period unless the move involved reclassification and passing a skills test. In that sense, the wage system in Canada and the United States was based both on occupation/classification and seniority. Nevertheless, it is the Japanese system that proponents of the three pillars theory have described as the "seniority-based wage system." Here we confront a classic example of cross-cultural miscommunication. The term "seniority-based wage system" is the standard translation of the Japanese term *nenkō joretsu chinkin*

14. Ibid., p. 295.
15. Nikkeiren, *Nikkeiren sanjū nen shi*, p. 430.

seidō. Nenkō has traditionally been translated as "seniority," but there is another Japanese term for seniority, *sennin* or *sennin ken*, which corresponds much more closely to the notion of seniority as it is used in industrial relations in Canada or the United States.

In other words, the term *nenkō joretsu seido* is misleading. Given management's own description, in which employers exercise discretion in deciding wage increases through their prerogative of employee evaluation, from a comparative perspective it is wrong to translate the term as "seniority-based wage system." Because management exercises discretion in the assignment of wage increases, the Japanese system is best described as an incentive or performance-based wage system. To be sure, workers do advance up a wage grid, but the rate of advancement is determined by management for the most part. Future research should be directed at workers' attitudes towards the incentive system and the proportion of the wage increase that is dependent on supervisors' evaluations. Dore's earlier study of the Hitachi plant is extremely valuable in this light. Dore found that less than one-third of employees supported the idea of such merit ratings.[16]

Managerial Workplace Control

Although managers debated the merits and demerits of wage systems and labor management councils, they agreed on one point: the sanctity of managerial rights. At certain factories, however, employer control remained tentative despite the 1949–50 offensive and the subsequent workshop defence movement.

One company where managerial control remained shaky was Nissan, the automotive manufacturer.[17] Like other major manufacturers, Nissan had managed to push through rationalization plans in 1949–50, but the cost was a radicalization of the union. Under the leadership of Masuda Tetsuo, the Nissan chapter of the automobile workers union (Zen Nihon Jidōsha Sangyō Rōdō Kumiai, or Zenji) developed a sophisticated shop committee system from 1950 on. One committee member was elected for approximately every ten union members. These committees had, by almost every account, become extremely powerful and acted as a democratic counterweight to managerial authority.[18] They were able to convene union meetings during work hours and could, at a moment's notice, mobilize the

16. Ronald Dore, *British Factory–Japanese Factory*, p. 192.
17. This sketch of Nissan labor relations is based on accounts in Kamii Yoshihiko, *Rōdō kumiai no shokuba kisei* [The influence of the enterprise union at the shop floor level] (Tokyo: Tokyo Daigaku Shuppan Kai, 1994); Nikkeiren, *Nikkeiren sanjū nen shi*; Sōhyō, *Sōhyō jū nen shi*; Maeda Hajime, "Nikkeiren ni ikita nijū nen"; and Michael Cusumano, *The Japanese Automobile Industry* (Cambridge: Harvard University Press, 1985).
18. Nikkeiren, *Nikkeiren sanjū nen shi*, p. 280.

membership to exert pressure on the company. The strength of these committees, the union's affiliation with Sōhyō in October 1952, and its opposition to Nissan's Korean War contracts attracted media attention as well as the attention of Nikkeiren.

The 1953 battle at Nissan began ostensibly as a wage dispute but quickly escalated into a pitched battle over the union's existence. In early June, Nissan dismissed the union's demands for wage hikes and two weeks later countered with demands for concessions, particularly concerning union meetings during work hours and the exclusion of section chiefs from the union. On August 5, Nissan locked out its employees and constructed elaborate barricades to preempt any attempts at production control. This led to clashes at the company gates, and Nissan conspired with city officials to have a number of union leaders, including Masuda, arrested for instigating violence. On August 21, Nissan's president, Kawamata Katsuji, fired Masuda and six other union officials for violating company regulations. Maeda Hajime recalled the incident: "We pondered the idea of firing these guys [Masuda Tetsuo and other union leaders] for a number of days. An advocate of quick and resolute decisions on firings myself, I urged Kawamata to make the move. In these cases if you fire the leaders you either irritate and create confusion or they simply disappear, floating up from the company and dispersing like grass without roots. I believed it would be the latter."[19] Despite Maeda's predictions, Nissan workers did not become confused, nor did Masuda disappear. Three days after the firings, union members voted 5,230 to 650 to continue the struggle and a nonconfidence motion in the executive also failed a few days later. At this point Nissan conspired to create a second union, just as had happened in the 1950 Suzuki struggle. Using funds provided by the Industrial Bank, Nissan offered employees who joined the new union 60 percent of their regular pay.[20] Dissident employees who, as early as 1949 had studied with the right-wing Institute for World Democracy (sponsored by Nabeyama and other ultrarightists), constituted the core of the breakaway union. As Kamii Yoshihiko meticulously documents, the breakaway union developed a base within the clerical and inspection departments and among lead hands and foremen, groups that had been unhappy to some extent with the policies of the original Nissan union.[21]

With their strike pay diminishing, workers gradually went over to the new union. The first union, facing bankruptcy and dwindling support, was forced to concede defeat in late September. With strong Nikkeiren support, Nissan had won.

19. Maeda Hajime, "Nikkeiren ni ikita nijū nen," p. 358.
20. Cusumano, *Japanese Automobile Industry*, p. 157.
21. Kamii Yoshihiko, *Rōdō kumiai no shokuba kisei*, pp. 96–101.

Maeda Hajime summed up the lessons from the Nissan struggle:

"First, reckless out-of-line demands such as a minimum wage of ¥10,000 for an eighteen-year-old or severance pay of ten million yen for thirty years service will never gain public support. Second, when the character of a dispute [changes and] is no longer an economic one about wages but is about demands based on wage principles motivated largely by political factors—demands such as implementing a minimum wage system, equal wages for workers doing similar job regardless of the company, or equal pay for women—then resolving the dispute becomes extremely difficult. Third, management will never accept so-called production control tactics whereby unions, taking advantage of the principle that union activities may be carried out during work hours, repeatedly carry out actions such as unspecified union meetings during work hours and still demand to be paid. Fourth, destructive and violent actions carried out as dispute tactics invite organizational splits and will only end in the self-destruction of the organization itself."[22]

Considerable evidence has been amassed to indicate that Nikkeiren and the hawkish faction of the Nissan executives conspired from about 1950 on to break the Nissan union.[23] The economic recession that accompanied the armistice in Korea afforded an appropriate opportunity for Nissan to make its move. Given this evidence and given Nikkeiren's role at Tōhō, at Tōshiba, and its coordinating role during the 1950 witch-hunt, such an assertion seems more than justifiable.

Labor's defeat at Nissan reverberated throughout the union movement. Not only had the most powerful union in the automobile industry been broken, the national federation of automobile workers went bankrupt. From this point on, the center of gravity of union organization in the automobile industry shifted to the enterprise. In certain companies, such as Nissan, the breakaway unions became the only organization for workers. At others, such as Toyota, there was no breakaway union but the union was taken over by a conservative leadership.

The Nissan scenario was repeated in 1954 at the Muroran works of the Japan Steel Corporation (Nikkō Muroran).[24] In this case the company attempted to break the Muroran local because it actively opposed layoffs. The union attitude ran counter to two Nikkeiren dictates—that employment levels were an exclusive managerial issue and that unions had no right to agitate on the shop floor against company policy. The company failed to force through the layoffs, however, even after locking out its employees. A breakaway union was then formed and affiliated

22. As quoted in Nikkeiren, *Nikkeiren sanjū nen shi,* p. 287.
23. See Cusumano, *Japanese Automobile Industry,* chap. 3. Cusumano conducted extensive interviews with Nissan executives as well as Maeda Hajime of Nikkeiren.
24. This account of the Muroron dispute is taken from Nikkeiren, *Nikkeiren sanjū nen shi;* Sōhyō, *Sōhyō jū nen shi;* and Zenrō, *Zenrō jū nen shi.*

with the newly established Japan Trade Union Congress (JTUC). With support from the Seamen's Union and JTUC, the new union worked with the company to break the strike and restart operations.

As these previous examples illustrate, the union-busting role played by Nikkeiren represented an attempt to set limits on the labor relations equation. Unions that advocated independent unionism and attempted to institutionalize their presence on the shop floor invited retaliation on the part of Nikkeiren. It would appear that one should not underestimate the role of coercion as an agenda-setting constraint in the evolution of labor relations in Japan, particularly in the 1950s.

A second phenomenon of significance was the use of breakaway unions to undermine labor. These organizational divisions occurred during disputes with regular frequency, as the experiences at Suzuki and at Nissan illustrated. The regulatory regime in Japan allowed for the formation of dual unions even during disputes, a practice that was not unheard of in the United States but which was more tightly regulated under the exclusive bargaining agent and unfair labor practices sections of the labor codes in the United States and Canada.

Resurgent Unionism

In the first half of the 1950s employers continued to break unions that challenged their control on the shop floor. But in certain sectors this was not possible because independent unions resurfaced to challenge management's agenda for the workplace. This section attempts to trace the rise and impact of independent unionism as it evolved in specific workplaces in the early 1950s.

Miike

The 1950s was a turbulent period for coalminers. The JCU had moved to the left during the 1949–50 upheavals, with over half of the national executive including its president affiliating with the left wing of the JSP. At Miike as well, large numbers of miners joined the JSP at this time. The Marxist, class struggle bent of the JSP in this period had an impact on labor relations. Not only did the coalminers' union play an important role in making Sōhyō a more militant force, but at the local level some miners also began to take union matters into their own hands.

At Miike the local union had rejected a 1949 Mitsui-wide agreement, which was supposed to involve 1266 layoffs at the Miike shafts. Through local negotiations the layoffs were reduced to 336. While the central and local unions had gone along with the 1949–50 purge of communists, by 1951 many unions actively opposed governmental measures, including further retrograde revisions of the TUL and the passage of the Subversive Activity Prevention Law.

Rank and file disenchantment grew after a series of disappointing wage agreements in the winter of 1950 and early in 1951, when Miike miners struck for eleven days. Miike miners were more than open to the class struggle orientation that the local executive tabled in June 1951. As they announced in their local union's action plan, "as organized labor, we will comply with the resolutions of higher organizations such as Tanrō and Sōhyō. But as a mining local, in order to achieve a deepening and enlarging of democracy and for the well-being of our members, we must resolutely undertake, in particular, educational activities to heighten class consciousness as well as struggles to improve our well-being."[25] On the educational level the plan called for regular, weekly labor lectures or research seminars for members of the executive; monthly lectures or research seminars for committee members and rank-and-file union members; organization of a womens' association affiliated with the union; purchase of a news broadcasting vehicle and film equipment; and uniform activities on the part of the education, editing, and political departments in order to reinforce education.[26] Regarding improving members' livelihood, the union called for wage increases, conclusion of a collective agreement, and an end to supervisors' harassment, among other things.

Sōhyō, at its second regular convention in March 1951, had called on unions to push for progressive collective agreements. At its convention that May, the JCU also took up this call and recommended its affiliates sign collective agreements that allowed for participation in management and a say in personnel matters. The Mitsui Miners' Federation decided to split off negotiations for a new collective agreement from wage negotiations and in the early summer conducted an educational campaign among the rank-and-file over collective agreement demands. A strike vote was taken in early August with 87 percent voting in favor of strike action if the company failed to conclude a collective agreement.[27] After a series of strike threats, the two parties signed the first collective agreement in three years. A key feature of the agreement was the establishment of a labor-management council to resolve grievances that arose during the contract period.

The Coal Operators Association had refused to engage in any form of industrywide bargaining since 1948, but the JCU resolved to establish sectoral bargaining for wage increases in the fall of 1951. To that end, the locals of eight major coal companies notified the Coal Operators Association that they had relinquished

---

25. Miike Kumiai, *Miike jū nen*, p. 251.
26. Ibid.
27. Ibid., p. 258.

their bargaining rights to the JCU and that all further discussions should be held with the central union. The coal companies refused this request, but after the union threatened strike action a deal was struck by which the Coal Operators Association agreed to negotiate a wage agreement with the JCU on the condition that formal collective bargaining would take place at the local level. The coal companies conceded that two members from the master bargaining committee would be allowed to sit in on the local negotiations. After protracted negotiations and mediation efforts and six days of strike action, the major companies signed an agreement giving underground miners a daily base rate of ¥550 and aboveground miners ¥350.[28]

During this period, the coalminers became involved in the Sōhyō-led struggle against rollbacks in the trade union laws. As early as December 1950 the government had begun to look into further revisions of the trade union laws. In the light of the San Francisco Peace Treaty and the imminent end of the Occupation, the government announced in May 1951 that it had appointed an advisory group to look into revisions of all laws brought in during the Occupation. Sōhyō established the Committee to Fight Revision of the Trade Union Laws (Rōtō) in August. On the 29th of that month, the government announced its intention to introduce bills in parliament to protect public security, restrict demonstrations, and ban general strikes. These bills were delayed by hearings and shelved with the end of the winter 1951 session of the Diet.

The issue reemerged, however, in the spring of 1952 when the government introduced a bill to curb "subversive activities." Sōhyō again took up the cause, and on April 18 over one million workers took various job actions to protest the bill. Miike miners along with coalminers in other regions took part in this job action. Mutō, the head of the JCU, had scuttled an earlier job action on April 12, and this came back to haunt his faction at the JCU convention later in the month when delegates pushed through a vote of nonconfidence in the executive. Mutō was forced to resign and a new executive was elected.

The government eventually pushed through amended versions of some of these bills despite continued job action by Sōhyō affiliates. Nevertheless, the 1952 political action campaign had established Sōhyō as a potent force and precipitated the demise of the Mutō faction within the JCU.

The militant trend was further reinforced at the local level with the establishment in early 1952 of regional union branches within the company housing compounds surrounding the Miike mines. Through these regional branches workers and their families articulated demands related to housing and community life. These demands were then taken up within the labor-management councils at each mine.

28. Ibid., pp. 261, 264.

The Miike local faced two other challenges in this period—the company's "workshop defence movement" and Mitsui opposition to the creation of a prounion womens' association. Mitsui's workshop defence movement was ostensibly aimed at stopping communist infiltration of the work site and eliminating those who might obstruct production, stabilizing labor relations, establishing control at the workplace, fostering a spirit of appreciation and respect for the mines and encouraging production through employee education and training, and protecting valuable or dangerous equipment.[29] To this end the company had already held a number of week-long retreats where a number of hand-picked employees absorbed a series of anticommunist diatribes from former communists such as Nabeyama Sadachicka and Sanō Manabu.[30] The Miike local registered its objection to this type of indoctrination, as did other Mitsui locals, and their opposition led to the demise of the workshop defense movement some months later.

The Miike local also pushed ahead at this time with its plan to foster a prounion womens' association in the company residences. The company attempted to block this initiative by refusing to allow women organizers to use its facilities. It was in this context that the local union attempted to organize its residential branches as a counter to company control.

At its fifth regular convention in May 1952, the JCU decided to push for master bargaining over summer bonuses. According to the Miike local, this was the first time that a union had systematized its bonus demand. According to the JCU resolution, the summer bonus constituted "a form of delayed wage payment, a distribution of profits, and a traditional custom" that the union had every right to institutionalize.[31]

That unions, including those with adversarial orientations, were demanding bonuses is significant. In this period, Nikkeiren and its affiliates were pushing hard to keep the base wage low. Unions attempted to overcome management intransigence by using custom as a wedge. In the past, bonuses had been mainly reserved for supervisory personnel, but unions argued that if they were to be treated fairly they had as much right to a bonus as anyone else. Thus instead of having protracted disputes over wages agreements, unions argued for constant renegotiation for bonuses. It was exactly this type of practice that drove some managers in Nikkeiren crazy. As we shall see, employers tended to acquiesce to union demands because bonuses did not raise the base wage, were one-time affairs, and could theoretically be revoked in the future. Unions, however, insisted that bonuses, once granted, be negotiated for each summer and winter, and as the bonus system became institutionalized employers lost the ability to revoke payments easily.

29. Mitsui, *Shiryō: Miike sōgi*, p. 114.
30. Ibid., p. 118.
31. Miike Kumiai, *Miike jū nen*, p. 291.

The Sixty-Three-Day Strike

In 1952, Sōhyō recommended its "market basket" formula for calculating wage demands. According to this formula, wage demands would reflect the real cost of living as determined by the actual costs workers encountered in their everyday lives. This formula did not, however, address the issue of the emerging wage structure other than to stress that affiliates should obtain much of the wage demand in automatic increases. The market basket formula was taken up by the JCU in its wage negotiations that began in the summer. Power utility workers (in the Densan union) also took up this struggle, which would climax in the biggest strikes (measured in lost days) in postwar Japan. Initially, the JCU demanded a base rate of ¥1060 for underground and 560 for aboveground miners. The Operators Association agreed to central negotiations in this round of wage bargaining: "It is believed that this attitude on the part of the Operators Association was due to its fear that, with separate negotiations, the weaker companies might fall prey to the JCU's pressure tactics."[32]

This is an important point because it illustrates how the relation of forces played an important part in determining forms of collective bargaining. Whipsawing—playing off one company or one union against the others—is a way in which one side can take advantage of divisions on the other. As in the coal industry case cited above, the demand for or acquiescence to centralized bargaining can reflect weakness not strength.

As events transpired, negotiations went nowhere. On October 26 the JCU commenced rotating strikes, which escalated into a full-scale walkout by the end of the month. Tens of thousands of electrical utilities' employees joined 282,000 miners on the picket lines in the two largest sustained walkouts in Japan's labor history. Management refused to budge, however, and the disputes escalated. Power blackouts occurred, and the JCU discussed the possibility of pulling out safety personnel from the mines. The government tabled back to work legislation in mid-December, and the strike was broken. Over 10 million man-days were lost in the course of the strikes. The wage issues were resolved through binding arbitration (through the LRB) with the final settlement giving coalminers a 7 percent wage increase and a signing bonus of ¥5,000.[33]

The sixty-three-day coal strike ended in defeat for the coalminers as well as for the electrical utility workers. This led to a rupture within the electrical utility workers union, Densan, and over the course of the next two years a breakaway union replaced the original union.[34] But at Miike the union had actually become stronger through the struggle. In the course of the strike, the union's regional

---

32. Miike Kumiai, *Miike nijū nen* [Twenty years at Miike] (Ōmuta: Miike Rōsō, 1969), p. 85.
33. Miike Kumiai, *Miike jū nen*, p. 323.
34. For details on the rupture see Kawanishi Hirosuke, *Kigyō betsu kumiai no riron*, pp. 193–202.

Table 11. Organizational strength of the Miike local, 1953

	Miyaura	Yotsu-yama	Mikawa	Office	Port	Machine shop
			Workshop councils			
Units	21	38	46	48	20	6
Members	3,415	2,789	5,619	2,414	1,320	1,527
Executive	344	304	598	315	170	219
			Regional councils			
Units	14	17	22	5	7	3
Members	1,880	2,255	3,662	1,120	653	462
Executive	208	119	370	76	60	39
			Womens' associations			
Units	13	13	20	6	3	3
Members	1,234	1,386	2,709	510	294	303
Executive	188	140	367	74	42	39

Source: Miike Kumiai, *Miike jū nen shi* (Ōmuta: Miike Tanko Rōdō Kumiai, 1956), p. 378.
Note: Rank-and-file members elected representatives to the workshop and regional council executives at an approximate ratio of 1 delegate for every 15 members.

committees had come to life and played a central role in organizing sustenance for the miners and their families. Womens' associations, composed mainly of the wives of miners, had overcome company interference in their attempts to organize and would go on to play a significant role at Miike. Table 11 illustrates the depth of organization at Miike.

This strong organizational base played a key role in the next major struggle Mitsui miners faced in the fall of 1953. With the armistice in Korea signed that year, Japan went into an economic recession, and the coal industry was hit with major layoffs.[35] On August 7 Mitsui management presented union representatives with its plan for coping with the recession. It called for 5,738 workers to be laid off at its six mines in Japan, including over 2,000 at Miike. The company called for collective bargaining to determine the criteria for layoffs. Refusing this, the union got the company to agree to enter into negotiations over its management plan and personnel issues.

The Mitsui Miners Federation had anticipated layoffs and had been preparing to take on the company. On August 7, miners at Miike began sit-down strikes at each of the work sites. On the 9th, 25,000 miners and their families participated in demonstrations at thirty-one sites in the residential areas. On the 13th, union

35. By the end of 1953, 48,417 miners out of a total of 688,249 had been laid off. Miike Kumiai, *Miike jū nen*, p. 368.

members began a mass sit-down at the Ōmuta rail station, an action which continued until August 19. Meanwhile, negotiations stalled, and on August 25 Mitsui tabled a new proposal. The new proposal, which the company threatened to implement unilaterally, reduced the number of layoffs from 5,738 to 4,563 and called for voluntary retirees (early retirement) to come forward between August 27 and 29, after which it would terminate those who refused to go along.

Of the 4,563 miners Mitsui hoped to discharge, only 22 percent came forward to take the early retirement package. To meet the challenge of the unilateral layoff notices that were to be delivered beginning on August 30, the Miike local issued a boycott notice prohibiting oral or written communication with Mitsui's 175 management personnel. The Miike local organized a huge demonstration on August 31 in which 30,000 workers and their families gathered at an Ōmuta park before walking to the city hall and then to the company headquarters. In the mines themselves, the workers organized slowdowns, sit-downs, and rotating strike actions, which dramatically reduced coal production throughout September.

The union attempted to win over public opinion, and miners from Miike went to Mitsui's Tokyo headquarters. In one dramatic instance miners occupied the boardroom, and one worker heaved himself onto a table. "Give me my leg back," he told the startled onlookers. Kurihara Fukumatsu, a twenty-one-year veteran of the mines, had lost his leg in a work-related accident in 1950. He had been one of a number of injured workers that the company was trying to lay off.[36]

Similar layoffs had happened at other mines. The Mitsui Miners Federation found itself battling Mitsui on its own, although the JCU gave it nominal support. Despite this drawback, the miners at the six Mitsui mines battled on into October. At this time a new challenge surfaced, this time from within the union. The company had publicly stated that a movement for a breakaway union was growing, and in September the local Minrōren group (a conservative union caucus) published a leaflet with the headline "Who will put an end to the anti-layoff fight at Mitsui Mining?" It accused the union executive of misusing funds, prolonging a useless struggle, and trying to delay elections.[37] In fact the union executive had wanted to delay elections, but it had failed to garner the requisite support. It sought a delay because it feared that candidates opposing the struggle would make substantial gains and that union dissension would undermine the struggle. Results of the October 22 election indicated firm support for the local and central union executives, however.[38]

36. Ibid., p. 420.

37. Ibid., p. 430.

38. Fifteen of 18 national executive members were reelected, as were 24 of 31 members on the local level. See ibid., p. 432.

This proved to be a decisive blow for the company, and finally, on October 27, Mitsui conceded defeat; 1,185 miners who had refused to accept the layoffs were reinstated in their positions. At Miike 408 miners accepted early retirement while 311 were reinstated. Kōno Kazuo, a union leader who hired on at Miike immediately after the war, considered the 1953 struggle the turning point for the Miike local:

> "Up until then the union gradually began to take on the real appearance of a union. Little by little, with experience in strikes, things were progressing. Strikes lasted from about twenty-four to forty-eight hours—well, with the exception of the sixty-three-day strike, that is. More than that, we didn't have confidence. When an order for a seventy-two-hour strike came down, we didn't have confidence. And even when we launched the 113-day strike [in 1953], we weren't too confident either. It was the year just after I became secretary-general in 1952."[39]

The Mitsui miners went on to win further battles in 1954 and 1955. In 1954 the Miike local forced Mitsui to abolish the prefect system (*sewagata seidō*) in the residential areas. This ended Mitsui control of what effectively had been a company town. Local actions also improved mining safety standards the same year.

In 1955, the government announced new measures to rationalize the coal industry, hoping to eliminate unproductive mines, increase productivity through mechanization, and lower the price of coal. The plan called for the elimination of thousands of jobs in the coal industry. The JCU and the Mitsui Miners Federation opposed this rationalization program with a political action plan. Once the related bills passed the Diet, however, the fight switched to the local level, where the JCU hoped to win long-term employment guarantees as a countermeasure to the rationalization program. This new fight called for a change in tactics. In April 1954 the Mitsui miners' union had called for the right to participation in management. In 1955 the call was not for participation in management but rather for the socialization of management, that is, making management socially accountable. This took the form of a protracted 143-day struggle to alter the management plan that Mitsui had presented in a series of meetings in the last two weeks of June. Mitsui's ten-year rationalization plan called for an increase in productivity from 13 to 18 tonnes per worker/month, a halt to all hiring except for graduates from the mining school, a reduction in personnel of 9,500 through attrition, and transfer of personnel from Bibai to Ashibetsu and from Yamano to Tagawa in line with changes in mine outputs.[40]

On August 6, the Mitsui Miners Federation executive met to determine its response to the rationalization program. It called for a struggle to maintain full em-

39. Kōno Kazuo, interview by author, 21 March 1990.
40. Miike Kumiai, *Miike jū nen*, p. 539.

ployment, to oblige the company to specify the details and responsibility for each part of its plan, and then to wage a struggle at the base to modify the plan. As the miners' bulletin put it: "This is an issue that will not be resolved simply through negotiations by the struggle committee; we can only be victorious in struggle when this becomes a mass struggle through . . . the elaboration of concrete demands at the worksite and in the mines."[41]

This strategy was implemented by forcing the company to explain itself to workers—to explain why, for example, it was contracting out work in the machine shop when port workers could have taken up the slack. After the company explained its position, port workers formulated and submitted demands to their foremen and obliged Mitsui to provide them with work. Similar demands were formulated at every level and then centralized into a bargaining platform.

Bargaining over specific demands took place at the work site, at each mine, and at the central level. Negotiations continued into October without resolution. On October 29, the union called for rotating strikes to begin on October 31. Mitsui at this point decided to accept the union's demands, and on November 5 a memorandum of agreement was signed. It included the following:

1. The union's demand for the full employment of miners would be the prime factor in the ten-year plan.
2. The union would be consulted about the implementation of the plan, and any internal transfers would be based on improving and not worsening working conditions.
3. New recruits other than from the mining school could be hired, and workers would be replaced as they left the mines.
4. Children of widows of deceased miners or the poor would be given priority in hiring upon union recommendation.
5. Children of those close to retiring or the infirm could replace their parents.[42]

Thus as early as 1955 the Miike union was able to force the employer to put job guarantees in writing with clear stipulations regarding hiring protocols. Nikkeiren, as we shall see, was virulently opposed to this type of agreement, because it held that employment levels were for management to determine exclusively.

The Moriguchi City Union

There is general agreement among labor historians in Japan that the Miike local and the JCU generally represented a key component of the adversarial current

41. Ibid., p. 547.
42. Ibid., pp. 558–559.

within the labor movement. But was it simply an exception that proved the general rule, namely that Japan's workers agreed to compliancy, docility, and loyalty in exchange for employee beneficence? Substantial evidence indicates independent unionism was as spontaneous as it was political.

At Moriguchi City Hall, the union remained relatively innocuous and under the control of white-collar supervisors who, according to the union's own history, "did little once the annual convention was over."[43] In the spring of 1951, however, younger workers took the initiative to form youth and women's bureaus. Initially these bureaus mainly engaged in organizing social activities, but when the Satellite City Federation decided to organize the workers at the Hirakata City Hall, members of the bureaus actively helped in the organization effort. In 1954 they contested the incumbent slate in union elections and called for an end to company unionism. Confronted with this message in posters and leaflets distributed in the city hall, the incumbent leadership withdrew from the elections. At the annual convention in June 1954, the new leadership initiated changes in the union bylaws and drafted an action program that emphasized solidarity and a persistent fight against reactionary powers in order to improve working conditions.

On the national level as well, the issues that had split the All-Japan Prefectural and Municipal Union Federation receded after independence, and the two national organizations moved towards unity once again in 1952–53. A formal unity convention was held in snow-bound Matsue in January 1954. One of the conditions for unity that both organizations had accepted was affiliation with Sōhyō. This was approved at the January convention, and Sōhyō accepted the 230,000-member federation as an affiliate in February.

The Moriguchi union was not yet a strong proponent of independent unionism, but its affiliation to Sōhyō indicated that the union members were open to change. When Miike miners confronted management at Mitsui in 1960, Moriguchi unionists were at their side.

The Women of Ōmi

The year 1954 constituted a watershed in spontaneous union struggles. Among the most famous of the struggles in this period was the strike at the Ōmi Silk mills. Employing 13,000, Ōmi Silk was one of the major textile enterprises in postwar Japan. The plant was unionized but the union was basically a company association. On May 25, 1954, twenty employees formed a new union and affiliated with the Federation of Textile Workers (Zensen Dōmei). New union locals sprang up in the other Ōmi plants, and on June 2 the new union submitted a list

43. Moriguchi Kumiai, *Moriguchi shi shokurō sanjū go nen shi*, p. 122.

of twenty-two demands to the company.[44] The workers, most of whom lived in company housing, demanded an end to invasion of privacy, freedom to marry, freedom of movement to and from dormitories, and similar rights. This strike, one that deserves our attention, represented a rebellion against the patriarchal factory regime of the prewar and wartime days. Restrictions on the the rights of employees, especially women, continued even into the 1950s and, in the context of the postwar liberalizing reforms, represented to some degree an anachronism.

The workers struck on June 4 after the company refused their demands. The company attempted to use its control over dormitories to exert pressure on the women. They also scabbed the operation and violence occurred on the picket lines. The union persisted and finally won union recognition after a 107-day strike. It won a first contract that fall.

By taking militant action, the Ōmi women were the architects of their own victory. Nikkeiren was actively involved in supporting the Ōmi management; but when the women challenged the patriarchal order, the struggle was seen as a fight for human rights (jinken sōgi), and some Nikkeiren leaders recognized that they were backing a loser. They ordered Maeda Hajime to instruct Ōmi management to settle, but the owner resisted this intervention for some time.

The strike at Ōmi illustrates how workers in certain sectors spontaneously gravitated towards adversarial strategies. Employees perceived their work situations as being worse than elsewhere and saw union organization and confrontation as a means to improve them. This process repeated itself in different industrial sectors throughout the decade.

Needless to say, managers were not pleased by this turn of events. Just when they thought they had things under control, disputes in new sectors occurred. As Maeda Hajime put it: "Around 1955 labor battles had changed quite a bit. In places where you wouldn't think struggles would occur, such as in banks, investment houses, hospitals, and schools, struggles began to break out."[45] More often than not, women played an important role.

These struggles included certification and first contract battles at investment dealers in Osaka, Tokyo, Nagoya, Kobe, Kyoto, Hiroshima, Fukuoka, and Niigata; strikes for wage increases in regional banks; and the fight against 17,000 layoffs at U.S. military installations.

Without further research it is difficult to discern how much impact these struggles had on the evolving labor relations. But it does appear that the success workers and their unions had in the Miike and Ōmi struggles may have been related to the strong bias in these two sectors towards the paternalistic regimes of the prewar

44. The twenty-two demands are reproduced in Kawanishi Hirosuke, Sengo nihon no sōgi to ningen [People and Struggles in Postwar Japan] (Tokyo: Nihon Hyōron Sha, 1986), p. 278.

45. Maeda Hajime, "Nikkeiren ni ikita nijū nen," p. 363.

period. Such regimes, with their overt control of workers through company residences and the like, were incongruous in the new, liberal-democratic society of postwar Japan. Even the conservative union at Ōmi was inclined to take up independent action when confronted with starkly transparent employer control. This may also explain why at both Miike and Ōmi managers were seriously divided about the future course of labor relations. It may well be that Ronald Dore's contention that Japan went through a social-democratic revolution after the war is simply a misreading of this very real transition from a paternalistic to a more open regime. This is not to say, however, that all struggles that took place in this period were simply the result of a transition from a paternalistic regime. Many of them were rooted in economic circumstances as much as anything else.

In any event, spontaneous struggles did give sustenance to Sōhyō's militant orientation. This orientation came under attack, however, from within the union movement itself.

Sōhyō: Splits and Shuntō

The resuscitation of independent, militant unionism between 1951 and 1955 led to further splits within the labor movement. As mentioned previously, the democratization movement had already fractured into left and right, with the left wing promoting political unionism and an independent foreign policy for Japan. The rise of the left wing to the leadership of Sōhyō in 1951 created ongoing tensions. Differences centered on several issues including international policy, strikes and wage policy, and political campaigns.

Sōhyō maintained the independent foreign policy position that it had tentatively adopted at its second convention in July 1951. It opposed a peace treaty that excluded China and the Soviet Union, it opposed rearmament, and it refused en bloc affiliation with the ICFTU. This prompted the ICFTU executive, meeting at New York in December 1952, to openly criticize Sōhyō for taking the path of the old NCIU.[46] This critique provided the right wing of the union movement with further ammunition, and they continued to press their case that affiliation to the ICFTU was the sine qua non of an authentic noncommunist union. Moreover, Sōhyō's decision to send representatives to attend May Day celebrations in Beijing in 1953 and to enter into discussions with the Chinese union movement further enraged conservative unionists.

The Sōhyō leadership and conservative unions such as the textile workers differed also on their outlook toward wage policy. Whereas Sōhyō emphasized aggressive wage demands and linked these to the political fight against rearmament,

46. Kōzuma Yoshiaki, *Shuntō* (Tokyo: Rōdō Kyōiku Senta, 1976), p. 5.

more conservative unions emphasized the consideration of industrial profitability and the national economy when formulating wage demands.[47]

Sōhyō's 1951–52 political campaign against revisions in the trade union laws and the subversive activities prevention bill also jarred conservative affiliates who abhorred direct, extra-parliamentary action by unionists. After Mutō withdrew JCU from the struggle in an attempt to compromise with the government over the subversive activities bill, both Mutō and the JCU executive were recalled by the next JCU convention. Although Mutō had nominally joined the left socialists, he retained close contact with Matsuoka and Katō; his waning influence within the JCU and his replacement as chairman of Sōhyō at the 1952 convention signaled the decline of this middle faction.

The final straw in the factional dispute was the outbreak of the strike by the JCU and power workers in late 1952. In a public statement issued December 25, 1952, four unions including the Textile Workers Union (Zensen Dōmei) and the Seamen's Union (Zen Nikkai) blasted Sōhyō for ignoring economic limits, for engaging in political struggles, and for generally being a dupe of the communists. The right wing coalesced in a new coalition, Minrōren, in February 1953. Then, after the Seamen's Union and Textile Workers Union split from Sōhyō, a new national labor federation, the Japan Trade Union Congress (Zenrō Kaigi), was established in April 1954.

The Rise of Shuntō

The cleavages in the union movement did not end with the formation of JTUC. Within the left wing of the union movement new tensions arose, ones with important repercussions for labor relations in postwar Japan. In 1953 Ōta Kaoru, the leader of the Chemical Workers Union (Gōka Rōren), began to challenge the strategic orientation of Takano Minoru, Sōhyō's secretary-general. This differences first emerged over foreign relations strategy. Takano preferred a united front (the peace force) against U.S. imperialism, whereas Ōta began to favor the new idea of a nonaligned movement as elucidated by Yugoslavia and India's Nehru. As events evolved, however, this debate became less important.

The breach in left solidarity broke wide open in late 1953 after Takano and Ōta ended up on opposite sides of a strategic debate within the Socialist Association (Shakai Shugi Kyōkai). This association wielded strong influence within the JSP left as well as within the union movement, and a number of its leaders had been called on to write a new program for the party. Sakisaka Itsurō penned the majority draft, which called for a one-stage revolution with the labor movement comprising the main force. But Shimizu Shinzō, another prominent intellectual

---

47. Ibid., p. 6.

with extensive union contacts, dissented and wrote a private draft that called for a democratic revolution by a broad united front to be followed by a socialist stage.[48] Takano lined up with Shimizu while Ōta aligned himself with Sakisaka. Takano and Shimizu left the Socialist Association, and this split was reproduced within the Workers Association (Rōdō Dōshikai), a caucus that had hitherto been able to exercise effective leadership within Sōhyō.

Within Sōhyō itself, however, the debate took on a different form. Strategies for socialist revolution were not on the union agenda. But what fundamentally galled Ōta and his ally, Iwai Akira of the railway workers union, was the fact that Takano had begun to ally himself with JCP activists in promoting the peace program. In doing so Takano had undermined the anticommunist basis of Sōhyō unity and, in Ōta's opinion, provided ammunition to the right wing.[49] Within Sōhyō, however, Ōta chose to do battle with Takano on the issue of wage struggles and their relative importance. At the Chemical Workers Union convention in March 1954, Ōta attacked Takano: "The Sōhyō leadership is in a hurry to take up political campaigns but is indifferent towards struggles that are important for workers to advance."[50]

At Sōhyō's fifth convention in July 1954, Ōta contested Takano for the secretary-general's position but lost 140 to 107. Excluded from the higher echelons of the Sōhyō leadership, Ōta persisted in organizing a united front around wage demands, and in December 1954 five unions—the Chemical Workers Union, the Japan Coalminers Union (JCU), the Private Railway Workers Union, the Power Workers Union, and the Pulp and Paper Workers Union—joined in a united front to press for wage increases. Takano and the Sōhyō leadership could not simply stand by; when Ōta indicated he was open to enlarging the united front, Sōhyō approved participation in the initiative. Three other unions joined what officially became know as the Spring Wage Increases Joint Struggle Council (Shunki Chin Age Kyōtō Kaigi). Ōta retained effective leadership over the council, however—its offices were located in the Chemical Workers Union and its secretary was from the same union.

The first Spring Wage Offensive, or *Shuntō* as it became known, was an attempt to develop a union united front through the articulation of joint demands and through coordinated tactics. The unions' wage demands for 1955 varied somewhat but the average figure represented an increase of about ¥1500 to ¥2000 per month. Regional meetings were held, and the unions were to escalate job action in three stages from late March to late April. No joint negotiations took place, however, and in fact the structure of negotiations was different in each in-

---

48. Sōhyō, *Sōhyō jū nen shi*, p. 424; and Kōzuma Yoshiaki, *Shuntō*, pp. 8–9.
49. This analysis is based on Kōzuma Yoshiaki, *Shuntō*, p. 11.
50. Sōhyō, *Sōhyō jū nen shi*, p. 425.

dustry. For example, in the private rail industry the operators association insisted on centralized bargaining for a master agreement while the union demanded a regional bargaining structure. In coal, the JCU demanded patterned bargaining, which the employers at first opposed but later were forced to accept after the JCU threatened strike action and after the CLRB mediated.[51]

The results of this first coordinated wage offensive were relatively meager. Of the eight participating unions, only the Chemical Workers Union made substantial wage gains, although all made at least slight improvements. On May 18 the Spring Wage Increases Joint Struggle Council published an evaluation of its 1955 activities prior to dissolving. The main points were (1) that job actions had been too limited and that other unions had not joined the offensive largely because the action plan had been developed too late; (2) that the action plan had not been linked to the general elections that occurred during the program; (3) that significant action had occurred in the industrial center but little in the large metropolitan areas and that future plans would have to reflect other unions' interests; (4) that the program was unable to break with a "top-down" approach and that the struggle was not embraced by the rank-and-file.[52]

Despite the weaknesses, the spring offensive strategy did gain support particularly because of the gains made by Ōta's Chemical Workers' Union. At Sōhyō's sixth convention in July 1955, Iwai Akira of the JNR union challenged Takano for the secretary-general's position. Iwai received more votes in the first ballot, 128 to Takano's 123, but since neither candidate obtained the required majority a runoff was scheduled. Takano, however, withdrew at this point on the recommendation of his union, and Iwai thus became the new secretary-general. Ōta became a vice-chair.[53]

The ascent of the Ōta/Iwai faction in Sōhyō was generally viewed as an indication of the rise of economic unionism as opposed to the political orientation promoted by Takano. As Sōhyō's Uchiyama Tashirō recalled: "The faction for trade unionism won, and from within this trend, Ōta felt that to give the union function some real life, enterprise unions alone wouldn't be enough, so the enterprise unions had to develop horizontal links and carry out industry-level struggles."[54] Although the new orientation was thus a departure from Takano's politics, it remained militant. The spring wage offensive would become institutionalized, but Sōyhō could not ignore the needs of its affiliates in the public sector. Many of these unions were denied the right to strike and bargain collectively. Furthermore, the conservative government that continued in power through the 1950s pursued political policies (support for U.S. bases, attempts to reinforce police powers, re-

51. Ibid., pp. 467–468.
52. Ibid., pp. 469–471.
53. Kōzuma Yoshiaki, *Shuntō*, p. 18.
54. Uchiyama Tashirō, interview by author, March 1990.

Table 12.   Union members as percentage of employed,
1949–1955

Year	Employed	Union members	Percentage
1949	11,930,000	6,655,483	55.8
1950	12,510,000	5,773,908	46.2
1951	13,360,000	5,686,774	42.6
1952	14,210,000	5,719,560	40.3
1953	14,470,000	5,842,678	40.4
1954	15,340,000	5,986,168	39.0
1955	15,780,000	6,166,348	39.1

Source: Rōdō Daijin Kanbō Rōdō Tōkei Chōsa Bu, *Rōdō kumiai
kihon chōsa hōkoku sho, 1959* [Report on the basic survey of labor
unions, 1959] (Tokyo: Rōdō Daijin Kanbō, 1960), p. 28.

vision of trade union laws) that obliged Sōhyō to remain directly involved in a series of extra-parliamentary struggles. It was precisely the political and social orientation of Sōhyō that infuriated not only employers but also the conservative
wing of the union movement. Thus, even if we accept the contention that the ascent of the Ōta-Iwai faction represented a strengthening of economic unionism,
given Japan's own specific dynamics, this should not be equated with the rise of
conservative "business unionism" in the United States in the 1950s.

If anything, what characterized this period was the resurgent labor movement
and the challenge it represented for employers. After having laid low during the
great offensive of 1949–50, independent unionists once again reasserted themselves within the labor movement. The basis for this revival was workers' spontaneous attempts to assert their rights at the workplace. In some cases, such as at
Nissan, workers had survived the management offensive of 1949 with an independent union. This set the stage for the 1953 conflict. The Mitsui Miners Federation
and Ōmi Silk workers won important victories in 1953 and 1954 respectively, as
they confronted the paternalistic regimes at their workplaces. And other workers
spontaneously aspired to improve their lot and turned to unions to help struggle.

That independent unionism reasserted itself there can be little doubt. The
strength of this current should not be exaggerated, however. Employers undermined it at every turn, and enterprise unionism became endemic in certain strategic industries such as automobile production. The enterprise union trend, with its
base among the breakaway unions, and in the conservative section of the labor
movement, also gained strength. The movement thus remained divided and unstable throughout this period.

Nor should it be forgotten that union members, in both independent and enterprise unions, remained a minority of the work force. Union membership slowly
increased after the rout of 1949–50, but by 1955 it still had not reached 1949 levels (Table 12). Employment, on the other hand, had increased, and as a result the

percentage of organized workers in the work force declined. With union membership concentrated in the male-dominant large enterprises, workers in small industry, particularly women, held less bargaining power. The effects of this dual industrial structure soon became apparent.

Conflict and diversity remained paramount in this period, but some features that would become part of the dominant industrial relations culture had already emerged. As will become evident in later chapters, the spring wage offensive became institutionalized and annual bargaining over the base wage established the contemporary norm. Since, additionally, negotiations for bonus payments took place at least once a year and often twice (in winter and summer), private sector wages were often being negotiated three times per year. This wage mechanism was uniquely Japanese.

5 Institutions Emerge: Tensions, Limits, and Challenges (1955–1959)

The confrontation and tension in class relations that characterized the first part of the decade continued between 1955 and 1960. Japan had not yet made the transition to a hegemonic regime, although certain structural features of a postwar compromise were beginning to take shape. The problem was that employers, under the leadership of Nikkeiren, persevered in a low-wage policy and in their hardline approach to independent unions. But their activities only served to reinforce the necessity of an independent union movement, a movement that Sōhyō with its adversarial approach had come to symbolize. Workers, in their continued support for unions, diverted employers from their headlong rush toward market despotism. The popularity and consolidation of Shuntō, although modest in its achievements, sent employers an important if unwelcome message: many of their workers had interests that not only were independent of but were often in conflict with their own interests as employers. The union movement pushed for and won some wage increases, but even these gains were offset by a general lengthening of the workweek during this period. Although Japan had entered its period of high-speed growth, life was not becoming much easier for workers. This constituted the economic basis for continuing conflict between employers and employees.

Tension and instability thus continued; yet, within the turbulence, important institutional features of postwar industrial relations in Japan emerged. Key ingredients of the wage-fixing mechanism became widespread, including a form of yearly national bargaining (the spring offensive) and regular, negotiated bonus payments that constituted an ever larger portion of the annual wage. These gains, mainly won through concerted labor action, were offset to a substantial degree by the institutionalization of the performance-based, incremental wage system in both the private and public sectors. The performance-based incentive formula, utterly under management's control, undermined the base-wage increases achieved through collective bargaining. Another significant institutional feature of the emerging compensation system was the progressively lower wage paid to women compared to men. On the employment front, some employers began to embrace the idea that layoffs should be avoided if possible, and Japan-specific job tenure patterns, based on a core of male workers, began to grow.

These features arose out of conflict and compromise, but they increasingly became institutional features of the postwar system of industrial relations, accepted by both labor and management, sometimes begrudgingly and often tacitly. Unions and employers might argue about the size of the bonus but not whether there should be one. Managers might hope for a two- or three-year wage agreement but would accept the annual system and the slight disruptions caused by job actions connected with Shuntō. Elements necessary to the consolidation of a hegemonic system were indeed emerging.

But on another level, independent unionism continued to challenge the sanctity of the market and the evolving hegemonic pattern as well. This was the workshop struggle movement that spread from the Miike local union and began to exert considerable influence among Sōhyō affiliates. With its focus on workshop activism led by an independent union that challenged management control at the workplace, this movement quickly attracted Nikkeiren's attention. Perceiving the workshop struggle movement as a renewed challenge to managerial rights, Nikkeiren made plans to crush it.

Parallel to this process, employers, government, and the conservative Japan Trade Union Congress (which apparently found more in common with employers than with the independent approach advocated by Sōhyō) began to develop a more collaborative relationship. This affinity of interests was clearly articulated when the JTUC joined the Japan Productivity Center (Nihon Seisan Sei Honbu) immediately after its founding in 1955. While this emerging entente remained peripheral in the period under discussion, it was a harbinger of what would become a new social contract between labor and management in the 1960s.

Signs and Sources of Conflict

Signs of a stabilizing pattern of labor-management relations were beginning to show in the late 1950s, but on the whole the these relations remained tenuous and marked by conflict. This continuing instability was rooted in the pattern of economic development that marked the 1950s. The thrust of government policy in the 1950s had been to give priority to heavy industry, particularly steel and shipbuilding. This reflected a bias toward the producer goods sector of the economy. Shipbuilding in particular became key. An end user of the developing steel industry and export oriented, it became one of the main links to the international marketplace. Given this thrust, employer organizations were able to make polemical mileage from their argument that keeping wages down was necessary in order to assure international competitiveness. Little wonder, then, that employers persisted in taking such a hard-line stance toward unions. Nor was it surprising that real wages did not increase much in this period, particularly if one factored in the lengthening of the workweek that took place between 1952 and 1957.[1] Symbolic of employer intransigence were the zero percent offers tabled by Japan's major steel companies in 1957 and 1959, which provoked futile strikes in the steel industry.[2] In other words, the dominant economic vision in the 1950s did not leave much room for workers or unions, since the consumption side of the economy remained generally undervalued. This was the economic background that gave rise to the complex and diverse patterns of industrial relations in this period.

Sōhyō and Shuntō

The ascent of the Ōta-Iwai faction in Sōhyō in 1955 and the central role that Sōhyō played in the labor movement (evident in Table 13) gave further impetus to the strategy of spring offensives.[3] In 1956, over three million workers took part in the action plan, the first led and fully supported by Sōhyō. Many nonaffiliated unions also took part, including the large Electrical Workers Federation. Furthermore, public sector workers for the first time declared their intention to join with their counterparts in the private sector in the spring activities. These included formulation of joint demands (¥2,000 across the board was the standard wage increase demanded in 1956) and a coordinated action plan including work to rule, on-site meetings, and strikes. The strength of the snowballing movement prompted Ōta to declare that the scale of the 1956 campaign would surpass that of the general strike planned for February 1947, which the Occupation had prohibited. While perhaps carried away by the moment, Ōta's historical analogy shocked the government and signaled the final split with the Mindō tradition, which had arisen out of the aborted 1947 movement.

1. For the length of the work week see Table 15 below. Yamamoto Kiyoshi estimated that the annual rate of wage increases in large enterprises actually declined from 13.8 percent in the 1951–1954 period to 5.4 percent in the 1955–1959 period before increasing to about 10 percent for the 1960–1973 period. See Yamamoto Kiyoshi, *Nihon no chingin, rōdō jikan* [Wages and work hours in Japan] (Tokyo: Tokyo Daigaku Shuppan Kai, 1982), p. 114.

2. See Kawanishi Hirōsuke, *Kigyō betsu kumiai no riron*, pp. 126–132, for details on this struggle. It was at this time that the steel industry began its practice of issuing a "one and only offer" (*ippatsu kaito*).

3. Sōhyō membership remained stable at about 50 percent of total unionized workers in this period. The rate of JTUC membership increased slightly more than Sōhyō, reflecting the inroads it was making, but Sōhyō still had over four times the membership of JTUC.

Table 13. Affiliated membership of national federations, 1954–1959

	Total union members	Sōhyō	Japan Trade Union Congress	Federation of Neutral Unions	Unaffiliated/ other
1954	5,986,168	3,003,127	595,091	—	n.a.
1955	6,116,348	3,093,513	624,251	—	n.a.
1956	6,340,357	3,137,551	661,965	—	n.a.
1957	6,762,601	3,410,228	782,459	1,029,011	1,554,275
1958	6,984,032	3,548,921	796,455	1,027,143	1,652,773
1959	7,211,401	3,666,357	826,642	1,082,511	1,690,367

Source: Rōdō Daijin Kanbō Rōdō Tōkei Chōsa Bu, *Rōdō kumiai kihon chōsa hōkoku sho* [Report of the basic survey of labor unions] (Tokyo: Rōdō Daijin Kanbō, 1954, 1955, 1956, 1959 editions).

Needless to say, employers were not enamored with the turn of events. Nikkeiren responded to the spring offensive in unequivocal if somewhat predictable terms:

> This wage offensive is in the end based on the wage demands of the unions in the big plants as well as the wages of the civil service and crown corporations, which are clearly higher than those in the private sector. The resulting price increases from the latter will no doubt fuel inflation. We hope the government will take a firm stand, and we also have no choice but to be resolute if we are to put Japan's economy on a solid footing. In particular, the fact that Sōhyō has stated that "wages are decided not on economic climate but on the basis of the relation of forces," and the fact it has on its own rejected productivity improvement can only lead us to conclude that this struggle is in essence a political struggle or class struggle parading in the guise of economic demands.[4]

The JTUC joined employers in their attack on the spring offensive. The conservative wing of the union movement had, in the wake of the 1952 strike by coalminers and power workers, clearly articulated that in their view wage demands should reflect the actual state of the economy. This explicit acceptance of the market as the determining factor in wage increases marked a fundamental departure from independent unionism and the view that wages should be socially determined. Furthermore, the JTUC's decision to participate in the employer-initiated Japan Productivity Centre (Nihon Seisan Sei Honbu) in 1955, and Sōhyō's opposition to it, clearly delineated the divisions in the workers' movement.

For its part, Sōhyō's rejection of the productivity movement was closely tied to its desire to overcome the limits of enterprise-by-enterprise bargaining through its

4. As cited in Kōzuma, *Shuntō,* p. 29.

spring offensives. And despite the opposition from employers and the JTUC, Shuntō thrived and became a central component of industrial relations in postwar Japan. In this early period a number of important trends emerged.

First, the issue of the right to strike and bargain collectively for the public sector became a central goal of the union movement after the government fired or disciplined 888 JNR employees including top union leaders for participating in job actions during the 1957 spring offensive. A similar battle occurred in 1958 between the post office and its employees.

Second, the spring offensive (peaking with job actions in March and April 1957) brought collective bargaining into sequential alignment. In 1957, for example, the steel and shipbuilding unions were still negotiating their annual wage agreements in the fall, outside the Shuntō framework. By the end of the decade, however, Shuntō became the vortex for union demands around which most unions, even those not affiliated with Sōhyō, began to orient themselves.

Third, horizontal bargaining (cross-enterprise or cross-industry union linkages) did develop to some extent but not in the same form as in the United States, where unions gained some control over the labor market by establishing standard rates based on job classifications within an industry, allowing for only small deviations based on enterprise size, etc. Pattern bargaining evolved as a means of maximizing subsequent wage increases, which were then transmitted, more or less, through the industry as a whole. Pattern bargaining also emerged as part of the Shuntō—in 1958, for example, the private rail unions were considered the best bet to set a positive wage increase pattern for other unions in other industries. This role for private rail unions as the lead-off batter, so to speak, was then codified when the Central Labor Relations Board used their settlements as a benchmark for mediated settlements in other sectors.[5]

Shuntō's legacy was institutionalizing annual collective bargaining and coordinating its demands and pressure tactics. It also provided a bridge between private and public sector unions. The formal collective bargaining process remained focused for the most part at the enterprise level, however, although by the mid-1960s sectoral-level consultations were taking place with increasing frequency.

Conflict Continues

Struggles between workers and employers often took place at the enterprise or sectoral level. Although Shuntō did not itself engender these conflicts, it did serve to focus some aspects through common articulation of demands and tactics. One

5. See Matsuzaki Tadashi, *Wage Negotiation in the Japanese Steel Industry: Key Bargaining in the Shuntō*, Pacific Economic Papers, no. 106 (Canberra: Australia-Japan Research Centre, Australian National University, 1983).

significant feature of the period was a decline in the average duration of strikes or job actions; but the number of incidents of job action and the number of workers involved continued to increase right into the 1960s.[6] This was another indication that the postwar system remained adversarial during this period, even though long strikes became the exception in cases of job action.

Wages and job security were often key issues in these disputes, but union security also remained an important source of conflict. Nikkeiren persisted in its campaign to stiffen employers' resistance to unions infringing on managerial control of the workplace. One of the most important of these battles occurred in 1958 at the Ōji paper mill. The formation of a breakaway union in the course of a wage struggle led to a protracted and bitter battle in which Nikkeiren was once again intimately involved. Just as the defeat of the Nissan union prompted the demise of the automobile union federation in 1954, the defeat of the original union at Ōji led to a split in the union federation for pulp and paper workers.

Around 1955, Japan entered a period of high-speed growth and rising productivity. This did not automatically lead to improved living standards, however. In fact, in some ways the opposite was occurring. Table 14 illustrates how the numbers of hours worked per month actually increased in mining and manufacturing into this period. Although the figures began to decline after 1960, workers were still working longer that year than they had in 1952. Of course, the expanding economy provided jobs and most workers were thankful to be employed, but the jobs did not necessarily deliver improved wages and working conditions.

And the fact remains that wage increases were hard to come by, since Nikkeiren had shaped a wage policy that promoted capital accumulation on the backs of workers. To be sure, through Shuntō some unions began to win wage increases. But the returns were meager and often came in the form of increased bonuses rather than increases in base wages. The disputes in the steel industry in this period illustrate the problem.

Steel: 1957 and 1959

One of the most important sectors in which confrontation dominated in this period was the steel industry.[7] From the early 1950s, business and government had targeted this industry as strategic to Japan's economic development, and money

6. For an analysis of this trend see Ōkōchi Kazuo et al., eds., *Workers and Employers in Japan* (Tokyo: University of Tokyo Press, 1973), pp. 309–326.

7. This account of the steel strikes is based on the following works by Matsuzaki Tadashi: *Nihon tekkō sangyō bunseki* [The Japanese steel industry: An analysis] (Tokyo: Nihon Hyōron Sha, 1982); "Tekkō sōgi, 1957, 1959" [The 1957 and 1959 steel struggles], in Rōdō Sōgi Shi Kenkyū Kai Hen, *Nihon no rōdō sōgi* [Workers' struggles in Japan] (Tokyo: Tokyo Daigaku Shuppan Kai, 1991), pp. 161–204; "Wage Negotiation in the Japanese Steel Industry"; and "The Japanese Steel Industry and

Table 14. Average monthly hours worked, 1952–1958

	Mining	Textiles	Transportation equipment	All manu-facturing
1952	183.9	193.1	197.2	194.4
1953	191.5	196.2	197.0	196.7
1954	190.2	196.7	192.9	195.9
1955	191.3	198.8	197.9	198.0
1956	193.8	204.1	208.9	204.4
1957	194.5	203.2	207.3	202.9
1958	191.6	201.6	199.7	201.4

Source: Rōdō Shō Rōdō Tōkei Chōsa Bu., Rōdō hakusho, 1959 nenban (Tokyo: Rōdō Shō, 1959), p. 289.

had poured in to upgrade the facilities. Between 1955 and 1960, output of crude steel increased from 9.4 to 22.1 million metric tons, bringing Japan close to Great Britain's output at the end of the decade. Despite increases in productivity levels, steel producers took extremely inflexible positions in wage negotiations with the steel unions in both 1957 and 1959. In 1957, for example, the steel union demanded a ¥3,000 per month average wage increase, but the major steel producers responded by offering zero. This prompted a strike wave in the fall of 1957. Despite CLRB mediation and its recommendation of a negotiated settlement, the steel companies held fast and refused to budge. Finally, after a series of strikes (eleven walkouts lasting between twenty-four and forty-eight hours beginning October 8, with the final walkout on November 30), dissension appeared among affiliates in the steelworkers federation, and the union was forced to concede defeat.

In 1959, the steelworkers federation aligned their negotiations with the spring offensive and demanded a ¥2,000 per month increase in the base rate. Major steel companies responded with an offer of ¥800 in the form of an incentive bonus (tied to sales or productivity levels) and no increase in the base rate. The steelworkers federation attempted to mount a campaign for better wages with a series of short strikes in March and April. After workers at Yawata Steel indicated they would accept the deal offered by the steel companies, the strike movement faltered and the steelworkers federation was again forced to capitulate.

The defeats for the steelworkers in 1957 and 1959 were significant for a number of reasons. First of all, as Matsuzaki Tadashi has documented, the hard-line stance of the major steel corporations was more than simply an attempt to accu-

Its Labor-Management Relations," Annals of the Institute of Social Science 21 (1980): 45–68, as well as Andrew Gordon, "Contests for the Workplace," in Gordon, ed., Postwar Japan as History (Berkeley: University of California Press, 1993), and Andrew Gordon, "Luttes pour le pouvoir dans les ateliers," Annales 49, no. 3 (May–June 1994): 531–533.

mulate capital on the backs of steelworkers. To be sure, the companies claimed poverty in the face of recession and the need to raise cash for further capital investment in plant and equipment. Supported by Nikkeiren, the steel corporations manipulated the ability-to-pay argument to their advantage. Although they chose to raise these funds by denying their employees wage increases, this choice was not forced on them. Even taking financial constraints into account, offering some monetary concessions to employees might have contributed to stable labor-management relations. But this long-term perspective was sacrificed. The steel corporations had their reasons: "We were disturbed and unhappy with the nature of the steelworkers' union, which was approaching the limit, becoming further left under the influence of Sōhyō and others. And so the expectation for a transformation of labor relations and of the labor movement, which was at a turning point, was part and parcel of the struggle."[8]

As Andrew Gordon has documented in his study of Nippon Kōkan in this period, the local steelworkers' union there had begun to build an independent presence in the workplace, empowering rank-and-file workers to confront supervisors on a host of issues including staffing levels, transfers, and work standards.[9] It was this issue, the fact that the steelworkers' union had developed a presence on the shop floor, that prompted the steel companies' tough stance, a stance that otherwise might be considered an irrational provocation of their employees.

After the union's defeat in the 1959 strike, leadership in the local union was taken over by conservative union caucuses, and the union's influence on the shop floor withered. This process occurred in other workplaces. Indeed, the steelworkers' union as a whole came to reflect the aspirations of the steel corporations for a cooperative partner in productivity improvement.

The steelworkers' union's turn towards pragmatism had tremendous ramifications for both the steel industry and the labor movement. Thanks to the union's moderate positions on wages and workplace change, labor costs per ton of steel in Japan actually dropped between 1957 and 1964. This, at a time when labor costs in Germany rose by nearly 40 percent over the same period. The steel companies' victories in 1957 and 1959 had propelled the industry into its high-productivity trajectory that would see it become the world's most efficient steel maker by 1975.

From an industrial relations perspective, the 1957 and 1959 steel disputes had lasting effects on two levels. First, the steel corporations thereafter institutionalized the practice of *ippatsu kaitō* (single-shot responses); they started this practice in 1957 when they offered a zero percent wage increase and refused to budge. Once they had tabled an offer, they refused to negotiate further: take it or leave it,

---

8. Shin Nihon Seitetsu, *Honō to tomo ni—Fuji Seitetsu kabushiki kaisha shi* [Firing up—A history of Fuji Steel] (Tokyo, 1981), p. 670, cited in Matsuzaki Tadashi, "Tekkō sōgi," p. 199.
9. Gordon, "Luttes pour le pouvoir," pp. 511–540.

they said. This does not mean, however, that discussions about wage and working conditions did not take place. The take-it-or-leave-it approach removed negotiations from the formal bargaining table, and an informal process of consultation came to supplement and at times replace collective bargaining. This approach, known as "Boulwarism" in the United States, was declared illegal by the United States National Labor Relations Board in the 1950s.

The steelworkers' turn towards moderation had another profound effect. As the new steel leadership embraced the politics of pragmatism, the union found that it had much in common with unions such as the electrical workers and automobile workers unions, organizations that had been formed in opposition to Sōhyō and its predecessor, the NCIU. The similarity in outlook eventually led to organizational ties through the establishment of the Japan Council of the International Metalworkers Federation (IMF-JC; Kokusai Kinzoku Rōren Nihon Kyōgi Kai, or Kinzoku Rōkyō) in May 1964. These unions—in steel, electricity, shipbuilding, and automobile manufacturing—would set the pattern for annual bargaining in subsequent years, undermining Sōhyō's traditional role.

New Standards in Industrial Relations

Some definable trends began to emerge out of the tumult of this period. New forms of collective bargaining and compensation developed within the cases we have studied.

Miike

Collective bargaining in the coal industry during this period was carried out on three levels. Sectoral bargaining over the annual wage increase was carried out by the JCU as part of the spring offensive. The coal companies took a hard line in bargaining, beginning with a lockout in 1956. Subsequent wage increases were generally below the levels won by other unions in this period.[10]

Because there was no master agreements, furthermore, the general standard wage increase reached at the joint bargaining sessions was only a guideline, and formal wage agreements were concluded at the enterprise level. This led to discrepancies in actual wages because in coal mining the piecework system based on job classification remained the dominant pattern. According to Mitsui statistics, the average wage at Miike was high because the wage for underground miners was

10. Ōkōchi Kazuo, *Shiryō: Sengo nijū nen shi* (Tokyo: Nihon Hyōron Sha, 1966), pp. 530–539, in Lonny Carlile, "Zaikai and the Politics of Production in Japan, 1940–1962" (Ph.D. diss., University of California, 1989), p. 389.

Table 15. Bonus agreements negotiated by JCU and major coal operators, 1956–1958

	Union demand	Agreement
1956		
Summer	10,300	10,250
Winter	14,500	14,450
1957		
Summer	22,700	20,500
Winter	25,000	23,500
1958		
Summer	n.a.	21,000
Winter	26,000	22,000

Source: Miike Kumiai, *Miike nijū nen* (Ōmuta: Miike Rōsō, 1969), pp. 152–226.

based entirely on output (there was no fixed base wage), which continually climbed during this period.[11]

Thus even after the general wage increase was set at the sectoral and enterprise level, negotiations still went on. Because of the output-based wage system, multiple classifications, and the job-action orientation of the Miike local, wage negotiations eventually ended up on the worksite, where specific work groups negotiated with foremen or supervisors over the details of the piece rate to be applied to their specific job category. Struggles over setting the rate became part and parcel of the compensation system at Miike and in other coal mines. This was an exception, as we shall see, to the general trend in compensation systems.

In this period the JCU had more success negotiating summer and winter bonuses than it did in improving base rates. Table 15 illustrates the results of sectoral negotiations over bonuses. By the winter of 1958 the coal industry had gone into recession and the bonus was down from the winter of 1957, but only slightly. Despite assertions that bonuses were a function of corporate profitability, companies found it difficult to make any substantial cuts in the bonus. As was mentioned earlier, the union actively pushed for higher bonuses, and at Miike the bonus came to represent an increasingly large proportion of the compensation package. This was a common trend for the period, although at Miike and other coal mines the piece-rate system diluted the actual importance of bonuses.

Moriguchi City

Government fiscal restraint in 1954 and 1955 prompted local governments to implement restraint programs in this period. In many areas this involved layoffs

11. Mitsui, *Shiryō: Miike sōgi,* p. 429.

(26,000 regular employees in 31 prefectures) as well as cuts in overtime payments and other allowances.[12] According to the Satellite City Federation (SCF), the union federation of municipalities surrounding Osaka, those most affected by the cutbacks were older workers and married women who were forced to quit their jobs.[13] At Moriguchi there were no major layoffs, but pay raises were delayed and travel allowances reduced.

Employees at Moriguchi increasingly focused on bonuses (see Table 16) as the means to improve their livelihood. Although the union was prohibited from signing a collective agreement, it circumvented this restriction by negotiating separately on specific issues. Demands that were formulated at the SCF level were then submitted to the council of local mayors (shi chō kai). Negotiations continued at this level until a general agreement was reached informally, at which point the bargaining switched to the local level. If problems arose, officials from the Satellite City Federation would join local negotiations, although this was often a last resort.[14] From 1957 on, the union did occasionally adopt militant tactics including sit-ins and work to rule.[15] As a result, according to the union, bonuses at Moriguchi exceeded those recommended by the National Personnel Authority.

In 1957, the Moriguchi union, in concert with the SCF, negotiated seriously for the first time for a general wage increase. On May 24, the SCF established a wage policy committee to take up the issue. The Moriguchi union's demands included an across-the-board increase of ¥2,000 per month, with the starting wage for a high school graduate of ¥6,900 per month. Regional negotiations between the SCF and the mayors' council ended in the following general agreement: a 6.2 percent general increase with a minimum guaranteed increase of ¥1,000 per month. Negotiations, as in the case of bonuses, then switched to the local level, at which time the union and city management agreed to an across-the-board ¥830 per month increase plus an immediate jump to the next highest increment with a corresponding wage increase.[16]

At the same time, the union negotiated an end to discrimination against outside workers (gengyōin, manual workers who were classified as day labourers). Nishimura Yasunori, a founder of the union among outside workers, re-

12. See Jichirō Ōsaka Fu Honbu, Eitōren nijū go nen shi [Twenty-five years of the satellite city union federation] (Osaka: Jichirō Ōsaka Fu Honbu, 1976), pp. 91–92, and Moriguchi Kumiai, Moriguchi shi shokurō sanjū go nen shi, pp. 137–139.

13. Eitōren nijū go nen shi, p. 93.

14. According to the Moriguchi union history, city officials as well as local union officials were reluctant to allow this type of participation.

15. In this case work to rule meant everyone left the city hall together after work. While perhaps tame in comparative terms, in the context of the time—when working extra hours was considered de rigueur—such an action was confrontational indeed!

16. Moriguchi Kumiai, Moriguchi shi shokurō sanjū nen shi, p. 145.

Table 16.   Bonuses of Moriguchi workers and of national civil service employees, 1955–1959

	Moriguchi	National
1955		
Summer	1.0 month (mo.)	0.75 mo.
Winter	1.5 mo. + 0.2 mo. + ¥3,000	1.5 mo.
1956		
Summer	1.0 mo.	0.75 mo.
Winter	2.0 mo.	1.65 mo.
1957		
Summer	1.0 mo. + ¥2,000	0.75 mo.
Winter	2.0 mo. + 0.15 mo.	1.8 mo.
1958		
Summer	1.0 mo. + ¥2,000 + alpha	0.75 mo.
Winter	2.15 mo. + ¥3,000 + ¥1,000	1.9 mo.
1959		
Summer	1.15 mo. + ¥3,000	0.9 mo.
Winter	2.15 mo. + ¥3,000	1.9 mo.

Source: Moriguchi Kumiai, *Moriguchi shi shokurō sanjū go nen shi* (Moriguchi, 1981), p. 144.

Note: "1.5 mo." indicates a one-time cash payment equivalent to 1.5 months of regular salary.

called the discrimination he and others faced: "So of course wages and benefits were different and we were supposed to get along with what we had. 'You're not much different than day labourers,' that's what those on top thought of us. We thought we were also human and also staff members. We thought we should be given the same treatment, get the same wages, without any discrimination and so we pushed for changes."[17] Nishimura helped found an association of outside workers in 1955, which then amalgamated with the inside workers in 1957. Negotiations resulted in their re-classification as regular employees (albeit on a separate scale, a source of contention later) with large increases in pay. As the union history succinctly stated: "Having received tens of thousands of yen, there were even some who bought a television which at the time was still quite a luxury for a worker."[18] The union also gained permanent status for cafeteria workers, who until this period had been classified as part-timers.

Union members did not confine their activities to local issues; in line with Sōhyō's aggressive political stances, they became active in the antinuclear move-

17. Nishimura Yasunori, interview by author, 14 October 1988.
18. Moriguchi Kumiai, *Moriguchi shi shokurō sanjū nen shi*, p. 145.

ment, which gained momentum in Japan after the Bikini atoll nuclear tests in 1954. As well, the Moriguchi union participated in the organization drive of Sanyō Electric workers, initiated by the electrical workers union (Denki Rōren). Sanyō's headquarters were located in Moriguchi and one of its main factories was nearby.

As in the case at Miike, bonuses at Moriguchi came to represent a progressively larger component of the compensation package, rising from the equivalent of 2.5 months of wages to 3.3 over the course of four years. Unlike Miike, however, performance evaluations came to play an important role in the annual wage increase at Moriguchi during these years. Elaborate wage grids were established, and making it up to the next wage increment depended on a positive rating by one's supervisor. This trend began with national government workers and became the standard for local government employees in this period. It would be challenged by the union in the early 1970s.

Negotiations over bonuses and wages became annualized. However, although the Moriguchi union did take part in the annual Shuntō, annual wage negotiations were delayed at the local level because of the emerging pattern for establishing wage rates for government employees. This pattern began with the National Personnel Authority investigating spring settlements in the private sector. Subsequently it issued a wage recommendation for national government employees, which then became the guideline for regional authorities in proposing wage levels for local government employees. The process of wage determination for local government workers such as those at Moriguchi often concluded in the fall as opposed to the spring for private sector settlements.

As in the coal industry, bargaining was tiered; negotiations took place regionally and then descended to the enterprise level for final determination. After negotiations were concluded at the enterprise level they did not descend to the actual workplace, however.

Suzuki: Looms to Motors

Suzuki's initial sortie into moped production in the early 1950s had proven successful, and in 1954 the company changed its name to Suzuki Motor Company, Ltd. The union at Suzuki subsequently changed its name to the Suzuki Motor Company Union. Suzuki began research into the prospects of automobile production, and in January 1954 it imported three European cars. Within a year, Suzuki had developed its own automobile prototype—the Suzuki Light.[19]

Research and development for auto production continued, but Suzuki concentrated on motorcycle production in the 1950s. In 1957 it opened its first motor-

19. Suzuki, *50 nen shi*, p. 50.

Table 17. Wage increases at Suzuki Motor Co., 1954–1960

	Base rate	Average wage[a]	Starting wage for high school grad (female)	Starting wage for high school grad (male)	Starting wage for university grad
1954	n.a.	16,938	n.a.	n.a.	n.a.
1955	n.a.	15,430	5,288	5,288	10,096
1956	n.a.	17,308	5,289	5,481	10,096
1957	13,875	18,486	5,958	6,176	12,000
1958	14,561	17,911	7,250	7,375	12,000
1959	n.a.	20,108	8,755	9,162	13,760
1960	n.a.	22,862	9,239	9,582	15,570

Source: Suzuki Jidōsha Kōgyō Rōdō Kumiai Shi Henshū Iinkai, *Nijū go nen shi* (Hamana Gun: Suzuki Jidōsha Kōgyō Rōdō Kumiai, 1976), p. 250.

[a] The average wage is before production bonuses and exclusive of allowances including summer and winter bonuses.

cycle assembly plant and by 1958 it began mass production with the installation of an automated assembly line that August. In the 1959–60 period it finally shifted to full-scale automobile production.[20] Diversified operations and the introduction of mass assembly led to constant increases in employment at Suzuki. The 1955 roster of 711 employees had increased to 1,361 by 1960, about 15 percent of whom were women.[21]

Collective bargaining at Suzuki centred on the enterprise. Katō Toshio, a veteran Suzuki employee and future union president, described the changed relationship between the union and company after the turmoil of 1950: "After that the company had to recognize the union to some extent. We wanted to make it an equal relationship but it was never really equal."[22] The Suzuki union had no affiliations with other unions in the automobile sector. During this period the focus of collective bargaining was on compensation and working hours. Table 17 gives a general overview of the trends in wage increases in this period. In 1955 the summer-winter bonus system was institutionalized as Table 18 indicates. These two tables highlight some important tendencies of the time. Wages were initially pegged according to educational level at the time of hiring, with significant differences between the starting wages of high school and university graduates. Wage increases were subsequently based on the annual increase negotiated between the

20. Ibid., p. 440.
21. These statistics are from Suzuki Jidōsha Kōgyō Rōdō Kumiai Shi Henshū Iinkai, *Nijū go nen shi* [Twenty-five years] (Hamana Gun: Suzuki Jidōsha Kōgyō Rōdō Kumiai, 1976), p. 250. Exact statistics on gender ratios were not available but according to union figures, 103 of 742 employees were female in 1955.
22. Katō Toshio, interview by author, 7 March 1990.

Table 18. Bonuses at Suzuki Motors Co., 1954–1959

	Average cash payment	Equivalent of average monthly wages[a]
1954		
Summer	17,700	1.0
Winter	n.a.	n.a.
1955		
Summer	13,000	0.8
Winter	16,000	1.0
1956		
Summer	18,050	1.0
Winter	22,000	1.3
1957		
Summer	23,500	1.3
Winter	30,100	1.6
1958		
Summer	30,425	1.7
Winter	31,726	1.8
1959		
Summer	40,000	2.0
Winter	44,846	2.2

Source: Suzuki Kumiai, Nijū go nen shi (Hamana Gun: Suzuki Kumiai, 1976), p. 249.

[a] The monthly equivalent was calculated by dividing the cash bonus by the average monthly wage as cited in the previous table.

union and management and an incremental increase assigned by a supervisor. Incremental increases during most of this period were haphazard.

The introduction of automatic transfer equipment and assembly line production in the 1957–61 period prompted Suzuki to carry out a thorough transformation of their compensation system. Up until this time, institutional discrimination between staff (shokuin) and production workers (kōin) had continued, with white-collar workers being paid on a monthly basis while blue-collar workers were paid at a daily rate. Blue-collar workers faced discrimination in salaries, promotions, transfers, and employment opportunities. According to Suzuki's own account: "These differences in rank among even permanent employees were a problem in terms of unifying the company's thinking and ran counter to building a system of united cooperation. It was an issue that called for rapid reform."[23] The story of those reforms is integrally related to the theme of scientific management and is fully discussed in a later chapter. One point is important in the context of emerging patterns of industrial relations, however. The 1959–60 reforms included the institutionalization of

23. Suzuki, 50 nen shi, p. 442.

performance evaluations as a major component of annual wage determination. By 1960 performance evaluations had become standard features in the compensation systems at both Moriguchi and Suzuki.

A second feature discernible in Table 17 was the institutional wage discrimination against women. Although the amount was not substantial, it did reflect the lower value managers assigned to women's work, particularly given the fact that wages for new hires were not pegged to specific job classifications. While wages for men and women were initially set at the same level in 1955, discriminatory rates began the following year; fifteen years later the original ¥192 difference had grown to ¥2,000.

Table 18 illustrates the dramatic increase in the role of bonuses in compensation packages at Suzuki. In the 1955 ratification vote for the summer bonus only 58 percent voted in favor of the settlement, and rank-and-file discontent over the low bonuses prompted the union to issue an "emergency declaration" during negotiations for the winter bonus the following year. Rank-and-file disenchantment thereafter focused on the bonus levels, and this issue was addressed in semiannual negotiations. The 1955 summer and winter combined bonuses equalled 1.8 months salary, less than national government employees (2.25 months) and Moriguchi workers (2.5 months) the same year. By 1959, however, Suzuki employees had more than doubled the size of their bonuses, receiving the equivalent of 4.2 months wages in semiannual instalments. They far exceeded Moriguchi employees, who received the equivalent of 3.3 months wages in bonuses in 1959.

Reliance on excessive, compulsory overtime became a major problem in this period, but the union's power to contain the extension of the workday was limited. Until 1958, the standard workweek was six eight-hour days Monday to Saturday. That year, Suzuki agreed to end the Saturday shift at 3 P.M. making for a 46.5-hour workweek. A 1960 agreement initiated by the union allowed for compulsory overtime of a maximum four hours per day or forty hours per month. Sunday overtime was restricted to half the Sundays in any given month. Theoretically, an employee could be limited to only two days off a month!

From this examination of general trends in the case studies, one can detect emergent patterns of industrial relations in the compensation system, collective bargaining, and union organization.

Emerging Patterns

Yearly springtime bargaining and job action became the institutionalized norm for determining increases in the base rate in the private sector. Often unions engaged in pattern bargaining by industry, with the private railway unions, for example, setting the pace in settlements. For the most part, however, the deals struck in centralized bargaining remained general, and the exact wage increase for any given year was determined by local circumstance. For example, a general percentage increase for coalminers was determined through national sectoral bargaining. This increase was then used as a guide for negotiations at the enterprise level. In the case of coalminers, wages for underground miners remained based on piece rates and job classifications. Thus the general wage increase was renegotiated on the local and even workplace level. Although not formally a part of the spring offensive, Suzuki followed the annual pattern, but negotiations were confined strictly to the enterprise.

In the public sector, the National Personnel Authority determined annual wage increases for national public employees based on the patterns set in private industry. For regional and municipal public sector workers, consultations based on the national pattern took place between a regional federation and the council of mayors to determine the general wage increase. This general agreement then acted as a guideline for local settlements. Because government workers, apart from employees of crown corporations, did not have the right to strike or to bargain collectively, the agreements reached were informal memoranda.

Thus in two of the three case studies, the collective bargaining process for the annual wage increase was tiered and involved more than one enterprise. Suzuki was the exception, with its untiered, enterprise focus. The diversity evident in the structure of collective bargaining also existed in terms of union organization.

The persistence of annual sectoral and regional bargaining reflects the fact that many unions continued to maintain broader affiliations, whether on the regional or industrial level, and that continued to play an important role in labor relations in Japan during this period. About half of all local unions (19,829) remained independent of any affiliation, whereas the rest (19,474) were amalgamated unions—ones that maintained affiliations with other unions through federations. The Suzuki union, for example, belonged to the former category and the Miike and Moriguchi locals to the latter. The Suzuki union itself would later affiliate with a newly constituted autoworkers federation, which would take part in sectoral level consultations over wages. This was not the case in 1959, however.

In 1959, of the various types of union organizations, 683 of nearly 2500 federations were enterprise based—the Mitsui Mineworkers Federation fitted in this category but, at the same time, it was also affiliated with an industrial federation, the JCU. The Moriguchi union was part of both an industrial federation, the AJMPWU (Jichirō), and a regional federation, the SCF.

Diversity in union organization was the pattern in Japan as it was for union organizations in Canada or the United States. The organizational bias of Japan's unions may have been weighted towards the enterprise, but the difference was quantitative not qualitative. Thus, we must go beyond organizational issues if we want to understand the real nature of enterprise unions.

On the other hand, the compensation system in Japan was indeed developing some distinct features. No single bargaining system existed for all sectors, but a number of trends were becoming clear. First, yearly bargaining or consultations were fixing a general wage increase ("base-up"). But this wage increase was a general figure based on a statistical average, which hid the discrepancy in individual wages that developed over time.

At Moriguchi and at Suzuki, a second trend was also emerging—yearly incremental increases up a wage grid either supplemented or began to determine the extent of any individual employee's return from the annual increase. Performance evaluations, controlled by management, became the determining factor in deciding the extent of incremental increases. The trend towards a performance-based, incremental wage system evident at Suzuki and Moriguchi in this period was not accidental. In fact, the years from 1955 to 1960 constituted a period of consolidation for this type of compensation scheme.

For example, in 1957 one of the most important political battles in postwar Japan erupted over the issue of personnel evaluations. As discussed earlier, government workers were subject to regular efficiency ratings prescribed by the public service laws. This provision had never been applied to teachers, however, who were under the control of prefectural school boards. When prefectural governments began to incur deficits in the 1954 and 1955, the Ministry of Education suggested that prefectures begin annual performance evaluation of teachers and accord incremental wage increases only to those teachers with top ratings.[24] The Ministry subsequently ordered this system institutionalized in all prefectures, which provoked a three-year running battle with the Japan Teachers' Union. Despite teachers' objections, the prefectural governments, in the end, implemented the ranking system. This struggle was well known in Japan and was documented by Benjamin Duke in his work on the teachers union. What is less well known, however, is the fact that employers in the private sector were resorting increasingly to this same system to contain their wage costs and as a tool of personnel administration.

Employers, especially in the monopoly sector, turned to regular employee evaluations (*jinji kōka*) as a means of internal stratification. According to the 1959 edition of the Labor Ministry's White Paper on Labor: "During the inflationary postwar period, wage increases occurred through an increase in the base rate, but in the last few years the proportion of wage increases based on incremental steps has increased."[25] Citing a National Personnel Authority

24. Benjamin Duke, *Japan's Militant Teachers* (Honolulu: University of Hawaii Press, 1973), pp. 138–155.

25. Rōdō Shō, *Rōdō hakusho 1959 nen ban* [Labor white paper, 1959] (Tokyo: Rōdō Shō, 1960), p. 137.

study of wages in the private sector, the annual report concluded that regular incremental wage increases, rather than an increase in base rates, were the most important factor in increasing firms' annual wage outlay. As for how workers received the increments, the report indicated that only 7 percent of firms allotted the incremental increases automatically, that is, on the basis of accumulated service or seniority as defined in the United States or Canada. The majority of firms used some form of personnel evaluation to determine the incremental increase.

The Ōhara Institute for Social Research's 1959 annual report also noted the trend towards the incremental system and the proliferation of personnel evaluations. Citing a study by the Kansai Employers Association, in which half of the enterprises surveyed used personnel evaluations, the report concluded: "[This system] plays an important role in proscribing the labor movement, because through it workers are under constant surveillance."[26]

Another element of the emerging compensation system was the escalating proportion that the semiannual bonuses constituted in the overall compensation scheme. In both the public and private sectors, twice annual bonus payments represented a greater proportion of the compensation package than in the past. As the case studies illustrated, unions pushed for this because many employers were more willing to acquiesce on bonuses than on increasing base rates, believing that bonus payments were more flexible and might be reduced in bad times. Thus most unions were negotiating or consulting over wage or bonus increases at least

Table 19.   Male-female wage gap in manufacturing, 1948–1958

	Average wage for males	Average wage for females	Ratio (%)
1948	5,456	2,363	43.3
1949	9,345	4,077	43.6
1952	15,008	6,392	42.6
1953	17,115	7,087	41.4
1954	18,014	7,600	42.2
1955	18,455	7,718	41.8
1956	20,419	8,257	40.4
1957	21,278	8,487	39.9
1958	20,935	8,390	40.1

Source: Rōdō Shō Rōdō Tōkei Chōsa Bu, *Rōdō hakusho 1959 nenban* (Tokyo: Rōdō Shō, 1959), p. 267.

Note: Data for 1950–51 were unavailable.

26. Ōhara Shakai Mondai Kenkyū Jō, *Nihon rōdō nenkan, 1959 nen ban* (Tokyo: Tōyō Keizai Shinpō Sha, 1959), p. 383.

twice and often three times a year, a practice that Nikkeiren had admonished employers about in the early 1950s.

A final aspect of the compensation system was the institutionalized discrimination in wages for women. Although this was blatant enough in the Suzuki case,
elsewhere it was even more serious. Women were streamed out of the work force
or into low-paying job ghettos. This occurred at Moriguchi, where it would be
contested by the union in the early 1970s. As Table 19 indicates, women's wages
as a percentage of men's wages were even lower in 1958 than they were in 1948,
regardless of factory size.

Labor Market Segmentation

The rate of wage increases remained low for workers in large enterprises prior
to 1960, but another important feature of the period was the wage drift occurring between workers in large and small enterprises. Table 20 illustrates the extent of the wage gap as it had evolved from 1950 to 1960. In 1950, workers in
medium-sized enterprises made 83.1 percent of the wages received by workers
employed in large enterprises, but by 1960 they were making only 70.7 percent.
The same trend can be noted for employees in the small enterprises employing
30–99 workers.

The issue of segmentation had important repercussions not only as an abstrac-
tion of labor force divisions but also as an issue for the enterprise. As Tokunaga
Shigeyoshi pointed out, in the 1950s many workers in the steel and shipbuilding
firms (between one-third and one-half depending on the period) actually were
contract workers who worked alongside permanent employees on a day-to-day
basis.[27] Although these workers were crucial to the functioning of the enterprise
by performing essential tasks, often on a long-term basis, they became a living example of an accepted hierarchy among workers.

Workers in smaller firms also waged important battles in the 1950s. The expanding economy and improved productivity did not in themselves lead to improved wages and working conditions. In Japan, as in other countries, workers
had to fight to improve their lot. Although Nikkeiren's Maeda Hajime may have
been surprised by the spread of conflicts into nontraditional sectors at this time,
from a comparative or historical framework it was not surprising that workers in
Japan spontaneously turned to unions for help. The silk workers in the northern
province of Yamagata are one example of this trend.

27. Tokunaga Shigeyoshi, "The Structure of the Japanese Labor Market," in T. Shigeyoshi and
J. Bergmann, eds., *Industrial Relations in Transition* (Tokyo: University of Tokyo Press, 1984), pp.
25–55.

Table 20. Wage gap in manufacturing, by size of workplace,
1950–1960 (percent)

	Over 500 employees	100–499 employees	30–99 employees
1950	100	83.1	67.3
1951	100	79.5	61.7
1952	100	79.1	58.8
1953	100	79.3	59.8
1954	100	77.6	59.9
1955	100	74.3	58.8
1956	100	72.1	56.1
1960	100	70.7	58.8

Source: Rōdō Shō Rōdō Tōkei Chōsa Bu, Rōdō Hakusho,
1959 nenban (Tokyo: Rōdō Shō, 1959), p. 268.
Note: Based on all cash payments to employees.

The Yamago Silk Workers

Kamiyama is a small town in Yamagata prefecture in northwest Japan. In March 1957 the three hundred mainly female employees of a small silk-reeling plant in the town, Yamago Industries, decided that they needed a union.[28] Wages were below the industry average, already among the lowest of any industry. Part of employees' wages were paid in the form of a meal allowance, which was then deducted at source. The company then retained ¥300 per month from the meal allowance in a compulsory savings scheme. Workers could not draw on the savings unless they explained to the plant superintendent what the money would be used for.

Union talk had been around for a while. One employee had already been fired the previous year for advocating a union. What really precipitated the union drive, however, was the company's decision to automate in 1957 and the subsequent layoff of sixteen young women on February 20. Rumor had it that over one hundred employees would be permanently laid off when the automatic silk-reeling machines were fully operational. Shortly after the first layoffs, employees contacted the prefectural labor federation (Yamagata Ken Rōhyō) and the Federation of Silk Workers. On February 23, the union president arrived in Kamiyama and the organization drive was on.

According to the union's account, the company's strategy was not to openly oppose the union but to attempt to block affiliation with the Federation of Silk

28. This account is based on Yamago Rōdō Kumiai, Teikō no seitō rōdō sha [Defiant silk workers] (Tokyo: Seni Rōren Tōhoku Shibu, 1977).

Workers or other regional councils. At the founding meeting of the union, male employees with close links to management attempted to control the meeting and block affiliation. Despite these efforts, members voted 206 to 119 for affiliation. Two of the three executive officers elected were male.

Two lines clearly emerged regarding the union immediately upon its foundation. The executive worked closely with the company, helped establish a joint disciplinary committee and refused to liaise with Federation of Silk Workers representatives despite the proaffiliation vote. The company also brought in Nikkeiren's Sakurada Takeshi to meet with union officials, and this resulted in the signing of a no-strike agreement.

These activities provoked the rank-and-file, and a group of young women began meeting with Federation officials to devise a counterplan. In response the company brought in a number of parents on March 19 to convince the young women to stop agitating. Instead of intimidating the workers, however, this tactic inflamed the situation, and workers spontaneously refused to return to work until later in the afternoon. The activists circulated a petition calling for a special general meeting and a recall of their executive; they gathered 198 signatures. The Federation representative submitted the request to the executive on March 26, but they refused to comply. That evening 160 employees gathered to found a second union and articulated a set of demands. These included an immediate wage increase, a severance pay package, an end to compulsory savings deductions, on-site union facilities, reform of the dormitory system to allow employee control and freedom of movement, and improvements in food provisions, among other things.

The company refused to enter into negotiations and, on the pretext of undertaking boiler repairs, effectively locked out the employees. The company cut off all services to the dormitories and attempted to force the women back to their homes and thereby break the union. The union responded by accusing the company of abusing the employees' human rights and, through the mediation of local police, obliged the company to keep the dormitories open. City officials and the local Labor Relations Board intervened, and on May 5 the lockout was lifted. The union did not win any contractual benefits, but it had survived the attempt to break it and had come out of the struggle intact and with strong support on the shop floor.

The two unions existed for a number of years, but eventually even the company union was obliged to take up some of the demands of its members. In 1960 the two unions amalgamated while retaining their affiliation with the Federation of Silk Workers. Kashiwakura Masako, a Yamagata organizer with the silk workers' union, spent three and one-half years working with the local union. She recalled that the workers were able to overcome their differences but that the company

Table 21.   Unions and members in medium
and small industries organized by Sōhyō,
1956–1963

	No. of unions	No. of members
1956	922	46,061
1957	1,076	48,061
1958	817	39,359
1959	1,126	59,844
1960	1,252	73,329
1961	1,705	102,982
1962	1,202	75,455
1963	1,076	68,722

Source: Nihon Rōdō Kumiai Sōhyōgi Kai,
Orugu (Tokyo: Sōhyō, 1976), p. 229.

persisted in its confrontational attitudes and in its discrimination against the independent union.[29]

The Yamago silk workers' story was part of the growing trend towards unionization that occurred in the late 1950s. Unions, I would contend, were perceived
as a necessary means to achieve a decent living even in an expanding economy. In
that sense, conflict remained very much at the heart of the labor-management relationship even during this period. And just as women at the Ōmi mills had used
a new union to break the grip of employer paternalism in 1954, Yamago women
also turned to an independent union to protect their jobs and counter the paternalistic control of their employer. Theirs was one of the few exceptions where a
dual union was used to break a company union.

But the tribulations of the Yamago workers to win and maintain a union also
illustrated the difficult task union organizers faced. Union organizers were cognizant of the convergence of interest between unions and unorganized workers:
unions hoped to increase their membership and expand their scope, while unorganized workers wanted to improve their livelihood. Thus in Sōhyō, for example, regional labor councils began organizational drives beginning in 1956 to
strengthen the unionization movement. This culminated in a central organization
campaign adopted by the Sōhyō convention in the fall of 1959 and the dispatch
of 263 full-time organizers into the field.[30] The campaign coincided with the
spontaneous upsurge in unionization of workers in small industry.

29. Kashiwakura Masako, "Watashi no Omoide," in Yamago Rōdō Kumiai, Teikō no seitō rōdō sha,
p. 25.
30. For details and analysis of the organizational drive see Nihon Rōdō Kumiai Sōhyōgi Kai, Orugu
(Tokyo: Rōdō Kyōiku Senta, 1976). Organizing the unorganized was a central but not the exclusive
task of these union officials.

As Table 21 illustrates, the average membership of new union locals was only about 50–60 workers. The Yamago workers, with the help of the Textile Workers Federation, did succeed in unionizing, but their case proved to be the exception. Sōhyō's organizational campaign peaked in 1961 and declined thereafter. Employer intransigence and the structural problems of organizing and maintaining small units proved to be prohibitive.

Nikkeiren had in the early 1950s remarked on the growing wage gap between workers in large factories and those in smaller ones. The development of the dual economy and the segmented labor market vindicated their perception, but their policy for correcting the problem was diametrically opposed to that of labor. Nikkeiren's solution was to reduce the wage gap by holding down wages in the large enterprises, not to help workers in the small enterprises improve their wages. The intervention of Nikkeiren's Sakurada on behalf of the company at Yamago further illustrated this point. In fact, one could make a strong argument that even as late as 1960 Nikkeiren, with its hard-line stance against independent unions and its low-wage policy, was inclined to move towards a form of market despotism. But the conflict provoked by this approach forced employers and policymakers to look for alternative visions of development.

Contesting Visions

Conflict remained endemic to this period and gave birth in the late 1950s to two conflicting visions for future labor-management relations. The first, articulated during the formation of the Japan Productivity Center (JPC) in 1955, perceived the need for smoother labor-management relations and attempted to develop a basis for future collaboration. The JPC vision did not dominate in this period, but the process leading to its formation and the articulation of what became known as the "Three Productivity Principles" was an important milestone in the history of postwar industrial relations. An alternative vision, one based on workers' desire for some control in the workplace, contested the JPC's perspective. The workshop struggle movement (*shokuba tōsō*) represented labor's continuing attempt to reestablish some form of union regulation of the enterprise.

The Japan Productivity Center

As outlined in previous chapters, Nikkeiren—the major employers' federation concerned with labor relations in the 1950s—vigorously pursued its attempt to break adversarial unionism right up to the 1960 Miike strike. Its conservative, authoritarian character is this period is conspicuous and increasingly well documented.[31]

In the early 1950s, however, however, a number of influential groups began to focus on productivity issues as a key ingredient for industrial reconstruction and reintegration of Japan into the world economy. The first of these groups was the Industrial Rationalization Council (*Sangyō Gōrika Shingikai*), which had been created by cabinet order as a consultative organ to MITI in September 1949. This council was mainly preoccupied with increasing industrial efficiency through cost reductions (including labor) and mechanization. However, it also studied the productivity movement that was being promoted in Europe as part of the Marshall plan, and in 1951 it recommended the establishment of a productivity center within Japan.[32] This proposal fell on deaf ears at the time.

A second source in the establishment of a productivity movement was the United States government. As part of the European recovery program administered by the Economic Cooperation Administration, productivity centers had been established in several European countries.[33] In late 1953, American embassy officials approached Ishikawa Ichirō, chairman of the powerful Federation of Economic Organizations, with a proposal to establish a technical exchange program between the United States and Japan with the objective of improving the latter's productivity levels.[34] Ishikawa was unenthusiastic.

At this point the third source of the productivity movement appeared on the scene. After the unsuccessful meeting with Ishikawa, American embassy officials turned to the Committee for Economic Development (CED, Keizai Dōyūkai) for help. The CED, unlike other management organizations, was not a federation of autonomous organizations but acted more as a think tank for younger managers who were affiliated on an individual basis. Its orientation, as outlined in its program for 1953, was to *(a)* promote a planned economy (rejecting classical liberal economic theory) in order to achieve balanced economic growth, *(b)* help put a stop to the intense class conflict between labor and management, and *(c)* continue to promote scientific management of enterprises.[35] At its sixth convention held in November 1953, CED delegates adopted a nine-point action program for the economy, including three points regarding labor. Delegates called for managers to recognize several facts: workers were participants in production, and without their

31. This perception is supported in Carlile, "Zaikai and the Politics of Production."

32. Nihon Seisan Sei Honbu, *Seisan sei undō 30 nen shi* (Tokyo: Nihon Seisan Sei Honbu, 1985), p. 27.

33. For an account of the productivity movement in Europe see Michael J. Hogan, *The Marshall Plan* (Cambridge: Cambridge University Press, 1987), chap. 4, and Nihon Seisan Sei Honbu, *Seisan sei undō 30 nen shi*, pp. 42–93.

34. Nihon Seisan Sei Honbu, *Seisan sei undō 30 nen shi*, p. 96.

35. Ibid., pp. 29–30.

cooperation it would be impossible to lower production costs; even firms with high labor productivity should not grant across-the-board wage hikes until higher productivity was stable; managers should not be overly concerned about layoffs from rationalization; and the government should provide relief for those laid off.[36]

A key figure in the CED was Gōshi Kōhei, a member of the prewar Takahashi Economic Institute. Just prior to meeting with U.S. embassy officials in late 1953, Gōshi had returned from a visit to Europe and came away impressed with the labor relations scene he had surveyed, particularly in Germany. He attributed the successful revival of the German economy not to labour participation in management but rather to three factors: a national predisposition to work for the country's prosperity; workers and unions were economically oriented and did not engage in political struggles; and management had come to respect unions because, even in the direst of circumstances, they worked for economic reconstruction.[37] These "blood ties" were the key to the labor-management cooperation in Germany, according to Gōshi.

Receptive to U.S. suggestions of a technical linkage to promote productivity, Gōshi and the CED vigorously lobbied other management organizations, and on March 5, 1954, four major management organizations—the Committee for Economic Development, the Federation of Employer Organizations (Nikkeiren), the Federation of Economic Associations (Keidanren) and the Japan Chamber of Commerce—reached an agreement in principle to embark on a productivity improvement project. In September both MITI and the cabinet gave their support to the project, promising financial and material support. A permanent liaison office was created that included government officials and representatives of the Japan Productivity Center. Furthermore, the cabinet document stated that "the Japan Productivity Center would carry out its concrete activities based on the program decided by the liaison office."[38]

With the assurance of government support, the JPC was formally established in February 1955. Its leadership was mainly from management but academics such as Nakayama Ichirō also played a prominent role from its inception. Its activities were to include

1. promoting a domestic exchange of knowledge, experience, and technology;
2. promoting an exchange of knowledge, experience, and technology overseas;
3. research and investigation;

---

36. *Keizai dōyūkai sanjū nen shi* (Tokyo: Keizai Dōyūkai, 1976), p. 62.
37. Nihon Seisan Sei Honbu, *Seisan sei undō 30 nen shi*, p. 31.
38. Ibid., p. 103.

4. education and training regarding scientific management and other means of improving productivity;
5. introducing and popularizing productivity-improving technology;
6. gathering and popularizing literature and research materials;
7. providing consultation and leadership for management;
8. public relations;
9. publication of research and literature;
10. supporting organization of the productivity movement;
11. other activities necessary to accomplish the goals of the organization.[39]

In the planning stages, labor had not been formally approached to participate in the JPC but tentative feelers had been put out. As early as February 1955 Sōhyō had announced its refusal to participate. Its opposition was based on the fact that part of the funding for the JPC was to be provided under the terms of the Japan-U.S. Mutual Security Agreement. Furthermore, it saw the JPC as providing a rationale for layoffs and low wages. On the other hand, representatives of the seamen's union and the JFL (Sōdōmei) participated as observers at the second directors' meeting.

The JPC-government liaison council met in May and, in response to Sōhyō criticism in particular, clarified the goals of the productivity movement by establishing three principles: First, improving productivity will eventually increase employment. Regarding temporary surplus personnel, however, the government and private sector must take national economic factors into account and must outline measures that will prevent unemployment to the extent possible. Second, labor and management should cooperate and consult in studying methods to improve productivity, which must be based on the actual conditions in each enterprise. Third, the fruits of improved productivity should be fairly distributed among management, labor, and consumers, taking into account the actual state of the economy. Not long after, the conservative side of the labor movement, including the seamen's union, the JFL, and the JTUC, announced their willingness to participate in or cooperate with the JPC.

Despite the ostensible unity among employer organizations in support of the JPC, Nikkeiren and hawkish managers remained skeptical of a social contract with labor and therefore persevered in their confrontational approach with labor. Nevertheless, the establishment and operations of the JPC were significant and need to be appropriately assessed for a proper understanding of how Fordism developed in Japan. On the one hand, the JPC embodied Japan's "new deal" entente between management and conservative labor, which eventually became the hallmark of labor relations in many large workplaces. This pact was

39. Ibid., p. 106.

based on the productivity pie theory: labor and management should cooperate to increase the size of the pie and then consult over its division. In exchange for unions accepting a largely consultative role, managers would attempt to minimize the disruption caused by layoffs due to rationalization.

At the same time, however, the content of JPC educational programs for managers reflected a fundamental adherence to the principles of "scientific management" first espoused by Taylor and later refined by others. The application of modern management in Japan's workplaces gave rise, however, to a different version of the Fordist workplace than in the United States or Canada.

JPC activities included dispatching study missions abroad (mainly to the United States), holding management seminars, publishing news and research on productivity, and generally spreading the productivity gospel. Gōshi Kōhei, reflecting on JPC activities in its first fifteen years, boiled its activities down to two points: "One lies in management education and the other extends to the modernisation of labor-management relations."[40] Gōshi's characterization of the content of JPC management education is important: "The curricula were mostly difficult for the participants to digest, but there was no denying that the American approach to problems, American thinking, American concepts on modern management, and American management philosophy deeply impressed the participants. This stirred their interest in modern management methods and techniques."[41]

Noda Nobuo, another prominent leader in the JPC, also emphasized the importance of the American role as "a leader with respect to business management." He pointed out how Japan's managers absorbed the works of Peter Drucker and W. E. Deming and the important role played by such works as *Top Management and Control*, by Holden, Fish, and Smith, and *Standard Oil Co., California: Management Guide*. "Japan," stated Noda, "while preserving those of her own traditions which should be preserved, has unhesitatingly adopted the good concepts and methods of the United States."[42]

As for modern labor-management relations, the JPC mainly emphasized joint consultation as a means of resolving labor-management contradictions. This was not an original concept. Indeed, as described in earlier chapters, management had always attempted to circumvent job-control unionism, in which independent unions spoke for workers on the shop floor and negotiated their working conditions through collective bargaining. The dilution of the union role in manage-

40. Gōshi Kōhei, "Successful Performance of the Productivity Movement in Japanese Enterprises," in British Institute of Management, *Modern Japanese Management* (London: British Institute of Management, 1970), p. 123.

41. Ibid., p. 125.

42. Noda Nobuō, "How Japan Absorbed American Management Methods," in British Institute of Management, *Modern Japanese Management*, p. 60.

Table 22.   Stages in the workplace struggle movement at Miike, 1954–1959

	First wave (spring 1954– winter 1955)	Workplace standardization (February 1956–April 1956)	Acute phase (July 1956–1959)
Union slogans	From a leaders' struggle to a mass struggle	Defend the organization	Showdown at the point of production
Demands	Improvement of wages and working conditions	Standardization of working conditions at all workplaces	An end to management control
Form of struggle	Workshop negotiations	Selective strikes	Local job action
Workshop action	Getting signed memos on issues	1,000 local demands	Control of job assignments/ productivity standards
Company response	Appeasement	Lockout	Enforcing workplace order

Source: Hirai Yōichi, "Mitsui Miike tankō ni okeru shokuba tōsō no jisshō kenkyū" (Ph.D. diss., Hōsei University, 1982).

ment councils and the transformation of these councils into consultative organs had been occurring throughout the 1950s. What the JPC did, however, was to anoint this consultative formula with the blessing of management and to attempt to institutionalize it on various levels.

The Miike Model: Workshop Control

The alternate vision that contended for the hearts and minds of workers was the resurgent workshop struggle movement. This movement dates back to the production control movement of the 1940s, and workers at Nissan and at Nippon Kōkan had continued to uphold the tradition. But it was the Miike local union's successful use of the strategy that breathed new life into the struggle for workers' control. This movement spread to other unions, particularly those affiliated with Sōhyō, and because it challenged managerial rights at the workplace it constituted a divergent path from the emerging trends in industrial relations. In historical terms, it represented the last fundamental challenge to the extensive managerial rights employers had gained in previous battles.

The Miike local (16,000 members) of the Mitsui Miners Federation had won a signal victory in the 1953 struggle against layoffs. Not only had this achievement won it a preeminent spot in the labor movement, it had invigorated union members to take on further battles. With the blessing of the local's leadership, rank-and-file union members began to take union functions into their own hands. This culminated in a running battle for control of the workplace, as workers came to realize that working conditions were inextricably tied to the production process. Hirai Yōichi, a contemporary authority on the Miike union, captured the flow of the workshop struggle movement (*shokuba tōsō*). His work is reproduced in Table 22.

The workshop struggle movement at Miike blossomed after the miners' 1953 victory over layoffs. Local divisions began to initiate small struggles over specific worksite issues. Normally, these issues would have gone up through the labor relations bureaucracy as grievances, but with the 1953 victory under their collective belts, local divisions demanded that grievances be resolved on the spot and were willing to back up these demands with local actions. Because of the relation of forces, on-site supervisors were obliged to resolve these issues by signing a chit authorizing the change in working conditions or work rules. Thus this type of action became known as "chit-struggles" (*memo tōsō*) and began to occur often in the 1954 and 1955.

However, the gains made through this process depended largely on the divisional level of organization and militancy, the role in the production process, and so forth. As the Miike local put it, "there were those work sites that fought and those that didn't, and the resulting imbalance began to be apparent."[43] This problem, and the fear that the company would attempt to take advantage of the differences, prompted the local to establish a special committee to investigate divisional conditions and to develop a plan to standardize work conditions throughout the Miike mines. This constituted the first organizational measure in preparation for the 1956 struggle to standardize work site conditions (*shokuba tōtatsu tōsō*).

This standardization struggle was articulated as the first phase in that year's national spring offensive. According to the national schedule, coalminers were set to begin partial strikes beginning on March 19. The Miike local decided to organize its standardization struggle in stages leading up to that date. The first stage called for articulation of divisional demands by February 21. The interesting point concerning these demands was that they were not new demands but rather demands that had already been won by other divisions. These had been centralized through a committee and then submitted to each work site or division to decide which they wanted to adopt as their specific demands. In the second stage, demands were to be submitted to company supervisors on February 25. The six divisions articulated a total of 892 demands, of which 435 were satisfactorily resolved through work site negotiations on February 27–28.[44]

43. Miike Kumiai, *Miike nijū nen*, p. 110.
44. Hirai Yōichi, "Mitsui Miike ni okeru shokuba tōsō no jisshō Kenkyū" [Corroborative research on workplace struggle at Mitsui Miike] (Ph.D. diss., Hōsei University, 1982), p. 85.

The third stage began on March 1, when work site delegations met with mine directors. At this point, however, negotiations stalled, and on March 5 the union called for rotating strikes at the various work sites. Prior to this, the union had assigned the "three rights" (to bargain, to strike, and to conclude agreements) to divisional and work site section leaders. With the onset of rotating strikes, the company contested this delegation of rights to the lower levels, accused the miners of illegal wildcats, and announced it would deduct wages because of the decrease in output. At this point the focus of contention had switched from the specific issues to the right of the lower union bodies to negotiate and call strikes.[45] The company demanded an end to all job actions as a precondition to reopening negotiations. This the union refused.

On March 16 Mitsui locked out the miners and three days later the other major coal operators implemented a general lockout of coalminers after negotiations over the spring wage agreement fell apart. The wage issues went to mediation and an agreement was reached on March 31. The general lockout was lifted on April 2. Mitsui also lifted the lockout at all its mines except Miike. The union insisted on resolving the outstanding issues. At this point, however, the Mitsui Miners Federation began to exert pressure on the Miike local to allow the MMF to represent the local in bargaining. Worried about Mitsui attempts to split the federation, the Miike local acceded to this request. The MMF established a schedule for sympathy strikes in the other Mitsui mines and began negotiations with the company. An agreement was finally reached on April 16. The main points included the following: outstanding issues would be resolved peacefully; wages for the March 5–15 period would be cut according to the fall in production; the respective parties' positions on the three rights was noted; 80 percent of the lost wages would be repaid if the lost production was made up in the next six months.[46] Although the Miike local accepted this agreement, it caused severe dissension among the miners.

Despite the setback, the workshop struggle movement continued at Miike. From 1957 on, Miike workers, particularly the underground miners, continued to press for work site reform. At the Mikawa mine, for example, the workers began to take over control of work assignments. Wage rates varied between jobs, and because rates were based on production levels, miners could easily wind up competing for those jobs that paid higher rates. This competition could be manipulated to speed up or intensify work with a subsequent decrease in miner solidarity. In order to avoid this the workers elected a delegate to take over job assignments. Workers were rotated through different jobs and wages were thus equalized for all the miners in the group.[47]

---

45. Miike Kumiai, *Miike nijū nen*, p. 605.
46. Miike Kumiai, *Miike jū nen*, p. 619.
47. For details see Hirai Yōichi, *Mitsui Miike ni okeru shokuba tōsō no jisshō kenkyū*, pp. 55–63.

The introduction of mechanized cutting equipment at Miike in 1958 offered a further opportunity for militant miners to appropriate control of production. They did this by setting the distance the double jib cutters would move in one shift.[48] Mitsui attempted to halt this practice, and when workers resisted it fired three union activists in September 1959. This dispute was one of a series that culminated in the 1960 lockout.

The Miike union local had, through the 1956 harmonization struggle, become the standard bearer for the workshop struggle movement. Of course, there were also problems with the movement. Union leader Kōno Kazuo recalled that workers at times conducted actions simply to get on the supervisors' case:

> Confrontation with *shokusei* was central—and even today I think this was a correct strategy, it's not possible to have a union movement without confronting supervisors. Miike gave this a whole new meaning. At the executive, I submitted a number of essays, warning them [that it was going to far]. If a supervisor was to give an inappropriate order, for example, to work in an extremely dangerous place, you feel uneasy because it would be dangerous, so you have to confront the supervisor on the spot. . . . it was absolutely necessary to confront supervisors when they gave inappropriate orders, but to go beyond that, to confront them simply to irritate them would really turn them against us. After all they were members of the staff union.[49]

Nevertheless the workshop struggle movement represented some power for workers at the workplace, and among Sōhyō affiliates the ideas embodied in this movement (mass struggles, strong union structures on the shop floor, workers' control) became a focal point for debate and, to some extent, action. After the 1956 harmonization struggle at Miike, Sōhyō established a commission to investigate and develop an organizational plan. The commission was headed by Shimizu Shinzō, a scholar-activist on the left wing of the JSP.[50] For two years, the commission travelled around Japan investigating the structures and practices of postwar unions. A draft organization plan, penned by Shimizu, was submitted to Sōhyō's 1958 convention.

Shimizu's draft plan (a two-hundred-page document) covered a whole range of issues, but it began by emphasizing the importance of the workshop struggle movement. Shimizu himself recollected that the plan contained two fundamental ideas that he felt remained valid. The first was that labor had to have

48. Ibid., pp. 63–73.
49. Kōno Kazuo, interview by author, 21 March 1990.
50. Shimizu's draft plan and his reminiscences of its elaboration are contained in Rōdō Kyōiku Senta, *Sōhyō soshiki kōryō to gendai rōdō undō* [Sōhyō organizational program and the contemporary labor movement] (Tokyo: Rōdō Kyōiku Senta, 1980).

influence not only in the private and public sectors but also among workers in small enterprises. The second was that union activities had to focus on the point of production, where workers had firsthand experience with capital.[51] The Shimizu draft both encouraged and reflected an upsurge among Sōhyō affiliates of the Miike model of workshop struggle. However, as Sōhyō's first director of organization later recalled, "the draft contained points which appealed to a large number of unions and activists and prompted many unions to draft their own plans. However, there were many points that were hard to implement, given the state of a large number of unions. So instead of being adopted as convention policy, it was simply accepted as a document to promote a broad debate."[52]

Nevertheless, the workshop struggle movement was taken up in a number of unions, and once again employers responded by emphasizing the primacy of management rights. In his address to Nikkeiren's 1958 fall convention, Maeda Hajime sharply criticized the worksite struggle trend: "Beginning with the Coalminers Union as well as the Private Railway Workers Union, a large number of federations are loyally implementing the directive on shop floor struggle. Already in one company over one thousand grievances have been submitted at one work site, and the foremen are going crazy."[53] In the same speech, Maeda attacked Sōhyō for radicalism and attributed this unwelcome phenomenon to four factors: communist infiltration; the syndicalism of Takano; the presence in Sōhyō of public sector unions, which tended to be more political than private sector unions; and the influence of the radical labor-farmer political trend among academics and cultural types within Sōhyō.[54] At the same time, however, Maeda praised JTUC for its reasonable approach to labor relations.

The 1950s was a tumultuous period for Japan, and the decade came to an end with workers and managers still articulating contesting visions of the workplace. The period's legacy was not a simple march of progress, conditions improving as productivity increased. High-speed growth may have begun, but most employers, under the leadership of Nikkeiren, continued to take a hard line on wages and working conditions and persevered in their attempts to undermine unions that contested their control within the workplace. This strategy bequeathed a dual legacy. On one hand, it engendered further conflict. As the decade came to an end, the tension in class relations erupted in a paroxysm of violent class confrontation at the Mitsui Miike mines. This dispute would have a profound impact on both labor and management in Japan. On the other hand, in certain strategic

51. Ibid., p. 15.
52. Ibid., p. 3.
53. Nikkeiren, *Nikkeiren jigyō hōkoku, 1958* [Nikkeiren annual report, 1958] (Tokyo: Nikkeiren, 1959), p. 48.
54. Ibid., pp. 49–50.

sectors such as the automobile or steel industry, independent unionism did suc-
cumb to employer attacks and cooperative, enterprise unionism became a fundamental feature of the workplace. Thus, as the economy expanded and mass
production took root, it did so in a labor relations soil different from that in the
United States or Canada. This gave rise to a different form of mass production—
the lean production model that would set new world standards for efficiency
twenty years hence.

6 Lean Production and the Quality Movement: Suzuki and Toyota

The patterns of industrial relations described in the previous chapters acted as midwife to the birth of the lean production system (also known as the Toyota system) which many, including the MIT authors of *The Machine That Changed the World*, herald as the next generation in production management. Employers around the globe are attempting to implement various facets of lean production though employee involvement programs, team work, just-in-time, or Total Quality Management, all based on the Toyota model.

According to U.S. scholars Martin Kenney and Richard Florida, lean production is not only efficient, it has also empowered workers and created the basis for a post-Fordist production paradigm:

> We contend that the social organization of production in Japan has reached a level of development that is postfordist, and we refer to this new and unique social organization of production as 'postfordist' Japan. Postfordist production replaces the task fragmentation, functional specialization, mechanization, and assembly-line principles of fordism with a social organization of production based on work teams, job rotation, learning by doing, flexible production and integrated production complexes.[1]

In their recent study, *Beyond Mass Production*, the authors shift their analytical framework somewhat but fundamentally maintain, in my opinion, their original

An earlier version of this chapter was published in *Studies in Political Economy* 45 (Fall 1994): 66–99, and in Steve Babson, ed., *Lean Work: Empowerment and Exploitation in the Global Auto Industry* (Detroit: Wayne State University Press, 1995).

1. Martin Kenney and Richard Florida, "Beyond Mass Production: Production and Labor Process," p. 122.

perspective and even go further, criticizing those who reject the post-Fordist theory for a "narrow focus on super-exploitation [that] misses the critical organizational innovations that have propelled Japanese industry to the forefront of global capitalism and have led to dramatic increases in living standards for Japanese workers."[2] The authors contend that new forms of work organization, including teamwork, multi-skilling and worker participation are far more significant than "issues related to labor costs or comparative levels of exploitation. The social organization of Japanese production is not simply a better or more advanced version of fordism; it is a distinct alternative to it."[3] Unfortunately, the authors tend to use what indeed may be positive features of the new production paradigm to dismiss the negative features.

In this chapter we will examine the genesis and characteristics of the new production paradigm as it developed at Suzuki and at Toyota, the prototype of the regime. The first part of the chapter traces the evolution of many facets of this production system at Suzuki Motors. The second part compares the Suzuki experience with that at Toyota, and the third summarizes the impact of the quality circle movement on the division of labor within the automobile factory.

The Suzuki Regime

In February 1957, the aging founder of Suzuki, Suzuki Michio, retired and was replaced as president by his son-in-law, Suzuki Shunzō. The younger Suzuki represented a new breed of manager. On March 1, the new chief convoked a general meeting of all employees to announce his management orientation. Tops on his list of five points was the modernization of management methods and a clarification of responsibilities. He also stressed the necessity of improving morale, cor-

2. Kenney and Florida, *Beyond Mass Production*, p. 25. The debate about Toyotism was originally integrated with the debate about flexible specialization sparked by Michael Piore and Charles Sabel's work, *The Second Industrial Divide* (New York: Basic Books, 1984). For an early review of the literature and an introduction to the scope of the debate see Stephen Wood's essay "The Transformation of Work," in Stephen Wood, ed., *The Transformation of Work* (London: Unwin Hyman, 1989), pp. 1–43, and also Martha MacDonald, "Post Fordism and the Flexibility Debate," *Studies in Political Economy* 36 (autumn 1991): 177–201. The debate has increasingly focused on Toyotism as it evolved in Japan and internationally. The literature is rapidly expanding but some central works in English include Dohse, Jurgens, and Malsch, "From 'Fordism' to 'Toyotaism'?" and Kenney and Florida's article cited above; Womack, Jones, and Roos, *The Machine That Changed the World*; Kenney and Florida, *Beyond Mass Production*; Parker and Slaughter, *Choosing Sides*; Koji Morioka, *Japanese Capitalism Today: Economic Structure and the Organization of Work*, special issue of *International Journal of Political Economy* 21, no. 3 (Fall 1991); Robertson, Rinehart, and Huxley, "'Kaizen' and Canadian Auto Workers," *Studies in Political Economy* 39 (Autumn 1992); Christian Berggren, *Alternatives to Lean Production*.

3. Kenney and Florida, *Beyond Mass Production*, p. 25.

rectly distributing profits, clarifying the difference between business and personal matters, and instituting a system of rewards and punishments.[4]

At a meeting of departmental and section heads a year later, Suzuki summed up the progress he perceived since beginning his stewardship. Managerial reform had been necessary, he stated, because some people still clung to the mistaken belief that the company was a clan. This perception had to be corrected: "The company is a public institution in society," he told his front line managers.[5] Over the course of the year, much progress had been made in instilling modern organizational methods and rationalizing production. But, he warned his staff, further efforts would be needed. "If we don't adopt management methods suitable to the organization of mass production, we will lose to the competition."[6]

Suzuki stated that there had been less disruption than anticipated in supervisory and personnel matters and that important progress had been made in installing a proper ethic based on the centrality of work and "everyone in their proper place." Some managers, however, had not made their charges work hard enough and he urged them to reflect on the fact that those managers who failed to study and exert themselves would become an impediment to the company's development.

That the younger Suzuki represented the new breed of "rational" managers imbued with the desire to modernize production management there is little doubt. He had been on one of the first delegations to study American management methods organized by the Japan Productivity Center beginning in 1955.

After becoming president in 1957, Suzuki made concrete changes in the organizational mode of his corporation, a mode hitherto strongly marked by informal and personal methods of organization. First, he created an executive board to run the day-to-day affairs of the company. The executive board reported only to the board of directors and was made up of the president and senior and regular managing directors. In March 1957 Suzuki proposed a planning department reporting directly to the executive board. The planning department became the nerve centre of the company and was responsible for overseeing the "managerial revolution." Subcommittees for design and production were created within the planning department, and in December a third committee to plan for the introduction of quality control was also established.[7] To round out the management structure, department heads joined managing directors in a planning conference. This was mainly a consultative forum that met irregularly to discuss Suzuki's over-

4. Suzuki, *50 nen shi*, p. 54.
5. Ibid., p. 124.
6. Ibid.
7. Ibid., p. 54.

all plans and issues relates to its implementation. It reported to the executive board. In 1958, the small personnel committee was expanded into a full-scale section to oversee human resource management.

Mass Production

The reforms that began at the top of the corporate hierarchy in 1957 began to be felt at the lower echelons as Suzuki moved into mass, assembly-line production in 1958. In terms of product development, the new management proceeded to emphasize motorcycle production while at the same time beginning development of small vehicle production. Thus the first assembly line at Suzuki was introduced in the motorcycle production facility in August 1958. Simultaneously, Suzuki began to fully Taylorize its operations. Suzuki's own chronicle unabashedly reported:

> As a result, the skills and types of jobs were restricted to a limited number of occupations such as pilot vehicle production, pattern makers, custom tool and equipment fabricators, as well as welding, fitting, and press operations. In many cases, operations such as assembly and machine processing required substantial amounts of labour, but not skills, and so standardized work operations were implemented.
>
> Work operations were minutely analyzed using work factors and the time, labor, and routines for the labor process and operations were standardized.
>
> For example, in order to assemble a designated part in a few seconds while the line flowed by, workers on the motorcycle assembly line were subject to a severe mode of production that did not allow even the slightest of margins. This sort of thing is standard everywhere in the automobile industry, but it underscored the necessity of reforming our system of labor management.[8]

Katō Toshio, who worked at the plant at the time, confirmed the impact of the assembly line: "Skilled workers went into other departments, the machining department for example, and inexperienced people, new hires were brought in to work on the line. Only the supervisors had any experience . . . on the line, if you weren't young, you couldn't keep up; more than skill you needed endurance."[9]

In order to implement assembly-line production, Suzuki created a job analysis committee in 1957 that undertook the work of delineating the standards for specific jobs. Part of the committee's task was also to assign job descriptions (*shokumu kijutsu sho*) for every employee, but according to the company history constant expansion led to confusion and job descriptions were never institutionalized, although standard operation routines were.[10] From a comparative perspective this

---

8. Ibid., pp. 440–441.
9. Katō Toshio, interview by author, 7 March 1990.
10. Suzuki, *50 nen shi*, p. 443.

was an important development. Adopting standard operation routines meant that assembly-line jobs would become similar to those in the United States. However, the absence of job descriptions for workers meant that Suzuki employees had no specific job assignment or classification and could be rotated or transferred relatively easily.

In order to respond to expanding production targets, Suzuki began to enlarge its facilities and increase employment. In 1960, for example, Suzuki produced 150,000 motorcycles compared to 5,824 four-wheel vehicles. However, Suzuki had clearly identified automobile production for strategic expansion. In 1959, a typhoon destroyed some of the main plant facilities and construction of a new plant for vehicle production, began immediately. But even this new facility was not enough to accommodate the anticipated expansion of vehicle production, and in early 1961 Suzuki began work on a new factory. The company also began to actively recruit new employees to staff its new facilities. Employment jumped from 880 in 1957 to over 2,000 in 1962.[11]

From a Status to a Performance-Based Wage System

Expanded markets, mass production, and the influx of new employees put into question the haphazard labor relations practices of the past. Suzuki characterized the system up to this time as remaining an individual status-based system (*mibun seidō*). Permanent Suzuki employees (*shain*) had been broadly classified into two categories. Office, technical, and managerial personnel constituted the white-collar staff (*shokuin*), while production workers were classified as simple labourers (*kōin*). Staff members were paid monthly, whereas labourers were still on a daily wage system. According to Suzuki, "prior to the introduction of the performance-based system, the wage structure included a base-wage determined by length of service, a bonus system based on output, and a series of special allowances."[12]

Production workers faced substantial discrimination in salaries, promotions, transfers, and employment opportunities. According to the company history, "These differences in rank, even among permanent employees, was a problem in terms of unifying the company's thinking and ran counter to building a system of united cooperation. It was an issue that called for rapid reform."[13]

The Suzuki union cooperated in the reform process. For most blue-collar workers, the changes represented a step forward from the arbitrary control exercised by supervisors in the past. Katō Toshio, who became president of the union in 1960,

---

11. Suzuki Kumiai, *Nijū go nen shi*, p. 250.
12. Suzuki, *50 nen shi*, p. 443.
13. Ibid., p. 442.

recalled how Suzuki had begun to include the union at regular company functions:

> The difference before and after was, well, we had that bitter experience, so labor-management consultation created a space for the union to have its say. At the president's New Year address the president would embrace the union president; or when new workers were brought in the union had an opportunity to be present and get itself known. Sales and problems would be discussed regularly, every month, in labor-management consultations so that the parties could come to an understanding and adopt necessary measures.[14]

The first step Suzuki took in abolishing divisions between white- and blue-collar workers was to put all employees onto a monthly salary beginning in 1959.[15] In the following year the company introduced a major reform, a uniform, performance-based incremental salary system. All employees were classified into office, technical, and production streams and then ranked on a scale in grades 20 through 1. An employee's starting rank was fixed according to educational level, and promotion up the ladder was thereafter based mainly on yearly evaluations by one's supervisor. These performance evaluations were then submitted to an evaluation screening committee composed of division managers.

The wage package at Suzuki thus became based on two major components, the base wage and the merit supplement. On the surface it would appear that the performance evaluation would only affect the merit supplement. In fact, however, the base wage was determined by ability, age, length of service, and performance evaluation, while the merit supplement was based exclusively on the performance evaluation. Thus, after the reforms of 1960 annual wage increases negotiated between the union and Suzuki management were neither across-the-board nor percentage increases. In other words, only a small percentage of the increase was automatic and an increasing proportion of the pay raise depended on the performance evaluations. In negotiations, the union pushed for maximization of the automatic portion of the raise, while the company insisted on maximizing the performance-based portion of wage increases.[16]

With the introduction of the performance system the productivity-based wage supplement system was gradually phased out. One part of the supplement, a production allowance, was folded into the grades. The second component of the

14. Katō Toshio, interview.

15. Upon reflection, the union's leaders at the time considered that Suzuki was among the first in the region to make this progressive step. See Suzuki, *Nijū go nen shi*, p. 245.

16. It was not possible to obtain historical documentation on the evolution of the relative weight of the components of the wage system. According to officials of Suzuki, however, of the ¥8500 average monthly increase negotiated for 1988, only ¥2610 was automatic or part of the "base-up." Nearly 70 percent (¥5890) was based on performance evaluations or managerial discretion.

wage supplement, a group-based productivity allowance, was altered to a company-wide system. In other words, workers received a small productivity allowance based on the performance of the company as a whole. Even this wage supplement was eliminated a few years later. The adoption of a uniform performance system did nothing to end gender-based wage discrimination. Starting wages for female employees continued to be pegged at lower rates than males with equivalent educational levels.

Onoda Itsuhiko, secretary of the Suzuki union at the time, recalled that Suzuki management also attempted at this time to introduce the Scanlon plan to calculate summer and winter bonus rates.[17] The Scanlon plan was a profit-sharing scheme developed by a former steelworker, Joseph Scanlon, and endorsed by the United Steelworkers of America in the 1950s.[18] Although later discarded, Suzuki's attempt to introduce the plan showed to what extent management was studying American management techniques.

The transformation of the wage system at Suzuki from one based on length of service and status to a uniform, performance-based system (also called a merit or incentive system in North America) was not an accident. As demonstrated in earlier chapters, many large plants had instituted a similar performance-based evaluation system in the 1950s. One might reasonably infer that, contrary to the assertions of the three pillars theorists, a central component of Japan's wage system particularly in the large manufacturing facilities was by 1960 not only length of service or seniority but also performance.

The centrality of the evaluation scheme in the wage system was such that it requires further comment. The fact that an employee's career development, wages, and bonuses became largely dependent on favorable evaluations by one's supervisors had fundamental implications for the nature of workplace culture. Management naturally viewed digression from its standards and values in a negative light. The fact that management could punish nonconformity through negative performance evaluations that would result in lower wages was a powerful weapon against an adversarial workplace culture. It does not take too much stretching of the imagination to realize that worker participation in management—in nonremunerated quality circle activities after work hours, for example—may have had less to do with some innate Japanese quality of loyalty or devotion to one's company than it did to scoring well on the next performance evaluation.

A second implication to the performance-based system was how it undermined employee support for unions. Whatever the general wage increase negotiated by the union may have been, its transmission to the individual worker was directly mediated by the performance evaluation. Thus the strong link between one's pay

17. See the roundtable discussion in Suzuki, *Nijū go nen shi*, p. 245.
18. For details of the Scanlon plan see Frederick G. Lesieur, ed., *The Scanlon Plan* (Cambridge: MIT Press, 1958).

check and the union-negotiated pay raise, as was found in the automobile industry in North America for example, was broken.

The management revolution that accompanied the assembly-line and mass
production methods at Suzuki brought about classic Taylorist management structures—standardized job routines and the performance-based incremental wage
standard. None of these developments were unique in themselves. Central planning departments and routinized jobs were legion in the U.S. automobile industry, and even the performance-based wage system was not unknown. Having said
this, however, two Japan-specific features should be noted.

First, job descriptions and classifications were never institutionalized. Nor
should it be assumed that they should have been. Classifications and job descriptions were very much part of the specific U.S./Canadian regime and were closely
associated with wage determination. The fact that job descriptions and strict wage
classifications were not adopted in Japan does not, however, mean that standardized jobs, job routines and cycle times did not exist. It simply means that a specific
person and wage were not attached to the job.

A second difference was the fact that Suzuki's performance-based wage structure, while not unusual in large factories in Japan, had increasingly been spurned
by organized labor in the United States and Canada.[19] As we shall see, the absence
of job-control unionism in Japan's factories combined with the performance-
based remuneration system were two crucial factors that permitted managers in
Japan to constantly change the production system and maximize employee involvement.

Production Management and Employee Involvement

At the same time Suzuki moved to introduce mass assembly-line production
and to transform its labor relations system, it also began to implement a quality
improvement program. The embryo of the program was a suggestion system
introduced by the planning department and personnel section in 1958. This program faltered early on, however, and the number of suggestions actually declined
from 236 in 1958 to 124 in 1959.[20] Rectification of the suggestion system only
occurred later as part of the quality movement that gripped the company in the
1960–64 period.

As mentioned previously, a quality control committee had been established
within the planning department in 1957. At the time, this committee limited its
activities to traditional quality assurance through inspection, sampling and statisti-

19. See Bernard Ingster, "Appraising Hourly Performance," in Milton Rock, ed., *Handbook of Wage
and Salary Administration* (New York: McGraw-Hill, 1972), pp. 5–27.
20. Suzuki, *50 nen shi*, p. 447.

cal verification. With expansion in the late 1950s, Suzuki attempted to develop a more systematic training program for its new recruits and also for its supervisory personnel. As part of this program Suzuki sponsored in-house courses on statistical quality control sponsored by the Japan Union of Scientists and Engineers (JUSE, Nihon Kagaku Gijitsu Renmei, or Nikka Giren) in 1960–61. In April 1960 a quality control section was established within the manufacturing division. That fall Suzuki designated November as quality improvement month. To this point, however, quality improvement measures remained piecemeal and technically oriented towards enforcing standardization in engineering, operations, and inspection.[21]

In this same period, however, Suzuki Shunzō became a convert to the quality movement. In January 1962, he issued a "Presidential circular concerning the promotion of total quality control."[22] The circular emphasized the importance of quality control and the necessity for all employees to thoroughly embrace the ideology of quality. As part of the new program, regulations concerning the supervision of work rules and implementing job standards were established and propagated throughout the company. A two-year education program was designed around an in-house journal, *Our quality control* (Watashitachi no hinshitsu kanri), and a slide show, both of which were used in meetings with every employee. The company carried out company-wide quality audits three times in this period.

The 1962 circular marked the transformation of statistical quality control from a technical engineering method of sampling into an employee involvement program with strong ideological dimensions. The quality control committee under the planning division was upgraded at this time to full departmental status. As part of its quality plan it called for the adoption of a company motto that would provide the basis for the quality movement and serve as a means of initiating new recruits to the Suzuki way. Suzuki's vision was most clearly articulated in the company motto, adopted on March 16, 1962, as part of the quality program. The motto included three parts:

1. take a consumer viewpoint, make products with value
2. through united cooperation, build a fresh company
3. work for improvement of the self, let's always progress with determination

In the explanatory note accompanying the motto, management articulated its concept of employee involvement:

The "scientific approach" to management and "democratization" constitute the [company's] foundation. . . . Employees must go all out in accomplishing their work

---

21. See ibid., pp. 332–335, for details on standards.
22. Ibid., p. 326.

and at the same time, by correctly discerning the organization's horizontal relationships and through united cooperation, work to build a company (workplace) that has
fresh appeal and that continues to develop. . . .

The human potential is limitless but the development of that potential is completely dependent on one's own effort and responsibility. The realization of one's maximum potential as an employee, as a human being, must wait for self-improvement
through endless effort and study. . . .

However, it is the responsibility of the manager concerned to evoke [in each em-
ployee] the consciousness and desire appropriate for members of an organization.
We must emphasize that crack human resources are built through effort and leadership.[23]

Thus what appeared as innocuous slogans in fact contained strong messages that
both reflected and shaped the workplace culture at the time. Democratization, a
powerful anti-trust demand of the labor and popular movements in the early postwar years, had now been appropriated by management. Employees, hitherto
viewed as little more than contract workers, were now acknowledged as members
of the firm, a status formerly accorded only white-collar workers. But even this
nominal status was not without strings. Workers were assigned the responsibility
of maximizing their potential and desire. Supervisors were accorded the role of
making sure this happened. In this context, the performance-based wage system
represented a powerful tool in management's arsenal of incentives.

The year 1963 was a watershed year for the quality movement at Suzuki. Supervisory personnel were all given fifteen hours of training in quality methods and
then all employees received a ten-hour course. Employees in other departments
were put through the latter course as well. By the end of the year, 1,384 employees had attended quality seminars. According to Suzuki, it was at this point that
the quality movement reached critical mass—workers began to spontaneously
form quality circles after work hours to improve production methods.

A closer reading of the documentation reveals, however, that quality circles
were neither spontaneous nor worker led. In fact, it was the lead hands (_hanchō_)
and the foremen who began to meet after hours. These meetings were fully supported by upper management and then used as a wedge for forming broader
groups.

Any thoughts of nonparticipation among the faint-hearted evaporated when,
in November, 1963, Suzuki Shunzō announced that the company would apply to
win the coveted Deming Prize for quality control. To win the Deming Prize, the
company had to go through a grueling audit of its entire operations to ensure they
conformed to the highest standards of quality control. As the Suzuki history put
it, "over the next year, the whole company exerted itself until blood literally

23. Ibid., pp. 74–75.

stained the floors."[24] Despite these efforts, however, the Deming Prize eluded the company, and the auditors reserved judgement on Suzuki's quality performance. The auditors encouraged Suzuki to continue its efforts and to be reassessed the following year, but this offer was declined. Although the company attempted to put the best light on this setback, the quality movement ran into problems at this time.

According to the company: "Beginning about 1965, activities in the circles became formalistic. Upon investigation it was learned that the main reason was that we had relied too much on the autonomous nature of the groups—group supervisors or leaders were not paying enough attention to the work."[25] Koguri Tadaō, a manager in the main plant production section put it in even blunter terms: "When looking for the reasons for stagnation of the circle movement, examination revealed that the major problems were that everything was being left up to the workers themselves, the guidance and concern of the control supervisors had deteriorated considerably, and the circle movement was not being viewed in the right way."[26]

The solution Suzuki seized upon was to introduce a formal evaluation system for quality circle meetings. Each circle was required to submit a written report at the beginning of each month. This report recorded the following:

number of suggestions
frequency of circle meetings
attendance rate
monetary savings and rank of suggestions
amendments to operation standards
reports given at conferences
published reports
violations of production standards[27]

Each category was assigned a point value and the results tallied and used in awarding yearly prizes. But this report was kept on file and was also used in the regular performance evaluations, since the names of all members of the groups were submitted with the form. Furthermore, personal self-evaluation forms could also be submitted along with the circle report. Formalizing the reporting mechanism not only created a competitive environment between groups but

24. Ibid., p. 78.
25. Ibid., p. 328.
26. Koguri Tadaō, "Providing Incentives to the QC Circle through an Evaluation System," in Asian Productivity Organization, *Japan Quality Control Circles* (Tokyo: Asian Productivity Organization, 1972), p. 168.
27. The assessment form is contained in ibid., p. 170.

integrated quality circle participation into the performance-based wage and promotion system.

Suzuki pointed to the evaluation system as the key in reforming its quality program. According to the company, employees were more conscious of quality and upheld production standards without direct supervision. The number of quality circles expanded from 125 in 1966 to 282 by the end of 1969. That year, Inoguchi Tadayoshi, a lead hand and quality circle leader from Suzuki, mounted the podium at the fifth annual national quality awards ceremony to receive the FQC (Quality Control for Foremen) prize from J. M. Juran, a U.S. expert on quality with a large following in Japan. The bitter memory of the failure to win the Deming prize in 1964 was washed away in the sea of applause for the Suzuki employee.

Clearly, the transformation of statistical quality control from an engineering statistical sampling method for inspectors to a shop-floor method of employee participation occurred at Suzuki. Questions remain, however, particularly regarding the spontaneous nature of the circle movement. That foremen and lead hands played the dominant role as circle leaders and that reports on employee participation in circles were integrated into the performance-based evaluation system indicate that this was a top-down incentive system that compelled employee participation. In that sense, Michael Cusumano's insight into the system at other automakers is particularly relevant: "Yet, the cases of Nissan and Toyota also suggest that stereotypes of decision making in Japanese firms as being 'from the bottom up,' that is, with initiatives rising upward from the lower ranks of the company, rather than 'top down,' need review."[28]

Other Aspects of the Production System

To this point I have attempted to outline the sequential relationship between Suzuki's adoption of mass production (a reaction to growth and perceived potential for expansion), the adoption of "scientific" management techniques, many of which were based on traditional U.S. industrial engineering, and its adoption of the performance-based wage and promotion system that was prevalent in Japan at the time. The combination of these factors created the basis for the specific regime at Suzuki, a Taylorist regime but one different from similar regimes in the United States in that management retained even more leverage over its work force. This leverage was based on two essential ingredients: union acceptance of almost exclusive managerial control over the production process and worker acquiescence obtained through the performance-based wage and promotion system. The importance of this leverage was demonstrated in the evolution of the quality program at Suzuki.

28. Michael Cusumano, *Japanese Automobile Industry*, p. 379.

Of course the specific production regime at Suzuki contained other elements besides those discussed above. For example, beginning in 1962 Suzuki management took an avid interest in value analysis. First developed by U.S. engineers in the late 1940s, value analysis as an engineering method was introduced to Japan in 1960. Suzuki began to study it in 1962. In 1963, Suzuki managers participated in a nine-day seminar on value analysis sponsored by the Japan Management Association (Nihon Nōritsu Kyōkai) and the Institute of Industrial Management (Sangyo Nōritsu Tanki Daigaku). The intensive course included worksite visits to factories already implementing value analysis techniques including a visit to a Hitachi plant.[29] Not long after, Suzuki implemented a value analysis program in which it trained management and workers alike to respect the value formula V = F/C (value = function or capacity divided by cost). This formula was used mainly as a cost-cutting guide for the elimination of waste (*muda*) particularly for suggestions made through the quality circle program.

Suzuki also developed its own methods of parts delivery and inventory control. This first involved the development of a central production plan from which was derived a parts ordering and delivery schedule. Gradually this process was duplicated at levels increasingly closer to the shop floor, and this resulted in a modified *kanban* or "tag" system. This closely resembled the Toyota innovation whereby assembly instructions (and parts reordering) followed vehicles throughout the production process on a paper or metal tag.

As production volumes increased, Suzuki attempted to minimize inventories and maintain constant flow through production leveling. It divided the production lines in two, one based on predicted volume production (using a three-month cycle) and a second line tailored to custom orders.[30] These two lines, while conceptually distinct, were integrated into a continuous flow process on the single assembly line.

As well, Suzuki developed a highly coordinated network of subcontractors or suppliers. The Suzuki supplier network was first formalized in 1956 with the founding of the Suzuki Supplier Cooperative Union (Suzuki Kyōryoku Kyōdō Kumia), which included forty-five businesses. Representatives from these companies met regularly with Suzuki management to iron out production-related issues. Gradually, Suzuki provided financing and training for many of these companies. The number of companies in the Suzuki cooperative network increased to sixty-seven by 1970.[31] Beginning in 1966, network members met on the twentieth of every month with officials from Suzuki's finance, production engineering, and quality control departments.

29. Suzuki, *50 nen shi*, p. 320.
30. Ibid., pp. 312–323.
31. Ibid., p. 315.

In 1961, Suzuki took advantage of a government incentive program for small and medium-sized businesses to develop an industrial park for its suppliers. It handpicked twenty subcontractors who were willing to move to the new site and then fronted the money for them to purchase space in the industrial park. From this point on, Suzuki directly influenced the management of these enterprises. In order to avoid undue reliance on any one firm, Suzuki maintained at least two suppliers for all major parts.

These features—the supplier system and subcontracting, *kanban* and inventory control, value engineering and production leveling—along with the performance-based wage system, the quality movement, standardization, and so forth are all part of what I have termed lean production at Suzuki. It grew out of a cross-fertilization of Taylorism with enterprise unionism that ceded management not only control of the labor process but also tremendous leverage over employees through the performance-based wage system.

The regime that developed at Suzuki was one variant of lean production. The prototype regime evolved first at Toyota, however. Suzuki learned much from Toyota, particularly through the network of subcontractors. To better understand the evolution of the lean variant of the Fordist regime and, in particular, to grasp how the absence of job control unionism was a precondition for its ascent, it is necessary to examine the Toyota example.

Lean Production: Toyota

Of all the automobile producers in Japan, Toyota has become the most famous for its version of the lean, flexible Fordist regime. Ogawa Eiji, a professor of economics at Nagoya University studied the Toyota system in the 1970s. In his assessment of the Toyota system, Ogawa emphasizes the following features:

supermarket-style demand-pull processing
small-lot production and transport
automated quality checking
education regarding constant waste reduction
conservative automation measures
the *kanban* system of production and inventory control
visual control systems (*andon*)
autonomous management[32]

---

32. Ogawa Eiji, *Modern Production Management: A Japanese Experience* (Tokyo: Asian Productivity Organization, 1984), pp. 127–128. This is a translation of Ogawa's *Gendai no seisan kanri* (Tokyo: Nihon Keizai Shimbun, 1982).

Ogawa summarizes the system: "A simple management mechanism, visual management and voluntary participation by workers are among the ingredients of this format. Waste should be excluded at the source, a concept foreign to the conventional management."[33] Ogawa's own critique of the system, however, highlights some important contradictions in this evaluation. The author emphasizes: "In terms of self-management, management authority is delegated extensively to supervisors and foremen, but not line workers." Furthermore, the organizational values lead to expulsion of those who did not fit in. Concretely this meant at Toyota, according to Ogawa, that "workers having value gaps, ill health, and weak minds became drop-outs."[34]

This analytical observation by a production economist is backed up through popular accounts such as that by Kamata Satoshi and others.[35] These accounts testified that Toyota line workers were put under severe stress through the process of constant rationalization, expanding job tasks, routinization of standard work movements, and long work hours. This led to a high accident rate, an elevated drop-out rate among temporary employees, and in a number of cases suicide. These accounts are not inconsistent with Ogawa's observations and oblige us to question seriously the claim that autonomous workers' participation forms the basis of lean production.

History of the Toyota System

Analyzing historically the relationship between Toyota's labor relations and its production management, one cannot help but be struck by the similarities with a number of features in the Suzuki experience.[36] The transformation of an adversarial union into an enterprise labor organization, the introduction of the performance-based wage system, and the development of the quality movement

33. Ogawa Eiji, *Modern Production Management*, p. 130.

34. Ibid., p. 130.

35. Akamatsu Tokushi, *Toyota zankoku monogatari* [The cruel story of Toyota] (Tokyo, Eru Shuppansha, 1982); Kamata Satoshi, *Jidōsha zetsubō kojō: Aru kisetsu kō no nikki* [The automobile factory of despair: Diary of a seasonal worker] (Tokyo: Gendai Shuppan Kai, 1973). The latter was translated and published in English as *Japan in the Passing Lane* (New York: Pantheon, 1982).

36. For information on Toyota and the automobile industry in general I have used Toyota Jidōsha Kabushiki Kaisha, *Sōzō kagiri naku, Toyota jidōsha gōjū nen shi* [Unlimited creativity, 50 years of Toyota Automobiles, Ltd.] (Toyota City, 1987); Nomura Masami, *Toyotizumu* [Toyotism] (Kyoto: Mineruba Shobō, 1993); Kamii Yoshihiko, *Rōdō kumiai no shokuba kisei*; Yamamoto Kiyoshi, *Jidōsha sangyō no rōshi kankei* [Labor management relations in the automobile industry] (Tokyo: Tokyo Daigaku Shuppan Kai, 1981); Totsuka Hideo and Tokunaga Shigeyoshi, eds., *Gendai Nihon no rōdō mondai* [Labor issues in contemporay Japan] (Kyoto: Mineruba Shobō, 1993); Totsuka Hideo and Hyōdō Tsutomu, eds., *Roshi kankei no tenkan to sentaku* [Transition and choice in industrial relations] (Tokyo: Nihon Hyōron Sha, 1991); and Cusumano, *Japanese Automobile Industry*.

bear marked similarities. I would contend that they constituted essential elements in the evolution of the lean production regime.

In the immediate postwar period, Toyota, like many other companies, attempted to switch from military to civilian production. Unlike Suzuki, Toyota had already begun producing four-wheel vehicles in the prewar and wartime period. On September 25, 1945, the Occupation authorized production of trucks for civilian production, and Toyota restarted operations, building eighty-two trucks in that month. Wartime production levels had been as high as 2,066 units in one month.[37] Workers at Toyota founded their union on January 19, 1946. Workers at Nissan and Isuzu Motors also formed unions in the same period. Instead of creating an industrial federations, the unions chose instead to affiliate individually with the militant NCIU. As the JCP influence grew within the NCIU, the Toyota union in particular decided to withdraw from the militant federation. It encouraged the Nissan union to do the same, and the two unions sponsored the creation of the Japan Automobile Workers Union (JAWU, Zen Nihon Jidōsha Sangyō Rōdō Kumiai, or Zenji) in April 1947.[38]

Despite their disaffiliation from the NCIU, the Toyota and Nissan unions remained relatively adversarial. Both unions actively fought the automakers' attempts to cut salaries and lay off employees as part of the 1949 employers' offensive. At Toyota, the union compromised by allowing for a 10 percent cut in wages in return for a written guarantee that Toyota would not resort to layoffs.[39] As events transpired, Toyota reneged on this agreement.

In January 1950, the Bank of Japan informed Toyota that it would not continue to finance the company unless it (a) allowed the creation of an independent sales corporation to handle Toyota marketing, (b) restricted production to quotas assigned by the sales division, (c) accepted a limit of ¥400 million for restructuring, (d) laid off redundant employees.[40] Toyota agreed to these terms. It raised the issue of a new sales company in the management council in early 1950. The union agreed to the separation as long as the company agreed to give the union certification and the same contract as existed at Toyota. By the spring, Toyota was failing to pay its workers their full salaries and it became evident that the company was contemplating layoffs despite the ironclad written assurances against such layoffs. On April 7, the union informed Toyota management that it would begin job action. Negotiations within the management council were terminated and collective bargaining began. On April 22, Toyota tabled an adjust-

37. Toyota, *Sōzō kagiri naku*, p. 191.
38. Cusumano, *Japanese Automobile Industry*, p. 144.
39. Toyota, *Sōzō kagiri naku*, p. 217.
40. Ibid., p. 219. It was also the banks that demanded Suzuki lay off hundreds of employees in 1949. Further research into their role during the 1949 crisis is necessary to fully understand the pivotal position finance capital played in this period.

ment package that called for plant closures and the voluntary retirement of 1600 employees. The union rejected this proposal and in early May applied to the courts for an order prohibiting layoffs based on a clause in the collective agreement (as opposed to the memorandum of agreement containing the early wage cut—no layoff tradeoff) that obliged the company to obtain union approval before laying off any worker.[41]

According to Toyota's account of this episode, company lawyers advised management in a late-night meeting that because the contract had not been properly signed it could be invalidated and thereby void the union veto over layoffs. Toyoda Eiji piped up at this point, stating that to use this legal technicality as an out would result in employees losing faith in the company.[42] Instead, the company simply sent out layoff notices and, in response to the union's legal challenge, ventured the opinion that the contract had expired![43]

Toyota employees carried out job-site actions to protest the layoffs, and in May only 304 trucks came off the line compared to 619 the previous month. Toyoda Kiichirō, Toyota president, decided radical action was necessary, and he made the largely symbolic gesture of resigning as company president to take responsibility for the crisis. Meanwhile, the company pressed ahead with its forced recruitment of early retirees, and by June 7 it had garnered 1,760 employees. The union had lost the battle to maintain jobs. On June 10 it accepted the company's adjustment program (including the closure of two facilities bringing the unemployed tally to 2146) and switched its bargaining focus to assuring that workers would not have pay deducted for on-the-job protests and to winning rehiring rights for those laid off.

In 1953, both the Nissan and Toyota unions underwent fundamental changes after they were defeated in a struggle to win a reformed wage system. That year, the autoworkers' union federation demanded a guaranteed base rate with incremental increases to be based solely on age. Of the two unions, the Nissan unit was the stronger. Here the company conspired with Nikkeiren to break the original union and create a new enterprise union.[44] At Toyota, the company also took a hard line, refusing any wage increases and docking workers pay when they took part in on-the-job protests. Unlike the situation at Nissan, however, the company was able to transform the union from the inside. During the 1953 confrontation the head of the engineering department at the main assembly plant

---

41. This clause was common to many contracts in the 1946–49 period, when the labor movement was on the rise.

42. Toyota, *Sōzō kagiri naku*, p. 229.

43. Because of the changes in the trade union law, contracts could no longer be automatically renewed. Toyota used this option, as had Suzuki, to break the contract instead of using narrow legal technicalities.

44. For details on the 1953 battle at Nissan see Cusumano, *Japanese Automobile Industry*, pp. 137–185.

was singled out for recognition of his efforts in helping to turn the union around and in making sure there would be no repeat of the 1950 struggle.[45] The company-directed plan to housebreak its union had begun much earlier, however. According to Toyota:

> During this period, general affairs director Yamamoto Masao and the auditing section chief Yamamoto Yoshiaki, devoted single-minded efforts to the transformation of labor relations. In April 1951, their efforts bore fruit with the establishment of a group based mainly among graduates of the technical training school (the predecessor of the Toyota Industrial Training Institute). Through the labor strife that had occurred, these people had come to realize that they were the ones who could make the company better. Realizing that everything depended on people, and painfully aware of the necessity to develop a meeting of the minds through direct contact with employees, Yamamoto and others were out meeting every night with groups they had formed around [employees'] workplace, educational affiliations, or place of origin. On holidays they would participate in softball tournaments.[46]

It was out of this attempt to overcome adversarial unionism and transform its labour relations that Toyota's "humanism" was born. "The idea of having this type of people at the center of things, having their hot blood pulse through the management structure, and having their knowledge reflected in management later spread to our suppliers, sales offices, and regional companies. Moreover, efforts continued to spread the concept of human relations into politics, government, and business."[47]

The defeats at Nissan and Toyota in 1953 led to the demise of the autoworkers' union federation in 1954. The Toyota union rejected any further industrial affiliations and, at its 1955 convention, adopted the slogan "the two wheels of progress are stability in workers' livelihood and the development of the industry and enterprise." A few months later, Toyota union representatives joined an overseas study mission to the United States sponsored by the Japan Productivity Center. This, according to Toyota, "was another indication of the rebirth of the union."

The years between 1949 and 1953 marks the transition between adversarial unionism and enterprise unionism at Toyota. By 1953 enterprise unionism had clearly gained the upper hand with important repercussions. For one, the new union abandoned the old demands for minimum wage guarantees and an aged-based incremental system. In its place, the union accepted a performance-based wage system similar in some respects to the one that Suzuki adopted in

45. Toyota, Sōzō kagiri naku, p. 308.
46. Ibid., p. 309.
47. Ibid., pp. 309–310.

1960.[48] At both Toyota and Nissan, worker control at the shop-floor level declined, although the Nissan union, under Shioji Ichirō, developed its own particular form of regulation.[49] At Toyota, management had a clearer field to develop the variations in Fordist methods that later became synonymous with the Toyota production system.

Making the Link: The Rise of Toyotaism

The rise of Toyota production methods coincided with the decline of adversarialism. Ōno Taiichi, the Toyota engineer credited as the leader in the development of the Toyota production system, provides further evidence for linking enterprise unionism with lean production. In his treatise on production, Ōno described the process of de-skilling that took place at Toyota in the late 1940s and early 1950s:

> It is never easy to break the machine-shop tradition in which operators are fixed to jobs, for example, lathe operators to lathe work and welders to welding work. It worked in Japan only because we were willing to do it. The Toyota production system began when I challenged the old system.
>
> With the outbreak of the Korean War in June 1950, Japanese industry recovered its vigor. Riding this wave of growth, the automobile industry also expanded. At Toyota, it was a busy and hectic year, beginning in April with a three-month labor dispute over manpower reduction, followed by President Toyoda Kiichirō's assuming responsibility for the strike and resigning. After this, the Korean War broke out.
>
> Although there were special wartime demands, we were far from mass production. We were still producing small quantities of many models.
>
> At this time, I was manager of the machine shop at the Koromo plant. As an experiment, I arranged the various machines in the sequence of machining processes. This was a radical change from the conventional system in which a large quantity of the same part was machined in one process and then forwarded to the next process.
>
> In 1947, we arranged machines in parallel lines or in an L-shape and tried having one worker operate three or four machines along the processing route. We encountered strong resistance among the production workers, however, even though there

---

48. The exact date Toyota introduced the performance-based system is not clear. Cusumano dates it from 1960. However, according to materials from Toyota Motor Sales, personnel evaluations were first introduced there in 1953 and "American-style training methods were introduced in 1955 with the implementation of programs such as TWI (training for workplace supervisors) and MTP (management training programs)." Toyota Jidōsha Hanbai Kabushiki Kaisha, *Sekai e no ayumi* [A world ahead] (Nagoya: Toyota, 1980), p. 235.

49. See Kamii Yoshihiko, *Rōdō kumiai no shokuba kisei.*

was no increase in work or hours. Our craftsmen did not like the new arrangements requiring them to function as multi-skilled operators.[50]

In his study of Toyota, Cusumano interviewed Ōno and confirmed this version of events. Through work reorganization and technical innovation one worker was operating up to seventeen machines at Toyota by 1953, up considerably from between five and ten in the 1950s. Even more fascinating was that Ōno recognized how union opposition to his schemes could have blocked his experiments. Ōno stated, "Had I faced the Japan National Railways union or an American union I might have been murdered."[51] Ōno's dramatic speculation regarding his own fate only serves to emphasize the significance he attached to the absence of independent unions.[52]

Judging from this study, from Ōno's own accounts, and from Cusumano's research, it seems reasonable to postulate that the classic Taylorist division of work into conception and execution, with engineers doing the conceiving and machinists executing the orders, was part and parcel of the emergence of Toyota's system. Even innovations such as flexible manufacturing, just-in-time and *kanban* were not so much deviations from Taylorism as they were ways of implementing Taylorist work methods when production volumes were relatively low. As Ōno described the system: "Kanban is a tool for realizing just-in-time. For this tool to work fairly well, the production processes must be managed to flow as much as possible. This is really the basic condition. Other important conditions are leveling production as much as possible and always working in accordance with standard work methods." Ōno began the process of standardizing work methods at Toyota during World War II. "Skilled workers were being transferred from the production plant to the battlefield and more and more machines were gradually being operated by inexperienced men and women. This naturally increased the need for standard work methods." According to Ōno, the standard work sheet detailed cycle time and work sequence, as well as standard inventory, and this had changed little over the past forty years. "I have always said that it should take only three days to train new workers in proper work procedures."[53] The standard work methods employed

50. Ōno Taiichi, *Toyota Production System* (Cambridge: Productivity Press, 1988), pp. 10–11. The interesting point in Ōno's observations is that, despite the lack of a craft union, Toyota craft workers apparently displayed opposition to "multi-skilling."

51. Cusumano, *Japanese Automobile Industry*, pp. 274, 306.

52. The historical insights Ōno affords us deserve further comment and research. It is clear that, despite the absence of craft unions in Japan, machinists at Toyota had embraced the principle of "one machine–one machinist" that was so highly valued and guarded by machinists' unions in Great Britain, the United States, and Canada. Whether the union at Toyota failed to protect this tradition because it lacked a craft perspective or because adversarialism was declining is not clear.

53. Ōno Taiichi, *Toyota Production System*, pp. 21, 22.

by Ōno were developed through classical Taylorist methods such as time-and-motion studies.[54]

Finally, a word should be said about the fundamental antilabor bias of the Toyota system. According to Ōno, the Toyota production system views "economy in terms of manpower reduction and cost reduction. The relationship between these two elements is clearer if we consider a manpower reduction policy as a means of realizing cost reduction, the most critical condition for a business's survival and growth." Ōno traces this propensity to reduce the work force to Toyota's experience with the 1950 layoffs and labor dispute. "Immediately after its settlement, the Korean War broke out and brought special demands. We met these demands with just enough people and still increased production. This experience was valuable and, since then, we have been producing the same quantity as other companies but with 20 to 30 percent fewer workers."[55] Automation, in this context, must be labor-saving in the sense of reducing the labor force: "But if it is simply used to allow someone to take it easy, it is too costly."

Toyota's Quality Program

In 1960 Nissan won the coveted Deming Prize for quality control. This inspired Toyota to begin its own formal quality program in 1961. Even prior to this, however, Toyota managers had studied quality theory. Managers such as Ōno resisted adopting traditional quality programs that emphasized the establishment of extensive sampling and inspection departments. Keeping staffing levels to an absolute minimum was essential, and thus from early on quality assurance was integrated into line responsibilities.

Under the 1961 quality program, Toyota began to promote quality circles, but as with Suzuki's program the circles initially languished. From 1968 to 1971, however, a major overhaul occurred. The employee suggestion program and circle activities were merged: "Like QC circle attendance, the practice [suggestions] stopped being voluntary after the 1960s; managers set quotas, kept records of who submitted suggestions and used these data when determining bonuses. Staff superiors also gave out awards for suggestions and criticized workers who failed to contribute their share."[56] Workers at Toyota, as at Suzuki, were obliged to conform to performance standards that were not of their own making. By 1971 Toyota had nearly 2500 functioning circles, compared to only 169 in 1967.[57]

54. Cusumano, *Japanese Automobile Industry,* p. 272.
55. Ōno, *Toyota Production System,* pp. 53, 68.
56. Cusumano, *Japanese Automobile Industry,* p. 357.
57. Ibid., p. 336.

Based on information provided by Toyota, Cusumano estimated that 65 percent of circle activity was directed at quality control procedures, costs, and efficiency, while 35 percent was aimed at safety and equipment maintenance. Workers received instruction in the use of Pareto diagrams, cause-and-effect diagrams, check sheets, histograms, dispersion and control charts, and graphs. These were standard tools promoted in most of Japan's quality programs.

Sequence or periodization is an important tool in historical analysis. In both the Toyota and Suzuki examples many aspects of the production system, including traditional Fordist methods of assembly-line production, standardization of job routines, and so forth, developed prior to 1965. Ōno Taiichi himself documented that his innovations were resisted by Toyota workers. Yet, extensive employee involvement through the quality movement developed mainly after 1965. Given this sequence, it seems reasonable to hypothesize that the quality movement, rather than being principally a vehicle for workers' aspirations, was in fact a mechanism for transferring management values as articulated under lean production into the minds and hearts of production workers. Of course, the process was multidimensional and the quality circles had to allow some leeway for spontaneous worker input. But the early difficulties in the quality circle movement at both Suzuki and Toyota indicate that workers had little enthusiasm for internalizing their own exploitation. Thus control mechanisms, particularly the enterprise union and the performance-based wage and bonus system, were essential to the smooth functioning of the system.

The Quality Control Movement and Taylorism

Ishikawa Kaoru contends that Japan's quality control evolved out of a rejection of Taylorism. According to Ishikawa: "The Taylor system ignores the latent potential of workers, ignores the human element and, in treating workers like machines, invites workers to react against work."[58] Ishikawa's critique appears to reinforce the post-Fordist theory that Japan has ruptured with classical Taylorism. And in a certain sense, Japan has. To the degree that workers were involved in conceptual activities, there was a break with the Fordist norm whereby workers were assigned a strictly operative role. But to what extent did this happen and to what extent did these activities represent a free flow of workers' ideas? Is it possible that the context of worker participation influenced the nature of participation?

58. Ishikawa Kaoru, *Nihon teki hinshitsu kanri* [Japanese Quality Control] (Tokyo: Nikka Giren Shuppan Sha, 1988), p. 35.

Quality control as a concept originated in the United States with the expansion of mass production.[59] Visual controls were no longer sufficient to assure standards when huge volumes were involved. Walter Shewhart, an engineer with Bell Laboratories, designed a statistical control chart and sampling methods to verify quality standards. These techniques spread in the 1930s.

Statistical quality control (SQC) was introduced into Japan by the U.S. Occupation. The army was concerned with the poor state of the telecommunications industry and introduced SQC into the electrical industry beginning in 1948. In 1949 the Japan Management Association, the Japan Standards Association, and the Japan Union of Scientists and Engineers (JUSE) conducted research and education on statistical quality control. All three organizations played an important role in introducing Fordism to Japan, but in quality control the third came to play the predominant role.

JUSE was established in 1946 by scientists and engineers, many of whom formerly had been part of the prewar Greater Japan Engineering Association, an organization dissolved by the Occupation. In 1949 JUSE established a quality control research group and began to conduct educational seminars on quality issues. JUSE invited prominent U.S. experts on quality control, including W. E. Deming and J. M. Juran, to lecture in Japan. In 1951 JUSE established the Deming Prize, which was awarded annually to the enterprise with the best quality control program. JUSE and Japan's national radio broadcaster, NHK, cooperated in introducing QC lectures in its shortwave programs. This later expanded into regular radio and television programs.

The years 1960 to 1962 marked a watershed in the quality control movement in Japan. Quality control evolved from being a method of statistical sampling used by engineers into an employee involvement program with the express aim of introducing management techniques into the work process. This began in 1960, when JUSE published a two-volume QC manual for foremen in an attempt to bring quality control to the shop floor. The drive to entrench quality control at the workplace accelerated in 1962 with the publication of a monthly journal *Genba to QC* (The shop and QC). In the inaugural issue of this journal, JUSE called for the establishment of quality circles at the shop-floor level. At the same time, JUSE began organizing annual QC conferences for foremen. In 1963

---

59. This account of the origins of quality control and its development in Japan is based on Cusumano, *Japanese Automobile Industry*; Wada Mitsuhiro, ed., *Nihon kaibō 2* (Tokyo: Nihon Hōsō Shuppan Kyōkai, 1987); Kumazawa Makoto, *Nihon rōdōsha zō* (Tokyo: Chikuma Shobō, 1981); *Quality Control Circles at Work* (Tokyo: Asian Productivity Organization, 1984), a translation of *QC Sakuru Katsudō no Jissai ni Manabō* (Tokyo: JUSE, 1982); and Ishikawa Kaoru, *Nihon teki hinshitsu kanri*. An earlier edition of Ishikawa's work has been translated into English by David J. Lu and published as *What is Total Quality Control, The Japanese Way* (Englewood Cliffs, N.J.: Prentice-Hall, 1985).

JUSE established the QC Circle Headquarters at its offices, which then expanded in 1964 with the establishment of nine regional offices.

Ishikawa Kaoru was one of the prime movers behind JUSE's quality control programs. The son of Ishikawa Ichirō (the founder of JUSE and later president of Keidanren), Ishikawa Kaoru graduated from and taught at the University of Tokyo after the war. He joined JUSE's quality control research group in 1949, and over the next two decades he became Japan's foremost consultant on quality control.

Proponents of the post-Fordist and flexible specialization theories point to Ishikawa's views and to the small-group activity that occurs in quality circles as hallmarks of the end of, or an alternative to, Fordism. Almost all sources recognize that quality control systems originated in the United States. How did the two systems diverge and what were the specific differences? How spontaneous or autonomous were small group activities and, probably most important of all, what did workers learn in quality circles?

Ishikawa Kaoru points to six features that distinguish quality control in Japan from that in the United States:

1. company wide quality control; full participation in quality control
2. education and training in quality control
3. quality circle activities
4. QC audits (Deming prize and presidential audits)
5. use of statistical methods
6. nationwide promotion of quality control[60]

These points reflect the integrated and systemic approach to quality control in Japan, particularly the attempt to bring quality control activities to the shop floor. They do not, however, explain the conditions that allowed these features to emerge, nor do they speak directly to how the movement developed or what specific differences there were in the content of quality reform.

Although Ishikawa contends that the quality circle was a form of voluntary, autonomous worker participation, the Suzuki case study and Ishikawa's own conclusion contradict this contention. As indicated in the Suzuki materials, worker enthusiasm for circles quickly wore thin, and closer supervision over circles was required after the failed attempt to win the Deming prize. Only after circle activities were integrated into the performance evaluation system did they consolidate. Ishikawa points out that circles were first devised for foremen as places to study and apply quality control techniques. This process was one of foremen setting norms that workers, in the absence of any alternative, were obliged to follow. Fur-

60. Ishikawa Kaoru, *Nihon teki hinshitsu kanri*, pp. 52–53.

thermore, total participation of workers was clearly identified as the goal of the groups. Participation may have been described as "voluntary," but in fact norms were being established over which workers had little input. Another QC expert in Japan described the essence of the QC movement there in terms radically different from Ishikawa's emphasis on voluntarism:

> In the firm, there is the saying that subordinates listen only to the person who conducts the evaluation to establish bonus payments. That is exactly the way it works. Whatever the top people are thinking regulates what the firm's employees do. So, even though we're often told that Japanese companies work from the bottom up, when QC activities are begun, they must begin from the top down. If you look for the reason, the fact is that QC demands extra work on top of the normal, everyday work.[61]

Even Ishikawa alluded to the rigid hierarchical managerial structure as a reason why the QC movement had to have a strong top-down component: "In Japan the vertical line authority relationship is too strong for staff members such as QC specialists to have much voice in the operation of each separate division."[62] One does not have to extrapolate much to posit that quality control circles may have been an extension of managerial control onto the shop floor rather than a form of worker autonomy.

Examination of the content and scope of the quality control movement lends further evidence to this hypothesis. Despite his critique of Taylor, Ishikawa refers to Taylor's concept of control as the basis for the quality movement: "Dr. Taylor used to describe control with these words, 'plan—do—see.' What does the word 'see' mean? To Japanese middle school students, it simply means to look at, and that does not convey Taylor's meaning. So we have rephrased it as follows: 'plan—do—check—action' (PDCA)."[63] According to Ishikawa, planning is exclusively a management function: "Unless policies are determined, no goal can be established. These policies must be determined by top management." One of the key methods to implement the policies is standardization, another management function and characteristic of Taylorism. According to Ishikawa, "the task of establishing standardization or setting up regulations should be done in order to delegate authority to subordinates. The key to success is to standardize aggressively those things that are plainly understandable and to let a subordinate handle them."[64]

The relative importance of QC circles is also secondary to the overall movement, which is predominantly management controlled. The tools that the circles

---

61. Karatsu Hajime, "QC to kigyō no katsudō," in Wada, ed., *Nihon kaibo 2*, p. 116.
62. Ishikawa Kaoru, *Nihon teki hinshitsu kanri*, p. 128 (Lu's translation).
63. Ibid., pp. 82–83 (Lu's translation).
64. Ibid., pp. 83, 90.

are given—Pareto diagrams, cause-and-effect diagrams, stratifications, check sheets, histograms, scatter diagrams and graphs, and control charts—all indicate that management attempted to limit the content of quality circle activity to strictly traditional industrial engineering methods. From a theoretical standpoint, then, there are problems with the contention that quality circles in themselves represented a significant break with Taylorist norms.

On the practical level, the quality circle movement apparently embraced varied tendencies. As Kumazawa Makoto has noted, struggle can and has taken place in the circles.[65] Using evidence from the steel industry, Kumazawa notes five specific types of circle activities: improving skills and knowledge, improving safety and eliminating hard jobs, reducing downtime and defects, improving efficiency, and eliminating labor. From the author's perspective, the first four categories represent areas in which improvement can benefit workers and even contribute to solidarity on the shop floor.

Other scholars who have studied the issue in Japan have emphasized the coercive nature of the system, however. Kamii Yoshihiko, an authority on industrial relations in the automobile industry, concluded, "The quality circle movement is a management-based system of personnel and production control. Generally it is initiated by management and supervisory personnel are the organizers."[66] Nomura Masami, an expert on Toyota, also contends that the image of workers and managers working together to *kaizen* (continuously improve) the workplace is mistaken.[67] Nomura suggests that getting workers involved in quality circles is just a form of "human relations activity," and not a serious institution that actually changes the nature of work. According to Nomura, workers' shop-floor initiatives are restricted to small changes in existing processes, while upper management and engineers continue to make the major decisions affecting production norms.

Historically, even enterprise unions have criticized the quality movement. The electrical workers union (Denki Rōren), for example, stated in a 1976 policy paper that the quality movement had "problems and limits where it tended to become a means for controlling workers according to company goals."[68] Indicating that the quality movement was far from "joint," the paper stated, "What we aim for in workplace participation is the transformation of a unilateral management system into a joint labor-management approach, which is inevitable." In fact, however, few enterprise unions were able to gain much influence over quality control. And where there was some influence, such as at Nissan, it led to labor-

65. Kumazawa Makoto, *Nihon rōdōsha zō*, pp. 111–164.

66. Kamii Yoshihiko, "Minkan daikigyō no rōdō mondai" [Labor Issues in large private enterprises], in Totsuka and Tokunaga, *Gendai Nihon no rodo mondai*, p. 78.

67. Nomura Masami, *Toyotizumu*, p. 126.

68. As cited by Kamii Yoshihiko, "Minkan daikigyō no rōdō mondai," p. 86

management conflict and to the union eventually boycotting the company's *kaizen* (continuous improvement) P3 program (participation, productivity, and progress).[69]

In light of the material presented in this study and the introductory discussion about Taylorism and Fordism, I would contend that Japan's employers, in the automobile industry at least, did depart from Taylor's ideas in some respects. In other respects, however, they adopted and reinforced Taylor's perspective. The net effect, however, was on the whole to reproduce the type of jobs and job routines that were conventional in the U.S. automobile industry and may have contributed to the intensification of labor that was partially responsible for the high productivity of the Toyota system. Further research on this issue is necessary, but the limited evidence suggests that a review of the empowerment theory inherent in the post-Fordist thesis is called for. Critical studies must also review the theoretical underpinnings of the critique of Taylorism, however.

If, for example, we take David Montgomery's functional definition of Taylorism, we find an analytical framework shorn of some of the ideological baggage that was specific to the emergence of Taylorism in the context of turn of the century America. Thus Taylorism becomes "(1) centralized planning and routing of the successive phases in fabrication, (2) systematic analysis of each distinct operation, (3) detailed instruction and supervision of each worker in the performance of that worker's discrete task, and (4) wage payments carefully designed to induce each workers to follow those instructions."[70] If one accepts this definition then what becomes clear is that the difference between the Ford and Toyota systems is not what is done but rather who does it! Furthermore, one could argue, in fact, that the wage system in Japan, which paid for individual performance, corresponded more closely to general Taylorist principles than did the wage system that evolved in postwar automobile plants in the United States or Canada, where compensation was no longer directly tied to performance.

But for many, such a definition will not suffice. What of worker participation, job rotations, and worker input into the production process? Surely the boundaries of Taylorism have been ruptured. To respond to these legitimate queries, its seems necessary to review Braverman's notion that employer control of the labor process is derived primarily through forms of work organization, that is, through the separation of conception from execution in the labor process and managerial control of the former.

69. This account of the Nissan situation is based on Kamii's *Rōdō Kumiai no shokuba kisei* and his essay in Totsuka and Tokunaga, *Gendai Nihon no rōdō mondai*, pp. 78–88; and an unpublished paper by Watanabe Ben, "Difference in Union Leadership between Toyota and Nissan."

70. Montgomery, *The Fall of the House of Labour*, p. 217.

In general terms, worker participation schemes under the lean regimes, such as at Suzuki, did not challenge or erode managerial control, nor did they challenge the fundamental norms of Fordism. Standardization of job routines and cycle times continued to be used and were strictly adhered to, even though workers occasionally moved from job to job. We should not forget that Suzuki historians themselves pointed to the grueling convergence of assembly-line production methods.

However, one must accept the fact that lean production has begun, if only partially, to break down the traditional, ironclad division between conception and execution so ingrained in the United States and Canada. Taken in isolation, this was a progressive historical development, long overdue. But as long as the boundaries of conceptual activities remained within management guidelines, worker participation in quality or continuous improvement activities did not and could not fundamentally alter the regime. Although such activities led to constant innovation in the production process and improved efficiency, they never led to the worker-friendly changes that were undertaken, for example, in Volvo's Kalmar and Uddevalla plants in the 1970s and 1980s and which led to a fundamental break with the assembly line, repetitive job routines, short cycle times and so forth.[71] If management in Japan relinquished partial control over conceptual activities, it compensated for this by exerting control in ways that differed from American Fordist norms. Those alternative methods included the entente regarding productivity and management rights that they enjoyed with enterprise unions and the performance-based compensation system. In that sense, employers maintained control, although in ways that departed somewhat from Taylor's prescription. But such was to be expected. Japan's quality movement and the movement for scientific management took place at different times in different circumstances. It would have been difficult for Taylor to have conceived of integrating workers into his system of control because he faced and understood the craft workers' tradition of autonomy from management. He was also surrounded by the nascent, independent union movement that was challenging managerial control. Japan in the 1960s was quite different. Employers had by this time won almost complete control over the shop floor, and the hegemonic regime that evolved allowed management to actually integrate workers into its production system.

Thus, it was no accident that quality circles arose only in the 1960s even though Japan's quality movement began in the late 1940s. History allows us to perceive the contingent nature of lean production as a variation of Fordism. Employer control of the workplace remained tentative and unconsolidated even in the 1950s, and thus the circle movement could only make its start later, after the consolidation of the hegemonic regime.

71. See Berggren, *Alternatives to Lean Production*.

Lean Production: Variation on a Theme

Stephen Meyer has pointed out that Fordism is in a state of constant revision: "The classic Fordist paradigm existed for less than the decade after the mid-1910s; a more flexible Sloanist variation quickly superseded it in the mid-1920s."[72] In a sense, the Toyota system is another stage in the evolution of the Fordist regime. The specificity of this variation is its advanced flexibility and the institutionalization of the appropriation of workers' knowledge through employee involvement programs. If Ōno Taichi put less emphasis on automation in the Toyota system, it was because he had the opportunity to use labor flexibly and was unencumbered by the web of work rules that obliged automakers in the U.S. to turn to automation as a panacea for production. In Japan, however, extended managerial control over workers and the labor process, buttressed by enterprise unionism, a coercive wage system, and motivational educational campaigns, allowed Toyota and Suzuki to develop highly efficient production systems.

But a critical argument in this book is that these systems hardly disposed with Fordist methods of exploitation. Work remained dictated by the standard work sheet with detailed instructions on cycle times, work movements, and job standards. The time-and-motion expert and industrial engineer remained an integral part of the production complex. What was different, however, was that workers were obliged to participate in the constant modification of the labor process instead of being excluded and potentially subverting changes. The top-down nature of the quality movement at Suzuki, with foremen and lead hands playing the dominant role, highlighted the limits of worker autonomy in the Japanese automobile industry.

This overview of the evolving relationship between production methods and labor relations at Suzuki and Toyota leads me to postulate that, instead of deviating from Fordist mechanisms, the automobile manufacturers in Japan adapted them to the specific conditions they faced in the 1950s and 1960s. This led to a new stage of production methods, one that is now often referred to as lean production. Two specific features of the period left an indelible impression on the systems. First, the poverty of production (small markets, limited resources, high fixed costs) obliged Suzuki and Toyota, for example, to adapt mass production methods to small-batch production. This led to the flexible manufacturing techniques (just-in-time, kanban, quick line and equipment changes, and so forth) that many management scholars have pointed to as the wave of the future. But the intent and result of these innovations was to achieve mass production, not circumvent it. Production leveling attempted to integrate the multitude of product variations into a single production process and thereby gain the inherent advantage from the

---

72. Meyer, "Persistence of Fordism," pp. 73–99.

economies of continuous assembly-line production. The general trend in mass production, be it in automobile factories in Japan or in North America, was to attempt to move towards a state of continuous flow.

To summarize, the regimes that emerged at Suzuki and Toyota were examples of the lean variant of mass production. Five specific features distinguished the regime from traditional assembly line production.

1. Flexible mass production: the ability to integrate diverse product lines into a continuous-flow, assembly-line production process based on technical innovations including quick die changes, kanban system of direction, and so forth.
2. Segmented production complexes: a heavily tiered production complex with the production of parts and some assembly largely subcontracted to nonunion suppliers. Major differences existed in the working conditions in the assembly plants and in the subcontractors.
3. Modified Taylorist labor process: jobs and job routines were standardized, cycle times for routines were short, and the work boring and repetitive, as in traditional automobile plants. However, the lack of job descriptions as part of a union contract gave management the ability to rotate workers through a group of standardized, routine jobs and easily transfer workers from one section to another.
4. Continuous Waste Elimination: a critical feature of lean production was the articulation of the necessity to eliminate waste through continual modification (*kaizen*) of the production process. "Idle time" was identified as waste, and this led in many cases to an intensification of labor. It also led to the creation of the just-in-time aspects of parts delivery.
5. Employee Involvement: through the quality movement workers, particularly those in the core work force, were expected to embrace the standards of lean production and apply them through the process of continual improvement.

These were the key features of the lean production system as it evolved from 1945 to 1973. But this modified version of Fordism could not have evolved without elaborate control mechanisms that were part and parcel of the production regime. The performance-based wage and bonus system, the enterprise union, and job tenure for the core work force (a facet of the hegemonic regime discussed in more detail in later chapters) were essential to the development of lean production.

7 Miike 1960:
The Limits of Coercion

In 1960 workers and employers in Japan confronted one another in what was arguably the most intense labor-management conflict in postwar Japan—the Mitsui Miike coal mine dispute. The bitter struggle pitted 15,000 miners at the Miike coal shafts in Kyushu against the large Mitsui Mining enterprise, one of the jewels in the Mitsui conglomerate's crown. The issue appeared at first to be impending layoffs in the coal fields caused by the energy revolution. It soon became apparent, however, that Mitsui and Nikkeiren were out to destroy the Miike local union, one of the most militant in Japan and renowned for its control in the workplace. One miner was killed and hundreds seriously injured after the company attempted to reopen the mine with scab labor. The JCU and Sōhyō mobilized thousands of supporters who traveled the length of the country to bolster the Miike picket lines. Going to the Kyushu mine became both a labor pilgrimage and an adventure in combat. At one point over 10,000 police stood face to face with 20,000 picketers. Class struggle was indeed alive and, if the Miike experience is any indication, even thriving as late as 1960.

The intensity, scope, and duration of the Miike dispute have elevated this confrontation to a central position in historical accounts of the evolution of labor-management relations. In Nikkeiren's own official history, for example, the year 1960 is characterized as "an epoch-making time for the postwar labor movement with the 1960 antisecurity treaty battle and the Miike struggle at the center."[1] No serious account of postwar labor-management relations can avoid coming to grips with this tumultuous episode in industrial conflict.

An early version of this chapter was published in *Bulletin of Concerned Asian Scholars* 23 (October–December 1991): 30–43.

1. Nikkeiren, *Nikkeiren sanjū nen shi*, p. 348.

Prelude to Confrontation:
Production Politics and the Energy Crisis

Economics and politics were inextricably linked as factors precipitating the Miike confrontation. The political elements—the militancy of the Miike miners, their ability to control some aspects of the work process, and the example they had become for the labor movement during the 1950s—have been described in the previous chapter. The antipathy for Miike-style unionism expressed by Nikkeiren has also been noted. By late 1958 Nikkeiren had become more aggressive towards the Miike miners. It began to use the *Nikkeiren Times* to openly criticize both Mitsui Mining and Mitsubishi Coal for the long-term employment guarantees they had signed with their respective unions. Ironically, a former U.S. union official working in Japan, Benjamin Martin, repeated Nikkeiren's criticism in a scathing attack on the Miike union published in an unprecedented full-page feature article in the English-language daily *Japan Times* in September.[2] As events unfolded, the political antagonism between Nikkeiren and the coalminers' union would determine the specific character of the 1960 dispute. Nikkeiren could not accept the fact that Mitsui had negotiated a long-term employment agreement with the Miike union and considered the nascent workshop struggle movement a threat to employers everywhere.

The initial events that precipitated the confrontation, however, were largely economic.[3] An economic recession and a decline in the price of imported oil in 1958 created problems for the previously protected coal industry. In 1955 the government had imposed oil tariffs and restricted construction of oil converters to protect the domestic coal industry. The government had also demanded that the industry rationalize, concentrate production in large, efficient mines, and become competitive with oil as an energy source.

The results between 1955 and 1958, however, were the opposite of what had been envisaged. Coal operators attempted to take advantage of rising coal prices in the wake of the 1956 Suez crisis. Mines in fact proliferated, prices rose, and coal companies pocketed substantial profits. Between 1955 and 1957, the price of regular thermal coal jumped nearly 20 percent from ¥5,537 to ¥6,436 per ton. Prof-

---

2. *Japan Times*, 1 September 1958. Martin accused the union of ultraleftism and using the negotiating process for political gains. Sakisaka Itsurō, the noted scholar and supporter of the Miike union, actually dates the beginning of the attack on the Miike local from the publication of this article. According to Sakisaka, Martin visited Miike in 1958 but never met or spoke with any of the Miike union's officials. Martin left Japan in 1960 and became a United States Information Agency field officer in Chile in 1961.

3. Economic policy was, however, politically determined. For a more detailed discussion on coal policy, see Laura E. Hein, *Fueling Growth: The Energy Revolution and Economic Policy in Postwar Japan* (Cambridge: Harvard University Press, 1990) as well as the next chapter.

its for eighteen major coal companies rose from an aggregate ¥4.5 billion in 1955 to ¥12.4 billion in 1957.[4]

With the onset of a short recession in late 1957, coal stockpiles began to rise, but coal companies attempted to keep prices high, sparking an outcry from major coal consumers including the steel, electric power, shipping, and rail industries. In August 1958 these latter groups formed the Federation to Oppose Crude and Heavy Oil Tariffs (Genjūyū Kanzei Hantai Dōmei) in a bid to lobby for importation of cheap oil. By the fall of 1958, coal operators were under heavy pressure for reductions in coal prices, and this prompted them to consider serious rationalization measures including large-scale layoffs of miners.

At the same time, however, coal operators insisted on continued protection from oil imports. The Federation of Economic Organizations (Keizai Dantai Rengō Kai, or Keidanran) intervened at this point to mediate the dispute between coal producers and consumers. It formed a discussion group of the concerned parties in the fall of 1958. Deliberations continued for over a year, but coal producers were no match against consumer industries, particularly the steel industry, which had come to occupy a strategic position within Japan's industrial structure by this time. In late 1959, the government was obliged to reverse its energy policy and allow major oil imports. Even prior to this, however, the coal companies came under intense pressure for price reductions. They reacted by introducing serious rationalization measures, which would have a dramatic impact on employment (the discussion of coal policy is further developed in Chapter 8).

Red Ink at Miike

Mitsui Mining announced losses of almost two billion yen for the first half of 1958 despite two profitable years in the preceding period. In September the company took the extraordinary measures of cutting executive and staff salaries and then refused to pay its workers the year-end bonuses that had been negotiated as part of the master agreement between the JCU and the Coal Operations Association that fall (the anticipated average ¥22,000 bonus was cut to ¥14,000). By this point reporters had caught scent of the impending crisis in the coal industry. In early October, the *Asahi* newspaper published a major article anticipating Mitsui's plans to deal with its losses. The Miike local responded by publishing its own assessment of the situation: "The company, from experience in previous struggles, will no doubt come up with new tactics. Recent labor battles have been plagued by organizational splits due to the formation of second unions, so we believe the company's main strategy will be to divide our organization and split the fight.[5]

4. Figures for prices and profits are from Mitsui, *Shiryō: Miike sōgi*, pp. 434, 436.
5. Ibid., p. 439.

The company formally tabled its "first company reconstruction proposal" (dai ichiji kigyō saiken'an) on January 19, 1959. The proposal included

increasing productivity by strengthening managerial control and discipline at the work sites,

halting recruitment of miners as stipulated in previous memorandums of agreements,

reducing expenditures by postponing or canceling construction projects for housing, a hospital, baths, daycare, sewers, and roads,

implementing reductions in labor-related expenses by cutting overtime,

if necessary, reducing the workforce by 6,000 through "voluntary retirement" (*kibō taishokusha bōhū*).[6]

Both the Mitsui Miners Federation (MMF) and the Mitsui Staff Federation (MSF) rejected the company proposals. Instead they resolved to struggle together against any deterioration in working conditions, to defend democratization of the workplace and residential areas, and to oppose layoffs. The two unions established a joint action committee in mid-February with the express objective of avoiding any splits in the face of the Mitsui proposals.

On the national level, the JCU attempted to link the fight against layoffs with that spring's wage negotiations: "The 1959 spring wage offensive is integrally related with resolving the fight against Mitsui's rationalization measures. These are not separate struggles and must be fought as one."[7] After a series of short work stoppages in March, the JCU launched an all-out strike over wages and the Mitsui layoffs on March 23.

The Central Labor Relations Board intervened at this point with an offer to mediate the wage issue. The JCU accepted the offer of mediation but added a stipulation that no wage agreement would be accepted until the Mitsui negotiations were satisfactorily concluded. The CLRB brought forward its wage proposal on March 31. Negotiations between Mitsui Mining and the two Mitsui unions (MMF and MSF) as well as with the JCU resumed at this time.

On April 6 the two parties reached a deal whereby the unions would accept voluntary retirements and reductions in welfare expenditures and Mitsui would withdraw its proposals to impose workplace control and cut back on overtime. In retrospect, this compromise constituted a key concession on the part of the JCU that would reverberate throughout the coal fields and undermine any basis for common action by coalminers. By accepting the voluntary retirements at Mitsui, the JCU had provided an opening through which other major companies soon

6. For the complete proposal see ibid., pp. 442–448.
7. JCU directive no. 44, 21 February 1959. Cited in Miike Kumiai, *Miike nijū nen*, p. 252.

poured. The Mitsubishi, Sumitomo, Furukawa, and Yūbetsu coal companies submitted voluntary layoff proposals to their respective unions one month after the April 6 agreement. Most unions accepted these proposals, as had the Miike union, but there was a key difference. Because of its militant tradition, the Miike local could undermine the layoffs by advising its members not to come forward to take early retirement, but this was not the case in the other mines. As a result, the employers' attack would come to focus on the Mitsui miners particularly in the Miike mine. Nor did the compromise stop Mitsui from trying to reimpose managerial discipline in the Miike mines. Ten days after initialing the April 6 agreement, Mitsui fired the head of the Mikawa workshop council for allegedly impeding production.[8]

Mitsui recruited voluntary retirees at its six mines during May and June. The company's goal was to get 6,000 miners to retire, but only 1,324 stepped forward to take the severance package. Staff, on the other hand, came forward in droves: 586 accepted early retirement, 26 more than Mitsui had called for. The company estimated that the low level of voluntary retirees among its miners would mean its savings over a six-month period would amount to only ¥862 million, far short of the ¥2.3 billion it had projected.

Contradictions among Managers

The inability of Mitsui to quickly implement its rationalization program, combined with escalating pressure for price reductions from coal consumers, created a new set of circumstances and brought new players into the fray. For this reason, the fight at Miike contains interesting lessons in the dynamics of class alignment.

After the failure of the April 6 agreement, powerful business leaders such as the president of Mitsui Bank, Satō Kiichirō, and Nikkeiren's Maeda Hajime began to intervene directly in the Miike dispute. As early as 1958 Nikkeiren had singled out the Miike union as a hot spot that required immediate attention. This position was reiterated at Nikkeiren's two regular conventions in April and October 1959. The active role of women within the JCU prompted Maeda Hajime to remark at the latter meeting: "There are some mines where women and youth groups are extremely strong, and in these places we can't guarantee major incidents will not occur that could quickly escalate into social unrest if things are not handled properly."[9]

Nikkeiren intervention at Miike brought it into conflict with Mitsui Coal's head of personnel, Yamamoto Asamichi. Essentially the dispute boiled down to

8. Ibid., p. 259.
9. Nikkeiren, *Nikkeiren jigyō hōkoku, 1959* [Nikkeiren annual report, 1959] (Tokyo: Nikkeiren, 1959), p. 61.

important tactical issues—Satō and Maeda wanted to open a frontal assault against the Miike local, while Yamamoto hoped to use informal mechanisms to purge Miike of its militant union. In his memoirs Maeda Hajime described his view of the Miike local in the following terms:

> There were two kinds of poisons that were eating at the roots of Mitsui Mining. One was the power of the union in the mines—they were so strong they could defy foremen's orders. The other was the influence the union had in the company residences—they were strong enough to eliminate company influence. Labor relations at Miike generally were unstable due to syndicalist ideas and action, and it was hopeless to expect a return to sound management without resolving this problem.[10]

Yamamoto later expounded on the factional fracas in a roundtable included in Nikkeiren's official history:

> Well, in the end analysis it became, as Ōta Kaoru put it, a general confrontation between capital and labor, but we had no such intention. We thought we had to resolve the disputes that arose by ourselves. We worked with the view that one way or another we had to stop the hemorrhaging on both sides and resolve the situation peacefully and quickly. Then, well, this is linked to Nikkeiren's motto 'managers: be strong and fair,' you see. My feeling was that we were entrusted with an industry which, as I had been told by Sakurada, was essential and therefore a national institution, and so workers and employers had to get together and put the industry before anything else. [The union] fought over issues it thought important, I guess, but if the company went under then the union members would lose their livelihood, and so this was the basis for my actions. But this issue of being a public institution was a little weird within the company. One thing was that we couldn't unite within the company. Then Nikkeiren—and this was proper education, mind you—brainwashed managers. The idea that managers had to purge the insolent types—like those from the red purge, the types who obstructed production or business—was pushed pretty thoroughly. Take my experience, for example. The type like Satō Kiichirō, who was head of Mitsui Bank at the time. I think he was a one of those very influential leaders through his close relationship with Keidanren and Nikkeiren. To us executive types he used to tell us in no uncertain terms that 'you'd better get rid of those rotten apples quick.' . . . As far as the dispute went *the fundamental issue became the firing of three hundred production obstructionists, but I never agreed and considered it an issue of layoffs due to economic reasons.*[11]

As events unfolded, Yamamoto's position became increasingly tenuous and the Satō-Maeda line of attack won the support of a majority of Mitsui directors in-

10. Maeda Hajime, "Nikkeiren ni ikita nijū nen," p. 364.
11. Nikkeiren, *Nikkeiren sanjū nen shi*, pp. 744–745 (emphasis added).

cluding the president of Mitsui Mining, Kuriki Kan. Nikkeiren's own historians described the dynamics thus: "the view that it was necessary to avoid a showdown with the Miike union held sway within the company at the beginning. However, once the plan for a showdown was decided on, the anti-agreement view triumphed with president Kuriki leading the way. This was due, among other things, to the fact that the other coal operators had prepared an unprecedented system of support and cooperation."[12]

As stockpiles of coal increased in late 1958, the government moved to have coal operators cut back production. It imposed an overall 20 percent cut in production levels and assigned specific quotas to the major mining companies that were to begin May 1, 1959, and continue for six months. At the same time oil prices continued to drop. In early April a Keidanren group that had been studying energy policy announced that while a thorough review of energy policy was necessary, it expected the coal operators to take immediate measures to rationalize over the interim. After mulling over the situation during the summer, coal operators met with labor representatives in September and informed them that they expected to lay off 100,000 of the 180,000 miners working for the eighteen largest coal companies.

The structural impact of the coal crisis elevated the Mitsui situation to a central place within employers' policy considerations. This was much in evidence at Nikkeiren's October meeting. The chairman of the Federation of Automobile Employers rose to present an emergency resolution on the coal crisis, which concluded: "To us this is not an issue which can be resolved by the coal industry alone. It will have important repercussions on every industrial sector, and we believe Nikkeiren must go all out and extend a helping hand and through concrete measures work to bring about a fundamental resolution."[13] Various factions of business interests, including the strategic steel and automobile sectors, had issued a mandate for Nikkeiren to bring about a speedy resolution of the coal crisis. In the fall of 1959 Maeda and Satō Kiichirō used this mandate to increase the pressure on Mitsui Mining and force it to take on the Miike union.

In July, Satō turned the screws a notch tighter, cutting off any further funds to cover Mitsui Mining's operating expenses. Summer bonuses went unpaid and the union rebuffed a Mitsui offer to pay the deferred wages in instalments. Mitsui implemented the plan despite the union's opposition. In September the coal operators met to discuss aid to Mitsui in the event of a work stoppage. The presidents of the major coal companies resolved not to take advantage of any such incident to steal Mitsui customers and promised Mitsui to provide coal shipments to cover its orders.[14]

---

12. Ibid., p. 355.
13. Nikkeiren, *Nikkeiren jigyō hōkoku, 1959*, p. 100.
14. Mitsui, *Shiryō: Miike sōgi*, pp. 551–552.

Hard Line Wins Out

At the Mitsui Miners Federation's convention in July 1959 the executive sub-mitted a proposal to deal with the layoffs. The proposal was a compromise that would allow Mitsui to recruit voluntary retirees while the union would refrain from obstructing production increases. Kōno Kazuo recalled: "At that point, the union leadership of the other five mines and Miike were at odds. The leaders of the other five mines were thinking that it would even be okay to make concessions in working conditions as long as layoffs could be avoided."[15] The proposal was ba-sically an attempt to cut a deal with Yamamoto that would prevent a full-scale as-sault against the union. It was predicated on the view that Mitsui would, in return, not resort to designated layoffs or firings (shime kaikō). The MMF vowed to wage an all-out battle if Mitsui Mining did resort to designated discharges. Del-egates from the Miike local of the MMF disputed this approach, however. They asserted that layoffs were imminent and interpreted the rationalization program as basically a political struggle targeting the MMF and the JCU. The final com-promise was a vague resolution to fight the company and, if the central struggle committee judged it feasible, to defeat the layoffs.

With pressure from Nikkeiren intensifying, Yamamoto attempted to avoid an all-out battle by submitting a second reconstruction proposal to the union. This proposal was tougher than the first, calling for 4,580 layoffs with set criteria for deciding who would be laid off. The layoffs would affect

those whose job was not essential for family support,
those unsuitable for work,
those considered unsuitable for collective life,
those in poor health,
those over 52,
those under 25,
those with less than five years continuous service.[16]

Each Mitsui mine had a quota for retirees (Miike was expected to lay off 2,210) and those who the company believed met the criteria would be "advised to retire" (*taishoku kankoku*). The new proposal also contained provisions for Mitsui to cut back on social benefits, overtime, and safety expenditures, and it also called for splitting off the machine shop from the Mitsui Mining operations.

This second reconstruction plan traced a very fine line indeed. The traditional approach to layoffs was to make a general appeal for voluntary retirees and then

15. Kōno Kazuo, interview by author, 21 March 1990.
16. Mitsui, *Shiryō: Miike sōgi*, p. 484.

resort to "shoulder tapping" (*kata tataki*) to get rid of unwanted employees. Concretely, an employee's supervisor or mentor would have an informal chat with the prospective worker, advising him/her that retirement would be best. This was the essence of the April 6 agreement. The strong Miike union presence on the shop floor, however, prevented this strategy from working. Thus for practical purposes and to appease Nikkeiren, Yamamoto had formulated strict criteria for deciding who would be laid off.

While Yamamoto continued to insist that this was not an attempt to break the union, the Miike local and the MMF saw things differently. Discussions on the second reconstruction proposal broke down on September 10. The JCU struggle committee called for rotating strikes at Miike and at two other mines beginning September 16 and for escalating limited strikes at fourteen major coal companies beginning October 1. The MMF reasserted its determination to reject designated discharges. It promised to guarantee the livelihood of those who refused to retire and called on union members to prepare for a company-inspired attempt to create a scab union.

In early October the JCU held its twenty-third convention in Tokyo. By this point it was apparent that 100,000 or more jobs were on the line. Delegates demanded a halt to the rationalization program and called for continued protection from cheap oil imports. The JCU had already gone on record as supporting voluntary retirements as an acceptable form of layoffs both at Mitsui and at Mitsubishi mines. Thus delegates left the convention with a mixed bag of resolutions calling for a general strike, shop-floor actions, and united class action, knowing full well that at individual mines deals were already being cut that would allow layoffs to proceed. This confusion would undermine the possibility of united action and eventually lead to the isolation of the Miike local of the MMF.

Discussions between Mitsui and the MMF broke off on October 7, and Mitsui began unilaterally to implement its second reconstruction proposal. At Miike the union's strength in the mines precluded "shoulder tapping," so the company resorted to dropping leaflets from airplanes calling on miners who met the retirement criteria to step forward. At its other mines, the company was able to exert direct pressure. The MMF, however, maintained its opposition to the forced retirements and backed up its opposition with a notice that those who accepted the notice would be subject to union disciplinary procedures. Mitsui reached its layoff objectives only at the Tagawa and Yamano mines, while at the others it fell far short, recruiting less than one-third of its target. Only 142 miners accepted retirement at Miike, far below the 2,210 volunteers the company had sought.[17] Mitsui was able to convince machine shop workers to split from the Miike local, however. At this point, the staff union also applied to the JCU for leave to settle with Mitsui.

17. Ibid., p. 518.

Negotiations resumed briefly on November 10 but quickly broke down. At this point the Central Labor Relation Board again attempted to mediate. On November 21, CLRB chairman Nakayama Ichirō tabled a seven-point plan that called for labor-management cooperation in raising production, "voluntary retirements" without company pressure or union interference, and further discussions if the retirement quotas were not met. By this time the Yamamoto faction within Mitsui Mining had lost control to the hard-line faction led by Kuriki and backed by Nikkeiren. On November 25 Mitsui formally rejected the Nakayama mediation proposal as a basis for resolving the dispute at Miike, although it indicated it would apply the mediation guidelines at its other mines.[18]

The historical record shows that Maeda Hajime and Satō Kiichirō were intimately involved in ensuring that Mitsui would reject the mediation proposal for Miike. Maeda recalled his fight with Yamamoto Asamichi over the proposal:

He [Yamamoto] probably thought that my opposition to the Nakayama mediation proposal was a big stumbling block, so he came to my office at Nikkeiren to give me an earful. In essence he said, "The problems at Mitsui Mining have to be resolved by the company itself. Interfering statements from the outside by third parties such as Nikkeiren are only causing problems, so please stop." But it was just at that time that Ōta Kaoru first made his statement that the Miike dispute was a fight between general labor and general capital. The issue had gotten to the point where it was now a social, no, even a national issue.[19]

Maeda and Satō had used their influence to convince the majority of Mitsui Mining directors that a showdown with the Miike local was inevitable.[20] Mitsui president Kuriki informed the various parties that the problem at Miike was not one simply of numbers but of "quality" and that three hundred "production obstructionists" had to be included in the layoffs. Of course these obstructionists were in reality the union's shop-floor organizers and activists, who constituted the very heart of the union. Having clearly set forth the company's objective, Mitsui Mining could not turn back from a head-on confrontation with the Miike miners.

While CLRB mediation was going on, Sōhyō held its thirteenth special convention. The coalminers' struggle and opposition to the proposed renewal of the Japan-U.S. Mutual Security Treaty (Ampō) were central issues at the convention. Delegates resolved to support the JCU financially by implementing a special levy of ¥300 per affiliated member by April 1960. Sōhyō leaders, including Ōta Kaoru and Iwai Akira, visited Miike on December 2 and pledged one billion yen in fi-

18. Ibid., p. 529.
19. Maeda Hajime, "Nikkeiren ni ikita nijū nen," p. 364.
20. For an analysis of the factions within Mitsui Coal, see Hirai Yōichi and Yamamoto Kiyoshi, "Mitsui Miike tankō sōgi ni tsuite," *Shakai Kagaku Kenkyū* 40, no. 3 (September 1988): 138–140.

nancial support. This visit was followed by a delegation of thirty-two leaders from many of Japan's largest unions who brought with them ¥75 million in cash. They assured the Miike local that they would raise another ¥1.8 billion in loans if necessary.

The same day that Ōta and Iwai visited Miike, Mitsui Mining mailed redundancy notices to 1492 Miike miners. Included in the list were 670 union activists, of whom 370 were union officials and 300 were shop-floor activists.[21] In the following days, the Miike union responded by organizing general meetings in the regional and workplace councils, which culminated in a twenty-four-hour general strike on December 8 (this was the seventeenth strike since the start of rotating strikes that fall). On the day of the strike, the union organized a large demonstration, which even according to company documents attracted at least 30,000 miners, family members, and supporters. Thousands cheered as the layoff notices were burned along with effigies of Mitsui president Kuriki.

Of 1492 workers mailed notices, 214 accepted the notices while 1,279 declined. On December 10 Mitsui mailed final notices to those who had declined the invitation to retire; failure to accept the severance package by December 15 would result in the miners being fired. On December 15, Mitsui discharged 1,202 miners including over 600 union activists. Of those fired 120 were Japan Socialist Party members and 31 Japan Communist Party members.[22] The Miike local continued its tactics of slowdowns and rotating strikes, and on January 7, 1960, it ordered its members to begin a disobedience campaign to protest the firings.

Mitsui Mining, with the backing of other coal operators, the Mitsui Bank, and Nikkeiren, had decided the time was ripe to destroy the militant Miike union. The company had not forgotten its bitter defeat at the hands of the Miike local in 1953. Its resolve had hardened over the years as the Miike miners had won further victories. The impending coal crisis had opened a window of opportunity. On January 25 Mitsui locked out all the miners at its Miike facilities except at the port. The union responded in kind, embarking on an all-out strike including the port facilities. A war had begun.

Phase One: Isolation and Division

By locking out workers at Miike but not at its other mines, Mitsui Mining and Nikkeiren revealed their true intentions—isolate the Miike local and crush it. They hoped to kill two birds with one stone: prevent a fightback against the im-

21. Shimizu Shinzō, "Mitsui Miike sōgi" [The Miike dispute], in Shiota Shōbe, Fujita Wakao, ed., *Sengo Nihon no rōdō sōgi*, rev. ed. (Tokyo: Ocha no Mizu Shobō, 1977), p. 522.
22. Sakisaka Itsurō, *Miike nikki* [Miike diary] (Tokyo: Shisei Dō, 1961), p. 117.

minent rationalization in the coal industry and root out a source of adversarial unionism that had begun to spread in other unions through the workshop struggle movement.

The fact that Mitsui moved to lock out its employees in January clearly indicates that it felt it had successfully isolated the Miike local union. As the battle developed, Mitsui attempted to split the Miike local and thereby get rid of what it considered the rotten apple in its union barrel once and for all. As events unfolded, this proved more difficult than Mitsui had anticipated. It was one thing to get the apple out of the barrel, quite another to crush it.

At first, the Miike local and the JCU seemed to underestimate the problems in the dispute. At the JCU convention in February, delegates resolved to provide further financial backing for the Miike local. Members of affiliates would be assessed an additional ¥600 per month (¥1,000 for MMF local members). On February 26 the JCU'S struggle committee even came to the unlikely conclusion that conditions were turning in the miners' favour. According to directive 194, JCU members were to prepare for a strike because various factors were converging that would provide an opportune time for industrial actions. These factors included a decrease in coal stockpiles, an upsurge in the mass movement against the security treaty, and increasing momentum in spring offensive activities.[23] The committee resolved to call an all-out coalminers' strike at the earliest possible moment.

In the meantime, however, divisions within union ranks began to make themselves felt. On March 3, the Mitsui Staff Federation communicated to the JCU struggle committee its refusal to pay the ¥600 per member assessment to support the Miike miners. One week later this fissure in union solidarity cracked wide open when opposition forces in the Miike local presented the executive officers with a petition calling for a special general meeting of the local executive to consider ways to end the dispute quickly. Of 254 members of the executive 96 had signed the petition. Local officials had no choice but to accede to the request, and a special executive meeting was set for March 15.

On the day of the meeting, thousands of miners and supporters from both sides gathered at the meeting hall. The dissident faction submitted a four-point proposal calling for an end to the strike and a reopening of negotiations; acceptance of voluntary retirement by those dismissed, for whom the company would help find new jobs and cover interim living expenses; legal redress for those who disagree with retirement; and a general poll of the membership on their proposal. A majority of the executive refused this request and the opposition left the hall.

On March 17 the opposition convened a special meeting at which time they founded the New Miike Mineworkers Union (Miike Tankō Shin Rōdō Kumiai). They immediately communicated with Mitsui Mining and cited an initial mem-

---

23. Miike Kumiai, *Miike nijū nen shi*, p. 327.

bership roster of 3,076 or about 20 percent of the workforce. The company immediately recognized the new union and negotiations between the two parties led to a March 24 agreement to start up production. All the issues in the dispute were left to future deliberations, the old contract was recognized and the lockout lifted.

That Mitsui Mining was intimately involved in the attempt to split the union there seems to be little doubt. To avoid the appearance of direct involvement that might result in legal action, however, Mitsui called on the services of professional union busters such as Mitamura Shirō. According to union sources, dissident elements in the Miike local attended special lectures and schools organized by Mitamura. Just prior to the creation of the second union, 280 miners attended a "labour university short course" in Fukuoka on March 12–13, sponsored by Mitamura.[24] Mitamura himself was closely aligned with other ultraright factions such as Nabeyama Sadachika, which had been involved in breaking the Nissan union in 1953. While the evidence remains circumstantial, union claims that Mitsui used Mitamura to organize the breakaway union seem valid in light of the fact that Mitsui Mining itself admits using Mitamura to organize anticommunist "lectures" in the early 1950s.[25]

In any event, the split in the Miike union had dire consequences. The day after the split occurred the Mitsui staff union (MSF) announced its intention to secede from the JCU and resolved to support the breakaway union at Miike. The JCU responded by issuing directive 203, which called for a general strike to begin in all coal mines on April 5 with the MMF going out earlier on April 1. This proposal met with stiff opposition within non-Miike locals of the MMF. At a meeting of the MMF struggle committee on March 26–27, the union decided that it was unable to implement directive 203. The Miike local, isolated within its own union, faced disaster. Although the strike would continue for another five months, the union's ability to exert economic pressure through concerted solidarity was thoroughly undermined.

In contrast to the divisions within the union movement, management solidified its ranks in the early period. In the months leading up to the lockout, Satō Kiichirō and Nikkeiren had set up an elaborate support network for Mitsui Mining. This network played a key role in minimizing the potential economic impact of a shutdown at Miike. It should be pointed out, however, that this network could succeed only to the extent that workers allowed.

By cutting off operating funds to Mitsui Mining in the summer of 1959, Satō Kiichirō played an instrumental role in forcing a showdown at the Miike mines. Once Mitsui Mining had resolved to lock out its employees, however, Satō was

24. Ibid., p. 330.
25. Mitsui, *Shiryō: Miike sōgi*, pp. 113–118.

more than willing to turn on the financial taps. Using his position as president of Mitsui Bank, Satō helped form a consortium of eight banks to underwrite the costs of the melee. Over the course of the struggle these banks provided Mitsui Mining with ¥6.9 billion in funds in three instalments.[26]

Coal operators, meanwhile, attempted to sabotage the JCU's attempt to raise strike funds among its affiliates by refusing to include the special Miike levy as part of regular dues checkoff.[27] At the same time, the other coal companies provided coal to Mitsui customers. Table 23 indicates how Mitsui was able to use the financing and support of other companies to replace coal normally shipped from Miike. Noteworthy is the fact that throughout the course of the struggle, Mitsui was able to cover nearly half of the normal Miike shipments from its other mines and through market purchases. The fact that miners at Mitsui's other coal mines remained on the job after Mitsui locked out the Miike miners seriously undermined the Miike union. Ironically, this breach occurred within an enterprise-based federation, where union solidarity was supposed to exist.

In his assessment of the Miike struggle, Shimizu Shinzō underscored a number of points which led to the isolation of the Miike local.[28] He noted that adversarial unionism had developed unequally within locals of the MMF. Indicative of this was the 1956 harmonization struggle, at which time the Miike local had gone on strike alone. This in itself did not isolate the Miike local, but its actions at the time highlighted the potential divisions within the enterprise federation. More serious, however, was the fact that Miike activists were perceived by other locals as being somewhat arrogant. Kōno Kazuo, secretary-general of the Miike local until 1958, at which time he became secretary-general of the MMF, recalled that the workshop struggle movement had created divisions because of its uneven development: "Other locals were also involved but not at the Miike level."[29] According to Kōno, this dynamic, the different levels of consciousness and mobilization among the union locals, left Miike vulnerable to criticism, justified or not. The Japanese proverb "The protruding nail will be hammered" aptly discribes part of the dynamic that came into play within the union federation. As much as the workshop struggle had been cited as a potential model for other unions, it had not consolidated within the MMF itself and this left the Miike local vulnerable to divisions within both the local and the enterprise federation. For Mitsui, the divisions meant it contiuned to have access to coal from its other mines.

Instead of overcoming these problems in the period leading up to the lockout, the Miike local failed to develop closer links with other locals. As Kōno recalled,

26. Nikkeiren, *Nikkeiren sanjū nen shi*, p. 357.
27. Ibid., p. 357.
28. Shimizu Shinzō, "Mitsui Miike sōgi," pp. 507–511.
29. Kōno Kazuo, interview.

Table 23. Replacement coal supplies, by source, July 1959–August 1960

Source	Tons
Replacement coal secured by Mitsui	
Hokkaido Ashibetsu	133,950
Yamano, Tagawa	133,911
Market purchases	52,178
Replacement coal secured by major coal operators	
From supplies at hand	47,547
Market purchases	18,246
Imports	
United States	23,696
Australia	96,341
Kyushu Power	
Market purchases	131,252
Total	637,121

Source: Mitsui, Shiryō: Miike sōgi (Tokyo: Nihon Keieisha Dantai Renmei Kōhō Bu, 1963), p. 551.

part of the reason for the divisions among the locals was objective: "The other mines were probably going to close, but the Miike mine was blessed with extensive resources, so that even in the wildest dreams the idea of closing, well, that wasn't really on.[30] Furthermore, the local was late off the mark in building a regional solidarity network within the Ōmuta region, where the Miike mine was located. Mitsui Mining, on the other hand, moved quickly to use its influence to build a citizens' group in the area that provided substantial support for the company during the course of the struggle. Shimizu also points to the weakness that the JCU showed in not developing the antirationalization struggle as a mass political movement for the nationalization of the coal mines in 1959. The absence of such a movement meant that coalminers' struggles could be isolated at the enterprise level, where coal companies could easily exploit sectional differences among coalminers.

These points all appear valid, but another factor, important in comparative terms, was the informal mechanisms that determined layoff procedures. Employers' attitudes towards layoffs were beginning to change. They continued to maintain that employment levels were purely management determined, but as the JPC three productivity principles adopted in 1955 suggest, large corporations in Japan were urged to avoid layoffs as a first resort in the case of economic downturns. Early retirement was the preferred route if job reductions were necessary. While this had some obvious advantages for core workers, it had the disadvantage of al-

30. Ibid.

lowing management wide discretion in deciding who was to be laid off. Early retirement was supposedly at the employee's discretion, but as we have seen, management could use shoulder tapping as an informal means to coerce unwanted employees to retire. A strong union, such as at Miike, could use its influence as a counterweight to management pressure. But without such a counterweight, management maintained tremendous power in deciding who would be laid off. Once the MMF and the JCU had agreed to allow voluntary retirements, it undermined any further possible basis of unity among coalminers.

In North America, on the other hand, employers resorted to layoffs as a quick remedy to economic distress. However, management was also obliged to strictly observe seniority provisions regarding layoffs. Seniority provisions severely limited employer discretion in deciding who was to be laid off, and this provided union activists with a strong measure of protection from employer repression. It was therefore much more difficult for a unionized American firm to use layoffs as the chief means to terminate union activists, for example.

In some ways, the struggle at Miike reflected the fact that the production regime in some parts of the coal industry had begun to defy the emerging orthodoxy regarding job tenure. First, the Miike miners had won, it should be recalled, a ten-year job security agreement in 1955 that Mitsui had wanted to tear up. Second, defending the agreement implied defying Mitsui's attempt to resort to early retirement as a layoff mechanism. The union's defiance in turn blocked Mitsui Mining from using informal means for forcing through layoffs. Mitsui thus attempted to set out strict criteria for deciding who was to be laid off, and when this failed it, resorted to naming names. In pursuing these actions, Mitsui exposed its intent to break the Miike union.

Phase Two: Breakaway Union

Having adroitly used the early retirement convention to undermine the potential for solidarity between the Miike local and other unions, Mitsui Mining had succeeded in splitting the Miike local. The JCU was left reeling from the split and from its inability to implement its own directives. Immediately after rescinding the strike order, the JCU applied to the CLRB to have it mediate both the Miike dispute and wage negotiations for all coalminers. With the momentum in its favor, however, Mitsui Mining declined to enter into any further mediation and said so to the CLRB chairman. Despite Mitsui's intransigence, the CLRB announced its intention to mediate, but only on the condition that the wage issue be dealt with separately from the Miike dispute. Once again, by disassociating the wage dispute from Miike, another opportunity for united action on the part of coalminers had been undermined.

The same day it declined the invitation to enter into mediation, Mitsui Mining attempted to restart operations using members of the breakaway union as strike breakers. This led to vicious clashes on the picket lines. In the early morning of March 28, 1500 miners attempted to charge the picket lines at the Mikawa shafts. They clashed with hundreds of miners and supporters of the Miike local, who were determined to keep the mines out of operation. Over one hundred people were injured in the confrontation. The evening headlines of the daily *Asahi* bellowed: "Unions clash at Mitsui Miike."[31] That evening Mitsui applied for and received from the Fukuoka District Court an injunction prohibiting the original union from entering the Miike mines and forbidding it to interfere with breakaway union members trying to get to the mines.

The Miike local contested the injunction, accusing Mitsui Mining of unfair labor practices for sponsoring the breakaway union, for negotiating with it, and for lifting the lockout. The picket lines remained, and on March 29 a procompany goon squad attacked picketers at the gates to the Mikawa shafts. Kubō Kiyoshi, a union picketer, was stabbed during the encounter and died shortly after. Miike made national headlines again.

Kubō's tragic death provoked widespread sympathy for the Miike local union and raised the confrontation to the heady plane of national politics. The *Asahi* editorialized: "Even in the Diet, criticism is being raised and the question asked, why did the company insist on restarting production when blood was surely going to be spilled? Even the bloody incident between the two unions on March 28 could have been avoided if the company had not attempted to start up again."[32] Kōno recalled how Kubō's death was a turning point:

> On the day that Kubō was killed, Hara and I had been sent by the MMF to Miike to convince them to give up the struggle. And then Kubō was killed, so the idea of suggesting a halt to the struggle, well, it just wasn't in the cards any more. I remember going to the Miyaura shafts that night, where I knew a lot of people; and hearing that I had arrived, a big group rushed up to ask me what was going on. Someone said, "Kōno what are you doing here? You're not here to tell us to give up the fight are you?" That's how intense things were. Well, especially after Kubō was killed, there was no turning back.[33]

Thousands of mourners gathered in memorial services for the murdered striker in the following days, but despite the adverse publicity, Mitsui refused to include itself in the CLRB mediation efforts then underway. The JCU and Sōhyō, how-

31. *Asahi shimbun*, 28 March 1960, p. 1.
32. *Asahi shimbun*, 31 March 1960, p. 2.
33. Kōno Kazuo, interview.

ever, took part in the mediation process, and in a meeting with the CLRB on March 30 Sōhyō leaders Ōta and Iwai made the following declaration:

1. By setting up a second union and employing goon squads the company is trying to destroy the first union. We won't yield and will fight to the end. The death of Kubō has reinforced the unity of workers there. Sōhyō also intends to step up the fight at Miike and will send in further reinforcements.
2. The company shows no remorse regarding the recent incidents. If it insists on re-opening the mine, the bloodletting can't be avoided. In order to avoid this worst-case scenario we expect a mediation proposal based on an impartial CLRB analysis.
3. to condone the firing of the 1200 workers is to legitimize future firings due to technological change. Moreover, it is a complete denial of workers' rights and a sub-mission to the current policy of making the union movement a hand-maiden to cap-italists.[34]

The CLRB released its mediation report in early April. The recommendation for a wage agreement for coalminers was released first and called for a ¥395 per month wage increase. This was accepted by both the coal operators and the JCU. The recommendations regarding the Miike dispute were tabled the following day. They called for Mitsui to rescind the dismissals, for those named to accept early retirement, for Mitsui to pay an additional ¥10,000 severance allowance, and for the company to help find laid off employees new work and to consider rehiring them once the company was back on its feet.[35]

Acceptance of the mediation proposals would have meant defeat for the Miike local. Nevertheless, it is quite likely that the MMF and even the JCU would have reluctantly accepted the deal had it not been for the death of Kubō a few weeks earlier. The stakes had indeed gone up.

The CLRB proposals were to be submitted to the JCU's twenty-fifth conven-tion, beginning on April 8. With the JCU struggle committee deadlocked over the proposals, however, the convention was delayed a day. Immediately after it opened, the convention recessed as various factions jockeyed for position. The MMF threatened to disaffiliate if the convention failed to ratify the proposals. The Miike local, whose executive had unanimously rejected the mediation report, sent its own delegation, which pleaded for the JCU also to reject the report. Sōhyō's chairman, Ōta Kaoru, opened the JCU convention and called on dele-gates to support the Miike local and reject the CLRB chairman's report. Sōhyō's general council met twice in emergency meetings just prior to and during the JCU convention, at which time new measures of support were adopted including a further ¥150 million in financial aide. After intense and painful debate, the JCU

34. As cited in Miike Kumiai, *Miike nijū nen shi*, pp. 368–369.
35. As cited in Mitsui, *Shiryō: Miike sōgi*, p. 613.

delegates voted to reject the Kobayashi report. The MMF walked out of the convention in disgust, and on April 18 the Miike local withdrew from the enterprise federation. As the Miike union later summarized, "The period from the formation of the breakaway union and the failure of JCU directive 203 to the rejection of the Kobayashi report caused qualitative changes in the nature of the Miike fight. It transformed a JCU dispute into a Sōhyō battle and brought about a new phase in the struggle."[36]

Phase Three: Nationwide Mobilization

Sympathy over Kubō's death and Sōhyō support breathed new life into the Miike local. At the mine itself, the confrontation centerd on control of the central hopper, through which all coal had to pass prior to being loaded for shipment. Members of the second union were mining coal, albeit at a reduced rate, but as long as picketers kept the hopper from operating, no coal could get out.

On April 20 picketers and strikebreakers clashed at the hopper and a number of people were injured. This was followed by a major incident on May 12 when police charged 2,000 picketers at the hopper. One hundred eighty workers sustained injuries in that violent encounter. Meanwhile, the town of Ōmuta was in a state of siege, as townspeople aligned themselves with either the company or the union. What sustained the miners in this trying struggle was the base of support that had been developed for and among women, most of whom were miners' wives. Women's associations had been built at both the local and national levels. The women played an active role not only in survival networks but in strategy deliberations. The Miike union's local paper always had one or two pages out of a total of four that were edited and produced by the Homemakers Association (Shufu no Kai).

As the confrontation continued, thousands of supporters flowed into the town to bolster the union's picket lines. In March, Sōhyō had called for the establishment of Miike support committees (Miike o Mamoru Kai) on a regional and industry-wide basis. Hundreds of such committees were established in all regions of Japan. They raised funds to support the strikers and hired buses to send down supporters to help on the picket lines. A typical sojourn of union supporters to the Miike front would last five or six days. The activists lived in billets or tents and spent endless hours bolstering picket lines or performing support services. Ogawa Keizō, a member of the Moriguchi union executive at the time, recalled his one week stint in support of the Miike miners that May:

36. Miike Kumiai, *Miike nijū nen shi*, p. 345.

At the height of the conflict, the Miike miners and young members of the youth action groups went toe to toe with people from the second union. I have experienced war, I was a soldier for six years. It was the same feeling as being at war, a land war with infantry and artillery, something I've experienced. It was like that. . . . We supporters from the municipalities, we followed the orders of the people there, and did what we were asked, but, generally, looking at it like it was a war movie, we provided support services in the rear. So we weren't that helpful, we didn't have any training. We were given a place to sleep, but because we didn't have any training they couldn't put us in the front lines. . . . So we brought lunch to people and did that sort of thing. Even then, in the middle of the night, we were there for eight days and during that period there were two or three severe clashes, so I believe we were there when things were heating up.[37]

In an extraordinary measure, Sōhyō opted to hold its fourteenth convention in Ōmuta from June 8–9, the first time it had been held outside of Tokyo. Uchiyama Tashirō, an executive member of the metalworkers' union at the time, recalled his trek to the convention and the tensions at the mine:

There wasn't enough room for everybody, so we stayed in tents. We heard that violent gangs were around; everyone, well, you know, we got magazines and wrapped them around our waists to protect ourselves. The Kyushu gangs they all carried knives. Kubō was killed with a knife, you know. So we stuffed about three layers of magazines, so that even if we were stabbed we'd be okay. It was a strange feeling. . . . But it, you know, there were a lot of big struggles after war, but it was really a national struggle, workers from all over the country came there. There were those that criticized the strategy, but still, every week or so, there would be new people arriving, staying in tents. It was June so tents were okay. Sometimes it would just be a plastic sheet.[38]

Even to these outside supporters, the role that women played at Miike was evident. When interviewed both Ogawa and Uchiyama spontaneously recalled the women at Miike: "The women were tough. Were they ever tough," Ogawa recalled. Uchiyama remembered his first impression of Omuta: "We went by sleeper car and arrived at Ōmuta the next morning. The women, the wives of the JCU, about five or six hundred came out to greet us in the square in front of the station."

Following the Sōhyō special convention, the JCU held its twenty-sixth convention on June 13 and 14 in the Kyushu city of Fukuoka, a short train ride from the Miike mines. While somewhat symbolic, the unions' convening of their annual conventions near Miike served notice that Miike was not simply a regional

37. Ogawa Keizō, interview by author, 9 March 1990. Ogawa, a retired Moriguchi union activist, traveled to Miike in May 1960.
38. Uchiyama Tashirō, interview by author. Uchiyama was a leader of the metalworkers' federation; he became deputy secretary-general of Sōhyō in 1978 and acting secretary-treasurer in 1983.

Table 24. Nationwide mobilization to support the Miike union

Period	JCU	Sōhyō	Total
March 17–April 20	33,804	15,017	49,821
April 21–May 20	35,577	32,123	67,700
May 21–June 20	22,141	24,260	46,401
June 21–July 16	21,746	16,526	38,272
July 17–July 25	22,040	21,680	43,720
July 26–August 20	7,423	7,928	15,351
August 21–	14,023	4,920	18,943
Total	156,754	122,454	279,208

Source: Shimizu Shinzō, "Mitsui Miike sōgi," in Shiota Shōbe and Fujita Wakao, eds., *Sengo Nihon no rōdō sōgi* (Tokyo: Ocha no Mizu Shobō, 1977), p. 581.

struggle but was considered a national political struggle, on the same scale as the antisecurity treaty struggle then in progress.

Tables 24 and 25 give some indication of the scale of mobilization of supporters who traveled to Miike in solidarity with the local union. Coalminers and members of Sōhyō affiliates constituted the largest bloc of supporters. As Table 24 indicates, the Miike local overcame its isolation within its own federation, the MMF, through the mobilization efforts of the JCU and Sōhyō. The scale of mobilization among coalminers clearly indicated that, had the layoff issue been handled differently, they might have waged a successful joint struggle. As events evolved, however, coalminers lost this option. Thus their opposition to rationalization in the mines took the form of mobilization in support of Miike miners.

The other base of support was among Sōhyō affiliates. A more detailed breakdown of the union affiliation of Sōhyō-dispatched supporters is provided in Table 25. The degree of mobilization was extraordinary, but the basis of support differed from that of coalminers. To workers outside the coal industry, the Miike local union had become a symbol of the enduring tradition of independent unionism. As Shimizu points out, many union activists perceived defending the Miike local from Mitsui attack to be a defense of independent unionism and of their right to carry on union activities at their workplace.[39] This perspective was closely linked to the popularity of the workshop struggle movement in the late 1950s, which Miike had come to symbolize.

39. Shimizu, "Mitsui Miike sōgi," p. 511. Shimizu also points out that one reason the Sohyō leadership went all out to support the Miike local was that the leadership in Sōhyō and the Miike local shared a common bond through their membership in the Shakai Shugi Kyōkai (Socialist Society), a left faction within the JSP led by Sakisaka Itsurō.

Table 25.   Sōhyō's Miike supporters, by affiliation

Affiliation	March 17–April 20	April 21–May 20	July 10–21
Public sector			
Postal union	4,081	4,331	3,678
Railway union	1,241	3,538	2,081
Telecom. union	2,825	6,065	2,095
Others	3,927	4,367	18,301
Total (public sector)	12,072	18,301	9,251
Private sector	2,172	2,622	1,345
Independent	1,728	1,302	3,200
Regional (labor council)	1,037	3,656	7,686
Other	52	205	65
Total	17,061	26,086	21,546

Source: Shimizu Shinzō, "Mitsui Miike sōgi," in Shiota Shōbe, Fujita Wakao, ed., Sengo Nihon no rōdō sōgi (Tokyo: Ocha no Mizu Shobō, 1977), p. 581.

Precisely because of the nature of the Miike struggle, the rival conservative union federation, JTUC (Japanese Trade Union Congress), actively intervened to undermine the Miike union. Although it is not clear whether JTUC conspired with Mitamura and other ultraconservative groups in setting up the breakaway union that March, JTUC actively supported it once it was formed. Not only did it send organizers to help the rival union, it actively campaigned against support for the original Miike union both domestically and internationally.

International support for the Miike miners came from both the International Mineworkers Federation and the International Confederation of Free Trade Unions (ICFTU), as well as from the older World Federation of Trade Unions (WFTU). Representatives of the latter two organizations visited Miike in May and June respectively. The ICFTU, at the request of the JCU, agreed to donate $10,000 out of its international solidarity fund to the JCU in support of the Miike union. This decision met with a stern rebuke from the JTUC and the Seamen's Union. The JTUC secretary-general, Wada Haruo, wrote to ICFTU executive member Walter Reuther (president of the United Automobile Workers) and others complaining about the ICFTU decision. Too long to reproduce here in its entirety, the five-page letter constituted a diatribe against the Miike local union. According to Wada, "The serious situation into which the dispute at Miike has plunged may partly be attributed to the employers' loose, easy-going way, but the union is [in] a position of bearing more than a half of the responsibility for it."[40]

---

40. Wada Haruo to Mr. W. Reuther, 22 June 1960, papers of the UAW Washington Office, International Affairs Department, 1956–1962, box 106, folder 22, Archives of Labor History and Urban Affairs, Wayne State University, Detroit (hereafter cited as UAW papers).

The letter accused the Miike local, the JCU, and Sōhyō of refusing to go along with rationalization of the coal mining industry and improving productivity. Such a policy, Wada insisted, would harm the coal industry, which was "in urgent need of levelling down the costs by means of rationalization and increasing productivity so as to increase the competitive power in relation to oil." Wada supported the breakaway union as a return to democratic unionism: "It is a deplorable fact that in the Japanese trade union movement the trade union democracy can by no means be established without the process of splitting and the formation of rival unions. But we must borne [sic] in mind and be well aware that, due to inexperience, this deplorable fact exists in the Japanese trade union movement."[41] In conclusion, Wada warned Reuther that continued support for the Miike local would seriously jeopardize the ICFTU's standing in Japan and that "a danger might arise of eventually bringing to naught all organizations and activities belonging to the ICFTU in Japan."

The JTUC also published a nine-page paper in English explaining its position of support for the breakaway union and distributed it to overseas unions. In this document, the JTUC accuses the militants of attempting to incite revolution through the strike: "[The Miike union and wives' association] were all completely spell-bound by a delusion of Marxism and were convinced that to bring to ruin the Miike colliery is a way leading to revolution of the Japanese economy."[42] The breakaway union, on the other hand, was "challenged with furious hostility and violence, but, refusing to accept the challenge, it concluded an agreement with the employers and completed their preparedness for resuming production." The JTUC also accused the Miike local of "provoking clashes with police officers."

Despite these attempts to undermine the Miike miners' struggle, international support remained solid. JTUC's conservative position and its support for what, in the eyes of many, was a scab union did, however, prompt Reuther and others in the ICFTU to attempt to reconcile the bitter factionalism in Japan's union movement in the early 1960s, an issue that will be dealt with in the following chapters.

Phase Four: Summer Showdown

As the humidity and temperatures rose in southern Kyushu that summer, so too did the Miike dispute intensify. Pitched battles were fought on the seas when the Miike local attempted to prevent Mitsui from bringing in strikebreakers and supplies to its island collieries near Kyushu. Responding to a Mit-

41. Ibid., pp. 2, 3.
42. Japan Trade Union Congress, "The Facts about the Strike of Miike Coal Miners and the JTUC's Attitude," May 1960, UAW papers, box 106, folder 22.

sui petition, the Fukuoka District Court meanwhile placed the area around the Mikawa hopper under the direct legal control of the courts. Armed with this special writ, Mitsui hoped to use the courts and police to completely eject the Miike strikers and their supporters from the hopper area. A bloody climax was in the works.

Sōhyō and the JCU responded to this latest crisis by mobilizing 10,000 union activists to defend the picket line around the hopper. They also called for a mass demonstration on July 17. Tensions reached a boiling point on that day as 20,000 unionists picketing the Mikawa hopper confronted 10,000 police in full riot gear. Not far away 100,000 Miike supporters gathered in a huge support rally. This mobilization led to a standoff, but Mitsui continued to demand that the riot squad enforce its injunction before the court order expired on July 21, just as a quarter century earlier General Motors had demanded National Guard troops roust the Flint sit-down strikers in 1937. In both cases the state declined to deploy its forces against such an organized force of workers, but the results were radically different.

On July 15 the Kishi cabinet resigned after having pushed through ratification of the security treaty. Kishi's replacement was Ikeda Hayato. Ikeda, a former finance minister and head of MITI, was inclined to try to diffuse the Miike time bomb. According to Sakurada Takeshi's biographer, Sakurada influenced Ikeda to appoint Ishida Hirohide as labor minister. On the evening of the 18th, Ishida worked with ministry officials and outlined three conditions or principles for resolving the Miike dispute: avoiding bloodshed, respect for the law, and resubmission of the dispute to the CLRB for binding mediation.

The Miike local, the JCU, and Sohyō accepted this fateful proposal, but as in the past, Mitsui was reluctant to relinquish its control. At this point, Ikeda, Sakurada, and Ishida stepped in. In an early morning breakfast meeting on July 20, Ikeda, Sakurada, and other powerful business leaders as well as officials from Mitsui convened to discuss the dispute.[43] Details of what exactly transpired at that meeting are not available, but, judging from later events, it appears that the business leaders convinced Mitsui to refrain from demanding enforcement of its injunction in return for an informal but powerful guarantee that the CLRB mediation would vindicate the company's position of purging the Miike local.

This meeting was followed by another at Mitsui headquarters. Attending were Ishida, Sakurada, Satō Kiichirō, other Nikkeiren officials (including possibly Maeda Hajime), Keidanren vice-president Uemura Kogorō, the head of the Japan Chamber of Commerce as well as Mitsui officials. There, the details of the compromise were fleshed out, and Mitsui subsequently announced that it would go along with mediation.

43. Ōtani Ken, *Sakurada Takeshi no hito to tetsugaku* (Tokyo: Nikkeiren Kōhō Bu, 1987), p. 144.

Picketers at the Miike hopper were confused when told of the decision to take down the picket lines. On the one hand, the fact that the injunction had been lifted was encouraging. But to abandon their front lines without knowing the contents of mediation would, they felt, leave them without recourse if arbitration failed.

On August 10 the CLRB came down with its ruling, which included the following points:

> The designated layoffs appeared unavoidable, and it was impossible at that stage to deal with each individual case to establish whether the layoff was justifiable;
> Workshop struggles had gotten out of hand and blame was attached to both the company and the union;
> Violence had gotten out of hand and was unacceptable;
> The company should rescind its designated layoffs, but those named should voluntarily retire;
> Those retiring and those named would receive ¥20,000 and ¥50,000 respectively;
> Those laid off could appeal their cases to the labor board or the courts;
> The government and company would work to find those laid off new jobs;
> The company and unions would form a committee to work out details to restart production, and the company would not discriminate between the new and old unions.[44]

Mitsui accepted the proposals with minor qualifications, but because the proposal permitted the layoff of union militants and relegated any further challenges to legal recourse only, the Miike local rejected the mediation proposal. The Miike local could not make the decision to reject the proposal and prolong the lockout/strike on its own, however. The issue would be thrashed out at the JCU's twenty-seventh convention, to begin in Tokyo on August 18.

The JCU was in an impossible position, and delegates soon found themselves in a deadlock. The convention adjourned temporarily as deliberations moved into the back rooms. Both rank-and-file delegates and union officials agreed that the Kobayashi proposals were unacceptable. Indeed, had a vote on the mediation package been taken, it probably would have been rejected. However, top union leaders felt that the tide had turned and that, even if delegates rejected the proposal, the union movement would be unable to mount the necessary campaign to sustain the fight at Miike. Instead of facing this question squarely, however, union officials maneuvred to shift the debate to the future struggle

---

44. A copy of the mediation proposal is contained in Mitsui, *Shiryō: Miike sōgi*, pp. 710–711.

against rationalization. In the wee hours of September 3–4 union officials
drafted a general proposal stating that *(a)* the JCU reaffirmed its plan to oppose
the rationalization program and its determination to halt the layoff of 110,000
miners, using force if necessary; *(b)* the union would institutionalize workshop
struggle under the direction of the appropriate union body; *(c)* the union would
demand the government and companies implement unemployment relief and
reemployment measures, and until the dispute was resolved the union would
support the Miike struggle and implement a JCU united strike. It authorized
the central struggle committee to call the strike at the appropriate time.[45] These
three points became the conditions in a conditional acceptance of the mediators
report.

The JCU convention reconvened in plenary session at 1:35 P.M. on September
6, and after some preliminary skirmishes the convention voted unanimously to
endorse the three-point proposal. It was, in effect, acceptance of the mediator's report. An *Asahi* journalist captured the agony of the historic moment:

> When the CLRB mediation proposal was adopted, the 60 people from the Miike
> local who were crammed into the back of the JCU convention remained silent, nei-
> ther clapping nor speaking. They appeared stupefied. Among the miners' wives
> with their white headbands, a few women cried. A number of motorcycle riders, of
> about ten or so who had come up to the convention in khaki suits and white hel-
> mets, struggled to take off white jerseys inscribed in bold letters "Reject the Medi-
> ation Proposal." Most of the Miike wives were in tears or were wiping their faces
> with handkerchiefs. It wasn't unexpected, but as one terminus in a long, bitter
> struggle—and having to swallow 1,200 dismissals—the disappointment went
> deep. Looking at those faces even I felt tears on the way. Later in the hallway wives
> hugged each other, crying. "Stop crying now, it's not a time for tears," Sakisaka It-
> surō softly chided them, his own eyes red with emotion. At that the wives burst
> out, tears rolling down their cheeks. The CLRB proposal was adopted amid Miike's
> tears of grief.[46]

Two hundred and twenty-six days after Mitsui locked out its miners, the struggle had come to an end. Following the JCU vote, the Miike local had little choice
but to go along with the mediation proposal. It took months, however, to work
out a return-to-work protocol and thus miners from the original Miike local only
reentered the mines on December 1, 1960. The original union survived, scarred
but resolute, and it continued to struggle to preserve its autonomy. Thirty years
later, the original union still existed, but it represented only a fraction of the remaining Miike miners.

45. As cited in Miike Kumiai, *Miike nijū nen shi*, p. 444.
46. *Asahi Shimbun*, 6 September 1960, as cited in ibid., pp. 445–446.

The intensity and scale of the Miike dispute challenges traditional periodization of industrial relations in Japan. Most conventional histories tend to portray industrial relations as harmonious and stable by 1955 or so.[47] But the Miike dispute and the extensive involvement of tens of thousands of workers from other unions indicate that stability was tenuous at best. In fact, the dispute at Miike exposed sharp cleavages within society in the late 1950s. This was partially due to the fact that employers, as represented by Nikkeiren, continued to rely on coercion to undermine independent unions in many instances. Furthermore, employers continued to take a hard line in wage negotiations, particularly in terms of base rate increases, as evidenced in the strikes in the steel industry in 1957 and 1959. Government workers chafed under the continued restrictions of their right to strike and bargain collectively. These factors all contributed to ongoing resentment among workers toward their employers and created a strong base for Sōhyō, which continued to occupy center stage in industrial relations despite attempts by JTUC to undermine it. And Sōhyō continued to emphasize that unions should maintain their independence from employers, develop intraunion bonds of solidarity, and undertake adversarial actions if necessary to win their demands.

From 1955 to 1960, however, employers continued to win some important battles including the Ōji Paper dispute in 1958, the steel strikes in 1957 and 1959, and finally the great coal battle at Miike in 1960. Employers remained intransigent and were often directly aided by enterprise unionism, as the Miike dispute showed. Labor's internal divisions seriously undermined workers' ability to resist employers, and the subsequent defeats further weakened the independent union current within Sōhyō. But the problem was that these battles did little to encourage an entente between employers and employees. Instead they engendered resentment and hostility, because employers consistently had to revert to coercion to win their points. The Miike battle was of such a scale that the highest echelons of the ruling elite came to realize that a continuation of Nikkeiren's aggressive tactics was not always in the best long-term interests of the system. In that sense, the Miike dispute marked a subjective recognition of the need to move from a coercive to a hegemonic regime.

If the Miike experience underscored the limits to coercion, it also pointed to some important insights about the nature of job tenure. Nikkeiren did not approve of written job security agreements such as the one that existed at Miike in the 1950s. Such an agreement, in Nikkeiren's view, was an infringement on managerial rights. Thus, the evolving managerial commitment to job tenure was often tacit. It was also contingent on the health of any given sector. In an immediate

47. For example, this was Andrew Gordon's interpretation. See Gordon, *Evolution of Labor Relations*, p. 367.

sense, the employers' victory in the Miike dispute gave the green light to the government and the coal operators to begin the massive rationalization and virtual elimination of coal mining as an industry in Japan. The postwar employment record in coal was one of disappearing jobs and deteriorating working conditions. However, the turmoil that arose also taught management that it should tread softly when jobs were at stake. The post-Miike coal story, the development of high-growth industries, and the consolidation of Japan's market hegemony are discussed and analyzed in the next chapter.

8 High-Speed Growth and Unequal Development

Most accounts of Japan's postwar history agree on one point: 1960 marked a watershed in socioeconomic affairs. The social unrest of that year was in opposition to the renewal of the security treaty with the United States and to the attempt to break the Miike union. It led to massive popular demonstrations involving millions of people, to the deaths of activists, and to the eventual resignation of the prime minister, Kishi Nobusuke. The social upheaval of 1960 wrote an indelible chapter in Japan's postwar development and acted as midwife to the birth of Japan's hegemonic regime. It was at this historical conjuncture that Ikeda Hayato came to the fore as the new leader of the Liberal Democratic Party. Ikeda assumed the mantle of government in the summer of 1960 during the heat of the Miike dispute. His ascent to power symbolized elite recognition of the need for a more sophisticated approach to labor and the triumph of a Fordist vision of development.[1]

Prior to 1960 the main thrust of economic development had been based on linking the Japanese economy to the world marketplace by making export development, particularly in heavy industry, the benchmark for economic

1. Not much has been written in English about Ikeda. For a brief account of his career see Chalmers Johnson, *MITI and the Japanese Miracle* (Stanford: Stanford University Press, 1982).

2. The emphasis on heavy industry began with the priority production plan in the late 1940s and continued in the 1950s through government financial support for capital construction in steel and shipbuilding. By the end of the decade, steel and ship exports were worth almost double that of textiles, hitherto the leading export commodity. See Table 17 in Nihon Bōeki Kenkyū Kai, *Sengo Nihon no boeki 20 nen shi* [Twenty-year history of trade in postwar Japan] (Tokyo: Tsūshō Sangyō Chōsa Kai, 1967), p. 36. For details on the capitalization and rationalization of heavy industry, see Yutaka Kosai, *The Era of High-Speed Growth* (Tokyo: University of Tokyo Press, 1986), pp. 80–92.

growth.[2] Capital accumulation to fund the technological and infrastructural aspects of this strategy occurred through a low-wage policy and extension of the workweek for all sectors of the work force, although workers in the smaller enterprises were most adversely affected. To the extent individual savings did occur, they were in large measure a by-product of the bonus system that unions developed as a countermeasure to the low-wage policy of employers.

Throughout the 1950s, employers in strategic sectors had hammered unions displaying signs of independence or militancy. The upshot of this process was the reinforcement of managerial control that was displayed in the performance-based wage system and in flexible job rules. Unions in many work sites were crushed or forced to abandon adversarialism and often became sounding boards or consultative bodies with relatively little power to regulate the workplace. Employers, for their part, displayed a propensity towards retention of a core work force and an abhorrence for the open labor market.

In terms of capital accumulation and international competitiveness, however, the economic strategy had worked. By the end of the 1950s, Japan's overseas steel shipments alone had reached 34 percent of all exports. Yet when Toyota began producing its first domestic car in 1955 it had been unable to purchase the necessary fine-grade steel for the roof and hood domestically and had to import it from the United States.[3] The producer and consumer-based sectors of the economy remained unlinked from a Fordist perspective. Furthermore, the export orientation left Japan vulnerable to downturns in the world economy and the strategy of rapid, extensive accumulation left little room for accommodation of domestic wage demands, demands that were becoming more vociferous through the organization of labor's spring offensives after 1955. Social tensions continued to escalate until they ignited in the 1960 Miike conflagration and the security treaty struggle. Ikeda's subsequent ascent to power reflected a recognition in the political elite of the need to avoid a repetition of the Miike debacle and to reach some form of social accommodation in Japan.[4]

Ikeda had made his reputation as an economic planner and in the 1950s played an important role in shaping some of the most important government-sponsored institutional mechanisms for capital accumulation, including the Japan Development Bank and the Fiscal Investment and Loan Plan. The latter allowed people to open tax-free savings accounts in the post office. With the development of the bonus system, this plan became a major source of investment finance.

    3. Yutaka Kosai, *Era of High Speed Growth*, p. 119.

    4. Ikeda's proposals were outlined in the September 5, 1960, statement "The Meaning of the General Election and an Outline of the New Policy," cited in Kent Calder, *Crisis and Compensation* (Princeton: Princeton Univeristy Press, 1988), p. 367. See Sheldon Garon and Mike Mochizuki, "Negotiating Social Contracts," in Gordon, *Postwar Japan as History*, pp. 160–161, for a similar perspective.

After taking office in 1960, Ikeda announced his famous income-doubling policy. This policy represented the adoption of classic Fordist policy—the attempt to link the producer goods sector with the consumer goods sector by increasing domestic consumption. Ikeda took his message directly to employers. He addressed the 1961 Keidanren convention and told employers that it was time to loosen the purse strings somewhat. In the previous decade, he declared, wage hikes had not in a single instance surpassed productivity increases; therefore increased wage levels could be justified.[5]

Ikeda's commitment to economic expansion through increased domestic consumption represented an attempt to establish some balance among different economic sectors and to defuse potentially dangerous social tensions. Although Ikeda recognized the need to release these tensions through consumerism, his commitment to domestic expansion was inspired not by latent egalitarianism or prolabor sentiments but rather by a nationalist appreciation of the mechanisms of Fordism. Japan, he knew, had to balance its export-oriented sectors with domestic expansion in order to continue to improve its international position.[6] Thus state intervention was directed mainly at helping to maximize accumulation through policies and institutions that promoted industrial rationalization, small business development, and finance. The government's new economic orientation, supported by both Ikeda and his successor Satō Eisaku, led to a decline in government support for basic industry through its Fiscal Investment and Loan Program.[7] More support was forthcoming, however, for residential land development and road building. That road building and land development became central to state intervention was consistent with the need to develop the Fordist consumption norm based on the automobile and housing. Road construction also reinforced the distribution infrastructure and, as Calder points out, represented a form of political patronage in Japan's countryside. These factors help explain how, by 1977, road densities in Japan were more than double that of Britain and nearly double that of West Germany. Government support for commodity production and circulation became central in this period.

Ikeda's policies stimulated domestic growth; Japan's economy continued its rapid expansion, and workers were able to press more effectively to raise wages. Expansion eventually created shortages in the labor market. One effect of these shortages was that employers in smaller firms were obliged to raise their wages relative to those in the large enterprises in order to obtain workers. Wage gaps that

5. Carlile, "Zaikai and the Politics of Production," p. 412.
6. This transition is illustrated best by the drop in plant and equipment investment in iron and steel production. Nearly ¥148 billion was invested in 1960, but a year later this figure had declined to ¥36 billion and in 1962 to only ¥10 billion. See Yutaka Kosai, *Era of High Speed Growth*, p. 115.
7. Credit afforded basic industry declined from 13.6 percent of total expenditures in 1960 to 5.7 percent in 1970. See Table 4.2 in Calder, *Crisis and Compensation*, p. 164.

had grown sharply in the 1950s—between women and men and between workers in small enterprises and in large ones—temporarily abated in the 1960s only to reemerge in the 1970s.[8]

Rapid growth and real increases in incomes in the post-1960 period consumated Japan's version of the Fordist pattern of economic development. While the state played an important developmental role in assuring economic growth, government support for basic human needs remained tentative at best. Although residential construction boomed, basic sewage and water treatment programs remained woefully inadequate. As for support for the reproduction of labor power through the implementation of welfare programs, Kent Calder concluded: "Even by the late 1960s, the Japanese government's welfare expenditures were only one-half the share of GNP of those in the United States and one-third the levels in France and West Germany."[9] It was precisely because of the underdeveloped welfare state that Japan was quite different from Sweden and why labor remained in an extremely dependent position. The unilateral emphasis on growth also meant that the state continued to intervene only weakly in labor issues (including a very weak minimum wage law) and avoided tampering with the modalities of production relations as they had evolved at the workplace between 1949 and 1960.[10]

Rapid growth also had its direct negative effects.[11] The most obvious and dramatic was rapid and extensive environmental degradation. The devestating effects of mercury poisoning from the Chisso chemical plant in Minamata and the protracted struggle of the victims for redress in the 1960s came to symbolize the cost of rapid development.[12] For years the government conspired with large corporations to avoid responsibility for the pollution problems. Students also rebelled against incorporation into the enterprise-centered society, and the fight against Japanese involvement in the Vietnam War was widespread during this period.

Thus considerable social unrest accompanied even the Fordist period of high-speed growth. The emerging hegemonic pattern could not erase the stamp of employer control that was the hallmark of the earlier period. Even though economic growth accelerated and family incomes increased, labor's position within the hegemonic regime remained tenuous. And growth itself created problems for workers, even for those in large plants in strategic sectors. Although many industrial sectors

8. There is some debate about the scale of the gaps but all sources confirm the general trend toward convergence in the 1960–73 period and growing wage gaps later. For a conservative estimate of wage gap trends see Japan Institute of Labor, *Japanese Working Life Profile, Statistical Aspects* (Tokyo: Japan Institute of Labor, 1989), pp. 30–31.

9. Calder, *Crisis and Compensation*, p. 349.

10. For a fascinating and pathbreaking comparative analysis of the history and politics of the role of the Fordist state see Esping-Andersen, *Three Worlds of Welfare Capitalism.*

11. See E. Patricia Tsurumi, ed., *The Other Japan: Postwar Realities* (Armonk, N.Y.: M.E. Sharpe, 1988), and Gordon, *Postwar Japan as History.*

12. See Margaret McKean, *Environmental Protest and Citizen Politics in Japan* (Berkeley: University of California Press, 1981), for information on the antipollution fight.

expanded, in a number of important industries declined. This chapter begins with an examination of growth in the automobile industry, using the Suzuki case study. This is followed by an analysis of developments in the coal industry and the public sector.

Uneven Development: Ascent of the Automotive Industry

If the 1920s represented the heyday of the automobile, the machine that changed the United States, the 1960s represented a similar benchmark for Japan's domestic automobile industry. In 1958, the industry produced less than 200,000 vehicles, but by 1970 vehicle production, directed largely at the domestic market, surpassed the four million mark.[13] The automobile industry in the United States went through the same leap into mass production between 1910 and 1922. A fundamental difference, however, was that Japan's automakers had already put in place the elements of the lean, flexible Fordist regime by the early 1960s. Thus Japan's automakers were able to take advantage of the economies of scope and scale on a level unprecedented in the history of vehicle manufacturing.

Suzuki Motors

The evolution of production at Suzuki Motors reflected this general trend towards expansion in the 1960s. Table 26 shows the dramatic production increases at Suzuki from 1959 to 1969. Motorcycles remained the mainstay of Suzuki business in the 1960s. Exports, particularly to Southeast Asia, increased throughout the decade. The domestic market for commercial and passenger vehicles developed quickly in the latter part of the decade. Four-wheeled vehicle exports remained marginal, however, not exceeding 700 units per year until after 1967.

Suzuki opened five new plants in this period and absorbed Nikkō Sangyō (Toyokawa Works) in 1971. Prior to the amalgamation, Nikkō Sangyō had assembled light commercial vehicles under contract to Suzuki. Table 27 highlights the domestic expansion of plant and equipment. In the 1960s, Suzuki also began to build overseas assembly plants particularly for reassembling knock-down units.

The heavy investment in new plant and equipment in the 1960s was dedicated to increasing production capacity to keep pace with the expanding domestic and export markets. As in the case of many large manufacturing companies, Suzuki hired new graduates (high school, junior and technical college, and university levels) each April. As the economy expanded, the labor market tightened in the Shizuoka area, and Suzuki's decision to build its new motorcycle assembly plant

---

13. Cusumano, *Japanese Automobile Industry*, p. 387.

Table 26. Fixed assets and production levels, Suzuki Motors, 1959–1969

Year	Fixed assets (billion yen)	Motorcycle units		Vehicle units
		Domestic	Exports	
1959	.927	66,906	737	1,157
1960	1.45	146,189	2,834	5,824
1961	2.47	158,740	6,867	13,283
1962	2.69	165,579	15,245	33,792
1963	4.96	270,985	29,421	39,846
1964	6.39	380,338	71,163	40,906
1965	6.71	334,364	98,800	42,037
1966	8.36	447,472	170,332	68,167
1967	11.65	402,541	124,562	116,192
1968	16.21	366,610	92,869	193,290
1969	19.68	400,617	—	238,165

Source: Suzuki Jidōsha, *50 nen shi* (Hamana Gun: Suzuki, 1970), pp. 510–512.

Table 27. Suzuki plant expansion, 1960–1971

Plant	Year	Location	Process
Headquarters	1921	Takatsuka, Shizuoka	Head office, machining, motorcycle engines.
Iwata	1967	Iwata, Shizuoka	Commercial vehicles
Otsuka	1969	Ogasa, Shizuoka	Aluminum castings
Kosai	1970	Iwata, Shizuoka	Assembly of passenger cars and light vans
Toyokawa	1961	Toyokawa, Aichi	Motorcycle assembly
Toyama	1969	Ōyabe, Toyama	Motorcycle assembly

Source: Suzuki Jidōsha, *50 nen shi* (Hamana Gun: Suzuki, 1970).

in Toyama in western Japan reflected its desire to tap new regional sources of labor. Table 28 charts the growth in employment at Suzuki from 1959 to 1974.

Employment opportunities expanded dramatically at Suzuki's main plants until the 1973 recession, after which jobs were cut, mainly through attrition. Besides increased employment, Suzuki workers also began to see some improvements in compensation and the length of the work week.

Wages

The incentive wage structure was slightly altered during the expansion period. In 1967 Suzuki eliminated all production-based bonuses and at the same time introduced an eight-step incremental scale for each of the twenty pay grades. The result was a wage grid with 160 steps. Movement through the grid remained a function of regular performance evaluations. In 1969 Suzuki introduced a small

Table 28. Employment at Suzuki, 1959–1974

Year	Employees	Net change	% change
1959	1,253	+136	12.2
1960	1,361	+108	8.6
1961	1,549	+188	13.8
1962	2,053	+504	32.5
1963	2,536	+483	23.5
1964	2,850	+314	12.3
1965	3,480	+630	22.1
1966	3,619	+139	4.0
1967	3,810	+191	5.3
1968	4,266	+456	12.0
1969	5,331	+1,065	25.0
1970	6,542	+1,209	22.7
1971	7,956	+1,414	21.6
1972	9,485	+1,529	19.2
1973	9,121	–364	–3.8
1974	8,875	–246	–2.7

Source: Suzuki Jidōsha Kōgyō Rōdō Kumiai, *Nijū go nen shi* [Twenty-five years] (Hamana gun: Suzuki Kumiai, 1976), p. 250.

allowance for particular jobs. This did not alter the basic pay structure, however, and the base rate and incremental level (both influenced by the performance evaluation) remained the two substantial components of the wage system. As the automotive industry expanded, Suzuki employees pressed for wage increases as part of the spring offensive. The result was a gradual rise in nominal and real wages, a trend that accelerated between 1969 and 1974 (Table 29).

By the early 1960s the bonus component of the wage package had reached its postwar peak, equal to about five months wages or almost 30 percent of yearly wages. Wage and bonus increases in this period reflected a standard formula of matching inflation plus a productivity increase. This formula was also followed in the automobile industry in the United States during the same period. Another significant trend was that starting rates increased at a faster pace, reflecting the increasing difficulty in recruiting in a tight labor market particularly in the late 1960s. At the same time, gender discrimination at Suzuki persisted. The gap between starting rates for female and male high school graduates increased from about ¥300 per month in 1960 to ¥3,000 in 1972.

Problems of Growth

Even as wages improved, workers faced serious problems in the workplace. The length of the workday, transfers, health and safety, and shiftwork were all thorns in workers' sides as well as challenges for the consultative model of labor-

Table 29.   Suzuki Motors wage and bonus increases, 1960–1975

Year	Average wage	Starting wage Male high school grad.	Starting wage Male university grad.	Average wage increase	Average bonus (yearly basis)
1960	22,862	9,582	15,570	1,740	119,528
1961	25,877	10,670	17,580	2,550	141,184
1962	25,346	12,103	19,268	2,500	121,289
1963	26,468	14,150	20,260	3,000	150,000
1964	30,425	15,025	21,620	3,500	160,000
1965	34,471	16,195	22,210	3,000	147,000
1966	38,194	16,785	23,380	3,100	159,000
1967	38,409	18,000	25,000	3,830	170,000
1968	41,495	20,000	29,000	4,927	184,000
1969	39,046	24,500	34,000	7,050	213,000
1970	46,221	28,000	38,000	8,700	255,000
1971	54,901	34,000	43,000	8,700	272,000
1972	64,398	41,000	51,000	9,900	312,000
1973	78,867	50,000	62,000	14,250	405,000
1974	103,611	66,000	81,500	24,500	515,500

Source: Suzuki Jidōsha Kōgyō Rōdō Kumiai, *Nijū go nen shi* [Twenty-five years] (Hamana gun: Suzuki Kumiai, 1976), pp. 249–250.

management relations. At times worker frustration overflowed, at which point the consultative model broke down and the enterprise union resorted either to repression or job action.

The Suzuki union considered the long workweek its major problem, and in 1961 it launched a major campaign to win a 40-hour workweek over a three-year period.[14] That year the workweek was reduced to 44.5 hours and then to 43 and 42 hours in 1962 and 1963 respectively. These decreases reflected a reduction in Saturday work hours from 6.5 to 4 hours. All employees continued working at least half a day every Saturday until 1964. But in 1964 the union's campaign stalled in the face of management intransigence. As part of the reduction to a 42-hour week, Suzuki had agreed to begin experimenting with alternating half-day Saturday shifts. In other words, employees would get a full weekend off every second week. On September 30, however, management advised the union that it would not continue with the experiment. The union protested and began formal negotiations, but it was unable to win its demand. It never resorted to job action to back its position, however, and as a concession the company increased annual vacations by four days. For the next ten years, until 1972, Suzuki employees did

14. Suzuki Kumiai, *Nijūgo nen shi*, pp. 262–264.

a daily shift of seven hours 35 minutes and went into work every Saturday for another half day, not including overtime. That the union was unable to win the 40-hour week at this time was an indication of the weakness of enterprise unionism, a weakness that left Japan's workers tied to the treadmill of production longer than workers in any other industrialized country.

In 1972 the company finally agreed to reinstate the program for alternate Saturdays off, but even then some workers were excluded from the program. For example, at the Iwata plant employees were unable to implement the plan as scheduled because they were too busy keeping up with new orders for light commercial vehicles.[15] The Toyama local also cites the work week as the principal problem in 1972. Finally in 1974, twelve years after the union had first called for it, the company conceded to a five-day, forty-hour week. Suzuki conceded on this issue partly because it wanted its employees to accommodate its increasing demands for shiftwork.

As mentioned above, the union had provisionally agreed to allow shiftwork in 1969, but the issue was constantly being renegotiated as new plants opened or as workers protested against the new system. Suzuki, in a desperate attempt to resolve the issue once and for all, tried to make its offer for the 1973 summer bonus contingent on full employee compliance regarding shiftwork. Much to its surprise, the union responded by calling a two-hour work stoppage in all the plants.[16] As the machines ground to a halt, employees gathered in courtyards of every plant to hear union officials explain how the company was unjustly trying to link the two issues. In the end the union gave in, however, and by summer 1973 most plants were operating with two shifts.

Another major irritant that developed in this period, particularly in the late 1960s, was transfers. In 1969 the company moved to increase its market share and transferred over one thousand employees to dealerships across the country; from there they went out door-to-door to drum up new business. Transfers also took place as the new plants came on stream in 1969 to 1971. As Suzuki rationalized its operations, workers had to accept permanent or temporary transfers to the new plants. As the union's Takatsuka local put it: "Problems relating to the transfer of union members occurred as the company grew, and we had numerous shop-floor and local executive meetings to negotiate with the company over work conditions and job placement for the transferees."[17]

Transfers were also used to balance production in response to market changes. For example, in 1972 demand for autos dropped while demand for motorcycles and commercial vehicles picked up. Suzuki consequently shifted personnel from

15. Ibid., p. 197.
16. Ibid., p. 154.
17. Ibid., p. 190.

Kosai to Takatsuka and from Takatsuka to Iwata. The Kosai local recalled: "All sorts of problems, including transfers to other plants and extensions of transfers, occurred as we switched to a regular shift at the beginning of the year because of the decline in compact cars." The festering problem burst into the open in the summer of 1973, when a number of workers went to court to stop the transfers. Not only were the employees unsuccessful in this, they also ran into problems with the union. The Takatsuka local described its version of events: "In July, a number of union members who had been ordered to transfer took on the company, applying for an interim injunction against the transfers on the basis that they constituted an unfair labor practice. The local made an effort to include the said workers in collective bargaining but [dissident] elements who attempted to split the union appeared."[18] The dissident workers' version of events remains to be told. What was clear, however, was that management's use of labor as a flexible component of the production system met with resistance.

Safety was another issue. In 1970 a worker was killed in the press section of the Kosai plant just after start up. Major accidents also occurred in the Iwata plant in the 1972 and 1973, and the union cited the company for 375 safety violations in 1973 alone.[19] A fire erupted in the paint shop of the Kosai plant in February 1973. These accidents led to a major campaign to improve safety standards under the direction of the health and safety committees, which according to labor law were joint labor-management committees.

The 1969–73 expansion brought changes in the organization of the Suzuki union. In 1970 the union began to establish local branches in each plant, and two years later it sponsored the founding of a federation of unions in Suzuki-affiliated subcontractors: the Federation of Suzuki Automobile Affiliated Unions (Suzuki Jidōsha Kanren Rōdō Kumiai Rengōkai, or Suzuki Rōren). But these new affiliates represented only a very small proportion of the workers employed in Suzuki subcontracting firms.

Suzuki and the Automobile Sector

Suzuki's mixed motorcycle, auto, and truck product line makes it impossible to compare the company's productivity directly with other vehicle manufacturers such as Nissan or Toyota. What can be said with reasonable certainty, however, is that Suzuki's expansion during these years was a general trend. As Table 30 indicates, automobile production finally came of age in the 1960s, and the main market was domestic sales. Even as late as 1970, 80 percent of all automobiles produced were sold internally. After the 1973–74 recession, however, exports ac-

18. Ibid., pp. 215, 192.
19. Ibid., p. 198.

Table 30. Japan's automobile production and exports, 1960–1973

Year	Total units	Domestic sales	Exports	% exported
1960	481,551	407,963	38,809	8.1
1965	1,875,614	1,661,856	194,168	10.4
1970	5,289,157	4,097,361	1,086,776	20.5
1973	7,082,757	4,912,142	2,067,556	29.2

Source: Michael Cusumano, The Japanese Automobile Industry (Cambridge: Harvard University Press, 1985), p. 4.

celerated at a rapid pace; and 54 percent of all vehicles produced in 1980 were sold overseas.

As at Suzuki, the rapid expansion of production led to increased employment opportunities at the major automobile manufacturers such as Nissan and Toyota. Employment at both automakers increased fourfold during the 1960s; Suzuki's increased fivefold. Wages at Nissan and Toyota increased at an even faster rate than at Suzuki, although all three producers loosened their purse strings in accordance with the Fordist imperative (articulated in Ikeda's income doubling plan) that the purchasing power of workers be increased in order to create the mass market necessary for mass production.[20] Living standards in Japan began to rise, but from the vantage point of international competitiveness, Japan retained an important edge because of its comparatively low labor costs. During the 1961–71 period, for example, wages at Suzuki (including bonuses) rose from $104 per month (Canadian) to $215 per month. The equivalent figures for Canadian transportation equipment workers was $380 to $692 per month.[21] In other words, Suzuki's wage bill per employee was about 27 percent of that of an automaker in Canada in 1961 and about 31 percent in 1971. Relatively inexpensive wage costs were an important factor that gave Japan an edge in the export market during the early 1970s. This advantage diminished later, however, as wages rose substantially in Japan from 1972 to 1975. Even more important was the appreciation of the yen after 1971, which seriously reduced Japan's wage advantage.

The significance of the ascent of Japan's domestic automobile industry only becomes clear, however, in comparative perspective. What was most dramatic was the phenomenal rise in productivity in this period. Table 31 gives a rough idea of the scale of nominal productivity increases: While GM and Ford appeared to stand still, productivity at Nissan and Toyota went up by more than 300 percent.

20. According to Cusumano (Japanese Automobile Industry, p. 170), in 1983 the average monthly wages at Toyota were ¥283,000, at Nissan ¥255,000, and at Suzuki ¥236,000.
21. Canadian figures are from Statistics Canada, Employment, Earnings and Hours, cited in J. Wood and P. Kumar, eds., The Current Industrial Relations Scene in Canada, 1978 (Kingston: Queens University Press, 1979), p. 460. The exchange rate was ¥360 per Canadian dollar.

Table 31. Nominal productivity, Japan and United States,
1960–1975 (vehicles per employee)

	1960	1965	1970	1975
GM (worldwide)	8	10	8	10
Ford (U.S.)	14	14	12	12
Chrysler (worldwide)	11	12	11	11
Nissan	12	13	30	41
Toyota	15	19	38	50

Source: Suzuki Jīdōsha Kōgyō Rōdō Kumiai, *Nijū go nen shi*
[Twenty-five years] (Hamana Gun: Suzuki Kumiai, 1976), pp.
249–250.

But as Cusumano points out, it would be truly miraculous if Japan's autoworkers
were four or five times more productive than American workers. And in fact they
were not.

The extremely high productivity levels mask the elaborate subcontracting
structure that was responsible for about 70 percent of the manufacturing costs for
cars sold under the Nissan, Toyota, and even the Suzuki brand label.[22] If one takes
the ensemble of the production complex in both countries, Japan's productivity
advantage drops from the nominal four of five times more productive to about 50
percent more productive. But even a 50 percent productivity advantage was lethal
in terms of international competitiveness.

Cusumano concluded that the primary forces that made automobile manufacturing in Japan more productive were extensive subcontracting, the need to
adapt mass production techniques to a small domestic market (rapid machine
setup and mixed assembly), and the extensive and innovative use of quality control processes. The conditions that permitted the emergence of lean, flexible
manufacturing were, according to Cusumano, "company unions" and protection
against imports.[23] My findings reinforce Cusumano's with further clarifications.
The incentive-based wage system, although slightly modified in the 1960s, provided the economic basis for employers' retaining substantial control over the labor force.

As described in previous chapters, the essential elements of the new production regime—flexible manufacturing and work practices, a performance-based
wage system, and enterprise unionism—had evolved in the 1950s. In the 1960s
the most notable development internal to the regime itself was the rapid spread
of the quality circle movement. Suzuki, Toyota, and Nissan institutionalized
quality circles as part of the production process, although many of the meetings

22. Cusumano, *Japanese Automobile Industry*, pp. 187–192.
23. Ibid., pp. 377–381.

were held after hours and workers were seldom compensated for the time spent in these meetings.

Despite the great strides in productivity and wage increases, life in the factory was no paradise. At Toyota, capacity utilization rates ran consistently over 100 percent. As Kamata Satoshi documented in *Japan in the Passing Lane* and as the Suzuki workers' own struggles indicated, workers were subjected to unwanted transfers, speedups, stress, and excessive overtime. While there were important distinctions among the regimes at Suzuki, Nissan, and Toyota, including differences in the functioning of the enterprise unions at each company, all three automakers shared many of the features of lean production. Lean manufacturing helped raise efficiency and productivity levels, but this did not necessarily mean an improvement in the quality of life for automobile workers—at times it was exactly the opposite.

Uneven Development: The Decline of Coal

On December 1, 1960, thousands of Miike miners walked into the coal shafts to dig coal together for the first time in 312 days. The work process may have obliged them to work collectively, but they remained prey to divided loyalties. Mitsui Mining, backed by the government, the CLRB, and the scab union, succeeded in purging its work force of hundreds of union activists. The 1960 defeat marked the onset of continuous discrimination against and decline of the original adversarial union. Deprived of a united voice in the workplace, Miike miners saw their jobs cut and their wages and working conditions decline dramatically relative to workers in other major industries. Safety conditions, which the original union had so assiduously helped to improve, deteriorated to the point where, within three years of the return to work, Miike miners would be beset by a catastrophe, one that was unprecedented even within the dangerous mining industry.

The experience of the Miike miners in the 1960s was the coalminer's fate writ large. The problems that hounded Miike dogged the industry as a whole. Between 1960 and 1973, six hundred mines closed, over 200,000 miners lost their jobs, and the coal industry became a major challenge in damage control for the ruling elite. The 1960s may well have been an era of high-speed growth for Japan as a whole, but industries like coal and to a lesser extent textiles declined with serious repercussions.

Of course, scholars in and out of Japan have not overlooked the decline of the coal industry. Paradoxically, their accounts of decline often obfuscate even more effectively than one-sided terms like "high-speed growth." For example, in his study of crown corporations, Chalmers Johnson concluded that miners' high wages and proclivity to strike caused the coal industry to lose its competitive advantage.[24] In other words, labor was responsible for the industry's decline. Similar accounts are found among scholarly works by economic historians in Japan such as Arisawa Hiromi.[25]

For others the decline of the coal industry in the 1960s represents the epitome of successful management of a declining industry. Ezra Vogel concludes: "The adjustment was painful, and the pain not over even two decades later. Yet considering the problems involved, Japan's success—in speed of adjustment to market forces, positive co-operation of many groups of people, and maintenance of a healthy society—was as striking in its way as the creation of competitive shipbuilding and machine tool industries.[26] To Charles McMillan, a specialist in business administration and former advisor to a Canadian prime minister, the government's management of the coal industry represented a "costly but ruthless recognition of comparative disadvantage in the industrial structure."[27] These accounts of the decline of the coal industry reflect either an antilabor bias or a glorification of the Japanese government and the ability of Japanese businesses to deal with structural change. A more balanced account reveals a radically different picture of decline.

Failure of Industrial Policy

Substantive state intervention in the coal industry in the post-Occupation period dates from 1955, at which time the government decided to protect the coal industry and minimize oil imports. In August 1955 the Hatoyama government passed the Coal Industry Rationalization Special Measures Law. The law called for a mine buy-back program, price-fixing mechanisms, a provision for cartels to implement production quotas if necessary, preferential treatment for efficient mines, and the establishment of the Coal Industry Advisory Council, which was attached to MITI (Ministry of International Trade and Industry). The council comprised representatives from the coal industry, consumers, and academics but none from labor. It was chaired by Uemura Kōgorō, vice-president of the Federation of Economic Organizations and head of its fuel policy committee.

The objective of the government's rationalization program was to reduce the number of mines, concentrate production in the more efficient mines, and reduce the price of coal for consuming industries. But in the first three years of the pro-

---

24. Chalmers Johnson, *Japan's Public Policy Companies* (Washington, D.C.: American Enterprise Institute for Public Policy Research, 1978), p. 128.

25. Arisawa Hiromi, *Shōwa keizai shi—ge* [A history of the Shōwa economy, vol. 2] (Tokyo: Nihon Keizai Shimbun Sha, 1980), and Arisawa Hiromi, *Nihon sangyō hyaku nen shi—ge* [One hundred year history of Japanese industry] (Tokyo: Nihon Keizai Shimbun Sha, 1967).

26. Ezra Vogel, *Comeback* (New York: Simon and Schuster, 1985), p. 96.

27. C. J. McMillan, *The Japanese Industrial System* (Berlin: de Gruyter, 1984), p. 88.

gram these objectives were utterly abandoned. With the Suez crisis in 1956 demand for coal increased, and MITI turned a blind eye as coal operators made a shambles of the rationalization plan. Small mines actually increased, as did their share of production. Prices increased, and the top eighteen coal operators showed a margin of ¥12 billion in operating profits for 1957 alone. The Japan Development Bank commented: "It is ironic that immediately after its implementation, the Rationalization Special Measures Law was unable to play much of a role due to the upturn in the coal industry."[28]

The boom in the coal industry between 1955 and 1957 created a production frenzy in which MITI as well as coal operators became embroiled. As late as August 1958, MITI itself predicted that coal production would reach 69 million tons by 1967 and that reductions in personnel, if necessary at all, could be achieved through attrition. It was under these circumstances that both Mitsui and Mitsubishi conceded to union demands for written long-term job guarantees for their miners in 1958.

Yet one year later the Coal Industry Advisory Council made a dramatic about-face. It demanded a ¥1200 reduction in coal prices, a production limit of 55 million tons, the layoff of 93,000 miners, and a reduction in the number of operating mines. These goals, even harsher than those established in 1955, were adopted as government policy in early 1960. What caused this dramatic reversal?

As noted above, many scholars have pointed the finger at labor costs or strikes, while others have portrayed the energy revolution as inevitable because of coal's price disadvantage compared to oil. Neither position is particularly convincing. Wages in the coal industry were about 70–80 percent of those in the gas or electrical industry in the 1957–58 period.[29] Steelworkers were making ¥29,000 per month in 1958 compared to 24,500 for coalminers.[30] Nor had high wages impeded the coal operators ability to make substantial profits in earlier periods.

As for coal's competitiveness with regard to oil, it is true that the per calorie price of coal was higher than oil, but this had always been the case in postwar Japan. The gap in price between coal and oil had in fact gone down during the 1950s. In 1952 coal cost ¥0.24 per calorie more than oil, but in 1955 it was only about ¥0.10 more expensive.[31] From the competitive disadvantage standpoint, coal should have been phased out in 1952, not 1960!

28. Nihon Kaihatsu Ginkō, *Nihon Kaihatsu Ginkō jū nen shi* [A ten-year history of the Japan Development Bank] (Tokyo: Nihon Kaihatsu Ginkō, 1963), p. 228.
29. As cited in Arisawa Hiromi, *Gendai Nihon sangyō kōza—III* [History of contemporary Japanese industry—3] (Tokyo: Iwanami Shoten, 1960), p. 268.
30. Rōdō Daijin Kanbō Rōdō Tōkei Chōsa Bu, *Rōdō tōkei nenpō—1958* [Annual report of labor statistics—1958] (Tokyo: Rōdō Daijin Kanbō, 1959), pp. 91–94.
31. See Mitsui, *Shiryo: Miike sōgi*, p. 434.

The real reasons for the shift in energy policy can be traced to changes in Japan's industrial structure. Whereas in the early 1950s the coal industry was a powerful force, by the late 1950s steel had emerged as the key pillar in the export-oriented sector of Japan's development strategy. Steel production had increased from 3.1 million metric tons in 1949 to 16.6. million in 1959. Even more importantly, steel as well as ships were Japan's leading edge into export markets. To maintain and improve their competitive positions, steel producers demanded a cut in energy costs. Thus when coal operators made the fatal mistake of attempting to maintain coal prices (and staggering profit levels) after oil prices began to drop in 1958, the steel industry pounced. They formed a powerful coal consumer lobby group and demanded an end to government protection of the coal industry. Theirs was the voice that Uemura Kōgorō, the Coal Advisory Council, and MITI would listen to in 1959–1960.

An additional element in the structural changes was the government position in the late 1950s. Foreign currency reserves had more than doubled between 1955 and 1960, thanks in large measure to steel and steel-related exports. Japan could thus afford an increased outlay of foreign currency for oil imports. Furthermore, the government was fortified by the economic growth in the latter half of the 1950s and was therefore less concerned about reliance on oil imports controlled by U.S. transnationals. Thus what had seemed impossible in 1958 became the reality of 1960. Resource-poor Japan began to abandon its coal fields, a process that would devastate mining communities.

It was at this conjuncture that the Miike lockout/strike occurred. The defeat of the Miike local (the JCU's largest affiliate) and the decision by other locals to negotiate the terms of layoffs (rather than attempt to halt them) severely hampered the JCU's effort to block the Ikeda government's plans to limit coal production.

In order to prevent complete chaos in energy policy, Uemura Kōgorō had been working behind the scenes to assure a stable transition from coal to oil. In June 1961 the Federation of Economic Organizations announced an agreement whereby the steel and electric power industries would contract for 13 and 20 million tons of coal annually until 1967, thus ensuring a reduced but stable market for coal while permitting an increase in oil imports. At the same time, however, MITI directed its Coalfields General Development Survey Commission to halt all exploration for new thermal coal deposits.[32] This reflected the government's long-term plan to phase out domestic coal as an energy source.

In September 1961 hundreds of miners marched through the streets of Tokyo in their work gear to protest the layoffs hitting the coal fields. The JCU subse-

---

32. Tsūshō Sangyō Shō Sekitan Kyoku, *Tanden sōgō kaihatsu chōsa hōkoku sho* [Report of the investigation into general development of coal fields] (Tokyo: Tsūshō Sangyō Shō, 1963), p. 5.

quently decided to begin a general strike on April 5, 1963, if the government did not reverse its energy policy. Under attack by the JSP in the Diet, the Ikeda government could not ignore the crisis, and Ikeda agreed to meet JCU and industry representatives on April 5. The following day the government announced the formation of a coal fact-finding commission to investigate conditions in the industry and to make recommendations for government policy. As part of the deal, the JCU withdrew its plans for a general strike, and coal operators were obliged to refrain from any further layoffs until the commission reported its findings.

The commission tabled its report on October 13, 1962. It upheld the reduced production target of 55 million tons per year and called for further rationalization of the industry, which it estimated would result in a further 75,000 layoffs. Coal prices would be cut by a further ¥1,200 per ton. Despite JCU protests, the Ikeda government adopted the recommendations in November. The JCU attempted to block this move by calling for a general strike on December 14. Although major work stoppages did occur, a general strike did not. All the wind had been taken from JCU's sails.

Government attempts to plan decline ran into severe problems in 1963 and 1964. The goal of coal policy was to maintain production levels at 55 million tons, cut the work force, and thereby lower coal prices. The only way to accomplish this in a short period was to attack labor. Layoffs were accompanied by speedups in the mines, wage cuts, and a serious deterioration in working conditions. Miners saw the writing on the wall, and a mood of abandoning ship—as government reports called it—spread through the coal fields. MITI had estimated that the mine labor force would be reduced by 38,000 miners in 1963, but over 28,000 miners had already quit or been laid off by the summer. In an ironic twist of events, a labor shortage developed.

This prompted the government to reactivate the coal industry commission to find out what was going on. The commission tabled its report in December 1964 and recommended reducing coal production to 52 million tons annually, increasing coal prices, and subsidizing interest rates on capital investment. The government adopted the new recommendations in early 1965. Within ten short years government policy had gone through four flip-flops. The 1955 rationalization plan, the 1958 expansion-at-any-price plans, the 1960 rationalization plans, and now the revised 1964 plans made a mockery of "planned decline."

The years that followed witnessed a litany of government "last words" on coal policy. In 1966, 1968, and 1972 the Coal Industry Advisory Council was called upon to provide advice on government policy as the industry lurched from crisis to crisis.[33] Each report was adopted with minor amendments by the government.

---

33. Details of the decline and government policies are contained in Nihon Kaihatsu Ginkō, *Nihon Kaihatsu Ginkō nijū go nen shi* [A twenty-five-year history of Japan Development Bank] (Tokyo: Nihon Kaihatsu Ginkō, 1976), pp. 375–402.

Table 32.   Basic coal industry statistics, 1960–1973

Year	Mines	Production (million tons)	Miners (thousands)	Productivity (tons/miner/mo.)
1960	682	52.6	244	18.0
1961	662	55.4	213	21.7
1962	608	53.6	179	24.9
1963	436	51.1	136	31.3
1964	322	50.8	116	36.4
1965	287	50.1	110	38.1
1966	239	50.6	104	40.3
1967	205	47.1	92	42.7
1968	168	46.3	80	47.9
1969	159	43.6	65	55.8
1970	102	38.3	52	61.0
1971	93	31.7	41	63.4
1972	77	26.9	34	66.0
1973	57	20.9	25	68.2

Source: Japan Development Bank, *Nihon Kaihatsu Ginkō nijū go nen shi* [Twenty-five-year history of the Japan Development Bank] (Tokyo, 1976), pp. 388, 391, 394.

The essence of the recommendations was a continual downward revision of production levels (from 52 million tons in 1964 to 20 million in 1972) and heavy subsidization for companies closing mines. Subsidy funds were provided through a 12 percent tariff slapped on imported oil, 10 percent of which went into a special coal account.

The effect of the substantial government subsidies for closures were such that coal operators bailed out en masse and mine closures proliferated, such that by 1972 only seventy-five mines were operating and about 34,000 miners employed. The scale of closures is demonstrated in Table 32. During the twelve-year period the government spent about ¥59 billion for relief measures for the unemployed. Direct subsidies to coal operators amounted to ¥260 billion for the same period.

The transition from coal to oil as Japan's primary energy source was neither efficient nor particularly well managed. What it did do, however, was provide massive subsidies to coal companies, which used a part of these funds to diversify into other operations. Miners, however, were left holding the bag.

The Effects on Miners

The chaotic decline of the coal industry played havoc with the lives of miners and their families. Over 200,000 jobs were lost in a decade, a tragic indictment of the popular myth of permanent employment in Japan. For those who

Table 33. Personnel reductions by the eighteen major coal mining corporations

Year	Miners		Office		Total	
1958	190,686	(100)	23,363	(100)	214,049	(100)
1968	55,521	(29)	8,536	(37)	65,057	(30)
Net loss	135,165	(71)	14,827	(63)	149,992	(70)

Source: Mitsubishi Mining and Cement Corporation, *Mitsubishi kōgyō sha shi* [History of Mitsubishi Mining and Cement] (Tokyo, 1976), p. 608.
Note: Figures in parentheses are percentages of base year, 1958.

remained in the pits things were little better, as wages fell, working conditions deteriorated, and mine explosions became endemic to the point of national scandal.

Table 33 illustrates the scale of layoffs in the major coal mining corporations. Seventy-one percent of all mining jobs were eliminated in the major companies in this decade. But this only captures the net job loss. It is estimated that between 1959 and 1968 the coal industry hired nearly 300,000 people while it laid off nearly 500,000.[34] The mines had become revolving doors, as miners wandered from site to site looking for work only to be laid off again.

The crisis in the mining industry clearly defined the limits of job tenure. Furthermore, structural decline undermined other methods of coping with unemployment, such as internal transfers and transfers to subsidiary companies. According to Labor Ministry statistics, 181,450 miners registered as job seekers between 1962 and 1970, of which fewer than 30,000 (about 16 percent) found alternative employment through their employers. Government employment offices placed about 116,000, while over 30,000 resorted to their own devices to find gainful employment.[35]

The scale of displacement and union protests obliged the government to provide special unemployment relief measures. In 1959 the Unemployed Mineworkers Extraordinary Measures Law provided some minimal relief through job placement programs, make-work projects, and special job training programs. This was followed by a consolidation of employment promotion measures under the authority the Employment Promotion Corporation in 1961. In 1963 the government instituted a passbook system (*teichō seidō*) for coalminers. Effective for three years once issued, the book made it unnecessary for miners to

34. Rōdō Shō Shokugyō Antei Kyoku Shitsugyō Taisaku Bu, *Tankō rishokusha taisaku jū nen shi* [A ten-year history of policy toward unemployed coalminers] (Tokyo: Nikkan Rōdō Tsushinsha, 1971), p. 340.
35. Ibid., p. 342.

reregister for unemployment benefits each time they were laid off. Miners simply showed their passbook to reenter the employment programs. Benefits for unemployed coalminers were set at a maximum of ¥450 per day, about one-third of their previous wages.

Although these relief measures were better than nothing, they did little more than veil the social upheaval that ravaged miners and their families. This was brought home to people across the country when the media picked up a letter from a miner's daughter to the prime minister Satō Eisaku. Known as "A letter of tears to Prime Minister Sato: Stop the Toyosato Mine closing," the letter captures the tenor of the times.

August 1, 1965

To Prime Minister Sato:

I am a girl in the sixth grade at Toyosato Elementary School in Akahira, Hokkaido. Our school is the one where the kids from the Toyosato mine go that's been in the papers and on TV every day. In class although we don't really know what's going on, we worry and we're always talking about it.

Thinking about it, I came up with the idea of asking you, Japan's most important person—the prime minister—so that the coal mine won't go under. I asked my Dad but he only laughed and said, "Forget it, even if you wrote it he wouldn't bother reading a letter from a kid." But I didn't give up—I heard a Diet member was coming to Toyosato, so I'm writing this letter with the idea that he'll be able to get it to you. When my Dad and the other workers get together you hear them talking about the "proposal" a lot. According to Dad, if things happen as they're written in that, thousands of people working in the mines will be left out and the Toyosato mine will be finished.

My teacher says that when the mine near where he taught before went under, a lot of people took up and went to Tokyo or Kawasaki. Some of them came back to the mine, though, because their new jobs didn't work out or their back pay ran out. I couldn't help thinking—digging coal is what mine people do best.

My Mom and Dad, everyone says they don't want to leave the mine. I heard my Dad came here in 1946. I worry whether he can do anything different after doing a job he's done so long. He's 51, so I also worry whether anyone else would hire my Dad. It's not just my Dad, everyone will have trouble. It seems the shopkeepers in Toyosato don't know what they'd do if the mine goes under. And good friends will be separated forever. The nice school where I and my brother and sisters studied will go too, I guess. The town where I was born will completely change. A lot of unhappy things will happen. Please help stop the mine from closing, help my Dad keep working just like now. Please help.

Kogawa Kikunae[36]

36. As cited in ibid., p. 301.

The letter did in fact get to the prime minister who responded promptly by saying that he would not abandon the mines and that the girl should reassure her parents. Six months later the Toyosato mine closed.

The fate of those miners who retained their jobs in this tumultuous period was not much better than those who lost them. Wage increases in the mining industry continually fell short compared to gains made in other sectors. For example, the wage increases in 1960 and 1961—¥395 and ¥1,341 per month increase respectively—were the lowest increases out of twenty-five industries surveyed by the Federation of Employers' Associations (*Nikkeiren*).[37] Bonuses also ranked among the lowest of those negotiated in the same period, with the summer and winter bonuses amounting to only one-half of the average for sixteen major industries. These low bonuses came at a time when productivity was soaring: labour output in the coal mines nearly tripled between 1959 and 1968. By 1964 worker productivity in Japan's coal industry had surpassed that of Belgium, France, West Germany, and England.[38] Given the short period under consideration, it is difficult to attribute the leaps in productivity to mechanization. The bulk of the increases were the result of an intensification of labor or speedups. While coal producers no doubt thought they were finally getting their money's worth, in the end the production-first mentality led to tragedy.

The afternoon shift was already on the job in the Mikawa colliery at Miike on that fateful day—November 9, 1963. The coal dust in the mine was pretty bad but living with it was a miner's lot. But at around 3:10 that afternoon, somewhere, somehow a spark ignited a pocket of gas and the dust disappeared, consumed in a thunderous explosion. Underground miners from the afternoon shift, and those exiting from the day shift but who had not yet reached the surface were trapped, forever. The final toll: 458 miners dead and 800 injured.

Substantial documentation ties the explosion to speedups and the subsequent deterioration in safety conditions that accompanied the rationalization program at Miike after the lockout in 1960. John G. Roberts charges in his book, *Mitsui*, that Mitsui Mining cut back on maintenance and safety personnel as part of the stringency program and that the water-spray system to damp down coal dust was poorly maintained.[39] After investigating the tragedy, the Fukuoka prosecutors office decided in 1966 that there was no clear basis to press criminal charges against Mitsui. Survivors of the disaster sued Mitsui, however, because of the carbon monoxide poisoning they suffered at the time. In 1974 the Fukuoka District Court found Mitsui guilty of "ignoring safety and failing to fulfil its re-

37. Nikkeiren, *Sangyō Rōdō Gensei Hōkoku* [Report on current conditions of industrial labor] (Tokyo: Nikkeiren, 1962), pp. 160–161.
38. Rōdō Shō, *Tankō rishokusha taisaku jū nen shi*, p. 351.
39. John G. Roberts, *Mitsui: Three Centuries of Japanese Business* (New York: Weatherhill, 1973).

sponsibility to prevent mine accidents" and awarded the plaintiffs substantial compensation.[40]

Miike was not the only mine to suffer tragedy linked to the massive rationalization plan. Even mainstream sources, such as the elite Japan Development Bank, were forced to at least acknowledge the human costs: "Going to excessive links to ensure coal production when there was a shortage of manpower, mine disasters multiplied, with 61 lives lost at Yūbari mine, 30 at Iōshima, and 237 at the Yamano mine."[41] These three disasters all occurred in 1965. The government's own figures indicate that the rationalization program and speedups were directly related to the mine tragedies. Whereas in every other industry the accident rate declined by an average of 40 percent between 1959 and 1969, in the coal industry the accident rate actually increased by 50 percent. "One can hardly say that the rapid increase in productivity had nothing to do with the mine disasters," was the way one labor department bureaucrat put it.[42]

That labor suffered the consequences of chaotic and often poorly managed industrial decline would seem beyond question. Economists' attempts to portray this as a consequence of poor competitiveness, that is, coal's inability to compete with oil, tells us little. As I have attempted to demonstrate, the decline of the coal industry was a political choice, just as the protection of the rice industry, despite its noncompetitiveness with foreign imports, was and still is a political choice. Politicians could have argued, as they had in the past, that preserving Japan's coal industry was a national trust just as preserving the rice industry. But this did not happen. Coalminers were not as important electorally for the LDP as rice farmers. Under pressure from the steel industry, the business community opted to abandon the coalminers while giving the coal companies extensive subsidies. The LDP was more than willing to accede to this strategy. Just as rice consumers had little input into the decision to protect rice, miners and other workers had little input into the decision to abandon coal, because these decisions were made within the highest echelons of big business and government. Neither conservative nor independent unions had much influence at these levels.

The tale of industrial decline also occurred in textiles, and later in steel and shipbuilding. But the adjustment process was smoother by then, although workers still paid a heavy price when transferred or obliged to quit. Competitiveness proved to be a transient phenomenon, and there was no guarantee of employment to long term. And even competitive, world-class sectors such as the automotive industry displayed important problems, raising once again the question: Is what is good for the company good for the employee?

---

40. As cited in Kamata Satoshi, *Saru mo jigoku, nokoru mo jigoku* [For those who left—a living hell; for those who remained—an inferno] (Tokyo: Chikuma Bunko, 1986), p. 151.

41. Nihon Kaihatsu Ginkō, *Nihon Kaihatsu Ginkō nijū go nen shi*, p. 390.

42. Rōdō Shō, *Tankō rishokusha taisaku jū nen shi*, p. 338.

The Public Sector: Moriguchi City

The 1960s witnessed the transformation of Moriguchi from a medium-sized, rural town into a bustling suburb of Osaka. As industry grew, so too did the population. Land formerly devoted to farming was gobbled up by residential and industrial construction. Table 34 gives some indication of the scale of growth. Between 1957 and 1967, the number of farming families declined by 32 percent. Of the farmland sold or leased between 1957 and 1967, 50 percent went to residential construction, 21 percent was used for industrial sites, and 23 percent was dedicated for warehouses, parking lots, and so forth. Only 6 percent was designated for public use. In 1956 National Highway One was built through Moriguchi, making the city an attractive site for investment. Between 1957 and 1972 the population nearly doubled.

The urbanization of Moriguchi exerted tremendous pressure for increased city services. Between 1960 and 1969 employment at city hall nearly doubled (555 to 1,087) and then increased by another 500 in the three years that followed. As in many large plants, new hires were recruited each April. Increasing the work force implied hiring for new posts and also replacing retiring workers. In the expansive years, the city was hiring as many as 250 new employees each April.

The larger work force and expanding services prompted the city hall to reorganize its management structures. In 1958, for example, the city operated with 13 autonomous sections and 23 departments. Ten years later, the city operated with five divisions, including general affairs, civil affairs, health and sanitation, construction, and engineering or waterworks. The mayor's office exercised supervision over the divisions. The 13 sections of 1958 had expanded to 23 and now operated under the divisions, and the number of departments jumped from 23 to 55 in this period.

According to the union's history, the 1961–1968 period represented a decline in union influence. Unionists of the Satellite City Federation, to which the Moriguchi union had been affiliated, came under attack after the federation pushed wage struggles in 1959 to 1961. Three union leaders at Sakai city hall, for example, were sacked in 1962 and twelve executive members were suspended for six months for their role in the wage dispute. At Moriguchi, management attempted to co-opt the union leadership by offering them managerial positions. The management hierarchy at city hall was amplified by eleven newly created posts (from assistant team leader to division head), each with some supervisory functions.

In the 1962 local union elections at Moriguchi only four candidates ran for eight executive positions, and none of the officer positions were filled. The 1963 local annual meeting failed to even achieve quorum, and the youth and women's division dissolved because of nonparticipation.

Table 34. Urbanization of Moriguchi, 1960–1972

Year	Households	Population	Businesses	Factories	City employees
1960	23,339	102,295	3,331	370	555
1966	41,177	144,558	5,379	687	819
1969	57,603	179,529	8,054	1,038	1,087
1972	61,138	184,259	10,036	1,792	1,519

Source: Moriguchi Shisei Yōran, *Moriguchi shi tōkei sho,* in Moriguchi Shi Shokuin Rōdō Kumiai, *Moriguchi shi shokurō sanjū go nen shi* [Thirty-five years of the Moriguchi Employees Union] (Moriguchi, 1981), p. 223.

Union atrophy at the local level was accompanied by a rightward swing within the All Japan Prefectural and Municipal Union Federation (AJPMUF). The Satellite City Federation, an autonomous regional block whose affiliates were also members of the national AJPMUF, was the focus of attack. In August 1964 the AJPMUF annual convention resolved to exclude the SCF, supposedly because it wanted to rationalize its organization and have only one regional body for each prefecture. Behind this organizational shakeout, however, an important political agenda was being carried out. The leadership of the AJPMUF basically wanted to wrest control of the Osaka area by getting rid of the JCP-influenced Satellite City Federation. It demanded that all its Osaka area locals affiliate with the prefectural headquarters. Some locals were reluctant to abandon the SCF, but eventually most did, including the Moriguchi union.

The decline in local union activism led, according to the Moriguchi union, to a change in the relation of forces and a relative decline in wages and working conditions at Moriguchi. Wage levels at Moriguchi had exceeded national civil servants wages and private sector wages in the Osaka region in 1962 and 1963, but they fell beneath them from the 1964 to 1968.[43] After 1965, neither the mayor nor his assistants even bothered to make an appearance during collective bargaining.

The decline in adversarialism in union-management relations at Moriguchi began to turn around as activists emerged among the new recruits hired in the late 1960s. These activists joined with female employees and outside workers to form a revitalized core of union militancy.

Over two hundred women worked for the city, many of them concentrated in the city-operated nursery schools and kindergartens. Women from the seven nurseries first became active in the union by organizing a discussion group, which created the impetus for a union women's committee in 1969. The committee's first plan outlines some of their grievances:

43. Moriguchi Kumiai, *Moriguchi shi shokurō sanjū go nen shi,* p. 220.

In the main facility, women are still required to come in early and fix tea or clean up. Cooks, who often suffer work-related injuries such as burns, are not given any sort of danger allowance. School employees always have to do overtime whenever there is a staff meeting, and they are often asked to work until noon on Saturdays. At the kindergartens, there are a lot of charges and never enough time to keep an eye on all the children. Even at the nurseries there is not enough time to have lunch. In these circumstances even the few women's rights that have been recognized by statute are not observed. For example, even though most women know that menstrual leave is necessary, given the circumstances they know they can't take it and have given up.[44]

In 1972, the women's committee, through the union, sent Mayor Kizaki a manifesto on childcare. They first demanded that children be respected as people, that they be valued as members of society, and that they be brought up in a proper environment. Specifically, they called for

clarifying the role of nursery supervisors and assuring at least one roving nursery attendant for each nursery and two for those with children still nursing,
guaranteed breaks,
room for breaks,
one attendant and cook for each nursery and a second cook for nursery with children still nursing,
recognition of childcare work as a distinct trade and appropriate change in rank,
provision of a special allowance,
recognition of past experience with adjustments for those currently working,
fixing child-supervisor ratios and limiting the number of children in each nursery,
provision of appropriate work clothes (t-shirts for summer, sweaters in winter, ballet shoes for footwear) instead of office wear.[45]

After discussions with personnel, the city agreed to a number of the women's demands (including special allowances) and the women's committee lost no time publicizing their gains in their in-house newsletter, *Women's Committee News*. In the same year, the women's committee, in its own name, presented specific demands concerning maternity leave. The women asked for paid leave for checkups during pregnancy, for eight weeks' leave before delivery and another eight weeks after, and for maternity replacements while on leave.

Two years after women became active, a new youth bureau was established within the union. Any male union member under thirty could join the bureau, which according to its regulations would work to build "fighting unity," provide

44. "1970 Women's Committee Action Plan" (June 12, 1970) as cited in ibid., p. 228.
45. Moriguchi Kumiai, *Moriguchi shi shokurō sanjū go nen shi*, pp. 229–230.

a lieu for study, develop workers' culture, fight for peace and democracy, and in conjunction with the women's committee build a militant union movement.[46] In September, 1971 the youth bureau presented the personnel department with a list of twenty-eight demands. It pressed the issue of overnight guard duty and eventually obliged the personnel department to abolish the practice of having new hires stay overnight at city hall to guard the premises.[47] The youth bureau also began to openly criticize the local executive for its lack of effective leadership in mobilizing the membership around the 1972 summer bonus.

The third component in the fight to rejuvenate the local were the nonregular employees, particularly the outside manual workers. Although the local had been able to convert 70 percent of the jobs into regular positions, a substantial number of casual positions remained. Furthermore, even the regular outside workers faced renewed discrimination when the city adopted a separate, lower pay scale for them. This pay scale was modeled after one the National Personnel Authority had introduced for national civil servants in 1963. Faced with this discrimination, manual workers in the waterworks department decided to split from the Moriguchi union in 1966. Other outside workers also began to caucus and discussed forming a separate union. After discussions with the national and local unions, however, an entente was reached in 1969. The outside workers gained a permanent representative on the executive, and the local agreed to allot funds to allow outside workers to organize. The outside workers maintained a permanent caucus, the Outside Workers Conference (Gengyō Hyōgi Kai), which also began to submit its own demands to the personnel department.[48]

1973: Watershed Year

Both political and economic factors sparked the resurgence of independent union activism at Moriguchi city hall. On the one hand, women and outside workers clearly saw themselves as disadvantaged within the system. Their demands and organization had spontaneous roots. At the same time, the JCP gained considerable support among younger employees and helped to organize the youth bureau. The three groups converged to reinvigorate the union as a vehicle for their aspirations. Another aspect to the emerging dynamic of confrontation was inflation, which by the early 1970s was seriously undermining wage increases won in the earlier period.

The simmerings of confrontation of 1969–72 boiled over in 1973, when the local union took an active role in the annual spring offensive and—even more sig-

46. Ibid., pp. 237–238.
47. Ibid., p. 241.
48. Ibid., p. 251.

nificant—articulated its own demands and pressed them through job actions including a work stoppage.

The year began with the local union submitting its wage proposals to the spring offensive coordination committee. Wage demands included (1) increasing the starting wage for high school graduates to a minimum of ¥62,000 per month (¥128,000 for an employee with seventeen years seniority); (2) adoption of the National Civil Service Administrative Wage Scale I excluding grades seven and eight (the low-end grades); (3) implementation of regular, incremental steps up the pay scale based exclusively on seniority; and (4) abolition of the Administrative Wage Scale II (a lower wage scale previously used for outside workers) and integration of those workers classified under the old scale into Wage Scale I.[49]

In articulating these demands, the Moriguchi union was fundamentally challenging the performance-based wage system, which had led to inequality in wages and had thereby divided union members. The accumulated inconsistencies in alloting annual wage increases through the performance-based or individual merit system had led to the situation illustrated in Table 35. As this table shows, although union members' wages clearly did increase with seniority (or age, a functional equivalent), they did so *unequally*. This provides further evidence to back the argument that it is quite inappropriate to describe the system as a seniority or age-based system when clearly performance evaluations and other factors led to fundamental differences in salaries received by individuals.

Negotiations over local demands did not take place until the fall because the local and prefectural civil service employees wage negotiations were conducted only after the National Personnel Authority (NPA) issued its annual report in late summer. In the meantime, Moriguchi city employees engaged in limited local job actions as part of the spring offensive. The main demands of the national spring offensive were wage increases, the right to strike for the public sector, a reduction in work hours, and pensions. The Civil Service Joint Struggle Committee and the AJPMUF had decided to participate in the national days of action called for April 17 (a sixty-minute work stoppage) and April 27 (a half-day general strike). At the local level, the Moriguchi union executive called on its members to book off for one hour on April 17 and to set up picket lines during that hour. Over one thousand employees took part in the work stoppage; instead of reporting to work they met at the community center just across the street from city hall. Buoyed by this successful job action, the local executive called for all-out participation in the half-day general strike planned for the morning of April 27. Despite intimidation by city officials, well over half the employees gathered at the community center in what amounted to the first successful general strike at Moriguchi city hall.

---

49. Ibid., p. 262.

Table 35.   Number of employees in each wage bracket, by age, Moriguchi City Hall, 1974

Wage (¥)	Age					
	22	27	32	37	42	47
66,000	6					
68,000						
70,000	23					
72,000						
74,000	49	1				
76,000		4				
78,000						
80–84,000		15	5	2		
86–90,000		19	6	2	3	
92–96,000		27	8	4	4	1
98–102,000			5	1	1	
104–108,000			11	3	3	
110–120,000			6	3	1	4
122–130,000				3		1
132–140,000					3	2
142–150,000					1	2
152–160,000					3	1
162–170,000						2

Source: Moriguchi Shi Shokuin Kumiai, *Dai 30 kai Moriguchi Shi Shokuin Kumiai teiki taikai, hōkoku-shiryō shū 1974* [Report and materials to the 30th regular convention of the Moriguchi City Employees Union, 1974] (Moriguchi, 1974), p. 68.

After the April 27 action, the last in the spring offensive, labor relations settled down to await the publication of the National Personnel Authority's summer wage recommendations. The NPA's annual report was directed only at civil servants on the national level, and even then it was subject to cabinet and Diet approval. Its recommendations nevertheless acted as a benchmark for wage negotiations for the whole of the public sector.

On August 9 the NPA released its 1973 report, calling for a 15.39 percent wage increase (a ¥14,493 average increase for national civil servants). Shortly after, the Osaka prefectural headquarters of AJPMUF held a representative council meeting to discuss the wage strategy for the fall. It called for wage agreements to be in place by September (through bylaw changes) and for retroactive pay to be disbursed by October. The regional union called for a sixty-minute walkout on September 13 to back up wage demands if necessary.

At this point, dissension appeared within the local executive over the bottom line in collective bargaining. Executive members with a support base among women, youth, and outside workers wanted to focus on local demands, including the abolition of the discriminatory Wage Scale II, automatic progression up the wage scale, and a standard minimum starting wage regardless of occupation. At the end of August the caucuses began a campaign at the workplace to popularize these local demands.

When collective bargaining began on September 3, Moriguchi city officials announced they would attempt to meet the wage standards set out in the NPA recommendations but were unwilling to discuss the local demands. On September 7 the local polled its members regarding the walkout planned for September 13. The proposed job action received ratification by a 55 percent majority. Even this slim majority support still indicated substantial support for militant unionism, particularly since all job actions in the civil service were illegal under existing labor laws.

From the 8th to the 19th of September local union activists stepped up activities at work sites. Union members wore headbands to work; meetings and demonstrations were held at lunchtime and after work. On September 13 union picketers closed the city hall in the morning, and hundreds of union members gathered at the community center. Here union leaders gave them an update on negotiations and local representatives of the JSP and JCP delivered messages of support. Negotiations became tense as union members began to congregate outside the meeting rooms. During breaks the members would swarm into the meeting hall in what appeared to be a reincarnation of the mass negotiations of the 1940s. Finally, on September 19, collective bargaining resumed, with hundreds of union members standing vigil outside the meeting room. The city officials caved in and agreed to (a) a uniform starting wage of ¥60,400, (b) automatic progression up the wage scale, and (c) abolition of the discriminatory Wage Scale II and coverage of all employees under Wage Scale I. All of these changes would be retroactive to April 1, 1973. The wage scale was amended and is reproduced in Table 36.

The victory in the 1973 wage battle led to wholesale changes in the local executive in the elections that followed. Opposition candidates representing the reform forces (women, youth, and outside workers) swept the slate, leaving only the former president and treasurer to maintain their positions by acclamation.[50]

In October the local union regrouped and called for further struggle over outstanding issues, for the winter bonus, and a supplementary wage increase. Collective bargaining resumed on November 13, initially over the winter bonus. The union called for a winter bonus equal to four months' wages plus ¥40,000 across the board. It had demanded as well an end to bonus additions based on performance evaluations (kinben teate or diligence allowance). Under pressure from the union, the personnel department disclosed the results of the diligence allowance on 1973 summer bonuses. According to this information, 22 people had received a supplemental .15 months' pay, 99 people had received a supplement of .12 months' pay, 128 people received an additional .08 months' bonus, and 258 peo-

---

50. Ibid., p. 275.

Table 36.   Moriguchi City employees wage scale, 1 April 1973 (yen)

Grade 1		Grade 2		Grade 3		Grade 4		Grade 5		Grade 6	
Step	Wage	Step	Wage	Step	Wage	Step	Wage	Step	Wage	Step	Wage
1	119,200	16	105,500	13	88,800	9	74,000	5	60,400	1	53,5
2	124,500	17	109.800	14	92,700	10	77,400	6	63,600	2	55,6
3	129,900	18	114,100	15	96,600	11	80,800	7	66,800	3	57,8
4	135,400	19	118,400	16	100,500	12	84,300	8	70,000	4	60,4
5	140,900	20	122,800	17	104,400	13	87,800	9	73,200	5	63,0
6	146,400	21	127,200	18	108,600	14	91,400	10	76,400	6	65,6
7	151,900	22	131,600	19	112,800	15	95,000	11	79,500	7	68,2
8	157,400	23	136,100	20	117,000	16	98,600	12	82,600	8	70,8
9	162,900	24	140,600	21	121,200	17	102,200	13	85,400	9	73,0
10	168,200	25	145,100	22	125,400	18	105,800	14	88,200	10	75,2
11	173,400	26	149,300	23	129,600	19	109,400	15	91,000	11	77,2
12	178,000	27	153,500	24	133,700	20	113,000	16	93,800	12	79,2
13	182,400	28	157,700	25	137,700	21	116,300	17	96,600	13	81,2
14	186,600	29	161,900	26	141,700	22	119,400	18	99,000	14	82,9
15	190,600	30	165,500	27	145,700	23	122,400	19	101,400	15	84,6
16	194,300	31	169,100	28	149,100	24	125,400	20	103,700	16	86,3
17	197,700	32	171,900	29	152,400	25	127,600	21	106,000	17	88,0
18	200,600	33	174,700	30	155,000	26	129,800	22	108,000	18	89,6
19	203,400	34	177,500	31	157,600	27	131,900	23	110,000	19	90,9
20	206,200	35	180,300	32	160,200	28	133,500	24	111,500		
21	209,000	36	183,100	33	162,800	29	135,100	25	113,000		

Source: Moriguchi Shi Shokuin Kumiai, *Dai 30 kai Moriguchi Shi Shokuin Kumiai teiki taikai, hōkoku shiryō shū 1974* (Moriguchi, 1974).

ple received a supplement of .04 months' pay.[51] This meant that more than 50 percent of all employees had received no diligence allowance at all, a fact not happily received by those workers who felt they had performed at least satisfactorily. Yamamoto Kikue, a school assistant, laughingly recalled her 1973 activism: "We wanted some sort of bonus allowance, and asked for it, *skoshi demo chodai* [even if just a bit], everyone came out, from 5 or 6 o'clock when we finished work we all got together, deciding on a gathering point then. And then from 7 o'clock things would get going, we'd gather in the hall just outside the mayor's office, and we'd send in our delegates to negotiate with them and we'd be sitting there with over one hundred or two hundred people, that's my memory."[52] In the early morning of October 20 the two sides finally reached an agreement: the winter bonus would be equal to 3.16 months' salary plus ¥21,000 prorated, plus an across-the-board lump sum of ¥2,000. The diligence allowance was abolished and part-time and temporary employees were also to be paid a winter bonus.

51. Ibid., p. 287.
52. Yamamoto Kikue, interview 14 October 1988. Yamamoto was a school assistant and union activist.

The struggles that occurred at Moriguchi in the early 1970s and the subsequent changes—the revision of the compensation system and the enfranchisement of women, outside workers, and part-time and casual workers—were significant. They become dramatic if one compares them to the developments, in the automobile industry. Compared to workers at Suzuki, Moriguchi employees had few rights. They did not have the right to strike, and their right to bargain collectively was severely restricted. One might have expected, therefore, fewer gains at the workplace. But the opposite occurred, and the question is why. One reason was that management was not as tough at Moriguchi as it was at Suzuki. Another was the nature of the unions.

I would argue that the Suzuki and Moriguchi unions were, on an organizational level, both enterprise unions. But in one case this fact restricted the scope of union action and in the other it did not. Organizationally the Moriguchi union was similar in its local character to the union at Suzuki. The difference was mainly in the orientation of the union. Despite the legal impediments, the Moriguchi union succeeded in mobilizing workers to fight for themselves. The union, whatever its problems, based itself among those who wanted change. It developed a concrete agenda reflecting an egalitarianism that the majority of workers supported. And it did not let itself be bound by the fetters of constraint and consultation that seemed so ingrained at Suzuki. In a word, it articulated a workers' agenda that was *independent* of the employer's. The Moriguchi union was, however, the exception that proved the rule of enterprise unionism as a political formation.

Hegemony and High-Speed Growth

As the history of the coal industry exemplified, decline was part of the high growth economy. But on the whole, job expansion and higher wages were two key elements that made the 1960–75 period one of relative consolidation for Japanese industrial relations. Wage increases were not automatic, however, and workers, regardless of union affiliation, had to struggle to recapture part of the benefits of high productivity. On the employment front, the labor force increased from about 45 million workers in 1960 to 52.7 million in 1974.[53] But this relatively small increase in the labor force hid some important transformations that were taking place. First, the increase was relatively small because a decreasing percentage of the population was entering the job market. Participation fell from 70.8 percent of the potential labor force (fifteen years of age and older) to 63.5 percent in 1974. The number of paid employees was increasing rapidly as the number of entrepre-

53. Rōdō Shō, *Rōdō hakusho, 1975* [Labor White Paper, 1975] (Tokyo: Okura Sho, 1975), p. 230.

neurs and family workers declined, however. Surprisingly, female participation in the paid labor force also declined over this period, from 54.9 percent in 1955 to 46.6 in 1974. This figure masks the fact, however, that more and more women were moving from the family farm to become paid employees. In other words, rapid growth brought the postwar industrialization process to a close, with agricultural workers declining from almost 30 percent of the labor force to just over 11 percent by 1974 while wage workers increased by nearly 60 percent. However, the decline in the percentage of the population that worked and the expanding economy created a relatively tight job market in Japan in the 1960s. This change in the labor market would have an important but temporary effect on the wage gap between men and women and between workers in small and large enterprises.

As the case studies reveal, however, not all industries experienced this tighter job market. The coal industry was a prime example of the instability of employment for workers in a declining industry. Furthermore, the failure of employers in the industry to place miners in alternative positions, despite massive government subsidies, is one example of the failure of the evolving system of employment tenure. In subsequent years there were other examples, in the shipbuilding industry for example, although the scale of disruption was much smaller.[54]

Nevertheless, employment with large employers in particular took on some aspects of long-term tenure, not because of employer benevolence but because the patterns of recruitment, the wage system, and workers' bitter resistance to layoffs made long-term employment patterns the only logical choice. Even then job security was only tacit—employers continued to eschew the idea of written job security agreements such as those that had existed in the coal mining industry in the 1950s. What arose instead was a normative commitment to avoid layoffs and, if they were unavoidable, to adjust staffing levels through restrictions of new hires, attrition, early retirement, transfers, and so forth. The Japan Productivity Center's first productivity principle—to achieve full employment and to mitigate against layoffs through transfers—had by the 1970s become a reality for male workers in larger enterprises.

To what extent workers in smaller enterprises enjoyed employment tenure remained a matter of debate. But one fact is certain, during this period women remained largely excluded from the tenure track. This exclusion was based not only on occupational segmentation or on their exclusion from large enterprises but rather on the expectation that women would quit their employment once they married or became pregnant. This, and the related phenomenon of nonpromotion, led to important legal actions by women. In 1966 the Tokyo District Court

54. See Nitta Michio, *When the Lifetime Employment Strategy Fails: Case Studies on the Japanese Shipbuilding and Coal Mining Industries,* Occasional Papers in Labor Problems and Social Policy, no. 12 (Tokyo: Institute of Social Science, University of Tokyo, 1992).

sided with Suzuki Setsuko in her landmark case against Sumitomo Cement for forcing her to retire upon marriage.[55] Despite this and other favorable decisions for women, Japanese enterprises continued to find informal ways of continuing this practice.

Wages, both nominal and real, increased in this period and the length of the workweek began to decline. At Suzuki, the average wage climbed from ¥46,000 per month in 1965 to approximately ¥175,000 in 1974. This roughly corresponded to the wage increase in manufacturing generally during this period. Over this same ten-year period the cost-of-living index increased by about 100 percent, however. But even taking inflation into account, real wages almost doubled.

The shortages in the labor market allowed women and workers in small and medium-sized industries to close the wage gap slightly with employees in large enterprises. Women's wages as a percentage of men's had fallen to a postwar low of 41 percent in in 1960. This trend was then reversed, and by 1974 women were earning about 50 percent of what men made.[56] Workers in smaller enterprises also closed the gap by about 10 percent over this period. At the same time, working hours in industry declined from an average of 202.7 hours per month (including overtime) in 1960 to 175.5 by 1974. The combination of increased real wages and a decrease in work hours marked a general break from the 1950s, during which wages increased marginally and the workweek actually lengthened until 1958.

Improvements in living standards reflected the imperative of a Fordist regime of accumulation: mass production demands mass consumption. The tight labor market and the pressure from labor to improve working conditions clearly had an effect in this period. At issue, then, is not whether living standards improved. From a strictly economic standpoint, clearly they did compared to earlier periods. At issue is how things improved and—in the context of the current debate regarding the appropriateness of Japan as a model of economic development— how much things improved from a comparative perspective. Table 37 draws on a detailed study of this issue by Yamamoto Kiyoshi.[57] The table illustrates real wage growth, productivity, and labor's share of productivity in four countries for the years 1952–70. These figures are rough approximations, but they do afford us some perspective on labor's return from productivity increases. Annual wage increases in Japan and Germany increased at a much higher rate than in the United States and Great Britain. Because Japan's productivity increases were much higher than even West Germany's, however, labor's relative share in Japan actually declined relative to other countries. Such figures are not surprising. Dore

55. For details on this and other cases see Alice H. Cook and Hiroko Hayashi, *Working Women in Japan* (Ithaca: Cornell University, 1980), chap. 2, and Sugeno Kazuo, *Japanese Labor Law* (Seattle: University of Washington Press, 1992), pp. 126–135.

56. Rōdō Shō, *Rōdō hakusho, 1975 nenban*, p. 261.

57. Yamamoto Kiyoshi, *Nihon no chingin, rōdō jikan.*

Table 37. Wages, labor productivity, and labor's share, 1952–1970

Country	Average annual wage increase	Annual increase, labor productivity	Labor's share of value added	Rate of increase in labor's share
Great Britain	3.3	2.9	63.9	0.5
United States	1.9	3.4	49.9	-1.5
West Germany	5.7	6.0	40.1	-0.3
Japan	5.4	10.0	33.2	-4.2

Source: Yamamoto Kiyoshi, Nihon ng chingin, rōdō jikan (Tokyo: Tokyo Daigaku Shuppan Kai, 1982), tables 9, 11.
Note: Labor's share is only for the years 1963–1969.

made a similar discovery about labor's returns from his comparative study of electrical works in Great Britain and Japan.[58] This was precisely why Sōhyō in the 1960s began to demand wage increases that would bring Japan's wages in line with those in Europe.

In the length of the workweek as well Japan began to fall behind. As the Suzuki documentation indicated, workers did not win the forty-hour work week until 1972 and even then its implementation was often delayed. In West Germany, I. G. Metall, the union representing transportation workers, demanded the forty-hour week as early as 1955 and won it in the early 1960s, although its implementation was delayed until 1967.[59] In larger enterprises in Japan, the forty-hour week did become the nominal standard in the 1970s, but overtime and economic dualism combined to put Japan's workers at the bottom of the heap in terms of actual hours worked.[60] Prolonged work hours, speedups, and transfers—important components in the flexible production regime—all acted to undermine the gains from the contractual shorter workweek and from enhanced job security.

The Labor Movement

Union membership increased in this period, reaching 12.6 million in 1975 (34.4 percent of the work force). As a result of limited unionization rates and increases in the labor force, the actual unionization densities continued to decline in

58. Dore, British Factory–Japanese Factory, pp. 330–332.
59. A. S. Markovits and C. S. Allen, "Trade Unions and the Economic Crisis: The West German Case," in Peter Gourevitch et al., Unions and Economic Crisis: Britain, West Germany and Sweden (London: Allen and Unwin, 1984), pp. 123–124.
60. In 1980 the average work week in Japan was 43.4 hours compared to 37.0 for West Germany. See Fujimoto Takeshi, Kokusai hikaku, Nihon no rōdō jōken [International comparisons, Japan's labor conditions] (Tokyo: Shin Nihon Shuppan Sha, 1984), p. 74.

this era of high growth, as they have, with few exceptions, throughout the postwar period. This was one indication of an institutional weakness to labor in Japan.

During the high-growth period, Sōhyō continued to act as a center for independent unionism; but industrial relations practices, particularly in the large, private enterprises, increasingly conformed to the enterprise model, and even some unions affiliated to Sōhyō had to conform to these standards. In exchange for union acceptance of the performance-based wage system and limited union input in regulation of the workplace, workers received some job security and annual wage increases. This "deal" had evolved at the workplace level in the 1950s, and although there were important exceptions, it did become the norm or pattern, particularly for the private sector.

In the post-Miike period another element was added to the pattern, the gradual expansion of joint consultation. On both the local and national levels, joint consultation as an alternative to collective bargaining began to flourish, and this process culminated in the establishment of labor-management consultative organs even on the sectoral level, particularly in the private sector (including mining, textiles, iron and steel, machinery and metal, shipbuilding, automobiles, and so forth).[61] A full assessment of joint consultation remains to be done, but it may well be that joint consultation did not provide labor with substantive input and thus, as Pempel and Tsunekawa conclud, the system in Japan reflects a form of corporatist intermediation that failed to develop into the forms of codetermination that developed in Europe.[62]

The defeats in steel in the late 1950s, the Miike conflict, and the subsequent decline of the JCU weakened Sōhyō's base within the private sector. Enterprise unions, on the other hand, attempted to refurbish their image, tarnished somewhat after the attempt by the conservative Japan Trade Union Congress to undermine the Miike miners. In 1962 the JTUC conservative was reorganized and renamed the Japan Confederation of Labor (JCL, Dōmei-Kaigi). This was followed in 1964 by another reorganization and a new name, Dōmei (still known as JCL in English). Private-sector unions in metal-related industries united in a loose

61. For an account of the development of joint consultation at the local level see Rōdō Sho, *Rōdō hakusho, 1973* [1973 White Paper on Labor] (Tokyo: Ōkura Sho, 1973), pp. 161–191. For background on the consultative bodies on the national level see Japan Institute of Labor, *Labor Unions and Labor-Management Relations* (Tokyo: Japan Institute of Labor, 1986), pp. 29–32.

62. See T. J. Pempel and Keiichi Tsunekawa, "Corporatism without Labor? The Japanese Anomaly," in P. Schmitter and G. Lehmbruch, *Trends toward Corporatist Intermediation* (London: Sage Publications, 1979). Pempel and Tsunekawa underestimate the development of joint consultation and also attribute the weakness of Japanese labor to enterprise unions as an organizational form. Nevertheless, their general observation, that unions in Japan did not exercise the clout of European unions, is accurate. There is also some evidence indicating workers were not at all satisfied with this form of representation. See S. J. Park, "Labor-Management Consultation as a Japanese Type of Participation: An International Comparison," in Tokunaga and Bergmann, *Industrial Relations in Transition.*

federation, the International Metalworkers Federation, Japan Council (IMF-JC, Kokusai Kinzoku Rōren Nihon Kyōgi Kai) in 1964. Over the next decade these organizations would come to play an increasingly pivotal role within the labor movement and actually dominate it after 1975.

The divisions in the trade union movement were also reproduced within the socialist parties. The old divisions between the JSP and JCP was further exacerbated by splits within the JSP itself. In 1959–60 a conservative faction of the JSP split off to form the Democratic Socialist Party, which obtained the support of the Japan Confederation of Labor (Dōmei). These political divisions further eroded the possibility for articulating a coherent labor program.

Further evidence that the hegemonic regime was undermining Sōhyō's independent orientation comes from the productivity movement. Despite Sōhyō's early critique of this movement and of the Japan Productivity Center, some of its affiliates began to participate in the activities of the Center as early as 1960.[63] The line of demarcation between independent and enterprise unions at the level of the workplace began to blur.

However, Sōhyō had not lost all its punch. It remained the leading force in Shuntō, the annual spring offensive that continued to play an important role in wage negotiations. As mentioned earlier, the steel unions aligned their negotiations with Shuntō in 1959, and the Federation of Independent Unions, representing about 10 percent of organized workers, also began to participate jointly with Sōhyō in the spring offensive. By the 1970s even the JCL was obliged to align negotiations of its affiliates with Shuntō, although it remained aloof from any direct organizational affiliation.

A number of significant developments related to Shuntō took place in this period. In 1964, Ōta Kaoru met with with Prime Minister Ikeda, at which time the government conceded that wage increases for public sector workers would be pegged to the agreements reached by unionized workers in large enterprises during Shuntō each year. On the one hand, this confirmed the second-class status of public sector unions, their right to full collective bargaining remained largely circumscribed. On the other hand, it assured public sector workers that they would remain in a similar wage bracket as their peers in large private enterprises. This gave them an ongoing incentive to unite with private-sector workers in Shuntō, because any concessions won by private-sector unions would be passed on to them.

Beginning around 1965, the four large metalworker unions—steel, shipbuilding, automobiles, and electrical machinery—had set the pattern for settlements in Shuntō. Also beginning around this time, the amount of the annual wage increase was going up every year, and this reached the point of institutionalization: the formula for the expected wage increase was last's years increase plus alpha. In other

63. For background see Nihon Seisan Sei Honbu, *Seisan sei undō 30 nen shi*, pp. 289–302.

words, unions were expecting that the rate of wage increases would accelerate every year. Inflation increased in the early 1970s and then spun out of control with the oil crisis of 1973. In 1973 and 1974 workers across Japan, regardless of union affiliation, banded together in limited but powerful Shuntō actions that, in 1974, won union workers in the private sector an average 32.9 percent wage increase. Inflation, running at about 25 percent in the spring of 1974, ate away much of the wage hike; but the increase, about ¥30,000 per month on the average, would be folded into the base wage, and the cumulative effect was significant for the long-term purchasing power of Japanese workers. Workers, we see, continued to fight for improvements in their living conditions right up to 1974, mainly through the mechanism of Shuntō.

Turning Point: 1975

Two events in 1975 significantly altered the course of the labor movement in postwar Japan. First, union leaders reined in the strike movement, which had gained such momentum in 1973–74. In 1975 the average Shuntō wage increase was about 13 percent while inflation was running at 15 percent. The decision to settle for what actually constituted a wage cut was carefully cultivated through the joint consultation system.

The first signs of a new wage entente came from the powerful metal unions. Prior to the 1975 Shuntō, Miyata Yoshikazu, president of the steelworkers union, announced at his union's August convention that it was no longer advisable for the union to continue its pattern of expecting a yearly wage increase equal to the previous year's increase plus alpha.[64] The JCL chairman, Amaike Seiji, also stated that autumn that the federation would be willing to engage in wage restraint if the government and employers would assist those socially disadvantaged.[65] Given the attitude of these key union leaders and the fact that, since 1965, the metal unions had set the pattern within Shuntō, it was not surprising that the 1975 wage pact fell as precipitously as it did, despite vigorous job actions that year. Enterprise unionism had planted the flag of self-restraint (jishuku) on its masthead as Japan headed into a period of slower growth.

The second momentous development in 1975 was the illegal eight-day strike that workers in crown corporations launched on November 26 to recover the right to strike, a right that had been taken away between 1948 and 1952.[66]

---

64. As cited in Ōtani Ken, *Sadurada Takeshi no Hito jin to tetsugaku,* p. 177.
65. See Sheldon Garon and Mike Mochizuki, "Negotiating Social Contracts," pp. 155–166.
66. This account of the 1975 strike is based on Takagi Ikujirō, "Kōrō kyō suto ken dakkan suto, 1975" [The 1975 strike to recover the right to strike in the public sector] in Rōdō Sōgi Shi Kenkyū

Those involved were employees covered by the Public Corporation and National Enterprise Labor Relations Law, including Japan National Railways, Nippon Telegraph and Telephone, and the Tobacco Monopoly as well as the Postal Service, National Forestry, National Printing, the Mint and the Liquor Monopoly.[67] The unions in these enterprises, under the banner of the Public Enterprise Labor Council (Kōkyō Kigyō Taitō Rōdō Kumiai Kyōgi Kai, or Kōrō Kyō) waged a series of actions throughout the postwar period to regain the right to strike. In 1975, they decided to begin a three-day series of rotating strikes beginning on November 26 to pressure the Miki government into granting them the right to strike. On the day the strikes began, however, a government-appointed blue-ribbon panel investigating the issue released its report, in which the majority recommended the status quo. The lack of movement infuriated many workers. Rail workers shut down the rail system completely, and the strikes lasted for another five days. On December 1 the government endorsed the majority report and refused to budge on the issue. Although some local government workers also walked off the job, labor support for the effort remained limited. The strikes inconvenienced many people, particularly employees trying to get to their work sites, and in some cases physical fights broke out between commuters and strikers. The nine unions involved in the strikes called off the effort on December 3.

For some, the 1975 strike looked like a futile effort in adversarialism. But there was much more involved than this simplistic perspective allows. In Canada, for example, similar strikes by public sector workers, such as the postal workers' strike in 1965 or the Common Front in Quebec in 1972, played a significant role in prompting the federal and many provincial governments to pass legislation giving public sector workers in Canada the right to strike. And in Japan there had been some indication that the government was willing to look at strike rights at least for workers in crown corporations.[68] But public-sector union leaders misjudged both the dynamics within the factions of the governing party and the change in the relation of forces that accompanied the onset of slow growth. The wage deal accepted by labor that spring, as part of Shuntō 1975, was a warning sign that Japan was entering a new era. The hawkish faction of employers and conservative union leaders became more assertive, and public sector workers were left to fend for themselves.

Kai, *Nihon no rōdō sōgi (1945–1980)* [Labor disputes in Japan, 1945–1980] (Tokyo: Tokyo Daigaku Shuppan Kai, 1991), pp. 345–381.

67. For background information on the public enterprises see Kōshiro Kazutoshi, "Labor Relations in Public Enterprises," in Shirai Taishiro, ed., *Contemporary Industrial Relations in Japan* (Madison: University of Wisconsin Press, 1983), pp. 259–293.

68. For details see Tagagi Ikujirō, "Kōrō kyō suto ken dakkan suto, 1975," pp. 361–363.

Post-1975 Developments

By 1986, Japan was awash in signs of prosperity. It had become the world's largest creditor nation; it controlled 30 percent of world automobile exports and over 50 percent of the total world exports in such fields as motorcycles, video recorders, cameras, and musical intruments. GNP per capita would soon overtake that of the United States, and Japan's trade balance was increasing year by year. These were also the tranquil years of labor relations. The number of worker days lost due to labor disputes plunged tenfold from an average six million days per year during 1970–74 to an average of just over 500,000 during 1980–84.[69]

To many Japanese, Japan had indeed undergone a dramatic transformation. But as Carol Gluck observes, "even when people shared the establishment's pride in national achievement, as they did by 1990, they felt deprived in their allotment of the touted goods, from housing to welfare—what is known as the 'rich Japan, poor Japanese' phenomenon."[70]

To be sure, many Japanese shared in the quest for economic prosperity. Employment levels remained high and wages increased. But as trade tensions with the United States increased, it became apparent that although Japan had perhaps won the competitive battle, it had also lost the race for well-being. These impressions—captured by the phrase "keizai taikoku, seikatsu shokoku" quoted by Gluck just above—were based on a reversal of trends that occurred in the post-1975 period.

Working hours, which had been on the decline in Japan until 1975, began to increase, and throughout the 1980s, Japan had the worst record among all industrialized countries.[71] The gap between women's and men's wages, which had declined in the pre-1975 period, began to grow again and in the early 1990s still remained greater than in 1975. This also placed Japan last among industrialized countries. In a related development, the spread in wages between workers in large and smaller enterprises widened again. Add to this list the high cost of housing, the extended periods spent commuting to work, the relative lack of social infrastructure, a recession, and continuous financial and political scandals, and it is little wonder that Japan entered a period of economic and political instability as it moved into the 1990s. Two events in 1989 were symbolic of the onset and contradictory nature of this transition. The Liberal Democratic Party lost control of the Upper House for the first time since 1955. And that same year Sōhyō, the flagship of independent unionism in Japan, voted to dissolve and join with other

---

69. Based on statistics in *Rōdō hakusho, 1975*, p. 304; *Rōdō hakusho, 1993*, p. 400.
70. Carol Gluck, "The Past in the Present," in Gordon, *Postwar Japan as History*, p. 76.
71. Rōdō Shō, *Rōdō hakusho, 1993* [1993 Labor White Paper] (Tokyo: Rōdō Kenkyū Kikō, 1993), p. 68.

federations, including the JCL, to form the eight-million-member Japan Trade Union Confederation (Nihon Rōdō Kumiai Sō Rengō Kai, or Rengō).

Internationally this crisis manifested itself in Japan's relations with the world, particularly its trading relationship with the United States. But domestically the focus is wider. Government and private agencies have become increasingly critical of what has been dubbed Japan's "corporate-centered" society and are demanding changes.[72] This phenomenon extended even to enterprise unionism. As was mentioned in the opening of this book, in 1992 the Japan Automobile Workers union acknowledged that its members were exhausted and the industry in crisis.[73] Shimada Haruo, advisor to the union and industrial relations scholar, concluded that unions had somewhere gone amiss: "Trade unions cooperated in this desperate competition for a share. Working hard, they lost their vision about for whom and what growth should be achieved."[74] A Rengō white paper also lamented the post-1975 record:

> Compared to 1975, productivity levels in manufactering, on an hourly basis, have increased 150 percent in real terms. The United States or Germany have gone up about 50 percent in the same period. On the other hand, real cash earnings in manufacturing have only gone up about 70 percent in Japan. In other words, the business foundation has been strengthened, competitiveness has been strengthened, but these things have not been reflected in wage improvements. Instead, the yen has appreciated in value and this is how international adjustment is being carried out.[75]

Yet, within a few months after the publication of labor's white paper, the results of the 1995 Shuntō showed that wage increases had dropped to their lowest level in postwar history. In Japan's steel industry, where productivity had far outstripped Germany and the United States over the past twenty years, 1995 brought no increase in base wages whatsoever.

72. For critical insights into these calls for reform see Osawa Mari, "Bye-bye Corporate Warriors: The Formation of a Corporate-Centered Society and Gender-Biased Social Policies in Japan," Occasional Papers in Labor Problems and Social Policy, no. 18 (Tokyo: Institute of Social Science, University of Tokyo, 1994).

73. Confederation of Japan Automobile Workers' Unions, "Japanese Automobile Industry in the Future" (Tokyo: JAW, 1992), p. 1.

74. Ibid., pp. 31–35. Shimada today is less inclined to see enterprise unions in a positive light. He still tends to see the issues from an organizational perspective (Japan's enterprise unions are unique), but he recognizes that their problems go beyond organizational issues. He believes they have become captive to an "industrial culture": "They are mentally restricted by the narrow scope of enterprise-level labor-management relations." See Shimada Haruo, "Japan's Industrial Culture," pp. 267–291.

75. Nihon Rōdō Kumiai Sō Rengō Kai, Rengō hakusho [Rengō white paper] (Tokyo: Rengō, 1995), p. 51.

9 Conclusion

In the course of this study, I came to the conclusion that Japan became neither a Sweden of the East, as Ronald Dore would have us believe, nor a revolutionary post-Fordist paradigm for the future, as Kenney and Florida assert. But the research also led me to reject the notion that Japan's workplace regimes in large enterprises had become havens of despotism, harking back to the satanic mills of early capitalism. The regimes that emerged from the crucible of postwar Japan were the result of conflict and compromise and thus bear the stamp of hegemony, that is, of accommodation as well as coercion. Workers and their struggles did make a difference, and we can trace the roots of the high-wage, full-employment economy in Japan to the struggles waged by organized labor for decent conditions in the 1950s, culminating in the 1960 Miike struggle, and for higher wages in the 1960s, culminating in the 1974 nationwide strike wave.

Of course, the stamp of hegemony reflected the specificity of Japan's own dynamics—economic, political, and cultural. This led to significant differences among the structures that emerged in the large workplaces. Women, whether they worked in these places or were excluded from them, were the most important group that remained largely isolated from the benefits of the system. But even for those who benefited, the workplace became an exercise in adaptation—survival and success depended on one's ability to embrace market norms and put the enterprise ahead of one's own interests or those of one's workmates.

This alignment of workers with the enterprise was the result of a complex set of structural incentives and disincentives. Enterprise unionism often facilitated acceptance of these control mechanisms. These levers of power placed management in a position to use workers "flexibly" and to innovate with quality circles. Flexibility for the employer, however, often meant sacrifices for workers. Extensive control, based on a blend of consent and coercion, was one of the key conditions for the rise of lean production. So, despite worker participation, neither repetitive work routines nor the assembly line disappeared in Japan's modern automobile factory. Instead, the system became tighter and work more intense. The significant difference from traditional Fordist practices was that in automobile factories in Japan, workers had to embrace to some extent the norms of capital accumulation. This led to high levels of efficiency and quality, but these standards exacted an intensification of labor. This is what struck outside observers such as the IMVP research team in their visit to Toyota; the team later admitted that work was harder in Japanese automobile plants than in North American plants. It also may explain why worker satisfaction levels at Toyota, for instance, were very low in the early 1990s.[1]

The difficulty workers had in finding an independent voice in the workplace is fundamental to understanding why lean production could not break with traditional Fordist practices, including the assembly line and short cycle times. The lack of an independent voice also compromised the workers' ability to cash in on the triumph of Japanese capitalism. It has now become commonly accepted in Japan that the returns to workers were neither commensurate with the costs to labor nor with the success of the enterprise. Kenney and Florida may argue that this is beside the point. These authors are not concerned with outcomes, nor with "the normative question of whether this model is 'better' or 'worse' than fordism or other Western economic arrangements."[2] There is a reason why Kenney and Florida avoid the normative. Despite their nominal acknowledgment of certain defects, they are more interested in "an objective theory of the Japanese production system."[3] But in their quest for the objective, they also eliminate workers and conflict, thereby eliminating the tension from the system and robbing it of its dynamic character. In the end, their work constitutes an immense effort in economic determinism, glorifying a system they believe would define the future of the advanced capitalist world. In so doing, they have misperceived the nature of Fordism, which is a regime based on politics as well as economics, on coercion as well as consent. Lean production may well take the world by storm, but if its mechanisms of control are reproduced and labor loses an independent voice, the future will be grim indeed.

This general conclusion, however, risks overshadowing what I believe are a number of other significant, specific findings that surfaced in the course of this

---

1. According to a Confederation of Japan Automobile Workers' Unions survey, less than 5 percent of autoworkers wanted their children to work in an automobile plant. As presented by Nomura Masami, "The End of Toyotism? Recent Trends in a Japanese Automobile Company" (paper presented at the Lean Workplace Conference, Port Elgin, Ontario, 1993), fig. 7.

2. Kenney and Florida, *Beyond Mass Production*, p. 10.

3. Ibid.

study. The historical approach to labor-management relations highlights the intense conflict that has shaped the postwar system of industrial relations. This pattern of conflict prevailed not only at Miike but also at Suzuki and Moriguchi. For Suzuki it was the 1946–50 period, for Miike 1950–60, and for Moriguchi 1970–73. In each case, these periods of conflict were fundamental in shaping later patterns of labor relations for better or for worse. What is the significance of this observation? Simply stated, the shape of contemporary labor relations cannot be understood except in a historical context that grants conflict its due place. From this perspective, one can conclude that many Japanese workers resorted to confrontation as one way to win some cooperation from employers and thereby improve their working lives. In fact, it was not until after 1975 that the contemporary stamp of labor-management collaboration really took root in a generalized way.

To be sure, conflict often seemed to end in defeat or victory. But regardless of the short-term outcome, the long-term impact usually reflected some elements of a compromise in class terms. Confrontation declined as Japan's Fordist regime consolidated, but conflict continued albeit in diluted and varied forms and over different issues. Today Suzuki unionists continue to haggle with management over how much of the yearly wage increase should be automatic and how much should be based on supervisors' evaluations of employee performance. This issue was resolved for Moriguchi employees in the 1970s. Struggle continued, but the nature, scope, and foci of conflict reflected differing regimes of industrial relations.

In this chapter I summarize our major findings through a comparative view of the case studies, I discuss the implications of our schema of Japan's labor and economic history, and I reassess our understanding of Japanese industrial relations.

Case Studies: Variations in Workplace Regimes

In the course of this study, we examined in some detail the production apparatuses in three workplaces—the Miike coal mine, the Suzuki automobile plants, and Moriguchi city hall. What were the important similarities and distinctions among these work sites? What shaped the diversity of these regimes?

Moriguchi

Suzuki and Miike were in the private sector while Moriguchi was in the public sector. The labor laws governing the regimes were therefore completely different. The public service labor laws prohibited government workers, even on the local level, to conclude collective agreements or to strike. In this way, the government constrained the public sector, in matters such as wages for example, to a level below that of the private sector. These were indeed impediments to some forms of union action. Paradoxically, however, the local union at Moriguchi appeared to thrive over the course of time; it developed its independence and even carved out arenas of contestation, specifically in gaining automatic movement up the incentive wage grid.

How did this happen? Even though the Moriguchi union had few regulatory rights, it flourished by incorporating the energies of younger workers, manual workers, and women who, under the system as it evolved in the 1950s and 1960s, faced discrimination in wages, bonuses, and so forth. To the extent that workers perceived discrimination, independent union action was possible. This discrimination existed at Moriguchi on a number of levels. Old status distinctions persisted, particularly those between office staff and manual laborers and between male and female work. One might interpret union activity in a cultural way: workers that faced discrimination yearned to have full membership in the community. The fact is that the material basis for the desire for change was rooted in the desire for equality and in that sense, the movement was a critique of the hierarchical community.

Thus, even though the Moriguchi union was precluded from signing collective agreements and from striking, it did begin to demand negotiations or consultations around specific issues including the yearly wage agreement. The process of wage determination for local government employees was and continues to be tiered. First, the National Personnel Authority decides on the annual average increase; then the local personnel board issues its recommendations; these are subsequently taken to the regional mayors council where the average wage increase is fixed for the region. However, there is some leeway in applying this average to local situations, and it is precisely in this niche that the Moriguchi union developed its own role.

That the union came under the influence of the Japan Communist Party was doubtlessly important. The JCP did not adhere to the politics of collaboration inherent in enterprise unionism. JCP adherents in the city hall union were willing to accommodate the aspirations of groups of workers within their jurisdiction and to channel these aspirations toward confrontation. Here we saw women and manual workers acting as catalysts for change.

On the other side of the equation, management at city hall may have been more flexible than employers in the private sector. Mayors, after all, were accountable to the electorate, not to the market. Furthermore, the management of labor relations at the city hall was less developed than at the personnel departments of larger enterprises. Again, precisely because many of the functions of the regulatory regime had been expropriated, the personnel department at Moriguchi appeared to be underdeveloped. Faced with a strong and organized union presence, management was happy to make some concessions that may well not have been tolerated in the private sector.

An often-asserted claim about unions in Japan is that public sector unions were more political because of their lack of rights. No doubt there is some truth to this, and for many years public sector unions, many of which were in Sōhyō, did continue to lobby and organize to win the same rights as their brothers and sisters in the private sector. It would seem, however, that the lack of union rights precipitated not only political action but also innovative reform of the regulatory system at the local level. Moriguchi workers' victory in de-linking yearly wage increases from supervisors' evaluations (allowing for automatic rise up the incremental wage ladder) was a small but significant change in the system. That this victory was won as part of a series of nominally illegal job actions is evidence of an alternative form of unionism at work.

The Moriguchi situation is one example of an approach to labor-management relations that departed from the enterprise unionism trend. I suspect there may have been many others in the public sector. The regimes at Nippon Telegraph and Telephone and Japan National Railways (until they were privatized in the late 1980s) are two examples that come immediately to mind and that bear further investigation. We see, then, that the political regimes of production may differ in the public sector not only because of state regulatory measures such as the restrictions on collective bargaining but also because independent unions continued to exist. In coping with their situations these unions transformed the politics of production in the public sector.[4]

Miike

The Miike story was an altogether different one. Three elements combined to create the conditions for intense conflict: an independent union, a regime bearing many of the markings of premodern industrial relations (including a piece-rate wage system and extensive company control of public life), and a declining industry.

The independence displayed by the Miike union had a broad foundation. First there was the political; the leadership of the union was very much a part of the left wing of the labor and socialist movements, and it carried out educational activities that clearly identified the interests of miners as separate from those of the mine management. But the form of wage negotiation also made an important

---

4. Mike Mochizuki has an excellent summary of labor relations in the railways and communications sectors in the 1980s in his article "Public Sector Labor and the Privatization Challenge: The Railway and Telecommunications Unions," in G. D. Allinson and Y. Sone, eds., *Political Dynamics in Contemporary Japan* (Ithaca: Cornell University Press, 1993), pp. 181–199.

contribution to energizing the rank and file. Even though average wage increases were negotiated at the industry and enterprise level, negotiations over specific job rates took place in the mines. It is little wonder that the Miike union never attempted to modify the wage system. As Burawoy reports in his study of Jay's and Allied machine shops, and as Tolliday and Zeitlin conclude in their study of automobile plants in Britain, when wage discussions descend to the shop floor they tend to provide a dynamic focus for rank-and-file action.[5] At Miike as at Jay's, production output and the compensation system were closely aligned. The third pillar in the Miike story was the mobilized group of women who supported and, indeed, helped direct the union. Firsthand observers who traveled to Miike as well as the miners themselves testified to the remarkable role played by the miners' wives during the 1960 dispute. But their role at that time was the result of a process of organization, one that had begun in the early 1950s as part of the union's strategy.

The union successfully overturned the paternal regime that permeated the workers lives. Miike was a company town (part of the city of Ōmuta), and Mitsui controlled the miners' debts and their housing. The Miike union put an end to this regime and began to carve out another, one that included substantial union control over the production process. As the Miike union began to stand out, it attracted the attention of top Mitsui management and Nikkeiren.

In 1958 imminent structural changes in the market, a united capitalist class, and a divided working class conspired to break the Miike union. The terrain of Japan's labor history is littered with the skeletons of independent unions. Pale shadows of them—enterprise unions—are often all that remain.

No objective observer can fail to see that the original Miike union represented the aspirations of a majority of its members. The before and after pictures of the Miike story are a tragic reminder that a union's acquiescence to the inevitable push for efficiency can have terrible consequences for workers. Might not the 457 miners who died in the 1963 mine explosion be alive today if the original Miike union had maintained its base in the mines?

It seems unlikely that there is any union in Japan that embodies the characteristics of the Miike union. Miike's legacy is indirect. It provoked a social crisis that caught the attention of top policymakers, who used the crisis to promote the agenda of the consent faction within the ruling elite. Thus Ikeda was able to promote his income-doubling plan over the protestations of Nikkeiren, and this gave unions more leverage in negotiations over wages for the next fifteen years. Furthermore, never again would employers consider large-scale layoffs as a first resort

---

5. Burawoy, *The Politics of Production*, pp. 128–137, and Steven Tolliday and Jonathan Zeitlin, "Shop Floor Bargaining, Contract Unionism, and Job Control: An Anglo-American Comparison," in Lichtenstein and Meyer, *On the Line*, pp. 219–244.

to resolving their economic difficulties. This strengthened the hand of the dovish faction of employers represented within the Japan Productivity Center. The three productivity principles came to the fore, and even Nikkeiren was obliged to tone down its antilabor rhetoric.

In the final analysis, the Miike case cannot represent the prototype of the dominant production regime in large, private enterprises in Japan. The Suzuki case study provided more insights into what many might consider a regime that typified the "three pillars" interpretation of labor-management relations.

Suzuki

The contemporary union at Suzuki has its origins in the destruction of an independent union during the great managerial offensive of 1949–50. Many other enterprise unions came into being, through dual unions or purges of the union, from the same era or afterwards. Hitachi, Tōshiba, Toyota, and Nissan are just a few.

After 1950 the Suzuki union accepted managerial control in the workplace and accepted the credo that what was good for the company was good for the workers. Its role was not to challenge management but to act as a sounding board, to play a consultative role. Concretely, this meant that it limited its role to discussions about the division of spoils, but even this became largely a ritual by the 1960s, since the formula for yearly wage increases was similar to one used in the United States (inflation plus an annual improvement factor). A second facet of the union's role was to act as a warning whistle, to sound the alarm when the company had pushed workers to the limits. When Suzuki began transferring workers helter-skelter in the early 1970s, the union intervened to sign a memorandum of agreement that would limit transfers to a six-month maximum. It also alerted the company to the problems of the extended workweek, and gradual reform began.

The Suzuki union accepted the performance-based, incremental wage system, even though this fundamentally weakened the union's impact in the workplace. Yearly increases for individual workers became dependent not so much on the union's ability to extract concessions from the company but on supervisors' evaluation of individual work performance. The union might haggle over what portion of the wage increase would be contingent on performance evaluations, but the basic structure was never challenged.

There were some signs that the union began to be informally integrated as a component of management. The chairman of Suzuki was a former leader of the breakaway union from 1950. And when workers in one Suzuki plant attempted to mount a legal challenge to transfers, the union recounted how they eventually left Suzuki employment. Further research is necessary, but the idea that enterprise unions integrate with management is hardly novel. Yamamoto Kiyoshi has documented this process in his work on Tōshiba.[6] However, the very nature of enterprise unions, not to mention the secrecy of private corporations, makes this type of documentation on any serious scale problematic. Nevertheless, the close ties between enterprise unions and employers deserve further scrutiny.

This brief summary of the variations among the case studies underscores the absolute necessity of breaking with stereotypes of industrial relations in Japan. No monolithic system predominates. Multiple systems have been shaped by many factors, including the impact of local unions, the legal framework, the size of enterprise, gender issues, and so forth. We may define certain parameters within which we construct a systems approach to analysis, but it is wrong to then substitute this analysis for reality. Recognition of diversity and variation must be the starting point for future research into work and workers in Japan. That the emphasis must shift to womens' experience and to the experiences of the 90 percent of the labor force who work in small and medium-sized industry should not have to be repeated.

Postwar History: Conflict and Compromise

From a regulationist perspective, I believe Japan's postwar labor history divides into the following periods: The 1945–48 period was one in which labor was in its ascendancy and union-articulated, indigenous forms of regulation were developing at the workplace; the 1948–51 period was one of reaction, when employers took the offensive, destroyed new forms of regulation that had evolved at the workplace, and eliminated, replaced, or transformed the unions that had inspired them; the 1951–60 period was a formative period during which the contemporary norms of regulation were established at the workplace—norms that bore the stamp of employer authoritarianism but which also reflected a sustained struggle and a resurgent but divided union movement; the 1960–74 period represented the consolidation of Japan's regime of market hegemony at the workplace and the consolidation of Shuntō, the annual spring offensive. The post-1975 era becomes the era of labor-management collaboration. Let us look more closely at this periodization.

Between 1945 and 1951, the state was under the control of SCAP, although other forces, including the Japanese government, had an important influence over some aspects of state dealings. Legislation related to labor was passed, in-

---

6. Yamamoto Kiyoshi, "The Japanese-Style Industrial Relations and an 'Informal' Employee Organization: A Case Study of the Ohgi-kai at T Electric," Occasional Papers in Labor Problems and Social Policy, no. 8 (Tokyo: Institute of Social Sciences, University of Tokyo, 1990).

cluding the Trade Union Law, the Labor Adjustment Law, and the Employment Standards Law. On the one hand, these laws constituted a triumph for workers, because for the first time unions, collective bargaining, and strikes became legal. But these reforms were very much stamped with the markings of the American production regime (although they went beyond the American regime by awarding government workers full rights including the right to strike). While the extensive rights accorded to labor corresponded in general to the aspirations of workers in the 1946–48 period, workers were only beginning to articulate more specific forms of workplace regulation bearing the stamp of a labor vision of the workplace.

We have partially reconstructed the workers' vision of the new regime through an analysis of their demands and their achievements in 1946–48. These include independent unions, the demand for parity in management councils (codetermination), a union veto over hiring and firing, perpetual duration of collective agreements, and a social wage tied to the age of an employee. These demands were stamped with the times. Extreme economic dislocation meant that workers had little concern for *how* layoffs were to be carried out—to be without a job at all meant extreme deprivation and invoked the specter of starvation. Thus the unions asserted the right to veto layoffs. As a result, Japanese unions did not concentrate on negotiating terms of displacement and displayed little attachment to seniority as a means of regulating the displacement process, such as it had developed in the United States or Canada. The union veto was abolished in the subsequent employer offensive, however, and in the absence of any other means of regulation, employers were able to use their power over hiring and firing as a means of eliminating union activists. This was demonstrated most clearly in the Miike dispute of 1960.

State regulation of labor-management relations protected labor only insofar as labor understood its rights and could manipulate the system to maximize outcomes. But a chasm separated the aspirations of workers in Japan and the rights potentially accorded them under the labor laws. Why workers were unable to have their aspirations articulated and enshrined through labor legislation is an issue worth exploring briefly.

Political and economic factors were of crucial importance. First, no political party was able to articulate the new labor-inspired forms of regulation. Of the two political parties linked to labour, the Japan Communist Party was not predisposed to promoting legalistic reforms. It was preoccupied with overthrowing the existing government or with realizing the immediate needs of workers, such as increased wages. Nor was structural reform through legislation a concern of the Japan Socialist Party, which at the time was under the control of the right wing of the party, which in turn was affiliated with the right wing of the labor movement. For these factions the main problem was containing the radicalism of the labor movement and maintaining good relations with the Occupation. Even when the JSP was in power in 1947–48, it was mainly concerned with taming the labor movement, in particular reducing the potential drain on government finances caused by vociferous demands by government workers for higher wages to keep up with inflation.

Finally, the Occupation itself stood as an immutable barrier to structural reform. The Labor Division's antipathy to the radical agenda of workers was consistent and crossed political lines. The prohibition of workers control at the Yomiuri newspaper in 1946, the banning of political strikes in 1947, and the abhorrence of labor's incursion into "managerial rights"—as expressed even by progressive labor bureaucrats like Valery Burati—testify to the intransigence of the Occupation regime to structural reform. It was to be the American way or no way.

The second factor inhibiting structural reform was the economic situation in Japan. Economic dislocation and the employers' early "capital strike" (hoarding and refusing to release capital) spawned many of the radical labor demands, but these same factors worked against a process of structural reform. The United States played a key role not only in elaborating the specific features of the new state but also in maintaining Japan economically through food imports, special procurements, and so forth.

Nevertheless, 1945 to 1948 must be recognized as a distinct phase of postwar history. The labor movement, in all its spontaneity and political diversity, played a significant role in what was essentially a struggle for power in the workplace. In retrospect, conditions clearly did not exist for workers' power, but that was not the essential issue. What was tragic was that many aspects of the workers' agenda (including codetermination) were lost in the ensuing conflict.

In the end, any prospect of enshrining labor's vision of the new regime came to an abrupt halt when the Occupation and the Japanese government shifted gears in 1947–1948. This was a period of realignment of class forces. Employers reorganized, and the labour movement split into antagonistic camps. Key turning points indicated the shift in the balance of forces: the aborted general strike of February 1947; and in 1948, the severe restrictions on the rights of public sector workers to strike and bargain collectively imposed in the summer of 1948; the formation of Nikkeiren; and the Tōhō dispute later in the year.

While carrying out its capital strike, the business community in Japan sought and successfully reestablished direct links with the business community in the United States. This alliance created the momentum for the reestablishing capitalist control and undermining the early Occupation reforms. The reforging of international business links culminated in the Dodge plan and labor code reforms in 1949, both of which signaled the onset of an intense, government-sanctioned employer offensive against labor. Let there be no mistake—there was acute labor resistance to the resurgence of managerial control. This was demonstrated in the struggles at Tōhō, Suzuki, Hitachi, Tōshiba, and many other workplaces in 1949 and 1950. But autocratic state intervention had tilted the balance of forces in favor of management, and prewar divisions in the labor movement quickly resurfaced, leaving the nascent union movement easy prey. The writing was on the wall and workers could read it; hence the relatively quick decline in support for the hitherto powerful NCIU. This reversal had a lasting and substantive impact on the nature of the workplace in Japan. The decline of labor and the resurgence of managerial control, sanctioned and supported by the state, was of a magnitude that far exceeded the difficulties faced by the postwar labor movement in any other industrialized country.

Employers were successful in their pursuit of control, but in their ruthless assault they undermined any possibility for significant labor-management cooperation. In fact, the effect of their assault was once again to radicalize labor: the 1950s were marked by instability and constant class conflict. The founding of Sōhyō, which subsequently became an independent and militant union federation, symbolized the ongoing tensions in labor-management relations. Employers continued to resort to coercion against independent unions, and workers spontaneously gravitated to unions for protection. Despite economic growth, wages were not rising much, and the workweek continued to be extended. As unstable as the general environment was, new forms of regulation were being worked out at the workplace. Many of these mechanisms, including the wage system, incorporated the stamp of employer control. But the forms of regulation also reflected the influence of peak organizations such as Sōhyō or employers' organizations. The founding of the Japan Productivity Center in 1955, for example, marked the recognition by some employers of the necessity to move from excessive coercion to hegemony, that is, to an accommodation with labor.

But this goal remained elusive; class relations were strained throughout the 1950s only to explode into national conflicts in 1960. The battle at Miike and the anti-Security Treaty struggle that year marked a turning point in Japan's development. The Miike miners lost their struggle. Although they had strong popular support, exceptional circumstances undermined support from other coalminers, and they lacked the necessary backing from enterprise unions in key industrial sectors. Sōhyō's acceptance of defeat at Miike was especially significant. That experience forced Sōhyō's leaders to recognize labor's own limits, imposed by shifts in economic structure and by the encroachment of enterprise unionism. They increasingly adopted a pragmatism that would, in the end, lead to the triumph of enterprise unionism and to Sōhyō's own dissolution in 1989. But employers also learned through the 1960 experience. While Mitsui wanted to use brute force against the Miike miners and their supporters, cooler political heads prevailed. Further coercion would have undermined the hegemonic role envisaged for the maturing state.

The post-Miike period from 1960–1974 witnessed the state playing an increasingly important, albeit indirect, role. Politicians berated employers for their hard-line attitudes, and the new prime minister, Ikeda, called for the doubling of incomes over the decade. Economic policy switched from being centered on leading-edge export sectors, such as shipbuilding, to the consumer goods sector, allowing the essential linking of the consumer and producer areas of the economy. The expanding economy created the conditions necessary for improved living standards generally. Real wages began to increase, the labor market tightened, and the wage gap between the core and peripheral work forces declined slightly. Shuntō became a central institution in this period and created the framework for a limited but significant strike movement in the 1973–1974 years.

In 1975, adopting the banner of self-imposed wage restraint, enterprise unionism finally came to the fore, wresting control of Shuntō away from Sōhyō and accepting what in fact amounted to a wage cut at the time. This, and the defeat of the public sector strike movement that fall, initiated a period of generalized labor-management collaboration. The formula that had evolved at the workshop level—union moderation in exchange for ongoing consultation—had become a social norm as labor-management consultative forums proliferated on the industry-wide level. As the world moved into the 1980s, Japan's enterprises clearly emerged victorious in the global competitive battle. From labour's perspective, however, victory remained elusive, and the popular saying of the period, "keizai taikoku, seikatsu shokoku" (powerful economy, impoverished life), reflected the imbalances created by a Fordist system that had scrimped on improvements in social infrastructure and, in the end, tethered workers to the treadmill of productivity with little independent voice.

To be sure, womens' labor has, as Nagoya Women's College professor Shibayama Emiko puts it, "been mobilized in a profoundly inhuman and discriminatory way from the Meiji period to now by aggressive labor market policies, whether they be to build a 'strong army-rich nation' or an 'economic superpower.'"[7] The stories that have percolated up through the research of the Ōmi strikers, the Yamago women, the Miike and JCU wives' associations, and the Moriguchi union activists, are all indications that women, through their individual and collective struggles, have been an important part of the history of resistance and the quest for change in Japan. Women today make up approximately 40 percent of the paid labor force in Japan, of which nearly 30 percent are part-time

7. Shibayama Emiko, "Josei rōdōsha" [Women workers], in Totsuka and Tokunaga, *Gendai Nihon no rōdō mondai*, p. 193.

workers. As any knowledgeable observer of contemporary Japan can attest, women continue to press for change, whether it be access to benefits for part-time workers or an end to sexual harassment.

Japan's Market Hegemony

The concepts of despotic and hegemonic regimes play an important role in the perspective that Burawoy and many others take on class relations under modern capitalism. The despotic regime that existed in nineteenth-century England was based on the super-exploitation of labor—what Aglietta and the regulation theorists would term a regime of extended accumulation. This regime was not viable in the long term because it eventually spawned intense conflict, which in turn created a growing awareness on the part of the working class that it was disenfranchised. Furthermore, the despotic regime's economic viability was also in doubt because of the continual crises of overproduction—the poverty of the masses created serious problems of realization of surplus value. In general terms the despotic regime creates the condition for its own transformation.

Hegemonic regimes came to replace despotic ones. The concept of hegemony in this case is the Gramscian notion of incorporation. The hegemonic regime allows for deal making on a grand scale. The bargain between labor and capital is characterized by consent on both sides, although this consent never excludes coercion. Workers through their unions consent to be managed, and employers consent to some union restrictions on their right to manage. Symbolic of these grand deals were the 1928 collective bargaining acts and 1938 Saltsjobaden Accord in Sweden, the 1935 Wagner Act in the United States, and the 1944 wartime legislation PC 1003 in Canada.

Question: When did Japan transform from its despotic to its hegemonic phase and what is the symbol of that transformation?

Some might point to the 1946 labor code, others to the 1955 founding of the Japan Productivity Center and the three principles of productivity. But neither of these perspectives are very satisfactory. The labor code could have symbolized the emergence of a hegemonic regime, but it was drafted in exceptional times when the postwar labor movement was not yet able to articulate its own agenda. And while the productivity movement did represent a certain consensus, in 1955 it really only reflected an agreement between the conservative section of the labor movement and employers. Even then, Nikkeiren persevered in its hard-line approach to labor relations right into the 1960s.

Japan, it would seem, did represent an exception to the general pattern of evolution from despotism to hegemony. Not that the transition did not take place, but rather that the transition was an extended one that occurred while the independent labor movement was in decline. Thus, the hegemonic features of postwar industrial relations were the result of the sporadic impulses from labor's receding tide. From a comparative perspective, this exceptionalism was due to historical circumstance more than anything else. It was not so much late development but rather the nature and relation of class forces over the period that the labor-management deal took shape in the 1950s and 1960s that seemed to dictate the specificity of the regime. In Japan's case, the ravages of war spawned intense class polarization with little room for reconciliation, and the state was under the control of a foreign power, the United States. This class polarization dated from the 1920s when employers, like their counterparts in the United States, rejected any form of class entente. Japan then moved towards absolutism and war, further repressing labor as an independent force. There was little sentiment for conciliation after defeat.

Instead, the state-endorsed initial period of democratic and even collectivist reform was one that allowed for union ascendency; but the same state also stood as a fundamental structural barrier to the formation of an alternative, indigenous regime. This period, labor's high tide, was soon followed by a period of reaction, which employers used to sweep away the labor reforms and to reimpose managerial rights in almost every arena. This antilabor offensive indelibly stamped the postwar regime with some of the rather despotic features discussed in this study. But there were also hegemonic features (job tenure based on convention, Shuntō, and the bonus system, for example) that, as time passed, became part and parcel of the postwar regime.

Male workers in large enterprises were the ones who most benefited from the hegemonic system, and even then their lot left much to be desired. But the requisite condition for their ability to rise within the system was a fiercely gendered division of labor. From a feminist perspective, "the company man not only owes a great deal to the assistance of his own wife, but also tramples upon the rights of his female colleagues at the workplace. A heavy concentration of female workers in simple, supplementary, and low-wage jobs with limited chances of promotion . . . has been indispensable for treating male workers on the basis of seniority."[8] The hegemonic regime indeed contained a strong patriarchal bent. Women and contract workers became the "other" upon whose shoulders would stand the workers in large, private enterprises.

Patriarchy and the divisions within labor, enshrined in the rival union federations and competing socialist parties, also undermined the ability of Japanese labor to shape government policy in such a way as to have lessened workers' dependency on their employers. In a pathbreaking study of the modern welfare state, Gosta Esping-Andersen classified the character of modern welfare states by assessing the impact of three political trends—conservative, liberal, and socialist

8. Ōsawa Mari, "Bye-bye Corporate Warriors," p. 17.

on a number of welfare programs.[9] In his assessment, Japan's strongest feature was its liberal orientation, its weakest was the socialist trend, and it scored in the medium range in terms of conservatism. Japan's liberal orientation and its weak socialist tradition (relative to Europe) helps to explain why Japan developed the type of minimalist Fordist support for labor that it did. In other words, labor's weakness in the workplace was also reproduced on the broader social level in a relatively weak welfare state that ended up reinforcing labor's dependency on the enterprise. Thus, Japan's hegemonic patterns reinforced the values of market capitalism. This was not the despotism of old, but a new form where the competitive logic of capitalism was garnished with the trappings of humanism, instilled in managers by the threat of workers' control from bygone eras.

Labor and Postwar Industrial Relations

This book does not attempt to establish the origins of many of the employment practices that evolved in postwar Japan. To be sure, many features, such as the bonus system for example, can be traced back to the prewar or wartime regimes or even back to pre-Meiji Japan. What this study attempted to do was to find out which practices became institutionalized and why. By examining case studies and following the trajectory of organized labor in postwar Japan, we gain a new appreciation of the mechanisms of labor-management relations. Although no single system spanned all workplaces important institutional features have taken on a normative role.

In many accounts, these features are captured in the three pillars typology of permanent employment, seniority-based wages, and enterprise unions. From a comparative and historical perspective, however, the three pillars emerge as sadly lacking in both depth and scope. Our objective in this concluding section is not to reformulate a new set of pillars but to reestablish the parameters of the multiple features of the regime, to deconstruct its normative characteristics, and to understand their dynamics and limits.

Enterprise Unions or Enterprise Unionism?

According to the theory of enterprise unions, Japanese workers were predisposed to forming unions at the workplace; their unions therefore became enterprise-based, and union locals generally shunned horizontal affiliations with other

9. Esping-Andersen, *Three Worlds of Welfare Capitalism*, p. 74. The author defines conservatism as the ideology of precapitalist elites, of which paternalism and corporatism were variations; liberalism was the ideology of nascent capitalism with its stress on individualism, free markets, and electoralism; and socialism was an anticapitalist ideology that stressed egalitarianism.

union locals. Enterprise unions, it is supposed, are the antithesis to industrial unions in the United States or Canada. The results from this study contradict that hypothesis. While it is clear that managers wanted to restrict unions to single enterprises, workers throughout the historical period tended to look for affiliations with other unions. Furthermore, as scholars like Solomon Levine and Matsuzaki Tadashi have stressed, there is a tendency to ignore or underestimate the extent to which industry-wide bargaining or consultation actually takes place in Japan.[10] Finally, if one places the Japanese unions organizational dimension within the comparative context of union organization in the United States or Canada, the idea that unions organized by enterprise are a distinctive feature of Japan dissolves quite quickly. This is not to argue that Japanese unions are not decentralized but simply that the differences are not so great that they constituted a fundamentally divergent pattern of union organization.

The original unions in all three of our case studies worked to establish either regional or industrial affiliations from the start. To be sure, close ties also evolved among workers at the three Mitsui mines in Kyushu, but these local affiliations were not counterposed to regional and industrial affiliations. Many factors contributed to the horizontal linkages. In some cases the CLRB directly intervened and promoted industrial and regional affiliations as a means of gaining consensual labor representation on regional labor relations boards. In other cases, such as at Suzuki, unions came together to organize around simple things such as celebrating May Day but then went on to organize further activities. To be sure, national labor organizations also played a role, campaigning to gain affiliates either on a regional or industrial basis. And finally, as workers and unions found themselves in struggles with employers, they spontaneously aspired to develop links of solidarity. Thus, from a historical perspective, the theory that workers somehow naturally embraced enterprise unions does not hold much water.

After the 1949 management offensive, however, employers attempted to limit outside influences and to proscribe the scope of the enterprise unions, which had replaced in many instances independent unions. But even here the natural drift was toward establishment of union affiliations on the local, regional, and national level. The reestablishment of the Japan Autoworkers Union in the early 1960s and the Suzuki union's affiliation to it, not to mention the establishment of wage consultations at the industrial and national levels, reflect a natural drift towards cross-enterprise affiliations. To be sure, power resides at the enterprise union level and collective bargaining is focused there. But there are many examples of joint or industry-wide bargaining that are often ignored in contemporary accounts of Japanese industrial relations. Unions in private railways, seamen's unions, and unions in

10. Levine, "Employers Associations in Japan," pp. 346–352, and Matsuzaki Tadashi, "Wage Negotiations in the Japanese Steel Industry."

the metal trades and in the public sector often engage in some forms of joint bargaining. Indeed Levine goes so far as to assert that decentralization is "only a formality," and Matsuzaki concludes that in the steel industry "formally speaking bargaining is on an enterprise basis [but] in practice it amounts to industry-wide bargaining."

Comparative studies of industrial relations indicate shed further light on this issue. Figures 5 and 6 are based on comparative data on the relationship between union centralization and union densities or the level of bargaining (national, industry or region, or enterprise or workplace based). These figures indicate that bargaining in Japan, Canada, and the United States are all relatively decentralized. These figures are further supported by studies of Canadian collective bargaining which indicate that 72 percent of all employees in large firms are covered by collective agreements negotiated with a single employer.[11] In other words, the purported industrial union model under which all unionized employees in a single industry negotiate together is, even in the United States and Canada, the exception rather than the rule. Some might argue that the contemporary decentralized model is the result of a decline in industrial unionism. There is some truth to that assertion but even leaders of the CIO at its inception were cognizant of the need for a multilevel approach to organizing. The AFL minority report on organizing, which was defeated at the 1935 convention and led to the eventual creation of the CIO, refers to organizing workers along "industrial and plant" or "industrial and enterprise" lines.[12] In historical perspective the industrial union ideal specifically embraced the concept of organizing along enterprise lines and thus the motto of the industrial union movement was "one shop–one union," or in modern-day union parlance, "wall-to-wall." This does not negate the ideal of industry-wide bargaining, nor does it deny the fact that in certain limited areas joint bargaining or industry-wide bargaining did develop. But, so too, in certain areas did they develop in Japan.

If the organizational dimension of enterprise unions was not quite so unique as our advocates of enterprise unions would have us believe, how then can we characterize these unions? Based on the evidence amassed in this study, I would suggest an alternative characterization that puts more emphasis on the orientation of such unions. Keeping in mind that not all unions in Japan pursue an enterprise orientation and that even among unions that do there are many variations, we might redefine enterprise unions historically as unions that:

    (a) were formed (either through purge or creation of a dual union) in order to break an independent union and had substantial employer support;

---

    11. Andersen, "Structure of Collective Bargaining," p. 216.

    12. "Minority Report of Resolutions Committee on Organization Policies: A. F. of L. Convention 1935," as reproduced in Litwack, *American Labor Movement*, pp. 49–51.

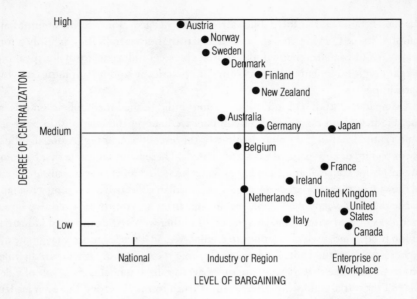

Figure 5. Union centralization and level of bargaining. Copyright © 1985 Ron Bean, from *Comparative Industrial Relations*, by Ron Bean. Reprinted with permission of St. Martin's Press, Inc.

(b) accepted managerial control of the workplace and identified with the goals and values of management;

(c) embraced the profit principle and subordinated workers' demands to the well-being of the enterprise and the national economy in exchange for a consultative role over wages and some working conditions;

(d) in some cases became integrated into the management structure through informal organizations, through duplication of steward/foreman functions, and through the use of the union as a stepping stone to management positions;

(e) avoided the organization of pressure tactics (job actions) especially those that had political overtones;

(f) generally tried to repress any opposition to company or union policies among workers.

Loosening enterprise unionism from the shackles of organizational determination places the focus on the historical determinants that gave rise to such a trend. And this would seem appropriate given that many enterprise unions were founded precisely for political reasons. Employers and some workers were adamantly opposed to independent, adversarial unions such as the NCIU in the 1946–49 period. Does this mean that enterprise unions became simply a hollow shell and were completely dominated by management? In other words, were they simply

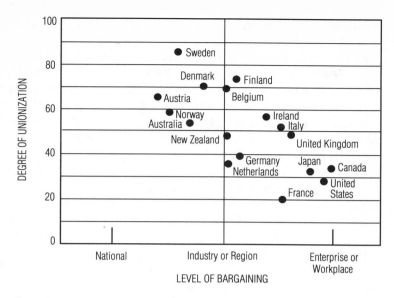

Figure 6. Unionization rates and level of bargaining. Copyright © 1985 Ron Bean, from *Comparative Industrial Relations,* by Ron Bean. Reprinted with permission of St. Martin's Press, Inc.

company unions similar to those that developed in the United States in the 1920s? The answer to that is both yes and no. Enterprise unions embraced certain management values that, while allowing them some legitimacy within the closed circle of the enterprise community, limited their room to maneuvre. Thus, instead of playing a role as a dedicated channel for articulating and fighting for worker aspirations, they became a mediator, a sounding board for management, and in certain cases a warning whistle against excessive exploitation. Enterprise unions in Japan were what company unions probably would have become had not the CIO been founded and incorporated the company unions in that era.

Enterprise unions also had a darker side. One of the essential roles of the enterprise union was to maintain stability, and this meant that internal opposition to enterprise unions had to be quickly eliminated. This is because close links with management rendered enterprise unions extremely vulnerable to being exposed. Debates over issues quickly escalate into discussions of the vary nature of the regime, and any challenge thus poses a threat to the very viability of the system. There is a distinctly corporatist bias to the enterprise as a community model, and union dissension is treated as an external virus that needs to be expelled from the corporate body.

Finally, we should keep in mind that we are talking about enterprise unions as an abstract notion. There are many variations on the theme. As Kamii and Totsuka remind us, the unions at Nissan and Toyota evolved into very distinct versions of enterprise unions, with important differences in the extent of union organization on the shop floor.[13] I would argue, however, that the unions at both Nissan and Toyota, like the Suzuki union, continued to share fundamental characteristics, including the commitment to profits and productivity first and a penchant for attacking dissent within their own ranks. A third shared feature was the commitment to a wage system that allows management considerable ability to control workers and pit one against the other in the fight for survival in the corporate hierarchy.

To put this historical definition in perspective, however, requires that we also define more clearly what is meant by independent or social unionism. Fundamentally, independent unions attempt to remove labor from the despotism of the market; that is, they try to promote the separation of the reproduction of labor power from the process of production or from performance in the workplace. Of course, on a practical level a complete separation is impossible—the ability of labor power to reproduce will always be tied to the general socioeconomic circumstances in which it finds itself. However, an independent union conceives of its members not as economic adjutants but rather as citizens with political and economic rights that should not be subordinated to profit and the marketplace. Unfortunately, after having fought for and won their independence in the 1935–50 period, some unions in Canada and the United States began to take their independence for granted, and the U.S. version of enterprise unionism, "business unionism," took root. Thus, in their pure forms social unionism and enterprise unionism represent two poles on a disjointed spectrum. The enterprise union represents the politics of market pragmatism constantly tempered by the aspirations of workers for independence, while independent unions represent the politics of social idealism constantly tempered by the realities of the market. Both forms of unionism existed on both sides of the Pacific.

The Performance-Based Wage and Bonus System

The wage system in postwar Japan has a number of notable features, including annual or semiannual performance reviews that determine one's status on an incentive wage grid; bonus payments that by 1975 provided four to six months' salary in two annual instalments (summer and winter); consultations/negotiations two or three time annually (once to determine the annual increase in the base wage and once or twice to determine the size of bonus payments); and a wage hierarchy based partially on length of service and partially on performance (new recruits are posted low on the wage grid, but to the extent that they receive favorable performance evaluations, they are able to climb to wages paying three to five times the starting rate).

13. See Totsuka and Hyōdō, *Rōshi kankei no tenkan to sentaku.*

CONCLUSION 279

The postwar determinants of this system were interlaced with the dynamics of class conflict from 1945 to 1960. In the early postwar period, managerial theorists favoured an American-style occupation-based wage system. Indeed, during the Occupation, the government introduced an occupation-based wage classification system for government employees. As the Occupation drew to a close, however, the government gradually abandoned this system and replaced it with a performance-based, incentive wage system.

In the early postwar years, the private sector pursued its own course, with the labor movement leading the way. Labor early formulated its theory of a social wage, that is, one that allowed workers to eat—something that could not be taken for granted in 1946–48, when the specter of starvation was real. This concept was further developed by the Densan wage formula (see Figure 4), which articulated what Kawanishi Hirosuke has called an egalitarian approach to salary determination. It proposed a base wage composed of a livelihood guarantee (principle and family) constituting 80 percent of the base wage, with accumulated service (seniority) and ability making up the remaining twenty percent. In order to balance potential employer favoritism, the union was prepared to intervene and negotiate about a given individual's ability. Union wage committees feared that competition between workers for higher wages would negatively impact on union solidarity so long as the employer played the role of arbiter.

History justified their trepidation. The rollback period of 1948–50 gave employers the upper hand. As egalitarian as it may have seemed at the time, the Densan wage formula's concessions on ability (merit) pay gave employers the opportunity to exploit this wage mechanism. Employers began to make extensive use of performance evaluations in both the public and private sectors. In the 1950s performance evaluations began to determine an ever increasing proportion of annual wage increases, and the proportion of wages determined by age declined. Thus, when Suzuki made wholesale renovations in its labor relations system in 1960, it adopted the performance-based, incremental system that by this time had become dominant within the automobile industry. The significance of this type of wage determination should not be underestimated. Not only did it give employers a strategic weapon for inducing conformity, it reinforced competitiveness among workers (individuals competed for wages and promotion) and thereby undermined potential worker solidarity derived from joint action for joint benefits.

There are other important facets to the wage system that evolved in the postwar period. The bonus system is of particular significance. Some commentators point to employers' historical benevolence as the source of the modern bonus system. But it would appear that this system may owe more to labor than to employers. Gordon goes so far as to assert that most unions were bargaining for semiannual bonuses as early as 1946. At Miike, however, the union contends that its attempt in 1947 to negotiate regular bonus increases was among the first. Furthermore the union perceived the bonus payment as a form of delayed wage payment, a way to share in profits, and also as a tradition that labor had every right to share in. A more contemporary source may also have been the one-time wage increases demanded and won by unions in the inflationary years of 1946 to 1948. Such demands may also have contributed to the momentum that prompted unions to institutionalize the demand for bonus payments.

No matter how the historical record resolves the issue of which unions started demanding bonuses first, the material from the case studies leads me to believe that the modern bonus system took its contemporary form and significance only in the late 1950s after continued bargaining by unions brought the bonus payment up to about 25–35 percent of the total wage. In one sense, the bonus system developed in a pressure cooker heated by Nikkeiren's pursuit of a low wage economy and labor's pressure for wage increases. The bonus was the compromise of the era. Bargaining continued over the size of the bonus, but by the early 1960s it had come to represent, at least in large enterprises, four to six months wages paid in two instalments, summer and winter. From 1960 to 1975 the system consolidated and remains in effect to this day. As with any negotiable item, management attempted to reduce the size of the bonus, but because it had become an acquired right and systemic, it was difficult to do so, although it did happen at Miike. Miike remains the exception that proves the rule that bonuses are difficult to cut. Many mortgage contracts have come to contain clauses for fixed balloon payments in summer and winter, coinciding with bonus payments. Any major shift in the bonus system would have had serious repercussions for the financial system.[14]

The bonus system was extremely significant both for labor and for the historical development of the national economy. Labor clearly perceived the bonus system either as a form of delayed wages or as a form of compulsory savings. Given that bonus payments represent from 25–35 percent of the total wage bill, employers profited directly from the interest saved on the amount of bonus retained. In other words, employers made money off the interest that the bonus funds accumulated, interest that labor would have received had the money been paid up front with regular monthly wages. The accumulated interest on the bonus of one worker was not huge, but when totaled for thousands of employees and then multiplied again by the thousands of employers, this became a substantial sum of money. Of course such a view is laden with comparative values. The fact is that unions negotiated or consulted over the size of the bonus payments, and what

14. Gordon also makes this assessment (*Evolution of Labor Relations*, p. 61). The bonus appears to have been institutionalized to some extent even in the small-business sector. As one supervisor from that sector summarized it, "The amount of bonuses, as with wage increases, depends on our President, but if business is poor, even in the red, the enterprise must pay this bonus. The President needs the confidence of the workers. He is well aware of this discipline" (cited in Chalmers, *Industrial Relations in Japan*, p. 143).

workers in Japan worried about was not that money was not being paid up front but that the size of the bonus was not right. In that sense, the bonus system was very much part of the hegemonic regime in Japan.

Another facet of the bonus system was the contribution it made to accelerated capital accumulation. In his study of the high-growth period from 1955 through the 1960s, Nakamura Takafusa concluded that the bonus wage system was the most important factor that contributed to the high savings rate during this period.[15] Only history allows us to remember that unions pushed for this system over (it should not be forgotten) the shrieks of Nikkeiren officials, who in the 1950s bemoaned the continual negotiations over wage and bonus payments.

The performance-based wage mechanism and the bonus were two key facets in the compensation system in Japan. But there were other significant features, including wage discrimination, annual wage negotiations, and exclusions from the system. Female workers in both the private and public sector faced blatant discrimination in wages, despite the best intentions of Occupation and government officials who drafted article 4 on equal pay in the employment standards legislation in 1947. In the case of Suzuki, the company and union quite openly advertised the wage discrimination as late as 1975; the wage grid specifically designated a different starting wage for high school and junior college graduates based solely on their gender. At Miike, discrimination in wages appeared mainly through occupational wage ghettos; women worked aboveground and thus received substantially lower piecework rates than underground miners, who were exclusively male. At Moriguchi, too, wage discrimination took place through the streaming of women into specific jobs, such as cook aides in schools or in day-care centers. The union, to its credit, did work with women members to convert many casual positions into regular ones, allowing women to gain benefits including job security, regular bonuses, and so forth. But wage discrimination based on gender continued to be an important part of the wage system right into the 1970s, and Japan's record on equal pay for women became the worst in the industrialized world.[16] Japanese women, supported by feminist groups, have increasingly challenged some of the discriminatory policies.[17] In many cases, unions found themselves defending male privileges which they had both negotiated, or in the case of informal discrimination, had helped perpetuate.

15. Nakamura Takafusa, *The Postwar Japanese Economy: Its Development and Structure* (Tokyo: University of Tokyo Press, 1981), p. 99.

16. See Fujimoto Takeshi, *Kokusai hikaku, Nihon no rōdō jōken*, p. 140, or Morley Gunderson, "Male-Female Wage Differentials and Policy Responses," *Labour Research Exchange*, no. 5 (December 1989), p. 2.

17. For an English-language source, see Alice H. Cook and Hiroko Hayashi, *Working Women in Japan: Discrimination, Resistance, and Reform* (Ithaca: Cornell University Press, 1980).

Another component of the wage system was Shuntō, the annual spring offensive or annual consultations/negotiations over base rate increases. The postwar genesis of this practice was clearly labor-based. It was under Sōhyō's Ōta and Iwai that the practice of annual wage and benefit bargaining became institutionalized in the late 1950s. Most major unions aligned the expiry date of wage agreements to the spring. It should be noted that the intent of Shuntō was to coordinate demands and job actions as well as to align the timing of the bargaining/consultation process. Although formal negotiations and consultation remained at the industry and enterprise level, the effect of Shuntō was to impart a centralizing component to the overall process and to institutionalize the annual nature of the consultations over wages and some working conditions. Shuntō played an important role in raising wage levels until 1975, at which point restraint became the watchword of enterprise unionism.

A final point regarding wage determination is that national and local government workers were excluded from the dominant enterprise pattern. They did not have the right to bargain collectively for their wages. Wage levels were largely determined by the government based on recommendations from national and local "personnel" agencies. In practice, these agencies have used as their standard the wage settlements in large private-sector firms, and thus government workers have to some extent seen real wages rise at a faster rate than those in the small subcontracting firms. There has been, however, some local adjustment to wage and bonus awards, and unions continue to be very much involved in this latter process.

The mechanisms of wage determination as they evolved in Japan become clearer and more distinct when compared with the wage systems in Canada and the United States. Put briefly, the U.S./Canadian wage structure probably combines two traditions. The first, upheld by craft unions, was the ideal of similar rates of pay for specific trades (occupations), with apprentices earning an incremental proportion of the journeyman's rate based on accumulated service. Taylorism, mass production, and unionization presented a new challenge to the system, which was transformed in the 1935–50 period into an elaborate matrix of comparative worth based on occupation, classifications, and detailed job descriptions. In the process two other distinct features emerged: women's work (clerical job classifications, for example) was consistently undervalued; and it became more complex (although still possible) for management to manipulate the system because unions could challenge the mode of regulation.

In Japan, on the other hand, unions never pushed for an occupational or job-based system. Instead, the relatively egalitarian Densan model eventually evolved into the performance-based, incremental system described in the previous section. What was common across the two systems, however, was how the wage systems could be manipulated to discriminate against women.

Job Tenure and Seniority

In terms of employment patterns, the case studies present a mixed record. Moriguchi and Suzuki saw employment grow from 1950 through 1973. The impact of the oil crisis led to a slight decrease in employment levels at Suzuki in 1973–74 with very slight increases thereafter. Moriguchi was less affected by the oil crisis and employment grew steadily if modestly into the 1980s. In most cases the issue of employment security is posed as one of "permanent employment," that is, whether workers enjoy cradle to grave job security once they have been employed. In this work I did not track separation rates within the case studies, so from a statistical point of view I have little to add. A historical appreciation of labor-management relations does provide some important insights, however, particularly into the role labor played on employment issues.

The Japan Productivity Center first articulated a managerial commitment to minimizing short-term layoffs in its 1955 statement on productivity: "Regarding temporary surplus personnel, however, the government and private sector, taking into account national economic factors, must outline measures such as job transfers and so forth which will prevent unemployment to the extent possible." This statement was in direct response to Sōhyō's criticism that the productivity movement would become a massive campaign of rationalization, in which labor would becine the ultimate victim through a loss of jobs. That this issue became central to the productivity debate in the mid-1950s was not a coincidence. Labor's fear of unemployment stemmed from the massive wave of dismissals that occurred in the 1949 management offensive and in the 1953–54 recession that accompanied the armistice in Korea. Workers and unions had not forgotten the experience of the early postwar period, where job loss and minimal government support posed the threat of starvation, and thus they vigorously contested job loss. In other words, at this historical conjuncture, labor's dependence on employers for their very existence was outlined in sharp relief. As Gōshi Kōhei later admitted, Sōhyō's criticism that productivity through rationalization would increase unemployment had "considerable effects."[18] Nevertheless, the JPC commitment to avoid redundancies remained peripheral in this period. Managers such as Maeda Hajime, who considered that employment levels were strictly a management concern, still represented the dominant employer perspective on this issue.

The 1960 confrontation at Miike reinforced the perception that eliminating jobs was extremely costly for employers. Evidence presented by Gordon and others indicates that employers justifiably feared that layoffs would lead to prolonged disputes, the expense of which might exceed the costs involved in transferring em-

18. Gōshi Kōhei, "Successful Performance of the Productivity Movement," p. 121.

ployees.[19] The evidence from Suzuki confirms that eventually some employers did indeed attempt to avoid short-term layoffs through job transfers—both internal (from production to sales) and external (from Suzuki facilities to subcontractors). However, disputes over transfers at Suzuki showed that workers perceived such policies as a harsh price to pay for their job security because of the disruption to work and family life.

But there were other factors that also influenced employers' commitment to jobs. The incentive, performance-based wage system directly contributed to the employment paradigm. Because the wage gap between new hires (usually recent school graduates from all levels) and top wages was substantial (equivalent today to a starting rate of $10 per hour and a top rate of $40 when bonuses are included), the wage system not only provided an incentive to stay (to leave would usually mean starting at a lower level on the wage grid at a different firm) but also created the expectation that one *could* stay. Permanent layoffs, or even longer temporary ones, would have destroyed the internal logic of the wage system. This is one of the keys to understanding why layoffs were so bitterly contested in Japan and why workers came to expect job tenure as an integral part of the employment equation.

By the 1960s the informal tenure track system and avoidance of layoffs had become the norm for male workers in large enterprises. But the wage and tenure system also came to have a normative role within society at large. An often neglected reason for this was the role that the courts came to play. As Sugeno explains in his study of Japanese labor law, major companies attempted to downsize during 1974 and 1975 in the wake of the oil crisis. This led to a rash of disputes that came before the courts for resolution. In making their rulings, the courts deemed that businesses had to prove that their business performance was so bad that they had to reduce personnel. Some rulings went so far as to recognize layoffs only after a corporation could prove that bankruptcy would have inevitably resulted had such measures not been taken. Even moderate rulings, however, precluded companies from paying large dividends or providing salary increases for managers around the time of layoffs, since these were taken as indications of bad faith on the part of employers. Furthermore, businesses had to establish that they attempted to avoid dismissals through other cost-cutting measures. These rulings helped to establish general norms that became propagated throughout society. For instance, employers—even small ones—received Labor Standards branch educational materials emphasizing that court rulings on dismissals meant that employers were not to free to lay off employees without valid reasons.

19. Gordon, *Evolution of Labor Relations in Japan*, pp. 386–411. Gordon also cites extensively from Yamamoto Kiyoshi, *Nihon rōdō shijō no kōzō* [Structure of the Japanese labor market] (Tokyo: Tokyo Daigaku Shuppan Kai, 1967).

Clearly, the tenure norms for employment in Japan came to differ from those in Canada and the United States.

But even in Japan there were basic limitations to the job tenure system. The 1960s experience in the coal industry spoke to one of those limitations. The onset of structural decline in coal was as much political as economic. Prodded by the steel industry and Keidanren, the government decided to liberalize oil imports and to end its protection of coal as a strategic industry. The ragged and disruptive decline had a devastating impact on coalminers—two hundred thousand were laid off in a decade. Less than two in ten found alternative employment through adjustment programs offered by their employer. The few miners that remained were subjected to speedups and a deadly deterioration in safety conditions. This was the legacy of the mismanagement of the coal industry decline. Clearly, job tenure or security of employment depended first and foremost on whether any given economic sector was in strategic ascent or decline. And for that there were no guarantees. The coal industry was the first economic sector to witness decline and employment loss, but it was later followed in the 1970s by textiles, steel, and shipbuilding. The stories of decline in those sectors were less traumatic than the coal experience because by then the mechanisms of adjustment, including transfers, early retirement, shortened workweek, and so forth had been established as norms. On the whole, however, the Japanese economy has continued to expand at a relatively high pace, and this created the possibility of continued job expansion into the 1980s.

The Miike story also helps us see the tacit nature of the job security convention. Long-term job security agreements had been signed in the coal industry, but such agreements were looked upon with consternation by Nikkeiren. Such explicit agreements interfered with managerial rights, the specific right to set employment levels in this case. Thus the job security facet of the hegemonic regime arose as a convention rather than as a contract, although some aspects of the adjustment mechanisms—transfer regulations for example—were laid down through specific labor-management accords.

It has become almost a truism that workers in smaller enterprises did not enjoy the same degree of job tenure as workers in large firms. When one considers that large enterprises employed only 15–20 percent of all workers in Japan, it would appear that most workers were excluded from the system. There is no doubt much truth to this assertion, but there were also factors that mitigated against this apparent discrimination. Koike documented, for example, that the number of workers with long seniority was only slightly less in small firms than in large ones.[20] Whether this was a result of persistent growth in the small business

20. Koike Kazuo, *Understanding Industrial Relations in Modern Japan* (New York: St. Martin's Press, 1988), p. 60.

sector, the impact of tenure standards established partially by the legal system, or other factors is not clear. Nevertheless, it would seem safe to assume that workers in small enterprises enjoy less security of tenure than those in large enterprises.

Another important limit to the employment pattern was the general trend to exclude women from permanent posts. At Miike women were excluded from underground mining, and at Suzuki only a small minority of production workers were women. At Moriguchi, women were seldom employed in career-track jobs particularly within city hall departments. The pattern at city hall was to employ women in adjunct, clerical positions and require them to retire after marriage or after becoming pregnant. Where women worked in day-care centers and so forth, they had to fight to win regular status. These four factors: tacit commitment to jobs, unequal development (and eventual decline), Japan's segmented enterprise system, and gender discrimination strictly limited the nature and scope of employment tenure.

One consequence of the evolving wage/employment paradigm may have been that employers in large enterprises realized that the creation of permanent positions involved a long-term commitment to the labor force. This may have been instrumental in attempting to keep the labor force in the enterprise as small as possible, particularly after 1975. The commitment to job tenure may thus have directly contributed to the creation of an extended dual structure and the extensive subcontracting system, a hallmark of the Toyota production system.[21]

Joint Consultation

By the 1970s, one of the fundamental features in Japan's union-management relations was the system of joint consultation. Employers' success in undermining independent unionism during their 1948–50 offensive resulted in conservative unions making two concessions that were fundamental to the shaping of the postwar union-management relationship. The first was the ceding of union rights in the workplace and the second was the explicit acceptance of the linkage of enterprise productivity/profitability to labor returns. These political developments and the subsequent consolidation of the wage and employment structure left little of substance for unions and employers to resolve. The new system could make little use of collective bargaining as it was defined in the United States or Canada. Uchiyama Tashirō, retired Sōhyō director, described the system that evolved in Japan:

21. As David Friedman points out, by 1977 less than 30 percent of the manufacturing work force in Japan was employed in large enterprises, compared to 60 percent in the United States. See David Friedman, *The Misunderstood Miracle* (Ithaca: Cornell University Press, 1988), p. 10. Between 1972 and 1981 employment in large enterprises dropped from 21.6 percent of the total work force to 18.6 percent. See Chalmers, *Industrial Relations in Japan*, p. 50. These statistics probably underestimate the shift because Chalmers uses government documents in which large enterprises are defined as employing three hundred or more.

In the case of Japan we have the labor-managment consultation system. This has spread and become part of the system, and so, how do we distinguish collective bargaining from prior consultation, how are they different? From my perspective, collective bargaining is bargaining that has as a background a strike or some sort of collective action. . . . The right to unionize, the right to bargain collectively, and the right to collective action are defined as basic rights in Japan, they come as a set. These days, the labor-management consultation system is such that even if discussions don't go well, there won't be any strike. This is the tacit understanding.[22]

In fact, what evolved was a system of consultation between the parties to resolve most issues (through labor-management committees) and the redefinition of collective bargaining (perhaps "applied definition" would be more appropriate) as either a confrontation of irresolvable differences between opposites or a pro forma adoption of the agreements reached through joint consultation. In other words, the onset of collective bargaining signaled a breakdown in the normal pattern of consultation and, unless a compromise was reached, confrontation appeared imminent. Otherwise, a one-shot session of collective bargaining signaled the conclusion to the joint consultation process. The system of joint consultation developed first at the workplace and later spread to the regional and industry-wide levels. As the system consolidated, even Sōhyō affiliates became incorporated into the process, particularly in the private sector.

There are of course many features of Japanese industrial relations that are not explored in this book. There is substantial evidence, however, even within the limited areas examined here, that labor had a significant impact in the shaping of the modern industrial relations system. The deeper one goes into the functioning of the system, the more glimpses we get of labor's impact on the enterprise and indeed the economy as a whole.

Lean Production

In undertaking this study, I made extensive use of Burawoy's postulate that production regimes might vary independently of the effects of competitive factors or workers' control (or lack thereof) of the labor process. The subsequent question was: once the existence of workplace regulation is established as an independent entity, how might it affect the larger picture of the production process?

Advocates of the post-Fordist thesis contend that the production regime in Japan's automobile industry has gone beyond Taylorism and that part of the reason for this was a social contract in industrial relations. In fact, most commentators discern correctly that there is an important relationship between the

---

22. Uchiyama Tashirō, interview by author, 6 October 1988. Uchiyama was formerly a Sōhyō director.

288   Japan Works

industrial relations system and Toyota production philosophy. I argue, however, that the post-Fordist advocates have misunderstood the internal, historical dynamics of industrial relations and, furthermore, that they have also incorrectly imputed a progressiveness to the Toyota system that one is hard pressed to document.

To prove that the Toyota system was able to develop a high-productivity, worker-friendly environment one must be able to document the transfer mechanism for worker aspirations. There are, in Japan's specific case, three possible mechanisms: paternal employers able to understand workers aspirations, enterprise unions, and workers themselves through employee involvement programs. None of these three possibilities stands the test of historical scrutiny.

Consider, first, paternal employers. In examining the employers' role in industrial relations and production management between 1945 and 1975, one is hard pressed to find much benevolence at work. Employers' rejection of the Dōyūkai's proposal for a workplace partnership in 1947–48, Nikkeiren's vigorous articulation of almost absolute managerial rights, the vicious antilabor offensive of 1949–50, the persistent attacks against independent unions culminating in the Miike debacle of 1960—all point to a class of employers determined to impose its control in the workplace. If there was any "fatherly" role it was that of establishing law and order in the family and making sure the children understood who was boss. By 1955 some employers realized that this trenchant and antagonistic approach threatened to unmask employers and destabilize the system. Conducting open class warfare tends to provoke further warfare. Thus there arose the concerted attempt to articulate a new labor-management partnership through the establishment of the Japan Productivity Center in 1955. This was not a vigorous attempt to strike a deal with labor (labor had no input in its conception), but it did articulate the employers' need to stabilize the system particularly through developing a stable work force based on long-term job tenure.

In the workplace, imposing and maintaining classic Taylorist control remained the name of the game even into the 1960s. One could argue that the Toyota production regime, or Suzuki's for that matter, evolved as an exception to the general trends. The evidence, however, points in the other direction. That is, as employers, Toyota and Suzuki conducted themselves in accordance with the general antilabor tenor of the times. The theory and practice of Ōno Taiichi, the engineer who spearheaded the production innovations at Toyota, displayed a clear antilabor bias and a penchant for Taylorism. Indeed, important organizations including the Japan Union of Scientists and Engineers actively promoted scientific management. In other words, it is difficult to sustain the argument that employer paternalism acted as the transfer mechanism for worker aspirations.

Perhaps the enterprise union acted as the transfer mechanism necessary for employee requirements? In some cases the enterprise union did act as a check on management's attempts to extend the workday or to transfer at will employees to other work sites. But such activities, the brighter side of enterprise unions, were constantly restricted by the historical niche occupied by such organizations. In most cases, enterprise unions came into being as a mechanism to displace an independent union. Employers tolerated them because such unions accepted and indeed enforced extensive managerial rights in the workplace and because they placed considerable priority on productivity improvements. This led, in some cases, to the integration of some enterprise unions into the structure of control at the workplace. In general, the ability of the enterprise union to act as conduit for challenge and change at the workplace was extremely limited.

On a theoretical level at least, a third potentially effective mechanism for integrating workers' needs into the production regime could have been the direct participation by workers themselves through employee involvement programs at the workplace. Indeed, employee involvement through quality circles in Japan has become the material of legends. But history once again confounds us. As demonstrated in Chapter 6, the most significant features of the Toyota system evolved in the 1950s or, in the case of Suzuki, between 1955 and 1965. Extensive employee involvement programs only developed in the late 1960s. Although employee involvement has in itself become one of the significant features of the system, other features including kaizen (continuous change) and the elimination of waste were established by industrial engineers such as Ōno Taiichi well before the quality circle movement had even been thought of. Furthermore, the evidence reviewed in this study suggests that employee participation programs, in the automobile industry at least, were strongly influenced by management.

It is difficult, then, to make the case that employer paternalism, enterprise unions, or employee involvement programs served as an effective mechanism for transferring workers' aspirations and values into the system. In fact, I would argue that there was no effective mechanism that allowed the free articulation and promotion of workers' aspirations. This does not mean that there was absolutely no struggle or no change. At each of the levels, among employers, in the union, and even in quality circles, debate and discussion about worker issues did take place. This was supplemented by pressures from the labor market and the state. These factors, the nature of Japan's hegemonic regime, and general social pressures have led to positive institutions including job tenure and high wages. And there is, as Christian Berggren noted, a nominal egalitarianism within the enterprise—everyone, managers and line workers alike, is expected to conform to the norms—and when sacrifices are necessary, managers must make the first move.[23] Furthermore, the concept of continual improvement

23. Berggren, *Alternatives to Lean Production*, pp. 50–51.

could, if freed from the shackles of market standards, be used as a means for shop-floor reform.

Unfortunately the system that was installed was not predisposed to major worker-oriented innovations. On the whole, workers' rights were not a "big ticket" item on the corporate agenda in Japan. Building an efficient production machine that could compete domestically and internationally was, and Japan was very effective at it. It gave birth to a new phase in production management, one that I believe should be correctly identified as a new stage in the evolution of Fordism.

In real life the system works as a comprehensive, integrated process. For purposes of analysis, however, we can distinguish five significant features of lean production.

(1) Flexible mass production. The Suzuki and Toyota production complexes did not abolish the assembly line nor have they adopted traditional batch-production techniques. What they did do was develop a sophisticated process whereby multiple variations of vehicles could be integrated into a continuous-flow assembly-line production process. This was accomplished through production leveling, kanban, accelerated technical flexibility, and other mechanisms. As Stephen Meyer pointed out, GM began this process in the 1920s. I would argue that the changes instituted under lean, intensified Fordism mark a qualitative leap in flexible integration. Contrary to post-Fordist theory, however, the changes did not eliminate the assembly line. For that, one would have to look to the experiments at Volvo's Kalmar and Uddevalla plants in Sweden in the 1990s, which effectively did eliminate the assembly line.[24] Furthermore, the idea of flexibility implied a "mobile" work force but, in the case of Suzuki at least, this mobility (the system of transfers and aid) was resisted by employees and became a source of contention in the system.

(2) Stratified production complexes. The production complexes at Suzuki and Toyota are notable for the small number of regular employees and the large number of workers employed by subcontractors. With expansion in the 1960s, the number of workers in the major assembly plants did increase but remained proportionately smaller than their counterparts in the Big Three. In other words, much of the value-added work is done by workers in subcontractors, and this is a crucial feature of the production complex. A small core work force and an extended peripheral work force cuts labor costs substantially but requires extra efforts in coordination from the central firm.

(3) Modified Taylorist labour process. Toyota and Suzuki both adopted classic Taylorist approaches to the work process. Jobs and job routines were standardized, cycle times for routines were short, and the work became boring and

24. See ibid.

repetitive, as in traditional automobile plants. This was true for the assembly line and in the machine shops as well. What Toyota and Suzuki did not adopt, and this is not a value judgement, was the job classification and description system that became institutionalized in the United States and Canada. Confusion arises when we equate Taylorism with job descriptions, as does Ishikawa. Job descriptions do reflect Taylorism in the United States but clearly one can do away with job descriptions or classifications and still have standardized job routines or boring and repetitive jobs. Thus, in its essence the work process retains its Taylorist bias. However, there have been modifications that relate to the next two specific features of the system.

(4) Continuous waste elimination. One of the most important aspects of the latest stage of Fordism was the articulation of the concept of kaizen (continuous change) with the express objective of eliminating waste (*muda*) in the system. Waste is defined as excess labor and/or resources. The concept can have certain benign or even positive applications (reducing oil consumption, for example) but if used to compress work cycle times and eliminate rest periods, it poses potential negative effects in the form of speedup and constant stress on the job. In the name of kaizen, furthermore, productivity improvements were defined as maintaining or increasing output (size or variety) with the same or smaller numbers of employees.

(5) Employee involvement. Extensive suggestion programs, quality circle activities, and work teams (*han*) became vehicles for workers to continuously develop the system. In a theoretical sense, these forums could have constituted a means for workers to articulate their own views and agenda. However, as the evidence presented in Chapter 6 suggested, management was able to control these forums by controlling the agenda-setting mechanisms. Such mechanisms included using team leaders and foremen to direct the groups; setting strict criteria for the types of acceptable suggestions; education in company values (including kaizen and muda) and the use of tools (Pareto charts and diagrams and so forth) that facilitated the types of changes the company wanted; using peer pressure and incentive programs to direct the suggestion systems into efficiency exercises; and integrating employees' participation into the regular performance evaluations. These sophisticated mechanisms resulted either in obligatory and resentful participation or in internalization and conversion to the system. In either case management was able to delegate duties formerly performed exclusively by industrial engineers to workers themselves. Workers began to undertake their own studies of job routines and redefine standards according to company values. Control was exercised not only through the study and appropriation of workers' knowledge by management, as in the classic Taylorist regime so eloquently critiqued by Braverman, but by getting workers to commit to management values through a subtle blend of coercion and consent.

The Future

Burawoy proposes that the hegemonic regimes in the United States and Britain are today in the process of transformation to what he calls a form of hegemonic despotism: "The new despotism is not the resurrection of the old; it is not the arbitrary tyranny of the overseer over individual workers (although this happens too). The new despotism is the 'rational' tyranny of capital mobility over the collective worker."[25] In other words, we are witnessing the third wave in production regimes. The first was the coercive and arbitrary regimes (of which market despotism was one form) of early industrialism; the second wave was the hegemonic regimes of Fordism; the third wave is a form of neo-Fordism in which consent must give way to commitment. Commitment to capitalist values, such as productivity improvement and competitiveness, was never an explicit part of the hegemonic regime. Except perhaps in Japan.

Japan's transition from a despotic to a hegemonic regime was partially aborted, and this gave rise to what might be termed market hegemony.[26] In a sense it represents both the past and the future. To be sure, there are despotic features to this type of regime, but that is not its main characteristic. The most significant feature of the neo-Fordist regime is that the market principles of Fordist societies have been explicitly embraced both ideologically and structurally within the production process. Workers must subordinate their own perspective to that of the enterprise and its values, which reflect the imperatives of market capitalism.

Herein lies one of the reasons why I believe the Toyota system represents a higher stage of Fordism. It has begun to break down the iron-clad division between conception and execution, albeit in a limited and controlled fashion. In doing so it brought to the fore the necessity of openly defining the values and standards upon which the system operates. Worker participation in functions that under traditional Fordism were the exclusive prerogative of management only occurred because of the sophisticated control mechanisms that obliged workers to commit to management values.

Control mechanisms were thus, in my opinion, just as important to the functioning, indeed to the very existence, of the system. The control mechanisms included the system of job tenure, enterprise unions, and the performance-based wage system described in detail above. The circle is complete and the relationship between the apparatus of production and the work organization begins to emerge. To the extent that employers can control labor through the industrial relations system, they can loosen the control exercised through the division of labor or

25. Burawoy, *Politics of Production*, p. 150.

26. I explicitly reject the terminology "hegemonic despotism" because it seems to imply a return to coercion. While there are coercive aspects to the lean system, including the form of compensation, the key aspect is that workers must commit to the values of production, in this case market values.

work organization. The two components of the labor process—the production apparatus and work organization—are dependent on one another, and the specific variations in industrial relations are one of the key reasons why the labor process evolved into the lean variant the way it did in Japan.

On a grander scale, the Toyota system has ushered in a new era. The first great turning point in the politics of production was the transition from regimes of coercion to regimes of consent that occurred mainly in Europe, the United States, and Canada between 1925 and 1950. Japan, for specific historical reasons, forged its own era of consent after employers gained the upper hand over labor. What emerged was a form of market hegemony that created a new stage of Fordism, the era of commitment. In doing so it surpassed the previous stage and put the issue of values and standards on the agenda for the rest of the world. In the past, world production standards largely conformed to the standards set by the most efficient regime. For most of the twentieth century, industrialists from around the world pilgrimaged to study the brash American Plan, the high-productivity processes symbolized by Henry Ford and Frederick Taylor that created the conditions for the specific hegemonic regime that later emerged with the Wagner Act. In the twenty-first century, will the world conform to the new standards? The control mechanisms are not in place, and to recreate them will cause tremendous upheaval. Yet, nonconformance will threaten the stability of the world system, which depends on ever increasing productivity. From coercion to consent to commitment. The battle for the hearts and minds of workers has been ushered onto center stage. The challenge of consciousness has arrived on a world scale.

Bibliography

Background Interviews

Harada Yōzō: Personnel Manager, Suzuki Motors (October 11, 1988)
Iribe Shōji: Moriguchi outside worker and union activist (October 14, 1988)
Katō Toshio: former president of Suzuki union (March 7, 1990)
Kōno Kazuo: Miike activist and former secretary-general of Mitsui Mineworkers Federation (March 21, 1990)
Kubota Takeshi: former vice-president of Miike local union (July 2, 1987)
Matsui Susumu: former Miike activist (March 15, 1990)
Matsuo Kamachi: former Miike activist (March 15, 1990)
Michiyama Fusahito: former Miike activist (March 19, 1990)
Nishimura Yasunori: Moriguchi union activist, former leader of outside workers, retired and chair of the Moriguchi Retirees Club (October 14, 1988; March 9, 1990)
Ogawa Keizō: former Moriguchi unionist, part of delegation to support Miike strikers in 1960 (March 9, 1990)
Sugita Tomoji: long-time member of Suzuki union executive, current president (October 11, 1988)
Uchiyama Tashirō: retired Sōhyō director (October 6, 1988; March 3, 1990)
Yamamoto Kikue: Moriguchi union, former school employee, now retired (October 14, 1988; March 9, 1990)

Archival Materials

Labor Division Papers, Supreme Commander of the Allied Powers, National Archives Depository, Washington National Records Center, Suitland, Md.
Valery Burati Papers, Archives of Labor and Urban Affairs, Walter P. Reuther Library, Wayne State University, Detroit, Mich.

U.A.W. Washington Office Papers, Archives of Labor and Urban Affairs, Walter P. Reuther Library, Wayne State University, Detroit, Mich.

U.A.W. International Affairs Department Papers, Archives of Labor and Urban Affairs, Walter P. Reuther Library, Wayne State University, Detroit, Mich.

Major Works in Japanese

Arisawa Hiromi. *Nihon sangyō hyaku nen shi—ge* [One hundred year history of Japanese industry, vol. 2]. Tokyo: Nihon Keizai Shimbun Sha, 1967.

——. *Shōwa keizai shi—ge* [A history of the Shōwa economy, vol. 2]. Tokyo: Nihon Keizai Shimbun Sha, 1980.

Fujimoto Takeshi. *Kokusai hikaku, Nihon no rōdō jūken* [International comparisons, Japan's labor conditions]. Tokyo: Shin Nihon Shuppan Sha, 1984.

Fujita Wakao. *Dai ni kumiai* [Breakaway unions]. Tokyo: Nihon Hyōron Shinsha, 1955.

Hazama Hiroshi. *Zaikaijin no rōdō kan* [Business views on labour]. Tokyo: Daiyamondo Sha, 1970.

Hirai Yōichi. "Mitsui Miike ni okeru shokuba tōsō no jisshō kenkyū" [Corroborative research on workplace struggle at Mitsui Miike]. Ph.D. dissertation, Hōsei Daigaku, 1982.

Hirai Yōichi and Yamamoto Kiyoshi. "Mitsui Miike tankō sōgi ni tsuite" [Concerning the Mitsui Miike coalmine dispute]. *Shakai Kagaku Kenkyū* 40, no. 3 (September 1988): 138–140.

Ishida Mitsuo, Inoue Masao, Kamii Yoshihiko, and Nitta Michio. *Rōshi kankei no hikaku kenkyū* [Comparative research in labor-management relations]. Tokyo: Tokyo Daigaku Shuppan Kai, 1993.

Ishikawa Kaoru. *Nihon teki hinshitsu kanri* [Japanese quality control]. Tokyo: Nikka Giren Shuppan Sha, 1988.

Jichirō Ōsaka Fu Honbu. *Eitōren nijū go nen shi* [Twenty-five years of the Satellite City Union Federation]. Ōsaka: Jichirō Ōsaka Fu Honbu, 1976.

Jichi Rōdō Undō Shi Henshū Iinkai. *Jichi rōdō undō shi, dai ikkan* [History of the prefectural and municipal labour movement, vol. 1]. Tokyo: Keisō Shobō, 1974.

Jinji In. *Jinji gyōsei nijū nen no ayumi* [Twenty years of personnel administration]. Tokyo: Ōkura Shō, 1968.

Kamata Satoshi. *Saru mo jigoku, nokoru mo jigoku* [For those who left—a living hell; for those who remained—an inferno]. Tokyo: Chikuma Bunko, 1986.

Kamii Yoshihiko. *Rōdō kumiai no shokuba kisei* [The influence of the enterprise union at the shop floor level]. Tokyo: Tokyo Daigaku Shuppan Kai, 1994.

Katō Etsuo. *Atarashii jiyū sekai rōren* [The new free world labor federation]. Tokyo: Kokutetsu Rōdō Kumiai Bunka Kyōiku Bu, 1949.

Kawanishi Hirosuke. *Kigyō betsu kumiai no riron* [A theory of enterprise unionism]. Tokyo: Nihon Hyōron Sha, 1989.

——. *Sengo Nihon no sōgi to ningen* [People and struggles in postwar Japan]. Tokyo: Nihon Hyōron Sha, 1986.

Keizai Dōyūkai. *Keizai Dōyūkai sanjū nen shi* [Keizai Dōyūkai: Thirty years]. Tokyo: Keizai Dōyūkai, 1971.

Koyama Kōtake and Shimizu Shinzō, eds.; *Nihon Shakai Tō shi* [A history of the Socialist Party]. Kyoto: Hōka Shoten, 1965.

Kōzuma Yoshiaki. *Shuntō*. [The spring offensive] Tokyo: Rōdō Kyoiku Senta, 1976.

Kumazawa Makoto. *Nihon rōdōsha zō* [Images of Japan's workers]. Tokyo: Chikuma Shôbô, 1981.

Maeda Hajime. "Tōshō Ichi Dai," [A fighter's life]. *Bessatsu Chūō Kōron, Keiei Mondai* 8, no. 2 (Summer 1969): 288–306.

———. "Nikkeiren ni ikita nijū nen," [Twenty years with Nikkeiren] *Bessatsu Chūō Kōron, Keiei Mondai* 8, no. 3 (Fall 1969): 352–368.

Matsuzaki Tadashi. *Nihon tekkō sangyō bunseki* [The Japanese steel industry: An analysis]. Tokyo: Nihon Hyōron Sha, 1982.

———. "Tekkō Sōgi (1957–59)," [Steel struggles (1957–59)]. In Rōdō Sōgi Shi Kenkyū Kai Hen, *Nihon no rōdō sōgi* [Workers' struggles in Japan]. Tokyo: Tokyo Daigaku Shuppan Kai, 1991), pp. 161–204.

Miike Tankō Rōdō Kumiai Jū nen shi Hensan Iinkai. *Miike jū nen* [Miike's ten years]. Ōmuta: Miike Tankō Rōdō Kumiai, 1956.

Miike Tankō Rōdō Kumiai nijū nen shi Hensan Iinkai. *Miike nijū nen* [Miike's Twenty years]. Ōmuta: Miike Rōsō, 1969.

Mitsui Kōzan Kabushiki Kaisha. *Shiryō: Miike sōgi* [Documents: the Miike dispute]. Tokyo: Nihon Keieisha Dantai Renmei Kōhō Bu, 1963.

Moriguchi Shi Shokuin Rōdō Kumiai. *Moriguchi shi shokurō sanjū go nen shi* [Thirty-five years of the Moriguchi Employees Union]. Moriguchi: Moriguchi Rōsō, 1981.

Nihon Bōeki Kenkyū Kai. *Sengo Nihon no boeki 20 nen shi* [Twenty-year history of trade in postwar Japan]. Tokyo: Tsūshō Sangyō Chōsa Kai, 1967.

Nihon Kaihatsu Ginkō. *Nihon Kaihatsu Ginkō jū nen shi* [A ten-year history of the Japan Development Bank]. Tokyo: Nihon Kaihatsu Ginkō, 1963.

———. *Nihon Kaihatsu Ginkō nijū go nen shi* [A twenty-five year history of the Japan Development Bank]. Tokyo: Nihon Kaihatsu Ginkō, 1978.

Nihon Rōdō Kumiai Sō Rengō Kai. *Rengō hakusho* [Rengō white paper]. Tokyo: Rengō, 1995.

Nihon Rōdō Kumiai Sōhyōgi Kai. *Orugu* [Organizing]. Tokyo: Rōdō Kyōiku Senta, 1976.

———. *Sōhyō jūnen shi* [Ten-year history of Sōhyō]. Tokyo: Rōdō Junpō Sha, 1964.

Nihon Seisan Sei Honbu. *Seisan sei undō 30 nen shi* [A thirty-year history of the productivity movement]. Tokyo: Nihon Seisan Sei Honbu, 1985.

Nihon Tankō Rōdō Kumiai Dōmei. *Tanrō jū nen shi* [Ten years of the JCU]. Tokyo: Rōdō Junpō Sha, 1961.

Nikkeiren. *Nikkeiren jigyō hōkoku, 1958* [Nikkeiren annual report, 1958]. Tokyo: Nikkeiren, 1959.

———. *Nikkeiren jigyō hōkoku, 1959* [Nikkeiren Annual Report, 1959]. Tokyo: Nikkeiren, 1960.

———. *Sangyō rōdō gensei hōkoku* [Report on current state of industrial labor]. Tokyo: Nikkeiren, 1962.

Nikkeiren Sanjū nen shi Kankō Kai. *Nikkeiren sanjū nen shi* [Nikkeiren: Thirty years]. Tokyo: Nihon Keieisha Dantai Renmei, 1981.

Nikkeiren Sōritsu Jū Shū Nen Kinen Jigyō Iinkai. *Jūnen no ayumi* [Ten years traveled]. Tokyo: Nikkeiren, 1958.

Nomura Masami. *Toyotizumu.* Kyoto: Mineruba Shobō, 1993.

Ōhara Shakai Mondai Kenkyū Jō. *Nihon rōdō nenkan, 1950 nenban* [Japan labor yearbook, 1950 edition]. Tokyo: Jiji Tsūshin Sha, 1950

———. *Nihon rōdō nenkan, 1951 nenban* [Japan labor yearbook, 1951 edition]. Tokyo: Jiji Tsūshin Sha, 1951.

———. *Nihon rōdō nenkan, 1952 nenban* [Japan labor yearbook, 1952 edition]. Tokyo: Jiji Tsūshin Sha, 1951.

———. *Nihon rōdō nenkan, 1953 nenban* [Japan labor yearbook, 1953 edition]. Tokyo: Jiji Tsūshin Sha, 1952.

———. *Nihon rōdō nenkan, 1959 nenban* [Japan labor yearbook, 1959 edition]. Tokyo: Tōyō Keizai Shimpō Sha, 1959.

Ōno Taiichi. *Toyota seisan hōshiki* [Toyota production methods]. Tokyo: Diayamondo, 1978.

Ōtani Ken. *Sakurada Takeshi no hito to tetsugaku* [Sakurada Takeshi: His person and philosophy]. Tokyo: Nihon Keieisha Dantai Renmei Kōhō Bu, 1987.

Rōdō Daijin Kanbō Rōdō Tōkei Chōsa Bu. *Rōdō tōkei nenpō—1958* [Annual report of labor statistics, 1958]. Tokyo: 1959.

———. *Rōdō Kumiai kihon chōsa hōkoku sho (1953)* [Report of the basic survey of labor unions, 1953]. Tokyo: Rōdō Daijin Kanbō, 1954.

Rōdō Kyōiku Senta. *Sōhyō soshiki kōryō to gendai rōdō undō* [Sōhyō organizational program and the contemporary labor movement]. Tokyo: Rōdō Kyōiku Senta, 1980.

Rōdō Shō. *Rōdo hakusho, 1959 nenban* [Labor white paper, 1959]. Tokyo: Rōdō Shō, 1960.

———. *Rōdō hakusho, 1975 nenban* [Labor white paper, 1975]. Tokyo: Rōdō Shō, 1975.

———. *Rōdō hakusho, 1993 nenban* [Labor white paper, 1993]. Tokyo: Nihon Rōdō Kenkyū Kikō, 1993.

Rōdō Shō. *Shiryō rōdō undō shi Shōwa 24 nen* [Documentation on the history of the labor movement, 1949]. Tokyo: Rōdō Shō, 1951.

Rōdō Shō. *Shiryō rōdō undō shi Shōwa 25 nen* [Documentation on the history of the labor movement, 1950]. Tokyo: Rōdō Shō, 1952.

Rōdō Shō. *Shiryō rōdō undō shi Shōwa 26 nen* [Documentation on the history of the labor movement, 1951]. Tokyo: Rōdō Shō, 1953.

Rōdō Shō Fujin Kyoku. *Hataraku josei no jijitsu, Heisei 5 nenban* [The facts about working women, 1993 edition]. Tokyo: Ōkura Shō Insatsu Kyoku, 1993.

Rōdō Shō Shokugyō Antei Kyoku Shitsugyō Taisaku Bu. *Tankō rishokusha taisaku jū nen shi* [A ten-year history of policy toward unemployed coalminers]. Tokyo Nikkan Rōdō Tsūshin Sha, 1971.

Rōdō Sōgi Shi Kenkyū Kai. *Nihon no rōdō sōgi (1945–1980 nen)* [Labor disputes in Japan, 1945–1980]. Tokyo: Tokyo Daigaku Shuppan Kai, 1991.

Sakisaka Itsurō. *Miike nikki* [Miike diary]. Tokyo: Shisei Do, 1961.

Shimizu Shinzō. "Mitsui Miike sōgi" [The Mitsui Miike dispute]. In Shiota Shōbe, Fujita Wakao, ed. *Sengō Nihon no rōdō sōgi*, rev. ed. Tokyo: Ocha no Mizu Shobō, 1977, pp. 479–584.

Shiota Shōbei, Fujita Wakao, ed. *Sengō Nihon no rōdō sōgi* [Labor disputes in postwar Japan]. Tokyo: Ocha no Mizu Shobō, 1977.

Shiota Shōbei et al., eds. *Sengo rōdō kumiai undō no rekishi* [History of the postwar Japanese labor movement]. Tokyo: Shin Nihon Shuppan Sha, 1970.

Shizuoka Ken Rōdō Kumiai Undō Shi Hensan Iinkai. *Shizuoka ken rōdō undō shi* [A history of the labor movement in Shizuoka prefecture]. Shizuoka: Shizuoka Ken Rōdō Kumiai Hyōgikai, 1984.

———. *Shizuoka ken rōdō undo shi, shiryō (jō)* [Documents, vol. 1, History of the Shizuoka labor movement]. Shizuoka: Shizuoka Ken Rōdō Kumiai Hyōgi Kai, 1981.

Sōhyō Chōsa Bu. *Nihon no seiji, keizai, rōdō bunseki, 1961 nenban* [An analysis of Japan's politics, economics and labor, 1961 edition]. Tokyo: Haruaki Sha, 1961.

Suzuki Jidōsha Kōgyō Kabushiki Kaisha. *40 nen shi* [Forty years in the making]. Hamana Gun: Suzuki, 1960.

———. *50 nen shi* [Fifty years in the making]. Hamana Gun: Suzuki, 1970.

Suzuki Jidōsha Kōgyō Rōdō Kumiai Shi Henshū Iinkai. *Nijū go nen shi* [Twenty-five years]. Hamana Gun: Suzuki Jidōsha Kōgyō Rōdō Kumiai, 1976.

Takano Minoru. *Nihon no rōdō undō* [Japan's labor movement]. Tokyo: Iwanami Shoten, 1958.

Takemae Eiji. *Sengō rōdō kaikaku, GHQ rōdō seisaku shi* [Postwar labor reform, a history of GHQ labor policy]. Tokyo: Daigaku Shuppan Kai, 1982.

Takenaka Emiko and Kuba Yoshiko. *Rōdō ryoku no joseika* [Feminization of the labor force]. Tokyo: Yuhikaku, 1994.

Totsuka Hideo and Hyōdō Tsutomu, eds. *Rōshi kankei no tenkan to sentaku* [Transition and choice in industrial relations]. Tokyo: Nihon Hyōron Sha, 1991.

Totsuka Hideo and Tokunaga Shigeyoshi, eds. *Gendai Nihon no rōdō mondai* [Labor issues in contemporary Japan]. Kyoto: Mineruba Shobō, 1993.

Toyota Jidōsha Hanbai Kabushiki Kaisha. *Sekai e no ayumi* [Stepping into the world]. Nagoya: Toyota, 1980.

Toyota Jidōsha Kabushiki Kaisha. *Sōzō kagiri naku, Toyota jidōsha gōjū nen shi* [Unlimited creativity: 50 years at Toyota Automobiles, Ltd.]. Toyota City: Toyota, 1987.

Tsūshō Sangyō Shō Sekitan Kyoku. *Tanden sōgō kaihatsu chōsa hōkoku sho* (Report of the investigation into general development of coal fields]. Tokyo: Tsushō Sangyō Shō, 1963.

Wada Mitsuhirō, ed. *Nihon kaibō 2* [Dissecting Japan 2]. Tokyo: Nihon Hōsō Shuppan Kai, 1987.

Yamago Rōdō Kumiai. *Teikō no seitō rōdōsha* [Defiant silk workers]. Tokyo: Seni Rōren Tō hoku Shibu, 1977.

Yamamoto Kiyoshi. *Jidōsha sangyō no rōshi kankei* [Labor relations in the automobile industry]. Tokyo: Tokyo Daigaku Shuppan Kai, 1981.

———. *Nihon no chingin, rōdō jikan* [Wages and work hours in Japan]. Tokyo: Tokyo Daigaku Shuppan Kai, 1982.

———. *Nihon rōdō shijō no kōzō* [Structure of Japan's labor market]. Tokyo: Tokyo Daigaku Shuppan Kai, 1967.

———. *Sengo kiki ni okeru rōdō undō* [The labor movement in the postwar crisis]. Tokyo: Ochanomizu Shobō, 1978.

Zenrō Jū Nen Shi Henshū Iinkai. *Zenrō jū nen shi* [Ten Years: The Japan Trade Union Congress]. Tokyo: Zenrō Kaigi, 1968.

Major Works in Western Languages

Abegglen, James. *The Japanese Factory: Aspects of Its Social Organization.* Glencoe, Ill.: Free Press, 1958.

Aglietta, Michel. *A Theory of Capitalist Regulation.* London: Verso, 1987.

Allinson, Gary D. and Yasunori Sone, eds. *Political Dynamics in Contemporary Japan.* Ithaca: Cornell University Press, 1993.

Anderson, John C., et al. *Union-Management Relations in Canada.* Don Mills, Ontario: Addison-Wesley, 1989.

Aoki Keisuke. "Flexible Work Organization and Management Control in Japanese-Style Management." In Koji Morioka, ed., *Japanese Capitalism Today: Economic Structure and the Organization of Work,* dedicated edition of *International Journal of Political Economy* 21, no. 3 (fall 1991): 49–69.

Asian Productivity Organization. *Japan Quality Control Circles.* Tokyo: Asian Productivity Organization, 1972.

Babson, Steve, ed. *Lean Work: Empowerment and Exploitation in the Global Auto Industry.* Detroit: Wayne State University Press, 1995.

Bamber, G., and R. Lansbury, eds. *International and Comparative Industrial Relations.* London: Allen & Unwin, 1987.

Bean, Ron. *Comparative Industrial Relations.* New York: St. Martin's Press, 1985.

Berggren, Christian. *Alternatives to Lean Production.* Ithaca: ILR Press, 1992.

Boyer, Robert. *The Regulation School.* New York: Columbia University Press, 1990.

Boyer, Robert, ed. *The Search for Labor Market Flexibility.* Oxford: Clarendon Press, 1988.

Bowen, Roger. *Innocence Is Not Enough: The Life and Death of Herbert Norman.* Vancouver: Douglas & McIntyre, 1986.

Braverman, Harry. *Labor and Monopoly Capital.* New York: Monthly Review Press, 1974.

Brinton, Mary. *Women and the Economic Miracle: Gender and Work in Postwar Japan.* Berkeley: University of California Press, 1993.

Briskin, L., and P. McDermott. *Women Challenging Unions: Feminism, Democracy, and Militancy.* Toronto: University of Toronto Press, 1993.

British Institute of Management. *Modern Japanese Management.* London: British Institute of Management, 1970.

Brody, David. *Workers in Industrial America.* New York: Oxford University Press, 1989.

Burawoy, Michael. *The Politics of Production.* London: Verso, 1985.

Calder, Kent. *Crisis and Compensation.* Princeton: Princeton University Press, 1988.

Carlile, Lonny. "Zaikai and the Politics of Production in Japan, 1940–1962." Ph.D. diss. University of California, 1989.

Chalmers, Norma. *Industrial Relations in Japan: The Peripheral Workforce.* London: Routledge, 1989.

Cohen, Theodore. *Remaking Japan: The American Occupation as New Deal.* New York: The Free Press, 1987.

Cole, Robert. *Work, Mobility, and Participation.* Berkeley: University of California Press, 1979.

Confederation of Japan Automobile Workers' Unions. "Japanese Automobile Industry in the Future." Tokyo: Japan Automobile Workers' Union, 1992.

Cook, Alice, and Hiroko Hayashi. *Working Women in Japan: Discrimination, Resistance, and Reform.* Ithaca: Cornell University Press, 1980.

Connaghan, Charles J. *The Japanese Way: Contemporary Industrial Relations*. Ottawa: Labor Canada, 1982.

Cusumano, Michael. *The Japanese Automobile Industry*. Cambridge: Harvard University Press, 1985.

Dohse, K., U. Jurgens, and T. Malsch. "From 'Fordism' to 'Toyotaism'? The Social Organization of the Labor Process in the Japanese Automobile Industry." *Politics and Society* 14, no. 2 (1985): 115–146.

Dore, Ronald. *British Factory–Japanese Factory*. Berkeley: University of California Press, 1974.

———. *Flexible Rigidities*. London: Athlone Press, 1986.

———. *Taking Japan Seriously: A Confucian Perspective on Leading Economic Issues*. Stanford: Stanford University Press, 1987.

Dower, John. *Empire and Aftermath*. Cambridge: Harvard University Press, 1979.

Duke, Benjamin. *Japan's Militant Teachers*. Honolulu: University of Hawaii Press, 1973.

Dunlop, J., and W. Galenson, eds. *Labor in the Twentieth Century*. New York: Academic Press, 1978.

Endo, Koshi. "Reflections on the Turnabout in Labor Relations Policy in Occupied Japan." *Annals of the Institute of Social Science* (Tokyo), no. 26 (1984): 78–101.

Esping-Andersen, Gosta. *The Three Worlds of Welfare Capitalism*. Princeton: Princeton University Press, 1990.

Farley, Miriam S. *Aspects of Japan's Labor Problems*. New York: John Day, 1950.

Fraser, S., and G. Gerstle, eds. *The Rise and Fall of the New Deal Order, 1930–1980*. Princeton: Princeton University Press, 1989.

Friedman, David. *The Misunderstood Miracle*. Ithaca: Cornell University Press, 1988.

Fudge, J., and P. McDermott. *Just Wages: A Feminist Assessment of Pay Equity*. Toronto: University of Toronto Press, 1991.

Gersuny, C., and G. Kaufman. "Seniority and the Moral Economy of U.S. Automobile Workers, 1934–1946." *Journal of Social History* (spring 1985): 463–475.

Gordon, Andrew. *The Evolution of Labor Relations in Japan: Heavy Industry, 1853–1955*. Cambridge: Harvard University Press, 1985.

———. "Luttes pour le pouvoir dans les ateliers." *Annales* 49, no. 3 (May–June 1994): 511–540.

———, ed. *Postwar Japan as History*. Berkeley: University of California Press, 1993.

Gourevitch, Peter, et al. *Unions and Economic Crisis: Britain, West Germany and Sweden*. London: Allen & Unwin, 1984.

Harris, Howell. *The Right to Manage*. Madison: University of Wisconsin Press, 1982.

Hein, Laura E. *Fueling Growth: The Energy Revolution and Economic Policy in Postwar Japan*. Cambridge: Harvard University Press, 1990.

Hogan, Michael. *The Marshall Plan*. Cambridge: Cambridge University Press, 1987.

Hyman, R. "Theory in Industrial Relations: Towards a Materialist Analysis." In P. Boreham and G. Dow, eds., *Work and Inequality*, vol. 2, *Ideology and Control in the Labour Process*. Melbourne: Macmillan, 1980: 38–59.

Japan Institute of Labor. *Japanese Working Life Profile, Statistical Aspects*. Tokyo: Japan Institute of Labor, 1989.

———. *Labor Unions and Labor-Management Relations*. Tokyo: Japan Institute of Labor, 1986.

Johnson, Chalmers. *Conspiracy at Matsukawa*. Berkeley: University of California Press, 1972.

————. *Japan's Public Policy Companies*. Washington, D.C.: American Enterprise Institute for Public Policy Research, 1978.

————. *MITI and the Japanese Miracle*. Stanford: Stanford University Press, 1982.

Kamata, Satoshi. *Japan in the Passing Lane*. New York: Pantheon, 1982.

Katz, Harry. *Shifting Gears*. Cambridge: MIT Press, 1987.

Kaye, Harvey. *The British Marxist Historians*. Cambridge: Polity Press, 1984.

Kealey, Gregory. "Labour and Working Class History in Canada: Prospects in the 1980s." In David Bercuson, ed. *Canadian Labour History: Selected Readings*. Toronto: Copp Clark Pitman, 1987.

Kenney, Martin, and Richard Florida. *Beyond Mass Production*. New York: Oxford University Press, 1993.

————. "Beyond Mass Production: Production and the Labor Process in Japan." *Politics and Society* 16, no. 1 (March 1988): 121–158.

Koike, Kazuo. *Understanding Industrial Relations in Japan*. New York: St. Martin's Press, 1988.

Kosai, Yutaka. *The Era of High-Speed Growth*. Tokyo: University of Tokyo Press, 1986.

Kumon, K., and H. Rosovsky, eds. *The Political Economy of Japan*. Vol. 3, *Cultural and Social Dynamics*. Stanford: Stanford University Press, 1992.

Levine, David. "Japan's Other Export." *Dollars and Sense*, September 1990, pp. 17–24.

Levinson, Edward. *Labor on the March*. New York: University Books, 1956.

Lichtenstein, N., and S. Meyer, eds. *On the Line: Essays in the History of Auto Work*. Urbana: University of Illinois Press, 1989.

Lipietz, Alain. *The Enchanted World: Inflation, Credit and the World Crisis*. London: Verso, 1985.

————. *Towards a New Economic Order: Post-Fordism, Ecology and Democracy*. Cambridge: Polity Press, 1990.

————. "Towards Global Fordism?" *New Left Review*, no. 132 (March–April 1982): 33–47.

Litwack, Leon. *The American Labor Movement*. New York: Simon & Schuster, 1962.

MacDonald Royal Commission. *The Royal Commission on the State of the Economic Union*. Ottawa: Supplies and Services Canada, 1985.

MacDowell, Laurel Sefton. "The Formation of the Canadian Industrial Relations System During World War II." In L. S. MacDowell and Ian Radorth, eds., *Canadian Working Class History: Selected Readings*. Toronto: Canadian Scholars Press, 1992.

McKean, Margaret. *Environmental Protest and Citizen Politics in Japan*. Berkeley: University of California Press, 1981.

McMillan, C. J. *The Japanese Industrial System*. Berlin: de Gruyter, 1984.

————. "The Japanese Steel Industry and its Labor-Management Relations." *Annals of the Institute of Social Science* (Tokyo), no. 21 (1980): 45–68.

Matsuzaki, Tadashi. "Wage Negotiation in the Japanese Steel Industry: Key Bargaining in the Shuntō." *Pacific Economic Papers*, no. 106. Canberra: Australia-Japan Research Centre, Australian National University, 1983.

Meyer, Stephen. *The Five Dollar Day: Labor Management and Social Control in the Ford Motor Company, 1908–1921*. Albany: State University of New York Press, 1981.

————. "The Persistence of Fordism: Workers and Technology in the American Automobile Industry, 1900–1960." In Nelson Lichtenstein and Stephen Meyer, eds., *On the Line, Essays in the History of Auto Work*. Urbana: University of Illinois Press, 1989.

Milkman, Ruth. "Labor and Management in Uncertain Times." In Alan Wolfe, ed., *America at Century's End.* Berkeley: University of California Press, 1991.

Montgomery, David. *The Fall of the House of Labour.* Cambridge: Cambridge University Press, 1987.

Moody, Kim. *An Injury to All: The Decline of American Unionism.* London: Verso, 1988.

Moore, Joe. *Japanese Workers and the Struggle for Power, 1945–1947.* Madison: University of Wisconsin Press, 1983.

———. "The Toshiba Dispute of 1949: The 'Rationalization' of Labor Relations." *Labour Capital and Society* 23, no. 1 (April 1990): 134–159.

Morioka, Koji, ed. Japanese *Capitalism Today: Economic Structure and the Organization of Work.* A special issue of *International Journal of Political Economy* 21, no. 3 (fall 1991).

Morton, Desmond. *Working People.* Toronto: Summerhill, 1990 edition.

Nakamura, Takafusa. *The Postwar Japanese Economy: Its Development and Structure.* Tokyo: University of Tokyo Press, 1981.

Nelson, Daniel. *Frederick W. Taylor and the Rise of Scientific Management.* Madison: University of Wisconsin Press, 1980.

Nitta, Michio. *When the Lifetime Employment Strategy Fails: Case Studies on the Japanese Shipbuilding and Coal Mining Industries.* Occasional Papers in Labor Problems and Social Policy, no. 12. Tokyo: Institute of Social Science: University of Tokyo, 1993.

Noble, David. *America By Design.* Oxford: Oxford University Press, 1977.

Nomura, Masami. "The End of Toyotism? Recent Trends in a Japanese Automobile Country." Paper presented to the Lean Workplace Conference, Centre for Research on Work and Society, York University, September 30–October 3, 1993.

Ogawa, Eiji. *Modern Production Management: A Japanese Experience.* Tokyo: Asian Productivity Organization, 1984.

Ōkōchi, Kazuo, et al., eds. *Workers and Employers in Japan.* Tokyo: University of Tokyo Press, 1973.

Ōno Taichi. *The Toyota Production System.* Cambridge: Productivity Press, 1988.

Organization for Economic Cooperation and Development. *The Development of Industrial Relations Systems: Some Implications of the Japanese Experience.* Paris: OECD, 1977.

Osawa, Mari. *Bye-bye Corporate Warriors: The Formation of a Corporate-Centered Society and Gender-Biased Social Policies in Japan.* Occasional Papers in Labor Problems and Social Policy, no. 18. Tokyo: Institute of Social Science: University of Tokyo, 1993.

———. *Feminization of Employment in Japan.* Occasional Papers in Labor Problems and Social Policy, no. 13. Tokyo: Institute of Social Science: University of Tokyo, 1992.

Ōtake, Hideo. "The Zaikai under the Occupation." In R. Ward and Y. Sakamoto, eds. *Democratizing Japan: The Allied Occupation.* Honolulu: University of Hawaii Press, 1987.

Palmer, Bryan. *Working Class Experience.* Toronto: Butterworth, 1983.

Parker, M., and J. Slaughter. *Choosing Sides: Unions and the Team Concept.* Boston: South End Press, 1988.

———. *Working Smart.* Detroit: Labor Notes, 1994.

Park, S. J. "Labor-Management Consultation as a Japanese Type of Participation: An International Comparison." In S. Tokunaga and J. Bergmann, eds. *Industrial Relations in Transition.* Tokyo: University of Tokyo Press, 1984: 153–167.

Pempel, T. J., and K. Tsunekawa. "Corporatism without Labor? The Japanese Anomaly." In Philippe Schmitter and Gerhard Lehmbruch, *Trends toward Corporatist Intermediation*. London: Sage Publications, 1979: 231–270.

Phillips, Gerald E. *Labor Relations and the Collective Bargaining Cycle*. Toronto: Butterworths, 1981.

Piore, M., and C. Sabel. *The Second Industrial Divide*. New York: Basic Books, 1984.

Price, John. "Valery Burati and the Formation of Sōhyō during the U.S. Occupation of Japan." *Pacific Affairs* 64, no. 2 (summer 1991): 208–225.

Radosh, Ronald. *American Labor and United States Foreign Policy*. New York: Random House, 1969.

Riddell, Craig, ed. *Labor-Management Co-operation in Canada*. Toronto: University of Toronto Press, 1986.

Rinehart, James. *The Tyranny of Work: Alienation and the Labour Process*. Toronto: Harcourt Brace Jovanovich, 1987.

Roberts, John G. *Mitsui: Three Centuries of Japanese Business*. New York: Weatherhill, 1973.

Rock, Milton, ed. *Handbook of Wage and Salary Administration*. New York: McGraw-Hill, 1972.

Schaller, Michael. *The American Occupation of Japan: The Origins of the Cold War in Asia*. New York: Oxford University Press, 1985.

Schonberger, Howard. *Aftermath of War*. Kent: Kent State University Press, 1989.

Shimada, Haruo. "Japanese Industrial Relations—A New General Model? A Survey of the English-Language Literature," in T. Shirai, ed., *Contemporary Industrial Relations in Japan*. Madison: University of Wisconsin Press, 1983.

———. "Japan's Industrial Culture and Labor-Management Relations." In K. Kumon and H. Rosovsky, eds., *The Political Economy of Japan*, vol. 3, *Cultural and Social Dynamics*. Stanford: Stanford University Press, 1992.

Shirai, Taishirō, ed. *Contemporary Industrial Relations in Japan*. Madison: University of Wisconsin Press, 1983.

Shirai, Taishiro, and Haruo Shimada. "Japan." In J. Dunlop and W. Galenson, eds., *Labor in the Twentieth Century*. New York: Academic Press, 1978.

Sōhyō. *This is Sohyo*. Tokyo: Sōhyō, 1985.

Stockwin, J. A. A. *The Japanese Socialist Party and Neutralism*. London: Melbourne University Press, 1968.

Sugeno Kazuo. *Japanese Labor Law*. Seattle: University of Washington Press, 1992.

Toffler, Alvin. *Powershift*. New York: Bantam, 1990.

Tokunaga, S., and J. Bergmann, eds. *Industrial Relations in Transition*. Tokyo: University of Tokyo Press, 1984.

Tolliday, Steven, and Jonathan Zeitlin. "Shop Floor Bargaining, Contract Unionism, and Job Control: An Anglo-American Comparison." In N. Lichtenstein and S. Meyer, eds. *On the Line: Essays in the History of Auto Work*. Chicago: University of Illinois Press, 1989.

Tsurumi, E. Patricia. *Factory Girls: Women in the Thread Mills of Meiji Japan*. Princeton: Princeton University Press, 1990.

———, ed. *The Other Japan: Postwar Realities*. Armonk: N.Y.: M. E. Sharpe, 1988.

Vogel, Ezra. *Comeback*. New York: Simon and Schuster, 1985.

Ward, R., and Y. Sakamoto, eds. *Democratizing Japan: The Allied Occupation*. Honolulu: University of Hawaii Press, 1987.

Watanabe, Ben. "Differences in Union Leadership between Toyota and Nissan." Unpublished paper, 1993.

White, Julie. *Sisters and Solidarity: Women and Unions in Canada.* Toronto: Thompson Educational Pubishing, 1993.

Windmuller, John P. *American Labor and the International Labor Movement, 1940 to 1953.* Ithaca: Cornell University Press, 1954.

Windmuller, J., and A. Gladstone, eds. *Employers Associations and Industrial Relations.* Oxford: Clarendon Press, 1984.

Womack, J., D. Jones, and D. Roos. *The Machine That Changed the World.* New York: Macmillan, 1990.

Wood, J., and P. Kumar, eds. *The Current Industrial Relations Scene in Canada, 1978.* Kingston: Queens University Press, 1979.

Wood, Stephen, ed. *The Transformation of Work.* London: Unwin Hyman, 1989.

Yamamoto, Kiyoshi. *The Japanese-Style Industrial Relations and an "Informal" Employee Organization: A Case Study of the Ohgi-kai at T Electric.* Occasional Papers in Labor Problems and Social Policy. no. 8. Tokyo: Institute of Social Sciences, University of Tokyo, 1990.

Yates, Charlotte. *From Plant to Politics: The Autoworkers Union in Postwar Canada.* Philadelphia: Temple University Press, 1992.

Index